Pensions

An ERISA Accounting and Management Guide

Second Edition

Pensions

An ERISA Accounting and Management Guide

Second Edition

Richard M. Steinberg
Harold Dankner

Coopers & Lybrand

A Ronald Press Publication

JOHN WILEY & SONS

New York • Chichester • Brisbane • Toronto • Singapore

This publication is designed to provide accurate and
authoritative information in regard to the subject
matter covered. It is sold with the understanding that
the publisher is not engaged in rendering legal, accounting,
or other professional service. If legal advice or other
expert assistance is required, the services of a competent
professional person should be sought. *From a Declaration
of Principles jointly adopted by a Committee of the
American Bar Association and a Committee of Publishers.*

Library of Congress Cataloging in Publication Data:

Steinberg, Richard M.
    Pensions: an ERISA accounting and management guide.

    Rev. ed. of: Pensions/Felix Pomeranz, Gordon P.
Ramsey, Richard M. Steinberg. c1976.
    "A Ronald Press publication."
    Includes index.
    1. Pension trusts—Law and legislation—United
States.   2. Pension trusts—Accounting—Law and
legislation—United States.   I. Dankner, Harold.
II. Pomeranz, Felix. Pensions.   III. Title.
IV. Title: E.R.I.S.A.

KF3512.S73 1982   344.73′01252   82-13396
ISBN 0-471-09798-5   347.3041252

Printed in the United States of America

10 9 8 7 6 5 4 3 2

Preface

Since the passage of the Employee Retirement Income Security Act (ERISA) in the mid-1970s, the entire area of accounting, auditing, and financial reporting for pension plans has continued to be a subject of much discussion and interpretative releases by governmental agencies and regulatory bodies. There is no question that ERISA has been one of the most important, as well as one of the most complex, laws passed in recent decades.

The need for an authoritative work in this field has been obvious from the start and was the basis for our earlier book on this subject (1975) and for this new work.

Many of the issues have now been clarified, and this book is designed as a reference for those involved with ERISA. It covers major accounting, auditing, and financial reporting issues related to the law and attempts to answer many basic and critical questions. Where no answer is presently available, we have pointed out the ramifications of the problem and attempted to provide some guidance or insights. While there are some conclusions set forth that are tentative, pending issuance of further regulations and accounting and auditing pronouncements, it is the authors' intent that this book will enable those involved with pension plans to better cope with the requirements and implications. We also intend that this book will stimulate public discussion of the issues.

Among the many issues covered in this work, there are some newer developments that may warrant special attention. These include FASB Statements Nos. 35 and 36 on accounting for defined benefit pension plans and disclosure of pension information by employers, new DOL and IRS regulations, and the forthcoming AICPA auditing guide. In addition, a special analysis of the provisions of the Tax Equity and Fiscal Responsibility Act of 1982 is included.

In producing this work, we gratefully acknowledge the contributions of Felix Pomeranz and Gordon Ramsey, partners in Coopers & Lybrand, who were co-authors, along with Richard Steinberg, of our first book on the subject. In this book, we had the valuable counsel and review of other Coopers & Lybrand professionals, with in-depth assistance from Paul Foster. Particular credit must go to Gerald Ackerman and Fred Schaefer, whose significant efforts in re-

v

searching and helping develop the manuscript played an important role in completing this project. In our actuarial benefits compensation consulting area, Jeffrey Perlmutter, Jeffrey Davis and James Ballard provided important technical review of relevant sections.

Also, Deanna Leap's editorial skills and administering abilities helped produce a professional product. Finally, we express appreciation to Mort Meyerson, for his role in visualizing and initiating development of this book as well as our firm's earlier work on the subject.

RICHARD M. STEINBERG
HAROLD DANKNER

New York
January 1983

Contents

Effective Dates. Maximum Deductible Contribution. Limits on Benefits and Contributions. *Penalties.* Back-Loaded Benefits. *Penalties.* Joint and Survivor Annuities. *Penalties.* Plan Termination Insurance. *Penalties. Effective Dates.* Multiemployer Pension Plans. Fiduciary Responsibilities. *Definition. Exemptions. Penalties. Effective Dates.* Enforcement. *How Penalties Apply.* Annual Registration.

Introduction. Participants and Beneficiaries. Accountants. *Independent Qualified Public Accountant. Financial and Other Information. Filing Under the Act. Filing Under the Alternative Method of Compliance. Comparison of the Two Methods. Discussion of Certain Requirements.* Actuaries. Providing Information to Administrator. Rejection of Filings. Exceptions. *Small Plans. Insured Plans. Unfunded Plans. Summary.* Penalties. *Applicability of Antifraud Securities Laws.*

Introduction. Historical Background. *Statements of the American Institute of Certified Public Accountants (AICPA). APB Opinion No. 8. FASB Statement No. 36.* Annual Provision for Pension Cost. *Minimum Provision. Maximum Provision. Calculation of Annual Provision. Valuing Vested Benefits.* Actuarial Factors. *Actuarial Cost Method. Actuarial Assumptions. Actuarial Gains and Losses. Actuarial Valuation Input Date. Differences Between Funding and Accounting.* Defined Contribution Plans. *Court Decisions. Employee Stock Ownership Plans.* Disclosures. *Accumulated Plan Benefits. SEC Requirements.* Accounting Effects of ERISA. *Liability for Unfunded Prior Service Cost. Liability for Unfunded Vested Benefits. Pension Expense. Liability to Acquiring Company.* Employee Stock Ownership Plans. *Accounting for the Debt. Measuring Compensation Expense. Earnings Per Share and Dividends. Investment Tax Credit. Poolings of Interests and Tainted Shares.* Special Situations. *Plant Closings. Business Combinations. Changes in Accounting. New Labor Agreements. Other Situations.*

Introduction. Basic Objectives and Audit Procedures. *Actuarial Information. Insured Plans. Audit Procedures Directly Related to ERISA. Accounting Impact. Compliance with ERISA.* Reporting Considerations.

Comparability and Consistency. Departures from the Opinion as Amended and Interpretation.

Introduction. Historical Background. *FASB Statement No. 35.* Methods of Accounting. Financial Statements. *Use of Averages or Approximations.* Plan Assets. Contributions Receivable. Investments. Operating *Assets.* Accrued Benefits. Reporting Actuarial Benefit Information. *Assumptions Used in Determining the Actuarial Present Value of Accumulated Plan Benefits. Disclosures.* Additional Financial Statement Disclosures. Internal Control. *Contributions to Multiemployer Plans. Investments. Benefits. Bonding Requirements. Administrative Expenses of Multiemployer Plans.* Illustrative Financial Statements.

Introduction. Independence. Contributions. *Multiemployer Plans. Employer Records. Alternative Procedures for Employer Records.* Investments. *Trusteed Investments. Contracts with Insurance Companies.* Benefit Payments. Administrative Expenses. Subsequent Events. Actuarial Information. Scope Limitations. Audit Requirements Due to ERISA. *Plan Compliance with ERISA. Transactions Prohibited by ERISA. Reporting and Disclosure Requirements of ERISA.* Other Audit Considerations. *Bonding. Taxes and Other Reports. Transaction Approval. Potential Plan Termination. Letter of Representation.*

Introduction. Standard Report. *Reporting on ERISA—Required Supplemental Schedules. Reference to Confirmation of Investments. Reference to Actuaries in Auditor's Report. Reference to Other Auditors in Auditor's Report.* Departures from the Standard Report: *Limited Scope Examination Pursuant to DOL Regulations. Scope Limitation—Employer Records. Investment Valuation. Internal Control Deficiency. Non-GAAP Basis.*

PART ONE

Pension Fundamentals and Provisions of ERISA

CHAPTER ONE

Introduction and Background on Pensions

HISTORICAL BACKGROUND

Payments have probably been made to retired employees ever since commerce and industry began. At first, payments were granted on an informal, almost casual basis. The amounts and the persons receiving them depended entirely upon the will of the employer. Early pensions were probably granted in recognition of past employee loyalty. Undoubtedly though, an important consideration was the removal of superannuated employees from the payroll.

This informal basis of dealing with pensions carried into the present century. The first formal pension plans were largely confined to government employees and employees of railroads and utilities. Even these early formal plans did not generally provide for advance funding, and pensions invariably were accounted for on a pay-as-you-go basis. The prevailing opinion was that the granting of a pension to a particular employee was a specific decision that related to the circumstances of the employee at the time of the grant, rather than to an established general policy.

As time went on, however, the granting of pensions gradually became a permanent part of employment policy. A pension grant came to imply that payments to the employee would continue throughout his retirement, and that similar consideration would be given to all other employees. Managements began to recognize the desirability of making some advance provisions during the active service lives of employees for pensions they expected to pay those employees upon retirement. Such provisions often took the form of contractual arrangements with insurance companies. Self-administered funding arrangements were also instituted. Enactment of Internal Revenue Code provisions making contributions to a qualified pension plan fund immediately deductible by an employer (while the resultant benefits would not become taxable income to the employees until actual pension payments were made) gave considerable impetus to the formation of self-administered funded plans.

Institution of wage and price controls during World War II resulted in the establishment or improvement of many pension plans, in order to increase total employee compensation while complying with the wage guidelines. From 1940 to 1945, over 2¼ million active workers were newly covered by formal retirement plans sponsored by private industry. In the late 1940s organized labor focused much of its efforts on the establishment of pensions, adding considerable impetus to the growth of private plans.

Two significant events in 1949 supported trade union efforts to gain pension plan participation for their members. First, the U.S. Supreme Court decided that pensions were a "bargainable" issue. Second, the Steel Industry Fact-Finding Board held that the industry was obliged to provide pension and welfare benefits for its workers under a "depreciation of human machinery" concept. The effect, by way of example, was that the mass production industries (e.g., automotive and steel) added more than 5 million participants to collectively bargained pension plans by 1950. More than 75% of the participants in collectively bargained plans made no contribution to the cost of the plans. Noncollectively bargained plans also expanded in the absolute numbers of plans and plan participants, although not as rapidly.

The growth of privately sponsored pension plans during the period from 1940 to 1973 can be illustrated as follows.

The number of covered retirees expanded from 200,000 to more than 6 million.

Annual benefits paid to retirees increased from $100 million to $10 billion.

The number of active covered employees increased from 4.1 million to 35 million.

Pension plan assets increased from $2.4 billion to $160 billion.

By 1975, total pension plan assets had increased to over $200 billion. From 1955 to 1974, corporate contributions to pension plans increased from $3.3 billion to an estimated $25 billion annually. Since then, plan assets and contributions have continued to grow at a rapid pace.

Despite this tremendous increase in corporate contributions to pension plans, accompanied by related growth in plan assets, the fact remained that a number of employees who expected to receive benefit payments upon retirement did not receive the anticipated benefits. There are numerous reasons why benefits were not ultimately received. In some publicized cases, employers terminated underfunded plans; in others, plan participants quit or were fired with few or no vested benefits. Officials of some plans made bad investments or used assets for their own purposes, leaving little for plan participants and beneficiaries.

It was largely the tremendous increase in the number, size, and importance of pension funds, coupled with instances in which employees failed to receive reasonably expected benefits, which led to development of the legislation resulting in ERISA.

The Employee Retirement Income Security Act of 1974, commonly known as ERISA, was the culmination of a decade or more of consideration and review by various government entities and others. It was the most complex and far-reaching legislation affecting pensions in over 30 years, and it has substantially changed the way in which employers are required to operate pension plans. ERISA accomplished the following:

> established funding requirements for some plans which had not previously been funded and increased minimum funding requirements for others;
>
> established minimum participation and vesting standards for the first time;
>
> required payment of insurance premiums to the newly established Pension Benefit Guaranty Corporation (PBGC), which guarantees certain vested benefits;
>
> increased substantially the disclosures and reporting required of pension plans;
>
> imposed substantial restrictions upon the manner in which pension plan assets may be invested; and
>
> required pension plans to provide annual financial statements audited by qualified independent public accountants.

These are only a few of the many requirements that were imposed by ERISA.

PENSION PLANS

A pension plan is an arrangement whereby an employer can provide for retirement benefits for employees in recognition of their service to the company. The arrangement may be informal, calling for voluntary payments to the retired employee in amounts and under conditions more or less at the discretion of the employer, or there may be a formal plan with the benefit payments and other features explicitly stated, susceptible to ready computation, or otherwise determinable. A formal plan is usually set forth in a written document, but an established policy with regard to pension payments may be sufficiently defined, constituting a formal plan.

One consequence of ERISA is that previously informal plans may, under certain circumstances, become subject to federal regulation. Plans subject to ERISA must be established and maintained pursuant to a written instrument.

An employer may establish a pension plan unilaterally (referred to as a *conventional* or *voluntary* plan) or as a result of collective bargaining between employer(s) and employees (referred to as a *negotiated* plan). A plan established by bargaining between a labor union and one or more companies is sometimes referred to as a *pattern* plan, where terms of the plan are adopted, perhaps with variations, by companies in the same or allied industries.

All plans are either those of a single employer or a group of affiliated employers (*single-employer* plans) or of several employers (*multiemployer* plans). Some single-employer plans are unilaterally established, whereas multiemployer plans are collectively established, usually pursuant to collective bargaining agreements and managed jointly by representatives of labor and management.

A *qualified* pension plan is a plan that conforms with Internal Revenue Service requirements. It provides certain tax advantages, including the deductibility of employer contributions to the plan as a business expense, deferment of taxes upon the employee for those contributions and the income therefrom until he actually receives retirement payments, exemption of the pension plan's investment income from taxation, and taxation of certain lump-sum retirement payments at more favorable (capital gains, 10-year forward averaging) rates.

A *contributory* pension plan is one in which both the employer and the employees make contributions. Employee contributions to a contributory plan may be mandatory or voluntary. A *noncontributory* pension plan is one in which only the employer makes contributions.

Employer contributions are usually based either upon actuarial calculations (*defined benefit* plan) or upon amounts or rates stipulated under the terms of the plan (*defined contribution* plan).[1] A defined benefit plan is one in which benefits are defined, and actuarial calculations are used to establish the amount of contributions required to meet those benefits. In a defined contribution plan, contributions are defined and the benefits which can be paid must be calculated. For certain types of plans such calculations must be made by an actuary.

---

[1] A common example of a defined contribution plan is the money-purchase plan (see "Normal Retirement Benefits," later in this chapter). Under ERISA, profit-sharing and similar plans, which were previously not normally considered to be pension plans, would fall into the defined contribution category.

It should be noted, however, that a plan that is called a defined contribution plan may be, in fact, a defined benefit plan. A common characteristic of the defined contribution plan is the requirement that the employer contribute to the plan pursuant to a stated formula (e.g., a fixed amount for each ton produced, so many cents per hour worked, or a fixed percentage of compensation). In most such cases the benefits for each employee are the amount that can be provided by the sums contributed for him, and it is clear that such a plan is a defined contribution plan. Where a contribution formula also provides for a contemplated scale of benefits, however, careful analysis is required to ascertain whether the plan should be considered to be substantively a defined benefit plan rather than a defined contribution plan. This determination may be important for accounting and auditing purposes.

PLAN VERSUS FUND

ERISA does not distinguish between the terms *plan* and *fund;* it describes a pension plan as "any plan, fund, or program. . . ." This lack of distinction created uncertainty with respect to important accounting and auditing matters, particularly with respect to whether financial statements of a *plan* as required by ERISA should relate to a plan or to a fund. Some observers believed that this distinction was significant. In their view, financial statements of a plan should contain data regarding future pension benefit payments and that these and related data should be audited, while financial statements of a fund should not include such data but rather should be restricted primarily to accountability for the assets managed by the fund trustees.

Inasmuch as ERISA requires reporting and disclosure by the *plan,* and the Financial Accounting Standards Board identifies the plan as the reporting entity, both the terminology and the substantive accounting uncertainties have been resolved. The *plan* is the reporting entity, and when generally accepted accounting principles are applied, data regarding future benefit payments must be included in plan financial statements.

PROVISIONS OF PENSION PLANS

Eligibility Requirements

The earliest date or age when an employee can become a participant in a plan and begin to accumulate pension credits is determined by the plan's eligibility provisions. Some plans provide that employees may become eligible immediately upon being hired, regardless of age or lack of prior service. Most plans, however, require a period of service or a combination of age and period of service (e.g., 25 years of age with at least one year of service). ERISA has established minimum waiting periods which a plan may require before employees can become eligible to participate. (See "Participation" in Chapter 4.)

Retirement Dates

A designated retirement age at which an employee may receive the normal pension is termed the *normal retirement date* or *age* (e.g., age 65, or age 58 with 30 years of service). *The mandatory retirement date,* also referred to as *compulsory* retirement date or *automatic* retirement date, is the date at which an employee must retire. The Age Discrimination in Employment Act generally precludes private employers from requiring an employee to retire prior to age 70.

Most plans provide for an *early retirement date* prior to the normal retirement age, at the election of either the employee or the employer. Benefits paid upon early retirement are usually less than normal retirement benefits. (See Figure 2-1 in Chapter 2 for discussion.)

A plan may permit an employee to postpone his retirement from the normal retirement date to a *deferred retirement date,* also referred to as a *delayed* retirement date or *late* retirement date. Late retirement may be at the employee's election, and may or may not involve higher than normal benefits.

Some plans also contain disability provisions which allow early retirement (at full or reduced rate) when a qualifying plan participant must terminate employment because of disability.

Vesting

When an employee's entitlement to benefits arising from employer contributions is not contingent on his continuing in the service of the employer until he is eligible to retire, he is said to have a *vested interest.* The applicable provision in the plan is described as a *vesting provision.* The vested benefits to which the employee would be entitled upon termination of employment are usually in the form of a deferred annuity income, with payments commencing at the normal (or early) retirement date. If the vested benefits are in an amount equal to the accrued pension rights determined up to the date when employment ends, the plan is said to provide for *full vesting.* If a portion of the accrued benefits is forfeitable, the term *partial vesting* is used.

Under ERISA, plans are required to vest accrued benefits of employees with specified years of service and/or age, even if those employees do not remain until their retirement or qualifying early retirement age. (See "Vesting" in Chapter 4.[2])

---

[2] Qualified profit-sharing plans have historically been required by the IRS to provide vesting comparable to or more favorable than requirements of ERISA.

Normal Retirement Benefits

A variety of methods are used to determine the amount of retirement benefits. Benefits may be the same for all participants with a specified period of service (e.g., $300 per month for participants with 20 or more years of service); this is known as a *flat benefit*. A variation of a flat benefit is a benefit based on years of service (e.g., $10 per month for each year of service). In many instances, however, benefits are specified in terms of percentages of each year's compensation, sometimes with fixed minimum and maximum amounts. The total benefit so accumulated is said to be on a *career-average* compensation basis. Alternatively, the compensation base may be determined by average earnings during a certain specified period such as the final three or five years of service. This is known as a *final average pay* or *final-pay* plan.

Many plans correlate or integrate retirement payments with federal social security retirement benefits. This may be provided for in the benefit formula by the application of a lower percentage to the part of earnings covered by social security or by reducing the benefit amount by a portion of the social security benefit.

In some cases, pension payments are determined as the amount of a retirement annuity purchasable by the contributions specified in the plan. This type of plan is referred to as a *money-purchase* plan.

Death Benefits

Some pension plans provide a *death benefit,* which is any benefit payable upon the death of an employee. In a contributory plan, the minimum death benefit would necessarily be the total contributions made by the employee, together with accumulated interest. In some plans, however, death benefits are related to the employee's anticipated pension benefits or the value of his accumulated pension credits, and hence may be substantial.

Duration of Retirement Benefits

A pension plan's retirement benefits may be either for the annuitant's remaining lifetime or for a longer period if the plan so provides. The annuity provided for the employee's lifetime is called a *life* (or *straight life*) *annuity.*

Annuities which may extend beyond the annuitant's lifetime generally are either:

period certain and life, or
joint and survivorship.[3]

---

[3] ERISA modified the use of joint and survivorship option provisions somewhat, as discussed in Chapter 4.

The former provide that if the annuitant dies before the end of a stipulated guaranteed period, payments (reduced from the straight life amount) will continue to the end of the guaranteed period to a named beneficiary, usually the annuitant's spouse. For example, if the annuity is a five-year certain and life annuity, the named beneficiary would receive benefits for two years if the annuitant dies three years after retirement and would receive nothing if the annuitant lived five or more years beyond retirement.

Under joint and survivorship options, the employee may elect to receive reduced retirement benefits with provision for a continuation of all or a portion of benefits to a named beneficiary (usually a spouse), whereby the named beneficiary receives benefits for the rest of his or her life. ERISA has established special requirements concerning the payment of joint and survivor annuity benefits. (See Appendix D.)

With respect to both period certain and life and joint and survivorship options, the option is elected prior to retirement. The benefit amount is usually (but not always) the actuarial equivalent of the normal benefit, generally based in the case of joint and survivorship options, upon the ages of the annuitants and the percentage reduction to the named beneficiary (*joint annuitant* or *contingent annuitant*).

In contributory plans, the annuitant is usually entitled to receive the full amount of his own accumulated contributions and interest thereon. Therefore, contributory plans commonly contain a *modified cash refund* annuity provision under which a deceased annuitant's named beneficiary receives any difference between the cash amount that would have been payable at retirement date and the pension benefits paid between retirement date and death.

FEDERAL INCOME TAX CONSIDERATIONS

Although ERISA introduced various changes to the Internal Revenue Code (generally to conform it with certain ERISA provisions, such as those related to participation, vesting, and funding), the code's requirements for qualified plans extend beyond ERISA's provisions. These requirements include the following.

A plan must not discriminate in favor of employees who are officers or shareholders or are highly compensated.

Benefits under the plan must be reasonable in amount when considered with other forms of compensation.

The plan must be a permanent written program.

Contributions to the fund must be exclusively for the benefit of participants.

There are special limitations on the amount of death benefits that a plan may provide. If a plan qualifies, contributions by the employer are currently deductible, income on accumulated funds held for a qualified plan is not subject to tax, and the employees will be subject to income tax on the resulting benefits only as payments are actually received. In addition, certain distributions receive favorable tax treatment, for example, capital gains and 10-year forward averaging.

It is customary to obtain a determination from the Internal Revenue Service that a plan is qualified, to avoid later difficulties in interpreting the technical qualification requirements.

PENSION FUND ADMINISTRATION

A pension fund is generally administered under a declaration of trust that sets forth the duties and responsibilities of the trustee(s), or in accordance with a contract between an employer and an insurance company.

ERISA requires that the pension plan "... instrument shall provide for one or more named fiduciaries who jointly or severally shall have authority to control and manage the operations of the plan." It further specifies that one or more administrators shall have full responsibility for the operation of the plan, and defines the term *administrator* to mean:

1 the person specifically designated by the terms of the instrument under which the plan is operated; or

2 the plan sponsor, if the plan instrument does not designate an administrator; or

3 such other person as the Secretary of Labor may by regulation prescribe, where the plan does not designate an administrator and a plan sponsor cannot be identified.

The term *plan sponsor* is defined to mean:

1 the employer in the case of a pension plan established or maintained by a single employer; or

2 the employee organization in the case of a plan established or maintained by an employee organization; or

3 the association, committee, joint board of trustees, or other similar group of representatives of the parties who establish or maintain the plan, where the plan is established or maintained either by two or more employers or jointly by one or more employers and one or more employee organizations.

Fund Policy and Operation

Responsibility for operation of a pension fund in accordance with the plan instrument, trust instrument, insurance contract, policies (e.g., as set forth in minutes of board or administrative committee meetings), and all applicable laws is normally held in a single-employer plan by an administrative committee and in a multiemployer plan by a joint board of trustees. The administrative committee usually consists of three or more officers or other responsible employees of the employer company acting for and reporting to the company's board of directors in matters pertaining to the plan. The joint board of trustees is generally composed of an equal number of employer and employee representatives.

The day-to-day administration of a single-employer pension plan, for example, determination of eligibility, payment of benefits, employee record maintenance, and so forth, is usually undertaken by the employer company. The benefits to be received, the conditions of eligibility for benefits, and other participants' rights are set forth in the plan documents. Broad policy decisions concerning the operation and interpretation of the plan are generally made by the administrative committee.

The joint board of trustees in a multiemployer plan generally has broad responsibility for determining benefits and other participant rights under the plan. Such trustees are responsible for: (1) collection of contributions, (2) payment of benefits, (3) management of the plan's assets, (4) maintenance of the plan's records, and (5) preparation of reports.

While retaining responsibility for the overall supervision of the fund's activities, the administrative committee or the board of trustees usually delegates the fund's day-to-day administration to one or more of the following:

the employer company;
a bank trust department;
an insurance company;
an independent contractual administrator; or
an employed administrator.

Administrative Expenses and Fees

Administrative expenses of a single-employer plan are generally borne by the employer company. This may vary from year to year under some plans that call for expenses to be paid by the fund unless the employer elects to pay them. Administrative fees of a multiemployer fund may be based on a percentage of contributions received, on a specified amount per participant per month, or on some other basis. Such fees and/or expenses are usually approved by the board of trustees. Where an administrative office manages several multiemployer plans for a single industry, appropriate provision must be made for an equitable allocation of administrative expenses among the several plans, since such plans are independent entities having their own assets, records, and reporting requirements.

Accounting Records

The basic accounting records for a pension plan should produce information necessary for effective management of the plan and provide the detailed information needed for financial reporting. In the case of single-employer plans, pertinent information is obtained from records similar to those used by other organizations; in the case of multiemployer plans, the following additional records are generally required:

Employers' Contribution Reports   Under collective bargaining agreements, employers must submit periodic contributions with an accompanying report listing the participants for whom contributions are submitted.

Contribution Records   The plans must maintain contribution records for each employer, showing all payments and accumulating the total annual contributions to be reported to the Department of Labor under ERISA. The contribution record is also used for determining delinquencies in employer contributions, and records are maintained to follow up on delinquent contributions or reports.

Participants' Eligibility Records   To ensure that each plan participant is properly credited with benefits earned (whether based upon hours worked, dollars earned or contributed, etc.), the plan must maintain separate records for each participant, to record and accumulate all pension credits earned. It is important that proper record retrieval and retention systems are in effect, since the accumulation of pension credits usually covers a long period of time. In the case of a single-employer plan, the eligibility records are generally part of the employer's payroll and personnel records.

ERISA provides for specific information on vesting to be included in participants' eligibility records. (See "Vesting" in Chapter 4.)

CHAPTER TWO

Actuarial Concepts, Assumptions, and Methods

INTRODUCTION

In defined benefit pension plans, pension costs must be ascertained by an actuary using various statistical, financial, and other techniques for computing the value of plan benefits, assigning costs to particular periods, evaluating and projecting actuarial experience under a plan, and periodically determining unfunded amounts. In defined contribution plans, actuarial computations may be needed for determining the amount of benefits the specified contributions will provide.

This chapter discusses the general nature of pension costs, actuarial cost methods, actuarial assumptions, and actuarial gains and losses.

THE GENERAL NATURE OF PENSION COSTS

The ultimate cost of any pension plan is determined primarily by the total pension benefits that will actually be paid to retired employees over their lives. This cost cannot be exactly determined so long as the plan continues to operate, since benefits for active employees are unknown and, for the retired, the duration of benefit payments is also unknown. Therefore, pension cost determinations are based upon *actuarial assumptions* and *actuarial cost methods,* which are used to establish total cost and assign that cost to periods of time. The portion of cost assigned to employee service in each year after the inception of the plan is called *normal cost.* The portion of cost assigned to years of service prior to the inception of the plan is called *past service cost.* At any later valuation date, the portion of cost assigned to prior years is called *prior service cost,* which includes as of the particular valuation date, past service cost, normal cost to date, and increases or decreases in plan cost arising from any amendments to the plan (e.g., to increase benefit levels).[1] Although most cost methods identify past service cost for separate amortization, some cost methods do not differentiate past service cost and instead assign all costs to years subsequent to the inception of the plan.

The concept of *present value* is basic to actuarial determinations of pension cost. Actuarial applications of the present value concept are described in Figure 2-1. Actuarial assumptions and actuarial gains or losses are discussed later in this chapter.

---

[1] Since amounts of increases or decreases in prior service cost arising from plan amendments are normally treated like past service cost, the term *past service cost* is sometimes used in this discussion to refer to both past service cost (arising upon adoption of a plan) and the amounts of any increases or decreases in prior service cost arising from plan amendments.

FIGURE 2-1

Present value applications to actuarial determinations

The present value (PV) principle permits the value at any future point in time to be expressed as the equivalent value at the present time under a given set of conditions. It also permits the computation of a series of financial transactions over a period of time to be expressed as a single

A general statement of a company's prospective pension obligation at any given time with respect to then covered employees, that is, the present value of future contributions required to meet retirement payments, may be expressed by the following formula:

$$\underset{\text{contributions}}{\text{PV}} = \underset{\text{benefits}}{\text{PV}} + \underset{\text{expenses}}{\text{PV}} - \underset{\text{on hand}}{\text{Funds}}$$

value at any point of time. The principle is particularly useful in dealing with financial transactions involving a time series, such as periodic contributions and retirement annuities.

The present value concept is frequently used for business purposes. For example, the present value of a debt of Y dollars payable X years hence is the amount that, with accumulated compound interest thereon for X years, would accrue to Y dollars. This illustration has a single assumption and is quite precise.

In contrast, actuarial use of the present value concept normally involves several factors and little of the certainty entailed in present value determinations in the preceding example. Actuarial determinations are based upon the interaction of various assumptions, such as mortality and severance of employment.

While many assumptions are normally involved when determining the present value of contributions as set forth in the preceding equation, actuaries' use of the present value concept may in other instances require the use of relatively few assumptions. For example, where a plan provides that the benefit at early retirement is to be the actuarial equivalent of the amount otherwise payable at normal retirement age, only the assumptions concerning income yield and mortality usually need be considered. The actuarial equivalent concept is used in any situation in which the value of a retirement benefit under one set of conditions is equated to one under a different set of conditions, for example, the conversion from a normal benefit to a joint and survivorship optional benefit.

ACTUARIAL COST METHODS

Actuarial cost methods fall into two general categories:

accrued benefit cost method, sometimes called unit credit, unit purchase, step-rate, or single premium method; and

projected benefit cost methods, sometimes called level cost or level premium cost methods.

The accrued benefit cost method considers as cost for a period (which may be a definite time interval such as a fiscal year) the present value of an annuity for each employee that would provide for retirement payments applicable to

FIGURE 2-2

Funding

Where there is a separate determination of past service cost, a plan's funding rate is commonly based upon normal cost plus some portion of past service cost. Plans commonly set the funding rate at a level which will amortize past service cost over a specified period of years ranging from as few as 10 to as many as 40.* Where there is no separate determination of past service cost, as is normally the case when the individual level cost method or aggregate method is used, there is a built-in funding of past service cost over employees' remaining service lives. Many plans differentiating between past service cost and normal cost previously delayed the funding of past service cost indefinitely by setting the funding rate at normal cost plus

the equivalent of interest on past service cost—the minimum previously required by the Internal Revenue Service for qualified plans. Not funding past service cost is generally no longer allowed under ERISA, which provides specific periods for amortizing past service cost.

Some plans in the past did not prefund benefits; in such cases, plan sponsors either used *terminal funding* or followed a pay-as-you-go policy. Under terminal funding, pensions are not funded until the date of an employee's retirement. At that time, a fund is established that is actuarially equivalent to all payments expected to be made to the retiree under the pension plan. Under a pay-as-you-go policy, benefits are paid to retired employees as due, with no advance funding. Under a variation of terminal funding, contributions are made in installments, giving such terminal funding some aspects of a pay-as-you-go method. Under ERISA, most pension plans must use some form of advance funding.

---

* ERISA has increased the deduction limitation from 10% of past service cost (12- to 14-year funding) to 10-year funding (12% to 14% of past service cost).

---

pension credits related to that period. Other things being equal, costs so calculated will increase with the advancing age of an employee because of the shorter time remaining for income accretions before retirement age and the greater likelihood of survival to retirement. Because of this ascending characteristic, this method is often referred to as *step-rate*.

Under projected benefit cost methods of calculating periodic pension costs, the effect of the ascending characteristics of the accrued benefit cost method is counteracted. Actuarial costs are based on providing for the present value of total projected benefits by level amounts or level percentages of compensation. Costs so calculated will, under normal circumstances, remain at a uniform rate unless pension benefits are revised.

The actuarial cost methods are used both for determining costs and as a basis for the advance funding of benefits, as discussed in Figure 2-2.[2] The following descriptions of actuarial cost methods include information on funding and funding agencies where deemed useful.

[2] The terminal funding method and the pay-as-you-go method described in Figure 2-2 have been used in certain instances as actuarial cost methods for funding and even for accounting purposes. The pay-as-you-go method is not an actuarial cost method, and neither of these methods is acceptable under ERISA (for funding) or under APB Opinion No. 8 (for accounting).

Accrued Benefit Cost Method

The accrued benefit cost method operates on the principle that the retirement pension is or may be divided into units of benefits, each unit being related to a year of employment service. The normal cost for each year of service is the amount needed to provide in full for the benefit unit or units assigned to that year.

The benefit units related to the various years of an employee's credited service are usually equal in amount or equal as a percentage of earnings. The normal cost applicable to an individual employee, however, increases with each advancing year, since it is increasingly probable that he will live, and will work for the employer, until retirement age, and there is less time to earn interest on the amount funded. The total annual cost for the group as a whole usually does not reflect the same pronounced step-up effect because of the effect of replacement, generally, of older employees upon their death or retirement by younger employees. For a mature population, therefore, the normal cost may be relatively uniform, while for an initially immature group, the normal cost will rise before ultimately leveling off.

The past service cost under the accrued benefit cost method is the single sum necessary at the inception of a plan to provide for retirement benefit units covering service credited prior to inception. Stated in present value terms, past service cost is the amount determined at the plan's inception date to be the present value of the units of benefit credited to employees for all years of service prior to the inception of the plan.

Past service cost may be funded in a variety of ways. A common method is to fund it on the basis of a series of uniform payments (which recognize interest) over a specified term. Some insured plans using the unit credit funding method provide that the initial past service cost for any individual must be fully funded by his normal retirement date. The group annuity type of insured plan frequently makes use of the accrued benefit cost method for funding, but the method is also used in self-administered (trusteed) or deposit administration plans.

Projected Benefit Cost Methods

The step-rate increases in normal costs that occur under the accrued benefit cost method as an employee ages, can be avoided by using one of the projected benefit cost methods which assign costs in level amounts to each year of service. These methods result in higher cost in the earlier plan years than under the accrued benefit cost method, and thus produce lower cost in later years. A level-cost method may use rates that are level in dollar amounts or use a level percentage of earnings. If level cost is determined as of an employee's current age to cover the benefits for all subsequent years, it is known as the *attained-age normal method.* If level cost is determined as of the age the employee could have entered the plan had it been in existence, it is known as the *entry-age normal cost method.*

Entry-Age Normal Cost Method

Normal cost under this method is the annual amount which would have been needed to fund pension benefits over the entire service life or lives of an employee or group of employees had the current pension plan always been in effect.[3] Past service cost is separately determined.

Past service cost under this method is sometimes defined as the fund that would have been accumulated at the inception of a plan if annual contributions had, in fact, been made over the entire credited service lives of employees up to that time. This is known as a *retrospective method.*

Past service cost is usually determined, however, by a prospective method in which the present value of the future normal cost is subtracted from the present value of all expected benefit payments, with the difference being the past service cost. If all elements were in accordance with the actuarial assumptions, this would equal the amount that would have been on hand if the plan had always been in effect. For any subsequent valuation, the value of all expected benefits is determined by the same procedure. The amount so determined, less the value of future normal cost and less the funds accumulated under the plan, would represent the then unfunded past service cost.

A modification of this method is often used, referred to as an *entry-age normal method with frozen initial liability.* The first-year costs are determined in the same way as under the entry-age normal method. Past service cost is not adjusted at any future time to recognize actual experience, and it is thus termed *frozen initial liability.* As a result, actuarial gains and losses are recognized in determinations of future normal cost amounts. In each year after the first, normal cost is computed as under the aggregate method (see below), except that the portion of the total liability represented by the unfunded part of the frozen initial liability is amortized by separate amounts.

The entry-age normal cost method is used in self-administered trusteed plans and for insured plans such as the deposit administration group annuity.

Individual Level Cost Method

This method uses the level cost approach, but fixes the level cost or level rate of compensation for each employee at an amount that would spread future pension costs over the remaining future service of each employee. Thus, this method includes past service cost in normal cost, rather than treating it separately. This method is also termed the *individual level premium method* or the *individual funding to normal retirement age method.*

Under this method, past service cost (not separately identified) is in effect

---

[3] The term *entry-age* derives from the fact that cost is determined on the assumption that the plan had always been in effect, and contributions commenced when the employee entered the plan.

amortized over the remaining service lives of employees. This usually results in very high costs in the early years because the past service cost associated with participants retiring in those years is amortized over a very short period. In later years, however, this method gives costs similar to those determined under the entry-age normal cost method.

The individual level-cost method is used in insured individual policy or group permanent plans and can be adopted for self-administered trusteed or insured plans.

Aggregate Method

This method is similar to the individual level-cost method, except that calculations are made on a collective basis. The total cost of future pension benefits for all employees covered at the inception of the plan is spread over their average future service lives. Costs are normally computed as a percentage of payroll.

Because cost is determined on a collective rather than an individual basis, past service cost, though not separately determined, is amortized over the average future service lives of all employees, thus avoiding the particularly heavy early-year costs involved under the individual level-cost method.

The aggregate method is used in self-administered trusteed plans and may also be used in an insured deposit administration plan.

Attained-Age Normal Method

This method's name derives from the view of normal cost as the annual amount necessary to fund future service benefits over the period beginning with the age the employee has attained at the date of the plan's inception, or at the date of initial coverage if he is employed thereafter. The attained-age normal method combines some features of the accrued benefit cost method and others of the aggregate method. As under the accrued benefit cost method, benefits are divided into units applicable to past and future service, and all units applicable to years prior to the inception of the plan are treated as past service cost. The cost of service in years after the inception of the plan, however, is spread over employees' future service lives in a manner similar to that of the aggregate method. Normal cost is usually determined as a percentage of payroll. Although normal costs tend to decline over a period of time, costs in the early plan years are generally not as high as under the aggregate method or individual level-cost method.

The attained-age normal method is used both in trusteed plans and in deposit administration contracts.

ACTUARIAL ASSUMPTIONS

Actual pension costs depend upon future occurrences, such as total years of employee service, mortality, compensation, and earnings on funds set aside for the future payment of benefits. Therefore, pension cost estimates are predicated on assumptions concerning those future occurrences.

Actuaries make these assumptions when evaluating the financial impact of pension plan benefits, suggesting appropriate funding arrangements, and determining pension costs. Some significant factors for which actuarial assumptions must be made are described in the following sections.

Mortality

Since pension benefits are not paid unless the employee lives to retirement, and may cease with the death of a retired employee, an actuarial assumption about expected mortality rates of covered employees (and of their coannuitants in the case of joint and survivorship options) is a major consideration in the determination of pension costs. Making allowances for future mortality is sometimes referred to as *discounting for mortality.* The value of any included death benefits also depends on the mortality assumptions.

Employee Turnover

An assumption is also made about the rates of future employee turnover, since termination of employment before retirement age generally reduces or eliminates benefits that would otherwise accrue, thereby reducing pension costs. Studies made of turnover rates usually involve recognition of the effects of age, sex, length of employment, and type of work. Making allowance for future employment severance is called *discounting for turnover.*

Retirement Age

When plans permit retirement at a date other than the normal retirement age, that is, at either an early retirement date or a deferred retirement date, assumptions about the number of employees who will retire at various ages may be needed. However, in many plans the benefits for early retirement are adjusted to amounts that are actuarially equivalent to those at normal age. It is then frequently assumed that all employees will retire at normal retirement age.

Salary Scales

When benefits are keyed to future salary rates, as in a percentage-of-compensation formula, assumptions may be made about future salary levels. This is essential in the case of a final-pay plan, where all benefits are related to earnings for the limited period of years immediately preceding retirement.

Interest Rate

Monies available to provide benefits result not only from contributions but from the income earned on investments in, and net gains or losses of, fund assets. The term *income yield* is sometimes used to describe all types of income. Recognition of future fund income is called *discounting for interest.*

Other Assumptions

Additional actuarial assumptions may be required, depending on the provisions of the plan. Thus, where plans provide for disability retirement or death benefits, or contain features dependent on marital status or changes in a cost-of-living index or social security benefits, appropriate assumptions are needed as to future events or status changes with respect to these conditions.

ACTUARIAL GAINS AND LOSSES

To the extent that actual experience after an actuarial valuation differs from the actuarial assumptions used in the valuation, actuarial gains or losses will arise. For example, if the actual experience is such that the contributions to the plan, as previously determined on the basis of assumptions at a particular valuation date, turn out to be larger than necessary, an actuarial gain would result. If the contributions turn out to be smaller than necessary, an actuarial loss would occur. For example, if more employees die prior to retirement or soon after retiring than had been anticipated, total benefits payable will be smaller than anticipated, creating an actuarial gain and reducing the otherwise required contributions. The opposite situation involves an actuarial loss.

When a plan's costs are computed, the effect of the difference between actual experience to date and the actuarial assumptions is automatically reflected in the new cost computation. From the valuation date on, however, the present value of projected benefits and other elements in the valuation may again be based on the same actuarial assumptions. It is thus necessary to determine when experience indicates that the actuarial assumptions themselves should be changed.

Actual experience may differ from the actuarial assumptions merely because of fluctuations occurring when the group is not extensive enough for averages to work out. On the other hand, the differences may arise because the assumptions used are no longer applicable to the group. For example, many plans that were started in the 1950s used an interest assumption of 2.5%, which at that time seemed as high as could be reasonably expected on a conservative basis. The investment returns have been above this for many years, and this rate is no longer applicable.

As indicated in Figure 2-1, the following formula is used in connection with determining the present value (PV) of future contributions required to meet retirement benefits:

$$\begin{array}{ccccc} \text{PV} \\ \text{contributions} \end{array} = \begin{array}{c} \text{PV} \\ \text{benefits} \end{array} + \begin{array}{c} \text{PV} \\ \text{expenses} \end{array} - \begin{array}{c} \text{Funds} \\ \text{on hand} \end{array}$$

This formula can also be used to illustrate the nature of actuarial gains and losses. Anything that reduces the present value of contributions more than anticipated by the assumptions can be considered a gain. Thus, such a gain would result if any of the following were greater than expected: (1) reduction in the present value of benefits, or (2) reduction in the present value of expenses, or (3) increase in the funds on hand. A gain would arise as a result of experience more favorable than the underlying actuarial assumptions would produce. For example, if investment income to date has been greater than assumed, the funds on hand will be larger than assumed, and the present value of contributions will be smaller. Similarly, if mortality to date has been greater than expected, fewer employees will survive to retirement, and the present value of benefits will be reduced. If employee turnover is higher than expected, the number of employees included in the present value of benefits will be lower, creating an actuarial gain. Conversely, differences between actual experience and assumptions that increase the present value of contributions would be termed actuarial losses.

Changes that result from causes outside the experience under the plan, however, would not be considered gains or losses. An example would be a change in the present value of benefits arising from a change in the benefit formula.

When a change is made in the actuarial assumptions, it affects the present value of benefits and therefore the present value of contributions.

Computing Actuarial Gain or Loss

Analyzing and computing the amount of gain or loss attributable to each actuarial assumption is more difficult than calculating aggregate net gain or loss on an overall basis. As part of the annual actuarial valuation of a plan, however, the actuary will frequently make the technical computations necessary to determine the sources of gains or losses, to compare actual experience with assumed experience. It is necessary to make these analyses from time to time in order to decide when adjustments should be made in the assumptions to be used in the future.

In the case of actuarial cost methods that reflect gains and losses as adjustments to past service cost, the aggregate gain or loss can be determined by comparing the actual unfunded past service cost at the valuation date with the unfunded past service cost that would have existed if experience had followed the actuarial assumptions used, taking into account the actual contributions made to the fund. In the case of actuarial cost methods that reflect gains and losses in future normal costs, the aggregate gain or loss can be determined by comparing the actual unfunded future normal costs with the unfunded future normal costs that would have existed if experience had followed the actuarial assumptions, again taking into account the actual contributions made. If the expected unfunded amount exceeds the actual unfunded amount, the difference is an actuarial gain; the opposite is an actuarial loss. See Figure 2-3 for an example of such a computation.

FIGURE 2-3

Illustrative computation of actuarial gains and losses

1. Expected Unfunded Past Service Cost

Unfunded past service cost at beginning of period	$100,000
Plus interest on above to end of period (at the assumed interest rate)	5,000
Total	105,000
Less contributions during period toward past service cost, and	10,000
Less interest on above from contribution dates to end of period at assumed rate	250
Expected unfunded past service cost at end of period	$ 94,750

2. Gain or Loss Determination

Present value of future benefit payments to employees for credited service to end of period	$300,000
Less actual fund at end of period	206,000
Actual unfunded past service cost at end of period	94,000
Less expected unfunded past service cost at end of period	94,750
Actuarial loss (gain)	($ 750)

Actuarial Gain or Loss Adjustment

Actuarial gains or losses may be used as adjustments to costs immediately, or be averaged or spread over a period of years. The methods by which pension costs are adjusted for actuarial gains or losses are discussed below.

Immediate Method

The first method, called the *immediate* method entails the immediate addition of an amount equal to the loss to (or subtraction of an amount equal to the gain from) the current or following year's normal cost.[4] Where there is a significant loss, however, it can be added to the unfunded past service cost, which is almost always done when the accrued benefit (step-rate) cost method is used.

Averaging Method

The second method, called the *averaging* method, involves averaging gains or losses over future periods. Under this method, an average of net gains and losses developed from those that have occurred in the past, with consideration of those expected to occur in the future, is applied to normal cost.

Spread Method

The third adjustment method, called the *spread* method, spreads the adjustment over future periods and is almost always used with the projected benefit cost methods (level funding). The gain or loss is spread by the basic actuarial

---

[4] See "Funding" in Chapter 4 regarding recognition of actuarial gains and losses for funding purposes, and see "Actuarial Gains and Losses" in Chapter 6 regarding restrictions on use of the immediate method for accounting purposes.

cost method over the same future period over which other remaining unfunded costs are spread. If the actuarial assumptions are being modified, the adjustment for prior actuarial gains and losses may be added to the effects of the new actuarial assumptions in order to arrive at a modified cost rate for future periods. Although the adjustment usually affects only future normal costs, in some situations it may be apportioned to the unfunded past service cost.

In either the individual level-cost method or the aggregate cost method, the spread technique is automatically used because costs are based on the present value of all unfunded future benefits. Thus, a revised cost rate at any valuation date automatically spreads the adjustment over future periods. Since the past service cost is not separately determined in the computation of the cost rate, either of these two methods, in effect, applies the actuarial gain or loss to all future costs.

VALUATION OF FUND ASSETS

The valuation of fund assets is a principal factor in the calculation of a plan's costs and actuarial gains and losses, and in the determination of any underfunding or overfunding. Thus, it is important to use an acceptable method of valuing the fund's assets.

In performing actuarial valuations, pension fund investment portfolios had traditionally been valued at cost, thus excluding unrealized gains or losses from the calculation until realized through sales. Since APB Opinion No. 8 specified that unrealized appreciation and depreciation should be recognized in the determination of pension cost for accounting purposes, employers have departed from the use of the cost basis for such purposes where the effect would be material. As a result, several techniques are in use for the gradual recognition of unrealized appreciation (depreciation). The most direct method would be to use market value in valuing fund assets, but the effects of short-term fluctuations often make this undesirable. The various techniques now used seek to smooth out these short-term effects. Such techniques include recognition of a portion of unrealized appreciation (depreciation) each period, and recognition of an average of unrealized appreciation (depreciation) over a number of years.

CHAPTER THREE

Agencies for Funding Pension Plans

INTRODUCTION

Pension plans may be funded either on a trusteed basis or an insured basis. This chapter describes the principles of trusteed plans and the various categories of insured plans commonly used.

Although the funding agencies discussed in this chapter are referred to as *plans,* in conformity with terminology commonly used by insurance specialists, actuaries, and others, such funding arrangements should not be confused with types of plans discussed in Chapter 1.

For operational guidelines for managing pension fund investments, see Appendix G.

TRUSTEED PLANS

A pension plan that uses a trust as its funding agency is called a *trusteed* pension plan. Other terms used for such a plan are *self-administered* pension plan,

27

self-insured pension plan, and *uninsured* or *noninsured* pension plan. Trusteed plans are generally set up under an agreement between an employer and a bank or one or more individual trustees. The agreement prescribes the terms under which the trust is to be created and administered. Subject to the plan's provisions, investment decisions may be made by the bank, by the employer company, or by others designated by the administrative committee or joint board of trustees.

Under a trusteed plan, contributions are made to the pension trust, and the fund so established is invested according to the terms of the trust agreement. Earnings serve to increase the fund, and the fund's assets are used to provide pensions or other benefits for employees. Retirement benefits may be paid out by the trust during the period of retirement, or an annuity may be purchased for the employee upon his retirement, thus transferring the obligation at that date to an insurance company. (See "Split Funding" at the end of this chapter.)

Retirement benefits to be paid are based upon the stipulations in the plan. Trustees assume responsibility for the proper administration of the trust, but do not guarantee actuarial adequacy, rate of income, or sufficiency of assets to pay benefits.

A trust agreement with a bank will normally specify that the bank is to provide services to the plan as a custodian, as a directed trustee or as a nondirected trustee. When acting as *custodian,* a bank performs only limited administrative services, such as retaining custody of securities, collecting dividends and interest, and providing the plan administrator with certain reports. As a *directed trustee,* a bank will perform the aforementioned custodial services and provide services to assist the portfolio manager and plan administrator in carrying out their duties. Such services normally include providing record-keeping services (e.g., portfolio transactions, balances, performance reports), providing the portfolio manager with economic and other data, and making benefit payments. The directed trustee also provides the plan administrator with information about developments in the employee benefits field and with information needed to prepare reports to be filed with regulatory agencies. When acting as a *nondirected trustee,* a bank will perform those services discussed above and provide portfolio management services. In most such cases the bank will make investment decisions, preferably based on policy guidelines set forth by the plan administrator and execute the transactions through stockbrokers.

Trust assets of several plans of the same sponsoring employer company are sometimes placed into one fund, called a *master trust.* In such cases the bank normally maintains the records necessary to determine accountability of assets for each plan. Similarly, one employer's plan assets may be pooled together with assets of other employer's plans into what is referred to as a *commingled* trust fund. In such cases each plan receives units of the commingled fund and shares in its income and expenses, in a manner similar to that of a mutual fund. The majority of large and medium-sized funded pension plans currently in effect are of the self-administered trusteed type.

INSURED PLANS

An arrangement with an insurance company may be used as a medium for the receipt of pension contributions, for the administration of a pension fund, and for payment of benefits. A plan that uses only an insurance company as a funding agency is called an *insured* plan. Under some insured plans, insurance companies contract to pay specific retirement benefits in return for certain set premium payments. Under others, the insurance companies receive and accumulate funds for use at subsequent dates, either to pay specified retirement benefits in return for certain set premium payments taken from the accumulated funds, or to pay benefits directly from the accumulated funds. The retirement benefits and eligibility for such benefits are established on the basis of the provisions of the pension plan.

Insured plans may provide either for individual policy contracts or for master group contracts. Some insured group plans may use segregated accounts, which accumulate funds separately from the insurance company's general assets. This procedure differs little from funding through a trust fund. Some of the more common types of insured plans are described below.

Individual Policy Plan

As the name implies, this type of plan involves the employer's purchase of a separate life insurance or annuity policy in the name of each covered employee. The premiums paid under such a policy are referred to as *level annual premiums* because they remain uniform for each employee through the period of coverage to retirement date. The premium is determined by reference to annuity benefits the employee will receive. When benefits are revised for any reason (e.g., changes in compensation), additional policies are issued and total premiums are changed accordingly. An annuity policy is sometimes referred to as a *level premium deferred annuity* or an *annual premium retirement annuity.*

Individual policy plans frequently use insurance policies that provide, for an additional premium, life insurance protection in addition to the annuity benefits. A policy that combines annuity and life insurance features is variously called a *retirement income policy,* an *insurance income policy,* or an *income endowment policy.* Such an individual policy provides for a death benefit before retirement equal to a specified sum related to monthly retirement income or to the cash value of the policy, whichever is greater. For an uninsurable employee, a policy is usually issued with a death benefit limited to the gross premiums paid or, if greater, the cash value of the policy.

A slightly different arrangement utilizes an *ordinary life policy* which provides death benefits and only a part of the retirement income. The balance of the retirement income is provided by a separate fund, often referred to as a *side fund* or an *auxiliary fund,* which is maintained either by the insurance company or in a trust. Although death benefits after retirement vary depending on a particular plan's provisions, a common practice is to provide a period certain and life annuity, the period usually being 10 years.

Individual policy premiums do not involve discounting for either mortality or severance of employment before retirement age. In the event of severance the employer is entitled to a refund, but this is considerably less than the amount credited for severance under a group annuity plan.

Because of the possible adverse tax consequences of direct ownership of the policies by either the employer or the employee, individual policy plans provide for a trust under which the trustee holds title to the individual policies and administers the plan in accordance with the formal plan document or a separate trust instrument.[1]

Group Permanent Plan

A *group permanent* plan normally provides ordinary life coverage under a single master policy issued to the employer. This type of plan often utilizes a side fund consisting of either a group deposit administration policy (see "Deposit Administration Group Annuity Plan," this chapter) or a trust fund, and is used primarily for plans of medium size (e.g., 10 to 100 participants). Group permanent plans have seen relatively little use because most employers who consider this funding vehicle will prefer the anticipated economies of the deposit administration concept.

Group Annuity Plan

Under this type of insured plan, the employer enters into a master contract with the insurance company which covers the entire group of eligible employees. The contract calls for the purchase each year of a fully paid-up deferred annuity in an amount equal to the benefit accrued in that year for each participating employee. This method of funding is the conceptual basis of the accrued benefit cost method for computing contributions.

When an employee retires, the total amount of his benefits will be equal to the sum of the separately purchased units of deferred annuity. This plan is often referred to as a *deferred group annuity plan* and sometimes as a *deferred annuity group annuity plan.* Because there is a direct correspondence between the premium and the amount of deferred annuity that is purchased by a given *single premium,* the group annuity plan is also said to employ the single-premium method of funding.

The premium rates applicable to the various ages under a group annuity plan are guaranteed by the insurance company for a fixed period, usually five

---

[1] Use of individual policy funding, which was one of the earliest funding techniques, has recently been limited to smaller plans (e.g., fewer than 10 participants) and to certain special situations.

years, after which a new premium structure may be established and guaranteed for a future fixed period.

Since group annuity contracts usually do not provide a refund of employer contributions upon an employee's death, premium rates related to these contributions reflect a discount for mortality prior to retirement. The employee's contributions, usually with added interest, are paid as a death benefit if the employee dies before his retirement date. Therefore, the premium rates used to determine the annuity available from employee contributions are set at a higher level because they do not involve a discount for mortality prior to retirement.

Group annuity plans do not discount for turnover. Instead, past employer's contributions which have been made for the account of those separated employees who do not receive vested benefits are credited against the employer's next premium payment, less a portion retained by the insurance company as a *surrender charge* to provide for applicable administrative expenses. Employees' contributions are returned, usually with interest.

The premium payment schedule for a given employee is usually of the step-rate type, that is, premiums increase each year with advancing age. However, the stability of the overall average cost for all employees depends either on the current and future age distribution of the group or on its degree of maturity.

Although not common, some group annuity plans may use a money-purchase basis for computing benefits. In such instances, the annual contribution applicable to each employee is determined by the plan. The amount of the deferred annuity that can be purchased for an individual each year with a constant amount of annual contribution will become progressively smaller as his age increases.

The provisions of a group annuity plan are ordinarily set forth in a master contract and individual employees receive *certificates* as evidence of participation.

At one time most insured plans were of the group annuity plan type. This type is now used primarily for small to medium-sized groups (e.g., 10 to 100 participants) or in special situations.

Deposit Administration Group Annuity Plan

Under this plan, as in the case of a group annuity plan, a master contract is drawn between the employer and the insurance company. This contract may be referred to as a *deposit administration contract,* a *deposit administration group annuity contract,* or, in abbreviated form, as a *DA contract.*

Contrary to what is done under a group annuity plan, under a DA contract no annuity units are purchased for the individual employee before the date he retires. Instead, the employer's periodic contributions are deposited with the insurance company in an unallocated fund, to which the insurance company adds interest at a rate guaranteed usually for five years, but subject to change thereafter. The rate, when changed, applies to funds deposited from the date of change, but the initial rate often continues to apply to previously deposited funds. When an employee retires, the amount required to buy an *immediate* annuity to provide for his pension is applied by the insurance company as a single premium from the unallocated fund. The premium rates for such annuities to be purchased in the future are also guaranteed by the insurance company on a five-year basis. The insurance company guarantees the pension payments on purchased annuities, but does not guarantee that the unallocated fund will necessarily be adequate to meet the cost of annuities to be purchased. The contract provides for periodic dividends (rate credits, if the company is a stock company) as determined by the insurance company at its discretion, on the basis of its experience under the contract. In effect, these dividends represent an adjustment of past premiums. Contributions to the unallocated fund may be determined by the use of any one of several actuarial cost methods.

Immediate Participation Guarantee Contract

This contract is an outgrowth of the DA contract and strongly resembles aspects of a trusteed plan. The master contract, if it is with a mutual insurance company, is called an *immediate participation guarantee contract* or, in abbreviated form, an *IPG contract*. If it is with a stock insurance company, it is called a *direct rerating contract*.

As in the case of a DA contract, the employer makes periodic payments into a fund maintained by the insurance company, and the insurance company credits interest to the fund and pays annuity benefits on employees' retirement. However, unlike the DA contract, which guarantees interest, the IPG contract calls for interest credits to be based essentially on the rate of the insurance company's earnings for the year on its investment portfolio after investment profits and losses are reflected. The insurance company charges expenses directly to the fund, whereas under DA contracts expenses are charged only in the determination of dividends or rate credits. Essentially, the IPG contract is intended to give the employer the immediate effect of experience under the contract, including the insurance company's investment results. At the same time, the insurance company makes fewer guarantees under such a contract.

The IPG contract is written in two forms with the same ultimate result. One form, like the DA plan, may provide for the actual purchase of single-premium annuities as employees retire. There is an adjustment each year for actual experience under the annuities, based upon the insurance company's analysis of mortality, benefits paid, and earnings. The annual adjustment for favorable or unfavorable experience is reflected by an addition to or a deduction from the fund.

In the other form, the IPG contract may achieve the same result through a different technique. When an employee retires, the retirement income payments to him are made directly out of the fund without the purchase of an annuity. However, the fund on deposit with the insurance company must be maintained at the amount required, according to a premium schedule in the contract, to provide for the remaining retirement benefits for all those on retirement at any time. Thus, if necessary, the fund could always be applied to buy all annuities in force. Under either form of IPG contract, the insurance company guarantees lifetime benefit payments to retired employees.

Separate Accounts

Legislation is now in effect in most states permitting an insurance company to offer separate accounts as an adjunct to one of the other insured plan contracts. The investments in these accounts are not restricted by insurance laws; they are used primarily for investing pension plan funds in equity securities. Such an account may be established solely for use in conjunction with the contract for one policyholder, in which case the term *separate separate account* is often applied. Usually, however, the account is pooled with funds of various policyholders and is referred to as a *pooled separate account*. Such a pooled separate account is similar in nature to a commingled trust and to a mutual fund.

The separate account facility can be used as a basis for the insurance company to offer investment services only, without necessarily being involved in the payment of plan benefits.

The availability of separate accounts with DA or IPG contracts has resulted in a considerable increase in the number of plans using insurance company funding facilities.

Guaranteed Income Contracts

Under a *guaranteed income contract,* the insurance company guarantees a specified return on amounts invested. The interest rate is guaranteed for the term of the contract, which normally runs from 5 to 12 years. In some cases, one rate will be in effect for the first part of the life of the contract, another (normally lower) rate for the next part, and another rate for the last part.

Under most such contracts, the guaranteed rate applies to any amounts invested during the term of the contract. Some contracts call for an increased rate to be applied to new investments if money market interest rates have risen during the contract period. However, such contracts usually apply a declining rate to the initial investment as described in the preceding paragraph.

At the end of the contract period, the investment may be withdrawn (normally with an option for a lump sum or installments) for transfer to another funding agency, or the contract may be renegotiated for a new contract period and at a new rate.

Guaranteed income contracts offer a fixed rate of return as high as or higher than that available from high quality fixed-income securities, and appeal to many plan administrators, particularly when the equity markets are performing poorly. While such plans offer an attractive interest rate with little risk, some administrators question whether the yields available under such contracts will keep pace with increasing salary levels over a number of years. Furthermore, if funds are withdrawn before the end of the contract period, the amount received will be limited to the lower of cost or the then current market value of the investment, plus accrued interest. Thus, if general interest rates rise, a loss will be incurred upon premature withdrawal.

It appears that guaranteed income contracts have been used most frequently in connection with profit-sharing and thrift-savings plans. In many such cases the participant may select between a fixed-income investment, represented by the guaranteed income contract, and an equity investment. When used with profit-sharing and savings plans, the insurance company normally allows participants to withdraw amounts invested at any time with no loss of principal, regardless of the then current value of the assets.

Split Funding

Many employers use both a trust fund and an insurance contract in an effort to obtain some of the expected advantages of each method. If this is done, the annuities to retired employees would usually be paid under the insurance contract, and all or part of the funds for active employees would be accumulated in the trust fund. The DA or IPG insurance contract is usually used for this purpose. If the contract calls only for the purchase of immediate annuities as employees retire, with all funds for active employees being accumulated in a trust fund, it is similar to the portion of the DA contract used to purchase annuities as employees retire.

CHAPTER FOUR

Principal ERISA Provisions

INTRODUCTION

In changing the requirements for private pension plans, ERISA affects both employer company financial statements and financial statements of pension plans.

This chapter summarizes the principal provisions of ERISA and the Multiemployer Pension Plan Amendments Act of 1980 relevant to accounting and auditing. Reporting and disclosure requirements are discussed separately in Chapter 5. Certain other matters which might be material for plan design, tax planning, and other purposes are omitted here. Significant questions outside the scope of this and the following chapter should be considered in light of the law itself and whatever rules and regulations may pertain. As a summary, this material cannot serve as a substitute for full reading of the act and pertinent regulations, and advice of legal counsel.

GENERAL COVERAGE OF ERISA

Prior to ERISA, the Welfare and Pension Plans Disclosure Act of 1958 (as amended) governed private pension plans. By the end of 1975, ERISA had replaced all provisions of the 1958 act. All ERISA provisions are currently effective except for certain provisions relating to minimum funding requirements, back-loaded benefits, and prohibited transactions. These provisions have effective dates as late as June 30, 1984, as discussed later in this chapter. Inasmuch as ERISA supersedes all state laws that might relate to plans covered by ERISA, pension plans are generally exempt from state requirements.

Most ERISA provisions apply to both defined benefit plans and defined contribution plans. See Table 4-1 for a summary of the applicability of ERISA to each of these types of plans.

PLANS COVERED AND EXCLUDED

Generally, the law applies to all plans established by sponsors engaged in interstate commerce except:

government plans, including state and local governments;

church plans, unless they elect to be covered by ERISA;

plans established and maintained solely for the purpose of complying with applicable workmen's compensation, disability insurance, or unemployment compensation laws;

plans maintained outside the United States, primarily for nonresident aliens;

unfunded excess benefit plans, that is, plans that are unfunded *and* are maintained solely for the purpose of providing benefits for certain employees in excess of the maximum benefit limitations imposed by the Internal Revenue Code.

PARTICIPATION

A plan may not require age and service standards for participation stricter than one year of service and the attainment of age 25. Alternatively, the plan may provide the age 25 requirement and a three-year waiting period provided that a participant's accrued benefits vest 100% thereafter. Furthermore, plans of cer-

Table 4-1 Applicability of ERISA provisions to defined benefit and defined contribution plans

Requirement	Defined Benefit Plans	Defined Contribution Plans[1]
Minimum participation and vesting standard	X	X
Limitations on benefits and/or contributions	X	X
Back-loaded benefits prohibition	X	
Minimum funding requirement	X[2]	[2]
Termination insurance	X	
Annual report	X[3]	X[3]
Actuarial statement	X[2]	[2]
Fiduciary standards	X	X
Limitation on investment in employer securities and real property	X	X[4]

1 Includes money-purchase pension plans, profit-sharing plans, and other individual account plans such as individual annuity contracts, thrift, and savings plans.

2 Does not apply to certain insured defined benefit plans, but does apply to money-purchase (including target benefit) plans.

3 A simplified reporting requirement is the only requirement that is applicable to unfunded deferred compensation plans for key executives.

4 Except for plans which meet specified requirements for exemption from limitation.

tain educational institutions that require no more than one year of service, with 100% vesting thereafter, may require the attainment of age 30 for eligibility to participate. Defined benefit plans and target benefit plans may exclude employees who are employed for the first time within five years of the normal retirement age under the plan (usually 65). An analysis of ERISA's minimum age and service requirements, including discussions of entry dates, maximum age limitations, and coverage tests used by the IRS appears in Appendix A.

Penalties

Failure to conform to ERISA's participation requirements (as well as to vesting, funding, limits on benefits, and certain other requirements described in this chapter) may cause the imposition of various penalties. These include possible civil actions by plan participants or beneficiaries to recover lost benefits and to clarify their rights to future benefits, and disqualification of the plan with concomitant loss of tax benefits. For a discussion of how these penalties may affect the plan administrator, employer company, and plan, see the section "How Penalties Apply," later in this chapter.

VESTING*

ERISA allows three alternatives for vesting normal retirement benefits derived from employer contributions. Under prior law generally, and in all cases under the new law, an employee's right to receive benefits derived from his own contributions is nonforfeitable. The three alternatives are:

1 *graded vesting* of accrued benefits, with at least 25% after five years of service, at least 5% each year thereafter for five years, and 10% each year thereafter, so that the employee's accrued benefits would be 100% vested after 15 years;
2 100% of accrued benefits after 10 years of service, with no vesting required before the end of the 10-year period (this vesting formula is commonly known as *cliff vesting*); and
3 a *rule of 45,* under which accrued benefits of an employee with five or more years of service must be at least 50% vested when the sum of his age and service equals 45, with 10% additional vesting for each year of service thereafter, provided that a participant with 10 years of service must be at least 50% vested and vest thereafter at a rate of not less than 10% per year of service.

* Beginning in 1984, accelerated vesting will be required in certain "top-heavy" plans. See Appendix H for a discussion of top-heavy plan rules.

In any event, accrued benefits derived from employer contributions must be fully vested at the earlier of the plan's normal retirement age or at normal retirement age defined by ERISA. According to ERISA, normal retirement age is the later of age 65 or the tenth anniversary of the commencement of participation.

A special minimum vesting schedule applies to class-year plans, that is, profit-sharing, stock bonus, or money-purchase plans providing separate vesting of contributions made in each plan year, or of the rights derived from them, and the withdrawal of these amounts on a class-by-class basis as they mature. Such plans must provide 100% vesting of benefits derived from employer contributions no later than at the end of the fifth plan year after the plan year for which the contribution was made.

Employee service before age 22 may generally be ignored unless the plan uses the *rule of 45,* in which case such service may be ignored only if the employee was not a participant in the plan during the years before age 22.

While the prescribed vesting requirements should prevail in a substantial majority of cases, it should be noted that more stringent vesting could be required administratively by the IRS in some cases. Where discrimination in favor of "highly paid" employees would occur under ERISA's vesting schedules, the IRS could require the use of stricter vesting standards to the extent needed to eliminate discrimination. As a general rule, however, adherence to one of the prescribed minimum vesting schedules should suffice unless (1) there has been a pattern of abuse under the plan (e.g., dismissal of employees before their accrued benefits become vested), tending to discriminate in favor of employees who are officers, shareholders, or highly compensated, or (2) there have been, "or there is reason to believe there will be," an accrual of benefits or forfeitures tending to discriminate in favor of such employees. But some uncertainty has been created in this area by virtue of a strict regulatory posture taken by the IRS. An analysis of ERISA's minimum vesting standards is presented in Appendix B, for use as a reference.

The rules for computing years of service are complex. Generally, an employee is considered to have a year of service if he has worked 1,000 hours in a 12-month period, subject to special provisions for breaks in service that cover when and under what circumstances service before and after a break must be included. See Appendix C for an analysis of the Department of Labor guidelines for computing periods of service.

If at least 50% of a participant's accrued benefits derived from employer contributions is vested, the withdrawal of his own required contributions will not cause him to forfeit his employer-financed benefits.

Record-Keeping Requirements

The employer is required to maintain records of each employee's years of service (including breaks in service) and vesting percentage. In the case of a multiple-employer plan, the data are to be submitted to the plan administrator, to the extent practicable. Multiple-employer plans are expected to meet the same requirements as single-employer plans. ERISA provides that the employer or plan administrator maintain such further records as may be needed to determine each employee's benefits. In most cases, data such as age, hours worked, salary, and employee contributions will be needed.

Many employers, especially those with high turnover rates, lack the adequate records of employee service history prior to ERISA, which are necessary to enable them to comply with the act's record-keeping requirements. In recognition of this problem, the Department of Labor allows a certain amount of judgment to be used in deducing past years of service from whatever records are available.

Penalties

Failure to comply with the record-keeping requirements can result in penalties imposed upon the plan administrator and/or employer of $10 for *each* employee with respect to whom such failure occurs.

Some of the other penalties which may be imposed for failure to conform to the vesting requirements summarized herein are described under "Participation," above.

FUNDING

For most defined benefit plans, employers' contributions must include (1) normal cost, (2) interest on unfunded amounts, and (3) a portion of unfunded original past service liability and of unfunded additional past service liability arising from plan amendments.

In determining the funding requirements, ERISA contains certain specifications, including the following.

> The value of the plan's assets shall be determined on the basis of any reasonable actuarial method of valuation which takes into account fair market value and which is permitted under regulations to be prescribed by the Secretary of the Treasury (except that, at the election of the plan administrator, bonds or other evidence of indebtedness not in default may be valued at amortized cost).
>
> Normal costs, accrued liability, past service liability, and experience gains or losses shall be determined under the method used to determine costs under the plan.
>
> All costs, liabilities, rates of interest, and other factors under the plan shall be determined on the basis of actuarial assumptions and methods which, in the aggregate, are reasonable (taking into account the experience of the plan and reasonable expectations) and which, in combination, offer the actuary's best estimate of anticipated experience under the plan.
>
> If the funding method or the plan year for a plan is changed, the new

method or plan year can be used only if the change is approved by the Secretary of the Treasury.

It should be noted that the Conference Committee Joint Explanation states "... a single set of actuarial assumptions will be required for all purposes (e.g., for the minimum funding standard, reporting to the Department of Labor and to participants and beneficiaries, financial reporting to stockholders, etc.)." Most authorities currently hold that ERISA does not contain this requirement, and this view is shared by the IRS. At present, the requirements in the statute, as they are interpreted by the IRS, require merely the same assumptions (and cost method and possibly asset valuation method) for minimum funding and tax deduction purposes.

Amortization Periods

Unfunded past service liability on the first day of the first plan year to which the minimum funding rules apply must be funded in equal annual installments as follows:

for plans in existence on January 1, 1974, over a period of no more than 40 years;

for single-employer plans (or multiple-employer plans other than a special type of such plans known as multiemployer plans) established after January 1, 1974, over a period of no more than 30 years.

Where unfunded past service liability increases as a result of plan amendments adopted in a plan year, single-employer plans must fund the increases over a period of no more than 30 years. Where unfunded past service liability decreases as a result of plan amendments adopted in a plan year, the amount of the decrease is amortized over the same number of years to reduce the amount otherwise required to be funded.

In addition, experience losses must be funded over a period of no more than 15 years by single-employer plans, with gains amortized to reduce the amount otherwise required to be funded.

Funding must also reflect losses resulting from changes in actuarial assumptions. Such losses must be funded over a period of no more than 30 years, with gains amortized to reduce the amount otherwise required to be funded.

Though there was some concern when ERISA was first enacted, it has now become fairly well established that the rules regarding amortization periods do not require amortization bases to be set up if that would run counter to the actuarial cost method in use. Rather, the rules merely prescribe the amortization *if* a base is established.

Funding Standard Account(s)

For the purpose of determining whether a defined benefit plan is meeting the minimum funding requirements, ERISA requires the plan to maintain a (memorandum) funding standard account and allows the use of an alternative account under specified circumstances. Requirements for maintenance of such accounts and examples of their operation are summarized in Tables 4-2, 4-3, and 4-4. The difference in the two illustrations in Table 4-3 is in the total value of plan assets. In the illustration in column A the value is $28,500,000; in the illustration in column B the value is $29,800,000. Table 4-4 is based on the illustration in column A of Table 4-3.

These accounts are not required to be maintained by profit-sharing and stock bonus plans, nor by certain other tax-qualified plans and insured plans funded exclusively by level premium individual insurance contracts or group insurance contracts having the characteristics of such individual insurance contracts.

For money-purchase plans (including target benefit plans), a funding standard account is generally required only to the extent that the employer is charged each year for the amount that must be contributed under the plan formula and credited with the amount actually paid.

Annual charges to the funding standard account are generally the following:

the normal cost for that year, and

amounts necessary to amortize:

    initial unfunded past service liability, increases in plan costs arising from plan amendments, experience losses, and losses resulting from changes in actuarial assumptions; and

waived funding deficiencies for prior plan years, if any.

Annual credits to the funding standard account are generally the following:

employer contributions made for that year;

amounts necessary to amortize portions of plan cost decreases resulting from plan amendments, experience gains, and gains resulting from changes in actuarial assumptions; and

the amount of any waived funding deficiency for the plan year.

If the funding standard account has an accumulated funding deficiency in a plan year following a year for which such deficiency was determined under the alternative minimum funding standard (see discussion below), any excess of the debit balance in the funding standard account over any debit balance in the alternative minimum funding standard account is credited to the account in that year and must be amortized as charges to the funding standard account over a five-year period.

In addition, the funding standard account and items therein shall be charged or credited (as determined under regulations prescribed by the Secretary of the Treasury) with interest at the appropriate rate consistent with the rate or rates of interest used under the plan to determine costs.

Waivers

The waiver item referred to in the credits to the funding standard account is based upon ERISA's provision that the Secretary of the Treasury may waive all or part of the minimum funding requirements for a plan year in which the minimum funding standard cannot be met without imposing substantial business hardship upon the employer(s), but only if failure to give the waiver would be adverse to participants' interests. The Secretary of the Treasury determines whether such hardship would occur, based upon various factors including certain factors stated in ERISA. ERISA limits waivers on all or part of the funding requirements to not more than five years out of any consecutive 15 years.

The amount of any waived funding deficiency is to be amortized as a charge over 15 years, beginning in the following year; such amounts being amortized may not themselves be waived.

Full Funding Limitation

To prevent contributions in excess of full funding, which would result in total plan asset values in excess of the plan's total accrued liability, ERISA provides that the funding standard account be credited with the excess of:

1 the accumulated funding deficiency (determined without regard to the alternative minimum funding standard account)

over

2 the excess of the plan's accrued liability (including normal cost) over the total value of plan assets.

This limits the year's contribution requirement to the amount that would fund 100% of the plan's accrued liability. The plan's accrued liability referred to herein is determined either by the plan's funding method or, if the liability cannot be directly calculated thereunder, by the entry-age normal funding method. Asset values are to be based upon the lesser of fair market value or the asset valuation method normally used by the plan.

In a plan year to which the full funding limitation credit applies, all "amortization period" items described in this section shall be considered fully amortized for purposes of all future years' calculations. If the plan is amended in later years to increase plan liabilities, however, a new amortization schedule would be established with respect to that increase in liabilities.

Alternative Minimum Funding Standard Account

Plans using a funding method which requires that contributions in all years are no less than those required under the entry-age normal funding method are permitted to use an alternative minimum funding standard account. However, the current position of the Internal Revenue Service is that the only funding method that meets this criterion is the entry-age normal funding method itself.

Table 4-2 ERISA requirements for maintenance

Annual Charges	Amortization Period (in Years)
Normal cost of the plan for the plan year	—
Amortization of (see Note 1):	
Unfunded past service liability under plan on first day of first plan year subject to ERISA:	
In existence on 1/1/74	40
Comes into existence after 1/1/74	30
Separately, with respect to each plan year:	
Net increase (if any) in unfunded past service liability under the plan arising from plan amendments adopted in such year	30
Net experience loss (if any) under the plan	15
Net loss (if any) resulting from changes in actuarial assumptions used under the plan	30
Waived funding deficiency for each prior plan year	15
Any amount credited to this account as an excess of any debit balance in this account over any debit balance in the alternative minimum funding standard account (as described contra)	5
Total for year	—
Debit balance (if any) from prior year	—
Adjusted total	—

1 Amounts required to be amortized may be combined or offset against each other, with the resulting amount amortized over a period determined on the basis of the remaining amortization periods for the appropriate items entering into such combined or offset amounts, pursuant to regulations to be issued by the Secretary of the Treasury.

of funding standard account (single-employer plan)

Annual Credits	Amortization Period (in Years)
Employer contribution considered made for the plan year: Amortization of (see Note 1):	—
Separately, with respect to each plan year:	
Net decrease (if any) in unfunded past service liability under the plan arising from plan amendments adopted in such year	30
Net experience gain (if any) under the plan	15
Net gain (if any) resulting from changes in actuarial assumptions used under the plan	30
Waived funding deficiency for the plan year	—
Excess (if any) of any debit balance in this account (prior to this credit) over any debit balance in the alternative minimum funding standard account (applies only where the accumulated funding deficiency was determined under the alternative minimum funding standard in the preceding plan year)	—
Amount of accumulated funding deficiency (prior to this credit) in excess of full funding limitation (see Table 4-3)	—
Total for year	—
Credit balance (if any) from prior year	—
Adjusted total	—

2 ERISA requires that the account (and items therein) be charged or credited, as determined under regulations to be prescribed by the Secretary of the Treasury, with interest at the appropriate rate consistent with the rate or rates of interest used under the plan to determine costs.

Table 4-3 Examples of funding standard account operation

	A Full Funding Limitation Inapplicable		B Full Funding Limitation Applies	
Description	Charges	Credits	Charges	Credits
Normal cost of the plan for the plan year	$1,000,000	NA	$1,000,000	NA
Amortization of:				
Unfunded past service liability	100,000	NA	100,000	NA
Net increase or decrease in unfunded past service liability arising from plan amendments	25,000	$ 30,000	25,000	$ 30,000
Net experience loss or gain	15,000	25,000	15,000	25,000
Net loss or gain resulting from changes in actuarial assumptions	10,000	45,000	10,000	45,000
Waived funding deficiency for each prior plan year	50,000	NA	50,000	NA
Any amount credited to this account as an excess of any debit balance in this account over any debit balance in the alternative minimum funding standard account	20,000	NA	20,000	NA
Waived funding deficiency for the plan year	NA	—	NA	—
Excess of debit balance in this account over any debit balance in the alternative minimum funding standard account	NA	—	NA	—
Employer contribution requirement[1]	NA	1,120,000	NA	200,000
Amount of accumulated funding deficiency in excess of full funding limitation[2]	NA	—	NA	920,000
Debit or credit balance from prior year	—	—	—	—
Totals (nets to zero balance)	$1,220,000	$1,220,000	$1,220,000	$1,220,000

1 Difference between total charges and total credits (before this amount).

Table 4-3   (continued)

2 Accumulated funding deficiency (before contribution and full funding limitation credit)		$1,120,000		$1,120,000
Plan's accrued liability, etc.	$30,000,000		$30,000,000	
Total value of plan assets (lesser of fair market value and value in accordance with use of asset valuation method)	28,500,000	(1,500,000)	29,800,000	(200,000)
Amount of accumulated funding deficiency in excess of full funding limitation		NA		$ 920,000

NA = Not applicable.

Table 4-4   ERISA requirements for maintenance of alternative minimum funding standard account and example of its operation

Annual Charges:
  Lesser of the following:
    Normal cost under the funding method used under the plan ($1,000,000; see Table 4-3)
    Normal cost determined under the unit credit method ($900,000) $ 900,000

  Excess, if any, of the present value of accrued benefits under the plan ($28,900,000) over the fair market value of the assets ($28,600,000)   300,000

  An amount equal to the excess, if any, of credits to this account for all prior plan years over charges to this account for all such years (applies only where this account was used in determining the accumulated funding deficiency)   —

  Total   1,200,000

Annual Credits:
  Employer contribution considered made for the plan year (see Table 4-3, column A)   1,120,000

Net balance—debit (credit)   80,000
Debit or credit balance from prior year   —
Adjusted net balance $ 80,000

1 It can be seen that the contribution required to avoid an accumulated funding deficiency (before the contribution) under the funding standard account ($1,120,000) is less than the amount that would have been required under the alternative minimum funding standard account ($1,200,000).

2 ERISA requires that the account (and items therein) be charged or credited, as determined under regulations (to be) prescribed by the Secretary of the Treasury, with interest at the appropriate rate consistent with the rate or rates of interest used under the plan to determine costs.

This alternative account is to be charged each year with the sum of the following:

> the lesser of normal cost under the plan's funding method or under the unit credit method;
>
> any excess of the present value of the plan's accrued benefits over the fair market value of plan assets; and
>
> any excess of credits over charges to the alternative minimum funding standard account for all prior years.

The annual credit to the account is the amount the employer has contributed for the plan year.

A plan that elects to use the alternative minimum funding standard account must also maintain the funding standard account. The basis for electing its use is that the year's minimum contribution may be lower than when the funding standard account is used alone.

If both accounts have debit balances at the end of a plan year, a funding deficiency exists in the amount of either the debit balance in the funding standard account or the debit balance in the alternative minimum funding standard account if less. No deficiency exists where either the funding standard account or the alternative minimum funding standard account contains a zero or a credit balance.

Penalties

Unless a contribution is made within two and one-half months after the end of the plan year (extended to eight and one-half months under certain circumstances) in at least the amount of the accumulated funding deficiency, a 5% excise tax based on that deficiency is levied upon the company. An additional 100% tax is subsequently levied where the initial 5% tax is imposed and the accumulated funding deficiency is not corrected within 90 days from mailing of a deficiency notice (or such other period allowed by the Internal Revenue Service). Payment of the tax alone does *not* correct an accumulated funding deficiency.

Some of the other penalties which may be imposed for failure to conform to the funding requirements summarized herein are described above, under "Participation."

Effective Dates

The minimum funding standards are generally currently effective.

MAXIMUM DEDUCTIBLE CONTRIBUTION

For qualified defined benefit plans, the maximum annual deduction is generally based on normal cost plus the amount necessary to amortize past service cost over 10 years (approximately 12% to 14% of past service cost, depending upon the actuarial investment yield assumption). The maximum annual deduction based on 5% of covered compensation has been eliminated, but the deduction based on level funding is still available. If the minimum funding rules require a larger dollar amount than the above, the larger amount would be deductible. The 15% limitation on covered compensation with respect to profit-sharing and stock bonus plans remains unchanged, except that where a profit-sharing or stock bonus plan is maintained together with a money-purchase pension plan or with a defined benefit plan, the maximum total limitation is 25% of covered compensation.

LIMITS ON BENEFITS AND CONTRIBUTIONS*

For qualified defined benefit plans, ERISA provides that the maximum annual benefit derived from employer contributions may not exceed the lesser of (a) $75,000 or (b) 100% of the participant's average compensation during his highest three years of compensation. The $75,000 limit is adjusted upward for cost-of-living increases and is not reduced for early retirement unless the participant retires before age 55. Regardless of the foregoing, the limit is generally not less than $10,000 if the employee has never participated in a defined contribution plan of the employer.

For qualified defined contribution plans, ERISA provides that a participant may be credited with no more than the lesser of 25% of compensation or $25,-000 per year. For purposes of calculating the limit, the individual's share of forfeitures (and in some cases a portion of employee contributions, if any) are to be included. Upward adjustments in the $25,000 limit for cost-of-living increases are provided for under ERISA.

If a participant is covered by both a defined benefit plan and a defined contribution plan of the same employer (multiple plans of the same type, e.g., two defined benefit plans of a single employer, are considered as a single plan), the total benefits permitted to accrue under the defined benefit plan and the contributions permitted to be made under the defined contribution plan with respect to a participant are limited as follows. The sum of (a) the accrued benefit (projected to normal retirement age) under the defined benefit plan as a percentage of the maximum amount permitted under ERISA plus (b) the amounts contributed to the defined contribution plan (for the current and all past years

* For years beginning after 1982, the limits on benefits and contributions have been reduced. See Appendix H for discussion of new limits.

of employment), as a percentage of the maximum amounts permitted to be contributed under ERISA cannot exceed 140%. For example, if 60% of the maximum amount permitted to be contributed each year was contributed for a participant under the defined contribution plan, the maximum amount of benefit that could be accrued under the defined benefit plan would be limited to 80% of the maximum permitted under ERISA for defined benefit plans.

Penalties

Some of the penalties which may be imposed for failure to conform to the summarized requirements are described above, under "Participation."

BACK-LOADED BENEFITS

ERISA contains provisions applicable to defined benefit plans which restrict so-called back-loaded benefits, a term which denotes a higher rate of normal retirement benefit accrued during an employee's later years of service than during his early years. An example of back-loading is a formula that provides for benefits to accrue at the rate of 1.5% of compensation for each year of service until age 55 and 2.5% thereafter. Other examples may include (a) final-pay plans that provide for reductions for social security benefits where the offset is subject to a maximum amount and (b) plans that provide for a minimum benefit after a specified number of years of service.

ERISA limits back-loading by prescribing that benefits provided must accrue at a rate which meets any one of three specified back-loading rules. The first rule basically requires accrual in each year of at least 3% of the maximum normal retirement benefit. The second rule generally prohibits accruals in later years which exceed 133.33% of the annual rate of accrual in any previous year. The third rule requires a service-based proration of the projected normal retirement benefit.

Penalties

Some of the penalties which may be imposed for failure to conform to these requirements are described under "Participation."

JOINT AND SURVIVOR ANNUITIES

ERISA requires that when a plan provides for a retirement benefit in the form of an annuity, the plan must provide for a joint and survivor annuity for married participants. The survivor annuity must be not less than one-half of the annuity payable to the participant during the joint lives of the participant and his spouse.

In the case of an employee for whom benefits are payable in the form of a life annuity, who retires, or who attains the normal retirement age, the joint and survivor provision is to apply unless the employee has elected otherwise.

In the case of an employee who is eligible to retire prior to the normal retirement age under the plan but who continues in active employment, the plan must offer a survivor's annuity but may require an affirmative election by the employee. Moreover, the plan need not make this option available until the employee is within 10 years of normal retirement age.

The employee is to be afforded an opportunity to exercise his election *out of* or, before normal retirement age, possibly *into* the joint and survivor provision before the annuity starting date or before he becomes eligible for early retirement. The employee is to be supplied with a written explanation in layman's language of the joint and survivor provision and of the practical dollars-and-cents effect on him and his spouse, of making an election either to take or not to take the provision.

The plan may provide that any election or revocation of an election is not to become effective if the participant dies within a certain period of time (not in excess of two years) of the election or revocation, except in the case of accidental death where the accident which causes death occurs after the election.

The plan may provide that the joint and survivor benefit is to be the actuarial equivalent of the participant's accrued benefit, in which case there would be no additional cost to the employer for the joint and survivor provisions.

A detailed explanation of the IRS regulations relating to joint and survivor annuities is provided in Appendix D.

Penalties

Some of the penalties which may be imposed for failure to conform to these requirements are described above, under "Participation."

PLAN TERMINATION INSURANCE

ERISA requires plan administrators to pay annual termination insurance premiums to the Pension Benefits Guaranty Corporation (PBGC) which, though within the Department of Labor, in practice operates autonomously. Premiums were initially set at $1 per participant per plan year (50 cents for multiemployer plans), with proratio for fractional years, commencing September 2, 1974. The premium rate for nonmultiemployer plans was increased (by statutory amendment to ERISA late in 1977) to $2.60 for plan years commencing in 1978 or later.

ERISA also contains provisions for further modifications of premium rates in later years so that they will be such "as may be necessary" to provide the PBGC with sufficient revenue to carry out its functions. Within limits, the PBGC in turn will insure the benefits vested according to the plan's terms at the time the plan is terminated (other than those benefits arising solely because the plan was terminated). The limit on the benefits to be guaranteed by the

PBGC under ERISA is generally the lesser of (a) 100% of the average wages paid to a participant during his five highest years of participation or (b) $750 per month (adjusted upward for cost-of-living increases). For plans terminating in 1982, the amount is up to $1,380.68. In addition, a phase-in rule limits benefit guarantees on all benefits stemming from new plans or plan amendments. The phase-in is at the rate of 20% per year or, if greater, $20 of monthly annuity per year.

ERISA establishes an employer liability of up to 30% of its net worth for losses the PBGC sustains as a result of payments made due to a single-employer plan terminated by the sponsoring employer. Net worth is to be determined as of a date (not more than 120 days prior to the date of termination) selected by the PBGC and on whatever basis the PBGC regards as best reflecting the current status of the employer's operations. The resultant liability thus imposed may be enforced by a priority lien on the employer's assets. PBGC has taken the position that the 30% liability applies only once where an employer has multiple plans terminated at the same time. With a controlled group of employers, the net worth of the whole family of companies is subject to the 30% test, not to the particular family member that maintained the plan.

Employers were theoretically allowed to insure this "contingent liability," as ERISA calls it, either with the PBGC itself or through private insurance carriers. However, as indicated below, through the Multiemployer Pension Plan Amendments Act of 1980, strong congressional sentiment repealed the provisions of ERISA that provide for this contingent employer liability insurance (CELI).

ERISA requires that certain events related to a potential plan termination be reported to the PBGC by the plan administrator. It is further noted that the plan termination insurance provisions generally pertain only to qualified plans and generally do not apply to defined contribution plans.

Penalties

Failure to pay the termination insurance premiums when due can result in the imposition of a civil penalty of up to 100% of the premium which was not timely paid, plus interest. Nonpayment of such premiums, however, does not result in loss of coverage.

Effective Dates

Generally, the plan termination insurance provisions became effective upon ERISA's passage (September 2, 1974) with some exceptions. For other than multiemployer plans, the provisions relating to benefit payment guarantees (but not the provisions for premiums or contingent liability) were also effective for plans that terminated after June 30, 1974, and before ERISA's passage. For multiemployer plans, benefit guarantees generally are not available for plans terminating before August 1, 1980.

MULTIEMPLOYER PENSION PLANS

A company withdrawing from a multiemployer pension plan may be exposed to unlimited liability, instead of the former 30% of net worth, as a result of the Multiemployer Pension Plan Amendments Act of 1980. In addition to repealing that ERISA provision, the new law, enacted in September 1980, has broadened the responsibilities of both multiemployer plans and the contributing employers. Although there are important retroactive features, the legislation was, for the most part, effective prospectively.

This highly complex law is the product of a statutory mandate dating from December 19, 1977, to the Pension Benefit Guaranty Corporation (PBGC) to study the desirability of reforming the treatment of multiemployer plans under ERISA.

Following is a summary of major provisions:

1 **Withdrawal** Determining the liability of an employer withdrawing from a multiemployer plan is no longer contingent on the plan's terminating within five years. In addition, the liability is now payable to the plan, not the PBGC. As mentioned earlier, the 30% ceiling on an employer's net worth has been eliminated.

2 **Insurable Event** Plan termination is no longer the insurable event in terms of benefits guaranteed by the PBGC. In fact, funding requirements still continue to apply to terminated plans. The insurable event for multiemployer plans will now be plan insolvency.

3 **Financial Difficulties** Multiemployer plans must now use new rules for identifying a plan's financial difficulties and classifying them. The law designates the more severe condition as "insolvency"; the less severe as "in reorganization."

4 **Higher Premiums** Termination insurance premiums to the PBGC will be gradually raised from 50 cents per year per participant to $2.60.

5 **New Benefit Guarantees** When a plan is insolvent, the PBGC-guaranteed portion of the plan benefits will be calculated by a radically different formula from that for single-employer plans. In general, that guaranteed amount will be smaller.

6 **Mergers and Spinoffs** Mergers and spinoffs involving multiemployer plans will merely have to protect the participants' accrued benefits, not the funded portion of the accrued benefits determined on a plan termination basis.

7 **Legal Responsibility** The employer's obligations to contribute to multiemployer plans have been upgraded into a legal requirement under ERISA.

8 **Repeal of CELI** ERISA's contingent employer liability insurance (CELI) provisions have been repealed. These allowed employers partici-

pating in single-employer and multiemployer plans to insure themselves against liability to the PBGC if a plan was terminated.

9 **Definition of Multiemployer Plans**   The definition of multiemployer plans has been expanded, although plans that had been filing with the appropriate government agencies as single-employer plans under former law may now elect to continue being treated as single-employer plans (actually, multiple-employer plans other than multiemployer plans).

10 **Immediate Deductibility**   The Internal Revenue Code has been clarified so that both termination liability payments by employers sponsoring single-employer plans and withdrawal liability payments by employers pulling out of multiemployer plans will be immediately deductible.

The Multiemployer Pension Plan Amendments Act of 1980 is a complex and comprehensive measure. In large part, the law has simply set the stage for procedures and implementation yet to come. These will be governed in the main by regulations from the PBGC and, to a lesser extent, the IRS.

FIDUCIARY RESPONSIBILITIES

ERISA contains detailed provisions for a plan fiduciary's responsibilities and transactions prohibited to him in fulfilling his responsibilities, as summarized in Figure 4-1.

These provisions include prohibitions against the fiduciary's engaging the plan in certain transactions with a party in interest. The term *party in interest* is defined broadly in ERISA and includes employers of plan participants, persons rendering services to the plan, unions whose members are plan participants (and their officers and agents), officers, fiduciaries, and employees of a plan, and certain relatives, agents, and joint venturers of any of the foregoing.

Definition

ERISA defines the term *fiduciary* as any person who:

1 exercises any discretionary authority or discretionary control over management of the plan or exercises any authority or control respecting management or disposition of plan assets;
2 renders investment advice for a fee or other compensation, direct or indirect, with respect to any monies or other property of such plan, or has any authority or responsibility to do so; or
3 has any discretionary authority or discretionary responsibility in the administration of such plan.

Additionally, ERISA provides that a pension plan must have a "named fiduciary" or provide a procedure for identifying the "named fiduciary," and it continues the requirements of prior law that fiduciaries be bonded. The fiduci-

FIGURE 4-1

Duties of and restrictions upon pension plan fiduciaries as established by ERISA

Fiduciaries of pension plans:

(a) Must manage assets solely in the interest of participants and beneficiaries;

(b) Must act with the care that a prudent man in like circumstances would exercise;

(c) Must diversify investments in order to minimize the risk of large losses (unless clearly not prudent to do so);

(d) May invest no more than 10% (less than 10%, if required by the diversification and prudence rules) of the fair market value of plan assets (as defined) in a combination of qualifying employer securities (stock and marketable obligations, as defined) and qualifying employer real property (see Notes);

(e) May not transfer assets outside the United States unless specifically permitted by the Secretary of Labor; and

(f) Are liable for those acts or omissions of cofiduciaries which constitute breaches of their fiduciary responsibilities in specified circumstances.

Notes:

1 Qualifying employer real property is defined as parcels of real property and related personal property which are leased to an employer or its affiliate and (a) a substantial number of the parcels are dispersed geographically and (b) each parcel of real property and the improvements thereon are suitable (or adaptable without excessive cost) for more than one use.

2 This provision became effective January 1, 1975, but the plan is allowed a 10-year transition period within which to comply with this requirement. Further, until June 30, 1984, under certain circumstances involving binding arrangements entered into prior to July 1, 1974, this provision will be complied with even when employer securities or real property that is not considered "qualifying" employer securities or real property is held or acquired. Acquisition or holding by a plan of certain employer debt securities such as bonds, notes, etc., is limited to certain percentages.

3 An exception to this requirement exists for "individual account plans" that are, in general, (a) profit-sharing plans, (b) thrift and savings plans, (c) money-purchase pension plans in existence on September 2, 1974, which held investments primarily in qualifying employer securities as of that date, and (d) stock bonus plans (including employee stock ownership plans), where such individual account plans are designed primarily to make, and specifically provide for, investments in qualifying employer securities or real property.

ary standards do not apply, generally, to unfunded plans for top executives, nor to an insurance company to the extent that the policy provides payments guaranteed by the insurer. Similarly, a mutual fund is not deemed a fiduciary merely because a pension fund holds shares in the mutual fund.

The rules on prohibited transactions do not prevent a plan fiduciary from:

1 receiving reasonable compensation for services to the plan unless he receives full-time pay from the employer or employee organization;

2 receiving benefits from the plan as a participant or beneficiary, as long as these are consistent with the terms of the plan as applied to other participants and beneficiaries;

3 receiving reimbursement for expenses; or

4 being an officer, employee, agent, or other representative of a party in interest.

Exemptions

Despite the rules on prohibited transactions summarized in Figure 4-2, ERISA provides various exemptions primarily to prevent undue restriction of the fiduciary's flexibility in managing fund assets.

Services

Banks and similar financial institutions are permitted to perform "ancillary services" for a plan, under specified circumstances. Payments to parties in interest for reasonable compensation for services necessary to operate the plan are also permitted.

Investments

ERISA permits investment of plan assets in interest-bearing deposits in a bank or similar financial institution, if such bank or other institution is a fiduciary of such plan and if (1) the plan covers only employees of the bank or institution and employees of affiliates of the bank or institution, or (2) such investment is expressly authorized by a provision of the plan or by a fiduciary (other than the bank or institution or affiliate thereof) who is expressly so empowered.

Loans

The plan may make loans to parties in interest who are plan participants or beneficiaries if the plan expressly allows such loans, if they are made on a non-

FIGURE 4-2

Transactions prohibited to pension plan fiduciaries by ERISA

Transactions Prohibited When Involving a Party in Interest

(a) A sale, exchange, or lease of property, except as noted in Figure 4-1, item (d).

(b) A loan or other extension of credit.

(c) The furnishing of goods, services, or facilities.

(d) A transfer of plan assets to a party in interest for the use or benefit of a party in interest.

(e) An acquisition of employer securities or real property, except as noted in Figure 4-1, item (d).

Other Prohibited Transactions

(a) Dealing with the plan assets in his own interest or for his own account.

(b) Acting in any transaction involving the plan on behalf of a party whose interests are adverse to the interests of the plan or its participants or beneficiaries.

(c) Receiving consideration for his own account from a party dealing with the plan in connection with a transaction involving the plan assets.

(d) With respect to fiduciaries who have authority or discretion to control or manage plan assets, permitting the plan to hold employer securities or real property, except as noted in Figure 4-1, item (d).

discriminatory basis at reasonable rates, and if they are adequately collateralized. Under certain circumstances, a party in interest may make a loan to an employee stock ownership plan.

Pooled Funds

The prohibitions of party-in-interest transactions do not apply to pooled funds under certain circumstances.

Life Insurance Companies

A life insurance company can use its own contracts to fund a pension plan for its employees.

Penalties

A plan fiduciary is liable to make good any losses to the plan resulting from a breach of fiduciary duties and to restore to the plan any profits which he made through the use of the plan's assets. In addition, parties in interest who participate in certain prohibited transactions are subject to an excise tax for the year of the transaction *and* for each subsequent year for which it is not corrected. This excise tax is equal to 5% of the amount of the transaction and may be combined with a tax of 100% of the amount of any such transaction if it is not corrected after notice from the Internal Revenue Service.

Some of the other penalties which may be imposed for failure to conform to the fiduciary requirements summarized herein are described under "Participation."

Effective Dates

The described fiduciary standards generally became effective January 1, 1975, with the exception of certain restrictions and limitations on holding or acquiring employer securities or employer real property, for which certain transitional rules apply.

ENFORCEMENT

The law gives both the Internal Revenue Service and the Department of Labor many methods of enforcing ERISA's requirements, providing both criminal and civil penalties as well as direct remedies for plan participants. In general, the Department of Labor is charged with the responsibility of looking after individuals' rights, while the IRS is responsible for overseeing whether funding, vesting, and other requirements are met by particular plans. ERISA provides many remedies and sanctions for its enforcement, including the opening of the federal court system to plan participants and the provision of assistance from the Department of Labor in enforcing their rights.

How Penalties Apply

Some of the penalties which may be imposed for failure to conform to ERISA requirements (as cited in earlier sections of this chapter, and also in Chapter 5) include possible civil actions by plan participants or beneficiaries to recover lost benefits and to clarify rights as to future benefits, and disqualification of the plan with concomitant loss of tax benefits.[1]

Although ERISA specifies that certain penalties are levied against the plan or against the plan administrator, the administrator is often the employer company and, even where that is not the case, it is likely that penalties would fall not upon the plan but rather upon the employer company. This evaluation is based upon the fact that Congress, in drafting the various provisions of ERISA, sought to protect plan assets for participants and beneficiaries, not to insulate the employer company from liability. In the case of a defined benefit plan, most penalties will in any event ultimately fall upon the employer company, if not directly, then indirectly via increased future contributions. The provisions of ERISA described in this chapter (and also in Chapter 5) are nevertheless important to the auditor of the plan as well as to the auditor of the employer company.

ANNUAL REGISTRATION

ERISA requires that all plans subject to the vesting standards file an annual registration statement with the Secretary of the Treasury. The statement must contain, among other things, the names and taxpayer identification numbers of the participants who separated from service and who are entitled to deferred vested benefits. This information is to be transmitted by the Treasury Department to the Department of Health and Human Services, which will notify claimants for social security benefits of their rights to benefits under the employer's pension plan.

---

[1] Past experience has shown that a company failing to comply with provisions of the Internal Revenue Code is normally allowed a period of time to take the necessary steps so as to be in compliance and thereby avoid disqualification of the plan.

CHAPTER FIVE

ERISA Provisions Relating to Reporting and Disclosure

INTRODUCTION

ERISA requires that specified reports be prepared and submitted to plan participants and beneficiaries and to various governmental agencies. Table 5-1 provides a summary of these reporting and disclosure requirements and the forms to be used. Information to be disclosed to participants and beneficiaries is summarized in Table 5-2. The major disclosure items are discussed and sample forms are provided in Appendix E.

PARTICIPANTS AND BENEFICIARIES

Due to ERISA reporting requirements, it is important to properly identify plan participants and beneficiaries, which is not as simple a task as one might initially anticipate.

The terms *participant* and *beneficiary* are defined broadly by ERISA to include any employee (or his designee) who is *or may become* eligible to receive a benefit from the plan. The following Department of Labor regulations relating to the reporting and disclosure requirements narrow the definition as follows.

1   For those plans providing for employee contributions or defining participation to include employees not yet retired, an individual becomes a participant on the earlier of the dates on which an employee contribution is made or the plan's age and service participation requirements are satisfied.

2   For plans that do not provide for employee contributions or define participation to include employees not yet retired, an individual becomes a participant on the earlier of the dates on which he completes the first year of employment that determines his benefit entitlement or the amount of his entitlement.

The regulations indicate that, *regardless of the above,* an individual is *not* a participant if:

1   the individual's entire benefit rights are fully guaranteed by a "regulated" insurance carrier, those rights are legally enforceable by the sole choice of the individual, and a contract, policy, or certificate describing the individual's benefits has been issued to him; or

2   the individual has received all benefits due under the plan; or

Table 5-1 Summary of reporting and disclosure requirements under ERISA

Form	Description	Who Must File	When Filed	Where Filed
5500	Annual return/report of employee benefit plan (with 100 or more participants at beginning of plan year).	Each plan administrator or employer maintaining an employee pension benefit plan (defined benefit or defined contribution) covered by ERISA. Includes HR-10s,[1] IRAs, TSAs (403(b)), and frozen plans.	On or before last day of seventh month after close of plan year. A two-and-one-half-month extension may be granted if Form 5558 is filed early enough for the IRS to act before the annual return's regular due date.[2]	IRS service center indicated on IRS instructions to Form 5500.
5500C	Annual return/report of employee benefit plan (with fewer than 100 participants at beginning of plan year and no owner–employee participant).	Each plan administrator or employer maintaining an employee pension benefit plan (defined benefit or defined contribution) covered by ERISA. Includes frozen plans, IRAs, TSAs (403(b)), and partnership plans where no owner–employee is a participant.	Same as Form 5500, except only sponsors with an employer identification number ending in 4, 5, or 6 should file Form 5500C. All other plans should file Form 5500R.	Same as Form 5500.

Table 5-1 (continued)

Form	Description	Who Must File	When Filed	Where Filed
5500K	Annual return/report of employee benefit plan for sole proprietors and partnerships (with fewer than 100 participants at the beginning of the plan year and at least one owner–employee).	Each sole proprietor, partnership, or plan administrator maintaining or administering a Keogh plan.	Same as Form 5500C.	Same as Form 5500.
5500R	Registration statement of employee benefit plan (with fewer than 100 participants at the beginning of the plan year).	Each plan administrator or employer maintaining an employee pension benefit plan (defined benefit or defined contribution) covered by ERISA.	Same as Form 5500, except only sponsors with an employer identification number ending in 1, 2, 3, 7, 8, 9, or 0 file Form 5500R. All other plans file Form 5500C or Form 5500K.	Same as Form 5500.
5500G	Annual return/report of employee benefit plan (for government and certain church plans) of any size.	Each plan administrator or employer maintaining a government pension benefit plan or a pension benefit plan for a church that has *not* elected coverage under Code Sec. 410(d).	Same as Form 5500, except for plans with funds pooled into a single fund for investment purposes, the year-end of the investment fund is used as the close of the plan year for filing purposes.	Same as Form 5500.

Schedule A (Form 5500)	Insurance information	Each employer or plan administrator of defined benefit or defined contribution plans must attach this schedule to Form 5500, 5500C, 5500K, or 5500R where any plan benefits are provided by an insurance company, insurance service, or similar organization. However, a plan covering only an individual or an individual and spouse need not file Schedule A if one or both own the trade or business. A plan covering only partners and spouses need not file Schedule A.	**Same as Form 5500, 5500C, 5500K, or 5500R**, whichever is appropriate.	Same as Form 5500.
Schedule B (Form 5500)	Actuarial information.	Each employer or plan administrator of a defined benefit plan subject to minimum funding standards (Code Sec. 412 and Part 3 of Title I of ERISA) must attach this schedule to Form 5500, 5500C, 5500K, or 5500R, as appropriate.	**Same as Form 5500, 5500C, 5500K, or 5500R**, whichever is appropriate.	Same as Form 5500.

63

Table 5-1 (continued)

Form	Description	Who Must File	When Filed	Where Filed
Schedule P (Form 5500)	Annual return of fiduciary of employee benefit trust.	Each trustee or custodian of a trust or custodial account that is qualified under Code Sec. 401(a) and exempt from tax under Code Sec. 501(a) who wants the statute of limitations to begin as provided in Code Sec. 6501.	Same as Form 5500, 5500C, 5500G, 5500K, or 5500R, whichever is appropriate, for the plan year in which the trust year ends.	Same as Form 5500.
Schedule SSA (Form 5500)	Annual registration statement identifying separated participant with deferred vested benefits.	Each plan administrator for any plan year having a separated participant with a deferred vested benefit under the plan.	Same as Form 5500, 5500C, 5500K, or 5500R, whichever is appropriate.	Same as Form 5500.
None prescribed.	Financial statements, schedules, and accountant's opinion (for plans with 100 or more participants at the beginning of the plan year).	Each plan administrator or employer maintaining an employee pension benefit plan (defined benefit or defined contribution) covered by ERISA. Includes HR-10s, IRAs, TSAs, and frozen plans, except those funded solely by allocated insurance contracts.	Same as Form 5500, 5500C, 5500K, or 5500R, whichever is appropriate.	Same as Form 5500.

Form	Title	Who Must File	When to File	Where to File
5330	Return of initial excise taxes related to pension and profit-sharing plans.	Employer failing to meet minimum funding standards for pension plans; disqualified person participating in a prohibited transaction; employer sponsoring a 403(b) (7) custodian account with excess contributions. Self-employed person or partnership who has made excess contributions to an HR-10 plan.	Same as Form 5500, 5500C, 5500K, or 5500R, whichever is appropriate.	Same as Form 5500.
5329	Return for individual retirement arrangement taxes.	An individual owing excise taxes because of an excess contribution, a premature distribution or an underdistribution from an IRA (after age 70½).	As an attachment to Form 1040 when that form is filed.	At the local IRS service center indicated in instructions to Form 1040.
PBGC-1	Annual premium filing.	Plan administrator of defined benefit plan subject to PBGC provisions of Title IV of ERISA.	Within seven months after the close of the prior plan year for the current plan year.	Pension Benefit Guaranty Corporation P.O. Box 2454 Washington, D.C. 20013
5500 5500C 5500K 5500R	PBGC annual report.	Plan administrator of defined benefit plan subject to PBGC provisions of Title IV of ERISA.	Same as Form 5500, 5500C, 5500K, or 5500R, whichever is appropriate.	Same as Form 5500.

Table 5-1 (continued)

Form	Description	Who Must File	When Filed	Where Filed
1099R	Statement for recipients of total distribution from profit-sharing and retirement plans.	Trustees of plan or other payor of total distribution.	By March 1.	Local IRS service center.
W-2P	Statement for recipients of periodic annuity, pension retirement pay or IRA payments.	Trustees of plan or other payor of periodic distribution.	By March 1.	Social Security Administration Office.
1096	Transmittal form (1099R).	Trustees of plan or other payor of distribution.	By March 1.	Local IRS service center.
W-3	Transmittal form (W-2P).	Trustees of plan or other payor of distribution.	By March 1.	Social Security Administration Office.
990-T	Exempt organization income tax return.	Trustees and every organization exempt from tax under Code Sec. 501(a) with gross income from an unrelated trade or business of $1000 or more.	By the fifteenth day of the fourth month after the close of the taxable year.	IRS service center indicated in instructions to Form 990-T.

Form	Title	Description	When filed	Where filed
5300[3] 5301 5303	Application for determination of defined benefit plan (Form 5300), defined contribution plan (Form 5301), collectively bargained plan (Form 5303).	Any employer or plan administrator may file to request a determination concerning the qualification of a new or amended plan (and trust).	Due the later of (a) the filing date for the employer's tax return (including extensions) for the fiscal year including the first day of the plan year involved or (b) the last day of the plan year.	IRS Key District Office for employer's principal place of business.
5302	Employee census.	Same as above. (See instructions for Form 5303 before attaching Form 5302.)	Same as Form 5300, 5301, or 5303, whichever is appropriate.	Same as Form 5300, 5301, or 5303.
5310 (Parts I and II)	Notice of merger, consolidation or transfer of plan assets or liabilities.	Every employer or plan administrator must file for any plan merger or consolidation, or any transfer of assets or liabilities from one plan to another.	At least 30 days before the plan merger or consolidation, or transfer of plan assets or liabilities.	IRS District Director for the employer's principal place of business.
5310 (Parts I and III and Schedule A)	Application for determination upon plan termination.	Any employer or plan administrator or fiduciary may file to request a determination concerning plan termination.	Any time a determination is desired.	IRS District Director for the employer's principal place of business.

Table 5-1 (continued)

Form	Description	Who Must File	When Filed	Where Filed
None prescribed (notice must include information in Reg. Sec. 2617.3(b), Part 2617, Chapter XXVI of Title 29, CFR).	PBGC reportable events (i.e., a plan amendment that decreases benefits payable, a reduction in the number of active plan participants, the inability to pay benefits when due, and a distribution to a substantial owner). Note: these and other reportable events are also reported on Form 5500.	Every employer or plan administrator of a defined benefit pension plan subject to the plan termination insurance provisions of Title IV of ERISA.	Within 30 days after the employer or plan administrator knows or has reason to know a reportable event occurred.	Office of Program Operations—Pension Benefit Guaranty Corporation Room 5300 A 2020 K Street NW Washington, D.C. 20006
None prescribed (notice must include information in Reg. Sec. 2604.4, Part 2604, Chapter XXVI of Title 29, CFR).	Notice of intent to terminate.	Every employer or plan administrator or duly authorized representative of a defined benefit pension plan subject to the plan termination insurance provisions of Title IV of ERISA.	At least 10 days before the proposed date of plan termination.	Office of Program Operations—Pension Benefit Guaranty Corporation Room 5300A 2020 K Street NW Washington, D.C. 20006

Item	
Summary Plan Description.	Filed with DOL and furnished to plan participants and beneficiaries within 90 days after becoming participants or after commencing to receive benefits in the case of beneficiaries. For a new plan, must be filed and furnished to participants within 120 days after the date of adoption. For all plans, a new summary plan description must be filed and furnished to participants and beneficiaries once every five years after the initial filing date if plan is modified; otherwise, must be filed and distributed every 10 years.
Summary of Material Modification.	Filed with DOL and furnished to plan participants and beneficiaries within 210 days after the close of the plan year in which the modification was adopted.

1 An HR-10 defined contribution plan of a sole proprietor or partnership that never had any common law employees or less-than-10% partners is exempt from annual reporting. This exemption does not apply to an HR-10 defined benefit plan.
2 For a single employer plan with the same tax and plan year, any extension granted for filing the employer's tax return beyond the due date of the annual report automatically applies to the annual report filing.
3 File short-form application (Form 6406) for determination on amendment of employee benefit plans.

Table 5-2 Summary of disclosures required to be made to participants and beneficiaries

Item	Description	Who Must Furnish	When Provided
Summary Plan Description (e.g., booklet); contents prescribed by regulations.	Summary of the provisions of the plan in language understandable to the average participant; gives details on the administrative operations and statement of ERISA protected rights.	Plan administrator of pension or profit-sharing plan.	New plans: 120 days after effective date. Periodic update: once every five years if plan is modified; once every 10 years regardless of changes. New participants after initial distribution: earlier of 90 days after becoming a new participant or first receiving benefits.
Summary Annual Report; contents prescribed by regulations.	Summary of Annual Report Form 5500, 5500C or 5500K (Form 5500R may be distributed for plans filing that form).	Plan administrator of pension or profit-sharing plan.	Nine months after end of plan year, or within two months after close of extension period for filing annual report, if applicable.
Joint and Survivor Coverage Notification.	Written explanation of the effect of electing preretirement survivor annuity coverage or post-retirement joint and survivor coverage.	Plan administrator of pension plan covered by qualified joint and survivor requirement.	For plans providing only post-retirement coverage, nine months before retirement age and election period must be at least 90 days. For plans providing for early retirement and early survivor election, six months before retirement age. For plans providing early retirement and automatic early survivor protection, nine months before retirement age.

Explanation of Claim Denial.	Written explanation of the reasons for denial of an application under the plan, the specific plan provisions on which the denial was based, and the procedure for appeal. Procedure for claiming plan benefits must be contained in the Summary Plan Description.	Plan administrator of pension or profit-sharing plan.	Within 90 days of initial claim for benefits (90-day extension is permitted if participant is notified of the delay within the initial 90-day period). Participant must be given 60 days to appeal, and final decision must be rendered within 60 days (60-day extension is permitted).
Notice to Terminated Vested Participants; contents prescribed by regulations.	Information provided to IRS on Schedule SSA (Form 5500 series) concerning participant's accrued benefit.	Plan administrator of pension or profit-sharing plan.	On or before due date for filing Schedule SSA (Form 5500 series).
Notice to Interested Parties; contents prescribed by regulations	Notice of application for letter of determination from IRS regarding qualification of a new or amended pension plan or the plan's qualification status after termination to allow participants to appeal to IRS and/or DOL concerning plan's qualification.	Plan administrator of pension or profit-sharing plan.	Between 7 and 21 days before mailing application if notice is posted in location frequented by participants; between 10 and 24 days if mailed to each participant.
Tax Information Returns (a) Form 1099R	Report of total and taxable amount of lump-sum distribution from a qualified retirement plan during the calendar year.	Trustees of plan or other payor of total distribution.	By February 1.

71

Table 5-2 (continued)

Item	Description	Who Must Furnish	When Provided
(b) Form W-2P	Report of total and taxable amount of retirement plan distributions and annuities paid during the calendar year.	Trustees of plan or other payor of periodic distribution.	By February 1.
Accrued Benefit Statement.	Statement of participant's benefit accrued to date based on the latest available data.	Plan administrator of pension or profit-sharing plan.	Within 60 days of request from participant. Need not be provided more than once in a 12-month period.
Copies of Plan Documents and Reports.	Copies of plan, trust agreement, and all government reporting forms, except those containing individual employee data.	Plan administrator of pension or profit-sharing plan.	Within 30 days of written request from participant. ($.25 per page may be charged for copying.)
Claims and Claims Review.	Procedure for filing claims and appealing denial of claims for participants and beneficiaries.	Plan administrator of pension or profit-sharing plan.	Within 90 days of claim. (Extension of 90 days under special circumstances.) Claims review: within 60 days of request for review. (Extension of 60 days under special circumstances.)
Plan Documents.	Copies of plan, trust agreement, bargaining agreement, contracts, etc.	Plan administrator of pension or profit-sharing plan.	All documents, except those containing individual employee data, must be available at the principal business office(s) during normal working hours.

72

Plan Description (Form EBS-1) and updated Plan Description (amended EBS-1).	Eliminated in 1979. Format prescribed by regulations.	Plan administrator of pension or profit-sharing plan.	All documents, except those containing individual employee data, must be available at the principal business office(s) during normal working hours.
Latest Annual Report (Form 5500 series) and attachments.	Annual report and schedules for the plan year.	Plan administrator of pension or profit-sharing plan.	Same as above.
Latest Request for Determination of Plan (Form 5300 series).	IRS application for determining plan qualification.	Plan administrator of pension or profit-sharing plan.	Same as above. *Important:* Form 5302, Employee Census, is not to be made available.
Terminal Reports.	Final Annual Report (Form 5500 series), Final PBGC-1 Schedule A (for years before 1978), Terminal Report (Form 5310 and Schedule A), Notice of Intent to Terminate, Request for Determination of Terminated Plan (Form 5300 series).	Plan administrator of pension or profit-sharing plan.	Same as above. *Important:* Schedule A of Form 5310 is not to be made available for public inspection.

3 an individual who was a participant and has no vested right to a benefit incurs a one-year break in service and has not completed at least one year of service after returning to employment.

ACCOUNTANTS

ERISA generally requires plan administrators to retain "independent qualified public accountants" on behalf of the plan's participants and beneficiaries. (Exceptions to the general requirements are discussed under "Exceptions," below.)

Independent Qualified Public Accountant

ERISA defines a *qualified public accountant* as:

1 a person who is a certified public accountant, certified by a regulatory authority of a state;
2 a person who is a licensed public accountant, licensed by a regulatory authority of a state; or
3 a person certified by the Secretary of Labor as a qualified public accountant in accordance with regulations published by him for a person who practices accounting in any state which has no certification or licensing procedure for accountants.

The Department of Labor announced guidelines for determining when a qualified public accountant is independent for purposes of auditing and rendering an opinion on the financial information required to be included in the annual report. An accountant will not be considered independent with respect to a plan if:

1 an accountant or a member of an accounting firm maintains financial records for the employee benefit plan; or
2 during the period of professional engagement to examine the financial statements being reported, or at the date of the opinion, the accountant or his firm or a member thereof had, or was committed to acquire, any direct financial interest or any material indirect financial interest in such plan or the plan sponsor; or
3 during the period of professional engagement to examine the financial statements being reported, at the date of the opinion, or during the period covered by the financial statements, the accountant, his firm, or a member thereof was connected as a promoter, underwriter, investment advisor, voting trustee, director, officer, or employee of the plan or plan sponsor; except that a firm will not be deemed not independent in regard to a particular plan if a former officer or employee of such plan or plan sponsor is em-

ployed by the firm and such individual has completely disassociated himself from the plan or plan sponsor and does not participate in auditing financial statements of the plan covering any period of his employment by the plan or plan sponsor.[1]

The DOL issued regulations stating that an independent qualified public accountant may permissibly engage in, or have members of his firm engage in, certain activities which will not affect the recognition of his independence. For example, an accountant will not fail to be recognized as independent if at or during the period of his professional engagement with the employee benefit plan he or his firm is retained or engaged on a professional basis by the plan sponsor. Also, the rendering of services by an actuary associated with an accountant or accounting firm will not impair the accountant's or accounting firm's independence. The subject of auditor independence is discussed further in Chapter 9.

Financial and Other Information

Department of Labor regulations generally provide that a plan required to file an annual report (Form 5500) has the option of either reporting the information prescribed by ERISA (as discussed under "Filing Under the Act" below) or electing an alternative method of compliance, in which case the plan is required to report information prescribed in the regulations (as discussed under "Filing Under the Alternative Method of Compliance" below). Certain requirements which pertain to both methods of filing are covered more fully under "Discussion of Certain Requirements" below. See the section on "Exceptions" below for certain types of plans that are excepted from some or all of the requirements. As discussed later, the rules for filing under the alternative method of compliance are more definitive and almost all plans now file under that method.

Filing Under the Act

A summary of the financial and other information that must be submitted when filing under the provisions of ERISA is presented in Table 5-3 (left-hand columns). The summary also shows which information must be covered by the accountant's opinion (which is required to be included in the annual report) and whether the opinion is required to be submitted on a form prescribed by the Secretary of Labor.

A combined annual report form has been issued by the Department of Labor and the Department of the Treasury. The annual report, Form 5500,

---

[1] The term *member* means all partners or shareholder employees in the firm and all professional employees participating in the audit or located in an office of the firm participating in a significant portion of the audit.

Table 5-3   Items required to be included in the annual report

Description	Filing Under the Act		Filing Under Alternative Method	
	Required (Note 1)	Form 5500 Item No.	Required (Note 1)	Form 5500 Item No.
Financial Statements				
Assets and liabilities (Note 2):				
Current year only	XC	—	—	—
In comparative form for beginning and end of year, at current value	—	—	XC	(Note 3)
Changes in net assets available for plan benefits, to include details of income and expenses and other changes	XC	—	XC (Note 4)	(Note 3)
Notes to Financial Statements	(Note 5)		(Note 6)	
Description of the accounting principles and practices reflected in the financial statements	—	—	XC	—
Description of variances from generally accepted accounting principles, if applicable	—	—	XC	—
Explanation of any differences between the separate financial statements and items 13 and 14 of Form 5500	—	—	XC	—
Description of plan including any significant changes in plan made during the period and impact of such changes on benefits	XC	—	XC	—
Funding policy (including policy with respect to prior service cost), and any changes in such policy during the year	XC	—	XC	—
Description of any significant changes in plan benefits made during the period	XC	—	—	—

Table 5-3 (continued)

Description	Filing Under the Act		Filing Under Alternative Method	
	Required (Note 1)	Form 5500 Item No.	Required (Note 1)	Form 5500 Item No.
Description of material lease commitments, other commitments, and contingent liabilities	XC	—	XC	—
Description of agreements and transactions with parties in interest	XC	—	XC	—
General description of priorities upon termination of plan	XC	—	XC	—
Information concerning whether a tax ruling or determination letter has been obtained	XC	—	XC	—
Any other matters necessary to present fully and fairly the financial statements of the plan	XC	—	XC	—
Supplemental Schedules				
Assets and liabilities aggregated by categories and valued at their current value, in comparative form with the prior year's figures, on either the cash, modified accrual, or accrual basis	XC	13	X	13
Receipts and disbursements (or income, expenses, and changes in net assets) during year, aggregated by general sources and applications, on either the cash, modified accrual, or accrual basis	XC	14	X	14
Assets held for investment purposes aggregated by issuer, borrower, or lessor, or similar party to the transaction, together with specified disclosures (including cost and current value)	XC	24	XC	24

Table 5-3 (continued)

Description	Filing Under the Act		Filing Under Alternative Method	
	Required (Note 1)	Form 5500 Item No.	Required (Note 1)	Form 5500 Item No.
Transactions with parties in interest (Note 7)	XC	24	XC	24
Loans or fixed income obligations in default or uncollectible	XC	24	XC	24
Leases in default or uncollectible	XC	24	XC	24
Reportable transactions, generally those exceeding 3% of the current value (generally fair market value) of the plan's assets (Note 8)	XC	24	XC	24
Other Information				
Form 5500	X (Note 9)	All	X	All
Insurance information, where any benefits under the plan are provided by an insurance company or a similar organization	X	Schedule A (Note 10)	X	Schedule A
Actuarial information, for defined benefit plans subject to the minimum funding standards for the year being reported on	X	Schedule B (Note 11)	X	Schedule B
When plan assets are invested in a common or collective trust or pooled separate account maintained by a "regulated" bank or insurance company (Note 12)	—	—	—	—
Information regarding value at year end, and purchases and sales during year, of units of participation (but information regarding the individual transactions of the trust or account is not required)	X	Various	X	Various

Table 5-3 (continued)

Description	Filing Under the Act		Filing Under Alternative Method	
	Required (Note 1)	Form 5500 Item No.	Required (Note 1)	Form 5500 Item No.
Most recent annual statement of assets and liabilities of such trust or account, or the employer identification number of the trust or account and a certification that the plan has received such statement (where the bank or insurance company files a copy of such statement with the Secretary of Labor)	X	—	X	—
Name of plan	X	5	X	5
If different from above, the name by which the plan is commonly known to its participants and beneficiaries				
The name and address of any employer having employees covered by the plan; the name and address of any labor organization maintaining the plan; or in the case of a plan established or maintained by two or more employers or by one or more employers and one or more employee organizations, the name and address of the association, committee, joint board of trustees, parent, or most significant employer of a group of employers contributing to the same plan	X	1	X	1
The name, business address, and business telephone number of the plan administrator	X	2	X	2

Table 5-3   (continued)

Description	Filing Under the Act		Filing Under Alternative Method	
	Required (Note 1)	Form 5500 Item No.	Required (Note 1)	Form 5500 Item No.
The number of employees covered by the plan	X	19	X	19
The names of fiduciaries (Note 13)	X	2 and 12	X	2 and 12
Detailed statement of salaries, fees, and commissions charged to the plan	X	12	X	12
An explanation of the reason for any change in appointment of trustee, accountant, insurance carrier, actuary, administrator, investment manager, or custodian	X	17	X	17
Such financial and actuarial information including but not limited to material described above as the Secretary of Labor may find necessary or appropriate	X	Various	X	Various
Report of independent qualified public accountant stating whether his examination was conducted in accordance with generally accepted auditing standards, and his opinion on the covered financial statements, schedules and other information (items marked "XC" in this table) and accounting principles and consistency of application (Note 14)	X	—	X Note 14	—

Table 5-3 (continued)

Description	Filing Under the Act		Filing Under Alternative Method	
	Required (Note 1)	Form 5500 Item No.	Required (Note 1)	Form 5500 Item No.
Report of enrolled actuary including his opinion whether the assumptions used are in the aggregate reasonably related to the experience of the plan and to reasonable expectations and represent his best estimate of anticipated experience under the plan (see Note 14 and Figure 5-3)	X	Schedule B (Note 11)	X	Schedule B

1 Items required to be included are indicated as follows:

X - Included, but not covered by accountant's opinion.

XC - Included, and covered by accountant's opinion. It should be recognized that while the "XC" notation is shown next to individual footnotes and schedules in this table, the accountant's opinion is expressed not on such items separately, but on the financial statements and such items taken as a whole.

An accountant's opinion is not required for plans with fewer than 100 participants at the beginning of the plan year.

2 Referred to by the authors in Chapters 8 to 10 as "Statement of Net Assets Available for Plan Benefits," which term is more appropriate from an accounting viewpoint.

3 May be presented in a format which may include (a) separate typewritten or printed statements, which need not be in the format of items 13 and 14 of Form 5500 but must include the items shown therein, (b) typewritten or printed statements which are reproductions of items 13 and 14 of Form 5500, or (c) a statement incorporating by reference items 13 and 14 of Form 5500.

4 This may be separate or combined statements of plan income and expenses and of changes in net assets.

5 When filing under the act, disclosures concerning these items shall be *considered* by the accountant. (The act does not *require* that these disclosures be made in all instances.)

6 When filing under the alternative method of compliance, disclosures concerning these items are *required.*

7 Regulations state that the supplemental schedule of transactions with parties in interest need not include any transactions that are exempted—either under ERISA or an administrative exemption—from the prohibited transaction rules.

Table 5-3 (continued)

8 Although the act is unclear whether the 3% criterion should be measured against the value of the plan's assets at the close of the plan's fiscal year or at some other date, regulations state that the 3% should be based on the value of plan assets at the beginning of the year (see "Supplemental Schedules," later in this chapter for discussion).

9 While the act does not specifically refer to Form 5500, it would appear that the DOL expects that form to be completed in its entirety regardless of the filing method.

10 Schedule A (Form 5500) appears to satisfy the act's requirement calling for inclusion in the annual report, where some or all plan benefits are purchased from and guaranteed by an insurance company or similar organization, of a statement from such organization enumerating (a) total premiums received, (b) total benefits paid, (c) administrative expenses charged, (d) commissions or other specific acquisition costs paid, (e) amounts held to pay future benefits, and (f) other specified information.

11 Schedule B (Form 5500) appears to satisfy the act's requirement calling for inclusion, in annual reports filed by defined benefit plans, of an actuarial statement prepared by an actuary, with his opinion as to whether the contents of the matters reported in the actuarial statement (see Figure 5-3) are in the aggregate reasonably related to the experience of the plan and to reasonable expectations, and represent his best estimate of anticipated experience under the plan.

12 See "Information Certified by Banks and Insurance Carriers," below in this chapter.

13 The act requires that the name *and address* of *each* fiduciary be furnished as a part of the annual report. Thus, when filing under the act, information in addition to that called for in items 2 and 12 of Form 5500 technically may be required. When filing under the alternative method, only the information called for in Form 5500 need be provided.

14 See "Reliance on Actuary/Accountant," below in this chapter.

15 The alternative method of compliance requires, in addition to the items listed, that the accountant's report (a) designate any omitted auditing procedures and the reasons for their omission, (b) identify whether or not changes in accounting principles are the result of DOL rules and regulations, and (c) be dated and manually signed, indicate city and state where issued, and identify (without necessarily enumerating in detail) the items covered by the report. Accountants would normally conform to (a) and (c) above in any event, even when the annual report is filed under the act. See also discussion under "Comparison of the Two Methods," below in this chapter.

"Annual Return/Report of Employee Benefit Plan," indicates that information on which the accountant is to express an opinion may be modified somewhat from that called for in ERISA. The annual report contains forms (items 13 and 14) for a statement of assets and liabilities and a statement of income, expenses, and changes in net assets, and it is not clear from the form whether those statements relate to the ERISA required *basic* financial statements (i.e., statement of assets and liabilities and statement of changes in net assets available for plan benefits) or to the *supplemental schedules* (i.e., statement of assets and liabilities and statement of receipts and disbursements). Although one might assume that the annual report combines the supplemental schedules with the basic financial statements, it would appear that the more reasonable explanation is that the forms for items 13 and 14 in the annual report are to serve as supplemental schedules and that the basic financial statements called for in ERISA would be attached to the annual report.

Filing Under the Alternative Method of Compliance

The requirements for filing under the alternative method of compliance are summarized in the right-hand columns in Table 5-3. The vast majority of plans file under this method, rather than under the provisions of the act. One reason is that the requirements under the alternative method are considerably more explicit than those under the act. Since the Department of Labor annual reporting regulations are silent as to whether they apply to any filing under the act, very few plans file under the act. The differences between the two methods are discussed in the following section.

Comparison of the Two Methods

According to the background paper accompanying its temporary regulations, the Department of Labor provides an alternative method for filing financial statements, schedules, and accountant's reports as part of the annual report because ERISA's statutory annual reporting provisions are unduly complex, confusing, and burdensome, and the absence of an alternative method would impose additional costs on pension plans without the commensurate benefit of more revealing financial disclosure or better fiscal safeguards. The DOL, in creating the alternative method, did not attempt to modify the requirements existing in ERISA. The alternative method represents what the DOL views as a reasonable set of reporting requirements. The right of plans to file under the act was left as an option, presumably for legal reasons or to accommodate plans that had already prepared their annual reports before the alternative method was introduced. Requirements for filing under the act are still somewhat confusing and subject to interpretation.

Annual Report

The more significant differences related to the annual report are as follows.

When filing under the act, the *schedules* of assets and liabilities and of receipts and disbursements are among those items that are required to be covered by the accountant's opinion. Under the alternative method of compliance those schedules still need to be included as part of the annual report (as items 13 and 14 in Form 5500), but they need not be covered by the accountant's opinion.

Under the act, the financial *statement* of assets and liabilities is required to contain information for only the current year, and there is no specific requirement as to the accounting method for valuing the assets. However, by requiring adherence to generally accepted accounting principles, the financial statement now, under FASB Statement No. 35 (see Chapter 8), must reflect investments at current value. Under the alternative method, that financial statement must be presented in comparative form and at current value.

The act requires that the accountant's opinion state whether the financial statements conform to generally accepted accounting principles, but there is no similar requirement under the alternative method. The regulations describing the alternative method, however, require footnote disclosure of a description of accounting principles reflected in the financial statements, any variances from generally accepted accounting principles, and an explanation of any differences between the separate financial statements and items 13 and 14 of Form 5500.[2]

While the act states that certain footnotes should be *considered,* the alternative method *requires* that the specified footnotes must be included.

Summary Annual Report

Until recently, differences existed in requirements for summary annual reports filed under the two methods. Department of Labor regulations, however, conformed the requirements.

The regulations provide that the summary annual report (SAR) must consist of a completed copy of a prescribed form (see Figure 5-1). The form is to be completed by inserting the required information from the annual report. The plan administrator may omit any part of the form which is not applicable to the plan and any information which is not included in the plan's annual report. If a

---

[2] The regulations are not clear as to what constitutes a difference. However, DOL representatives informally confirmed the authors' view that different categorization of amounts with identical totals would not constitute a difference requiring explanation. Thus, for example, if total assets are the same, no explanation is needed even if the categories of assets presented are different. On the other hand, differences that do need to be explained would include, for example, presentation of separate financial statements on the accrual basis and items 13 and 14 on the cash basis.

FIGURE 5-1

Form for summary annual report
relating to pension plans

Summary Annual Report for (name of plan)

This is a summary of the annual report for (name of plan and EIN) for (period covered by this report). The annual report has been filed with the Internal Revenue Service, as required under the Employee Retirement Income Security Act of 1974 (ERISA).

Basic Financial Statement

Benefits under the plan are provided by (indicate funding arrangements).

Plan expenses were ($).

These expenses included ($) in administrative expenses and ($) in benefits paid to participants and beneficiaries, and ($) in other expenses. A total of (   ) persons were participants in or beneficiaries of the plan at the end of the plan year, although not all of these persons had yet earned the right to receive benefits.

[If the plan is funded other than solely by allocated insurance contracts:]

The value of plan assets, after subtracting liabilities of the plan, was ($) as of (the end of the plan year), compared to ($) as of (the beginning of the plan year). During the plan year the plan experienced an (increase) (decrease) in its net assets of ($). This (increase) (decrease) includes unrealized appreciation or depreciation in the value of plan assets; that is, the difference between the value of the plan's assets at the end of the year and the value of the assets at the beginning of the year or the cost of assets acquired during the year. The plan had total income of ($), including employer contributions of ($), employee contributions of ($), (gains) (losses) of ($) from the sale of assets, and earnings from investments of ($). [For plans filing Form 5500K, omit separate entries for employer contributions and employee contributions and insert instead "contributions by the employer and employees of ($)."]

[If any funds are used to purchase allocated insurance contracts:]

The plan has (a) contract(s) with (name of insurance carrier(s)) which allocate(s) funds toward (state whether individual policies, group deferred annuities or other). The total premiums paid for the plan year ending (date) were ($).

An actuary's statement shows that (enough money was contributed to the plan to keep it funded in accordance with the minimum funding standards of ERISA). (Not enough money was contributed to the plan to keep it funded in accordance with the minimum funding standards of ERISA. The amount of the deficit was $.)

[If the plan is a defined contribution plan covered by funding requirements:]

(Enough money was contributed to the plan to keep it funded in accordance with the minimum funding standards of ERISA.) (Not enough money was contributed to the plan to keep it funded in accordance with the minimum funding standards of ERISA. The amount of the deficit was $.)

Your Rights to Additional Information

You have the right to receive a copy of the full annual report, or any part thereof, on request. The items listed below are included in that report: [Note: List only those items which are actually included in the latest annual report.]

1   an accountant's report;
2   assets held for investment;
3   transactions between the plan and parties in interest (i.e., persons who have certain relationships with the plan);

FIGURE 5-1 (continued)

4   loans or other obligations in default;

5   leases in default;

6   transactions in excess of 3% of plan assets;

7   insurance information including sales commissions paid by insurance carriers; and

8   actuarial information regarding the funding of the plan.

To obtain a copy of the full annual report, or any part thereof, write or call the office of (name), who is (state title—e.g., the plan administrator), (business address and telephone number). The charge to cover copying costs will be ($) for the full annual report, or ($) per page for any part thereof.

   You also have the right to receive from the plan administrator, on request and at no charge, a statement of the assets and liabilities of the plan and accompanying notes, or a statement of income and expenses of the plan and accompanying notes, or both. If you request a copy of the full annual report from the plan administrator, these two statements and accompanying notes will be included as part of that report. The charge to cover copying costs given above does not include a charge for the copying of these portions of the report because these portions are furnished without charge.

   You also have the legally protected right to examine the annual report at the main office of the plan (address), (at any other location where the report is available for examination), and at the U.S. Department of Labor in Washington, D.C., or to obtain a copy from the U.S. Department of Labor upon payment of copying costs. Requests to the department should be addressed to: Public Disclosure, Room N4677, Pension and Welfare Benefit Programs, Department of Labor, 200 Constitution Avenue, N.W., Washington, D.C. 20216.

plan administrator believes that additional explanation of some of the prescribed information is necessary, the explanation may be added at the end of the form and must be headed "Additional Explanation."

   The regulations provide a cross-reference table which matches each item of the SAR to the corresponding line item of the annual report. Although the act stated that the summary material required to be furnished to participants and beneficiaries was to be covered by an auditor's opinion, the regulations eliminate that requirement. Similarly, although the act stated that the supplemental schedules of assets and liabilities and of receipts and disbursements were required to be included in the SAR, the regulations eliminate that requirement. Instead, the prescribed form includes a notice concerning the availability of the financial statements and accompanying notes included in the annual report and of the full annual report. (See Figure 5-2.)

Discussion of Certain Requirements

Reliance on Actuary/Accountant

In offering his opinion upon the financial statements, schedules, and other material, the accountant is allowed by ERISA to rely on the correctness of any actuarial matter certified to by an enrolled actuary, if he states his reliance. While not explicitly stated, it appears that this provision would apply to filings under the alternative method as well as to filings under the act. It is important to note, however, that under generally accepted auditing standards (as prescribed by

FIGURE 5-2

The summary annual report (SAR) under ERISA:
a cross-reference to the annual report

SAR Item	Form 5500 Line Items	Form 5500-C Line Items	Form 5500-K Line Items
1. Funding arrangement	11	11	11
2. Total plan expenses	14(l)	14(k)	13(d)
3. Administrative expenses	14(j) Column b	14(i)	N/A
4. Benefits paid	14(h)	14(g)	13(e)
5. Other expenses	14(i) plus 14(k)	14(h) plus 14(j)	N/A
6. Total participants	7(f)	7(b) (ii)	7(b) (ii)
7. Value of plan assets (net)			
a. End of plan yr.	13(m) Column b	13(l) Column d	13(g)
b. Beginning of plan yr.	13 (m) Column a	13(l) Column b	13(a)
8. Change in net assets	14(o)	14(n)	13 (g) minus 13(a)
9. Total income	14(g)	14(f)	13(b) plus 13(c)
a. Employer contributions	14(a) (i)	14(a) (i)	13(b)
b. Employee contributions	14 (a) (ii)	14(a) (ii)	13(b)
c. Change in sales of assets	14(e) (ii) Column b	14(d) Column b	N/A
d. Earnings from investments	14(d) (iv) Column b	14(c) Column b	N/A
10. Total insurance premiums	14(h) (ii) or Sched. A Part II Item 5(b)	14(g) (ii) or Sched. A Part II Item 5 (b)	Sched. A, Part I Item 5(b)
11. Funding deficiency			
a. Defined benefit plans	Sched. B, Item 8(d)	Sched. B, Item 8(d)	Sched. B, Item 8
b. Defined contribution plans	21(b) (iii)	20(b) (iii)	19(b) (iii)

Note: This format for cross-referencing the SAR to the annual report is reproduced from the final regulations, issued April 3, 1979. Therefore, revisions made to the 5500 Forms subsequent to this date are not reflected.

the Auditing Standards Executive Committee of AICPA in its Statement on Auditing Standards, No. 11) an accountant is *precluded,* when expressing a standard or "clean" opinion, from stating reliance on the work of an actuary.

Similarly ERISA provides that, in making his certification, the enrolled actuary may rely on the correctness of any accounting matter as to which a qualified public accountant has expressed an opinion, if he states his reliance.

Insurance Information

Instructions to Form 5500 provide for the inclusion of Schedule A, "Insurance Information," when any benefits under the plan are provided by an insurance company, insurance service, or similar organization. The information contained in Schedule A does not need to be covered by the accountant's opinion.

Supplemental Schedules

Regulations describe the manner in which the required supplemental schedules (see Table 5-3) are to be prepared. The more significant schedule requirements are discussed below.

With respect to the schedule of assets held for investment purposes, the regulations provide that the schedule must include *all* investments held by the plan on the last day of the plan year.

In addition to the supplemental schedules specified in the act and in past temporary regulations, final regulations also call for a schedule of assets acquired and disposed of *within* the plan year. That schedule must include investments purchased and sold during the plan year except for the following:

1 debt obligations of the United States or any of its agencies;
2 interests issued by a company registered under the Investment Company Act of 1940;
3 bank certificates of deposit with maturities of not more than one year;
4 commercial paper with maturities of nine months or less if ranked in the highest rating category by at least two nationally recognized statistical rating services and issued by a company required to report under Section 13 of the Securities Exchange Act of 1934;
5 participation in a bank's common or collective trust fund;
6 participation in an insurance company's pooled separate account;
7 securities purchased from a broker-dealer.

Investments purchased in a preceding plan year and sold during the current plan year need not be reported on the schedule.

With respect to the schedule of party-in-interest transactions, the regulations state that the schedule need not include transactions that are exempted from the prohibited transactions rules[3]—under either the act or an administrative

---

[3] The footnotes to the financial statements called for by the act and regulations include a description of agreements and transactions with parties in interest (see Table 5-3), and those

exemption. Thus, in effect, only prohibited transactions would be reported on this schedule.

Regarding the schedule of reportable transactions, as indicated in Note 8 to Table 5-3, ERISA is not explicit as to what constitutes a reportable transaction. The regulations, however, clarify the issue by defining the following reportable transactions:

1 a *single* transaction within the plan year involving an amount of more than 3% of the current value of plan assets;

2 a *series* of transactions *in other than securities* within the plan year with or in conjunction with the same "person" that, in the aggregate, involves more than 3% of the current value of plan assets;[4]

3 a *series* of transactions within the plan year with respect to securities of the *same issue* that, in the aggregate, involves more than 3% of the current value of plan assets;

4 all *security* transactions within the plan year with or in conjunction with a "person" if any other *single* security transaction with that same person within the plan year exceeds 3% of the current value of plan assets; exceptions to this general rule are discussed below.

The *current value of plan assets* is measured at the beginning of the plan year. Transactions during the year are valued at the respective transaction dates, which may be either the date the trade is executed (trade date) or settled (settlement date), provided that one method is used consistently during the plan year. *Security* is defined to include a unit of participation in a common or collective trust or a pooled separate account. It is important to recognize that the phrase *with or in conjunction with a person* is defined extremely broadly in the regulations to include any person who benefits from, executes, facilitates, participates in, promotes, or solicits a transaction involving plan assets. That definition includes broker-dealers.

With respect to the fourth category of reportable transactions the regulations state that *triggered transactions* need *not* be reported in the reportable transactions schedule if either:

1 the *triggering* single 3% transaction involves a bank or insurance company regulated by a federal or state agency, an investment company registered under the Investment Company Act of 1940, or a broker-dealer registered under the Securities Exchange Act of 1934, *and* involves:

---

provisions are *not* affected by this regulation. And, although the footnote requirement is usually interpreted to mean a general description of significant transactions or types of transactions, not a detailed listing, consideration should be given to the footnote disclosure requirements of SAS No. 6, "Related Party Transactions" and, as of March 1982, Statement of Financial Accounting Standards No. 57, "Related Party Disclosures."

[4] A simultaneous transfer of property (that is not a security) and execution of a related loan agreement should be treated as two transactions to be aggregated for the 3% test.

(a) debt obligations of the United States or any of its agencies with maturities of not more than one year *or* with maturities of longer than one year if purchased or sold under a repurchase agreement having a term of less than 91 days; or

(b) interests issued by a company registered under the Investment Company Act of 1940; or

(c) bank certificates of deposit with maturities of not more than one year; or

(d) commercial paper with maturities of nine months or less if ranked in the highest rating category by at least two nationally recognized statistical rating services and issued by a company required to report under Section 13 of the Securities Exchange Act of 1934; or

(e) participation in a bank's common or collective trust; or

(f) participation in an insurance company's pooled separate account; or

2 the *triggered* transaction satisfies the conditions described in subparagraph (1) above; or

(a) the person involved in the triggered transaction (the same person connected with the reportable single 3% transaction) is a broker-dealer registered under the Securities Exchange Act of 1934; and

(b) the triggered transaction involves the purchase or sale of securities listed on a national securities exchange registered under Section 6 of the Securities Exchange Act of 1934 or quoted on NASDAQ; and

(c) the broker-dealer neither purchases nor sells the securities for its own account or the account of an affiliated person.

Information Certified by Banks and Insurance Carriers

ERISA provides that the accountant's opinion need not cover the annual statement of assets and liabilities of common or collective trust, or, in the case of a separate account or trust, certain other information, if the bank or insurance carrier is regulated and supervised and is subject to periodic examination by a state or federal agency and such statement or other information is certified as accurate by such bank or insurance company and (1) is made a part of the annual report or (2) is filed with the Secretary of Labor by the bank or insurance carrier. (See Table 5-3.)

Some accountants interpreted that ERISA provision to mean that financial statements of the *plan,* as well as the statement of assets and liabilities of the common or collective trust or separate account, need not be covered by the accountant's opinion. DOL regulations, however, remove any uncertainty in this regard.

In its explanation of the regulations the DOL points out that although the accountant's examination and report need not cover information required to be transmitted and certified to the plan administrator, this does *not* mean that a plan need not engage an auditor to render an opinion on the financial statements of the plan. An audit report must accompany the financial statements, but that report is not required to extend to the specified information. This limitation on the scope of an accountant's examination applies to plans sponsored by a *regulated* bank or insurance carrier for its own employees, as well as to plans of unrelated parties.

The AICPA has developed a form of auditor's report acceptable to the DOL for dealing with situations where the auditor is asked not to cover information certified by a bank or insurance company. (See "Scope Limitations" in Chapter 9.)

Master Trusts

The final master trust reporting rules require each plan participating in a master trust to report net figures reflecting that plan's participation in the trust. A master trust is defined as a trust maintained by a bank or similar financial institution to hold the assets of several plans that are all sponsored by a single employer or by several employers which are under common control.

More detailed financial information on the master trust itself must be filed separately with the Department of Labor. Although the plan administrator of each participating plan is responsible for filing the master trust information, the plan administrator can designate another participating plan administrator or the trustee of the master trust to do the filing.

ACTUARIES

ERISA requires plan administrators to retain *enrolled actuaries* on behalf of the plan's participants and beneficiaries. The term *enrolled actuary* is defined in ERISA as an actuary enrolled by a Joint Board for the Enrollment of Actuaries (established jointly by the Secretary of Labor and the Secretary of the Treasury under ERISA's requirement for such establishment). ERISA further requires that the joint board establish reasonable standards and qualifications for persons performing actuarial services for plans subject to ERISA and enroll an applicant if the joint board finds that he satisfies the standards and qualifications.

Different standards are specified for persons applying for enrollment before January 1, 1976, and for those applying on or after January 1, 1976. Regulations for individuals applying before January 1, 1976, require the applicant to have qualifying experience within the prior 15 years of (1) at least 36 months of "responsible pension actuarial experience" (as defined) or (2) at least 60 months of "total responsible actuarial experience" (as defined) including at least 18 months of responsible pension actuarial experience and other qualifications as follows: (1) specified educational degree or (2) specified organizational qualifications or (3) satisfactory completion of an examination prescribed by the joint board.

Regulations for individuals applying after December 31, 1975, require the applicant to have (1) qualifying experience within the prior 10 years of (a) at least 36 months of "responsible pension actuarial experience" (as defined) or (b) at least 60 months of "total responsible actuarial experience" (as defined) including at least 18 months of responsible pension actuarial experience, (2) basic actuarial knowledge qualifications of (a) specified educational degree, or (b) successful completion of a specified basic examination prescribed by the joint board, or (c) successful completion of a comparable examination given by an actuarial organization, and (3) pension actuarial knowledge qualifications of (a) successful completion of a specified pension examination prescribed by the joint board or (b) successful completion of a comparable examination given by an actuarial organization.

ERISA requires (with respect to most pension plans) that an actuarial statement and the actuary's opinion thereon be filed with the Secretary of Labor as part of the annual report. Figure 5-3 summarizes ERISA's requirements for information needed for the actuarial statement that must be included in the annual report filed with the Secretary of Labor and covered by the actuary's opinion. The actuary's opinion shall be based on his making an actuarial valuation of the plan for every third plan year, unless he determines that a more frequent valuation is necessary to support his opinion. The Department of Labor (and the Internal Revenue Service) has issued Schedule B to Form 5500, "Actuarial Information," to be used in filing the actuarial statement. The instructions to Schedule B state that it must be filed only for defined benefit plans subject to the minimum funding standards for the year being reported on.

PROVIDING INFORMATION TO ADMINISTRATOR

Regulations require insurance companies that provide plan benefits and insurance companies, banks, or similar institutions holding plan assets to transmit to the plan administrator, and certify the accuracy of, information needed by the plan administrator to file the annual report. This provision applies to institutions holding plan assets in a common or collective trust or pooled separate account (common trust or account), separate account or separate trust, or a custodial account. It also applies to plan sponsors.

In the case of a common trust or account, the bank or insurance company must provide the plan administrator with a copy of the statement of assets and liabilities of the common trust or account (for the fiscal year of the trust or account that ends within the plan year for which the plan's annual report is filed) and a statement of the value of the plan's units of participation. In the case of a separate trust or separate account, the bank or insurance company must provide a list of all transactions of the separate trust or account and, upon request of the administrator, any other information contained within the ordinary business records of the bank or insurance company needed by the plan administrator to complete the annual report.

FIGURE 5-3

Information required to be covered by the actuary's opinion

1 The date of the plan year, and the date of the actuarial valuation applicable to the plan for which the report is filed.

2 The date and amount of the contribution (or contributions) received by the plan for the plan year for which the report is filed and contributions for prior plan years not previously reported.

3 The following information applicable to the plan year for which the report is filed: the normal costs, the accrued liabilities, an identification of benefits not included in the calculation, a statement of the other facts and actuarial assumptions and methods used to determine costs, a justification for any change in actuarial assumptions or cost methods, and the minimum contribution required under Section 302 (minimum funding standards).

4 The number of participants and beneficiaries, both retired and nonretired, covered by the plan.

5 The current value of the assets accumulated in the plan, the present value of the assets of the plan used by the actuary in any computation of the amount of contributions to the plan required under Section 302, and a statement explaining the basis of such valuation of present value of assets.

6 The present value of all of the plan's liabilities for nonforfeitable pension benefits allocated by the termination priority categories as set forth in Section 4044, and the actuarial assumptions used in these computations. The Secretary of Labor shall establish regulations defining (for purposes of this section) *termination priority categories* and acceptable methods, including approximate methods, for allocating the plan's liabilities to such termination priority categories. (*Note:* The Secretary of Labor has issued regulations which waive these requirements.)

7 A certification of the contribution necessary to reduce the accumulated funding deficiency to zero.

8 A statement by the enrolled actuary that:

   a to the best of his knowledge the report is complete and accurate, and

   b the requirements of Section 302(c)(3) relating to reasonable actuarial assumptions and methods have been complied with.

9 Such other information regarding the plan as the Secretary of Labor may by regulation require.

10 Such other information as may be necessary to disclose fully and fairly the actuarial position of the plan.

The requirement to provide, upon request, needed information contained in the ordinary business records also applies to insurance companies providing plan benefits and to bank custodial accounts. The regulations limit the additional information that must be provided to that which is contained in the banks' and insurance companies' ordinary business records. But there is a question as to whether banks and insurance companies are required to specifically identify transactions that need to be reported in the annual report schedules (e.g., party-in-interest transactions, reportable transactions). Although the commentary accompanying the regulations implies that banks and insurance companies should, to the extent that they have pertinent information, specifically identify transactions to be included in the schedules accompanying the annual report, there is no such requirement set forth in the regulations themselves.

Plan sponsors must provide the plan administrator with all transactions engaged in by the sponsor that directly or indirectly affect plan assets and any other information needed by the plan administrator to file the annual report. The information to be supplied by the plan sponsor is not limited to that which is contained within its ordinary business records. The deadline for providing plan administrators with required information is 120 days after the plan year end.

REJECTION OF FILINGS

The Secretary of Labor may reject any filing if he determines that there is any material qualification by an accountant or actuary contained in an opinion submitted pursuant to requirements of ERISA. In certain instances where the annual report is deemed inadequate, the Department of Labor may retain an independent accountant to perform an audit, and/or an enrolled actuary to prepare an actuarial statement, with their expenses to be paid by the sponsoring plan.

EXCEPTIONS

The Secretary of Labor has issued regulations providing certain exceptions from the reporting and disclosure requirements discussed in the above sections of this chapter. Such regulations are discussed below.

Small Plans

The most significant exception applies to pension plans with fewer than 100 participants at the beginning of the plan year. Such plans need not engage an accountant to perform an audit and are required to file only a simplified annual report in lieu of the regular annual report. The majority of these plans are required to file Form 5500-C, the exception being owner-employee (Keogh) plans with fewer than 100 participants and at least one owner-employee participant, which are to file Form 5500-K.

Effective with plan years beginning in 1980, revised Forms 5500-C or 5500-K are to be filed only every third year. Form 5500-R, a brief registration statement designed to ensure that the DOL receives certain minimal information each year to permit the continuous review of small plans, is required to be filed in intervening years. In addition, plans must still file Schedules A, B, and SSA every year.

Three filing exceptions, however, will be permitted. The first allows the option to change the filing cycle by filing Form 5500-C or 5500-K before the year it is otherwise due and then filing Form 5500-R for the next two plan years, thus creating a new cycle. The second exception permits pension plans which have 80 to 120 participants (inclusive) as of the beginning of the plan year to file the same category of form (either Form 5500 or the category consisting of Forms 5500-C, K, and R) as that filed in the previous year. In addition, plan administrators are permitted to ignore the filing cycle and file Form 5500-C or Form 5500-K, as applicable, each year.

Insured Plans

Another significant exception to the general reporting and disclosure requirements applies to certain insured plans funded exclusively through insurance contracts, which plans are exempt by regulation from the financial reporting and audit requirements. The exempt plans are not required to file financial statements and supplemental schedules and need not engage an independent accountant to perform an audit. Other annual report items, however, including Schedule A of Form 5500, are required to be filed. To be exempt from the financial reporting and audit requirements, a plan must satisfy all of the following conditions.

1 Benefits are provided exclusively through allocated insurance contracts where benefits are fully guaranteed by the insurance carrier and the premiums for which are paid directly by the employer or employee organization from its general assets (premiums may also be paid partly by the participants).
2 Contributions by participants are forwarded by the employer or employee organization within three months of receipt.
3 For plans that provide refunds of contributions to participants, refunds are returned to them within three months of receipt by the employer or employee organization.

Individual Policies and Deferred Annuity Contracts

Most individual policy plans and deferred annuity contracts (see Chapter 3) would seem to meet at least the first criterion set forth above, and probably the others as well.

Deposit Administration and Immediate Participation Guarantee Contracts

Temporary regulations provided an exemption from audit for wholly insured plans if, among other things, the payments received by the insurance company were held solely in its general account. This requirement caused many requests

Table 5-4 Exceptions to general reporting and disclosure requirements for material to be filed with Secretary of Labor or to be furnished to participants and/or beneficiaries

Types of Plans	Exceptions, Based on Number of Participants at Beginning of the Plan Year	
	Under 100	100 or More
(a) Insured plans that provide benefits exclusively through allocated insurance contracts or policies where benefits are fully guaranteed by the insurance carrier, and the premiums for which are paid directly by the employer or employee organization from its general assets (premiums may be paid partly by the participants) provided that (1) contributions by participants are forwarded by the employer or employee organization within three months of receipt, and (2) for plans that provide refunds of contributions to participants, such refunds are returned to them within three months of receipt by the employer or employee organization (see "Insured Plans," above in this chapter).	1,2,3,4,5	2,4,5
(b) Insured plans (other than above) that provide benefits in whole or in part through insurance contracts or policies issued by an insurance company.	1,2,3,5	
(c) Unfunded plans, for which benefits are paid solely from the general assets of the employer or employee organization maintaining the plan [other than (d) below] (see "Unfunded Plans," above in this chapter).	1,2,4,5,6,8	2,4,5,6,8
(d) Plans maintained by an employer primarily for the purpose of providing deferred compensation for a select group of management or highly compensated employees ("top hat" plans), and are (1) unfunded, with benefits paid solely from the general assets of the employer, or (2) insured, with benefits provided exclusively through insurance contracts or policies, the premiums for which are paid directly by the employer from its general assets, or (3) partly unfunded and partly insured [as described in (1) and (2)].	7	7
(e) All other plans subject to reporting and disclosure requirements.	1,2,5	—

Table 5-4 (continued)

Exceptions:
1 Required to file a simplified form (Form 5500-C, or Form 5500-K for owner-employee Keogh pension plans), in lieu of Form 5500.
2 Not required to include within the annual report the financial statements and schedules [but, when filing Form 5500-C or Form 5500-K, all schedules called for therein are required unless otherwise excepted in (4) below].
3 Not required to include in the annual report data with respect to insurance commissions or fees (e.g., names and addresses of insurance agents or brokers to whom commissions or fees were paid, and related amounts) (applies only to the annual reports required to be filed for plan years beginning in 1975 and 1976).
4 Not required to complete items 13, 14, and 24 of Form 5500; 13, 14, and 16 of Form 5500-C; or 12 and 14 of Form 5500-K, as appropriate.
5 Not subject to audit requirements.
6 Not required to furnish a summary annual report.
7 Deemed to have satisfied reporting and disclosure requirements by (a) filing specified information with the Secretary of Labor within 120 days of inception of the plan or, for plans in existence on May 4, 1975, by August 31, 1975, and (b) providing plan documents, if any, to the Secretary of Labor upon request.
8 Not required to furnish a summary plan description or a summary of material modification or changes.

to the DOL for clarification as to whether the exemption applied to pension plans funded through certain types of insurance contracts, particularly deposit administration and immediate participation guarantee contracts (see Chapter 3).

As stated above, the final regulations make it clear that the exemption for pension plans only applies to plans funded entirely with allocated insurance contracts where benefits are fully guaranteed by the insurance company or organization that issued the policy. Thus, the exemption clearly does not apply to the typical deposit administration or immediate participation guarantee contract.

Unfunded Plans

The explanation to the temporary regulations states that unfunded plans, that is, plans which are funded solely from the general assets of the employer or employee organization, are exempt from the financial reporting and audit requirements and from the requirement to furnish a summary annual report. Although these exemptions are not set forth in the final regulations, the explanation accompanying the final regulations states that the exemptions contained in the temporary regulations are preserved. Accordingly, it seems clear that such plans are not required to file financial statements and supplemental schedules, furnish a summary annual report to participants and beneficiaries, or engage an independent public accountant to perform an audit, but they are required to file other annual report items.

Summary

Table 5-4 contains a summary of the exceptions to the reporting and disclosure requirements (including the exceptions discussed above) that are set forth in the regulations. The table contains a description of various types of plans with cross-references to exceptions described in the latter portion of the table. A particular plan should fall under only one of the types of plans described.

PENALTIES

Failure to comply with the reporting and disclosure requirements may lead to fines of up to $100,000, and fines of up to $100 *per day per participant or beneficiary* for failure to comply with the requests for information. As is the case with certain other penalties which may be imposed under ERISA, the penalties related to reporting and disclosure are imposed upon the plan administrator. But, in many cases, the employer company may ultimately become liable for such penalties, as discussed in Chapter 4. Other penalties which may be imposed for failure to conform to the ERISA reporting and disclosure requirements are also discussed therein.

Applicability of Antifraud Securities Laws

The Supreme Court ruled in *International Brotherhood of Teamsters* v. *Daniel* that the Securities Act of 1933 and the Securities Exchange Act of 1934 do not apply to compulsory, noncontributory pension plans. In a unanimous decision, the Supreme Court reversed the Seventh Circuit Court of Appeals ruling that a participant's interest in such a plan is a security for purposes of the antifraud provisions of the securities laws. The Supreme Court, reversing a lower court decision, refused to extend the coverage of the securities laws to pension plans that are funded entirely with employer contributions. However, *Daniel* does not address the status of contributory plans under the securities laws, and it is therefore possible that the SEC may attempt to regulate all plans which provide for employee contributions.

PART TWO

Employer Company Accounting, Auditing, and Financial Reporting

CHAPTER SIX

Accounting for Employer's Pension Costs

INTRODUCTION

As indicated in Chapter 1, in the early part of this century pensions were invariably accounted for on a pay-as-you-go basis. The only charge to income for the cost of pensions was the amount of benefits paid to retired employees during the accounting period.

The concept of past service cost became an element in determining the amount of funding contributions to related funds upon the adoption of formalized funded pension plans. Among accountants, this gave rise to considerable uncertainty and some difference of opinion about the nature of contributions made for past service. The question arose whether these contributions should be charged to retained earnings at the time they were made, or to current expense, which was the generally accepted procedure for contributions for current services.

This chapter discusses the methods companies have developed to account for the cost of their pension plans.

HISTORICAL BACKGROUND

Statements of the American Institute
of Certified Public Accountants (AICPA)

The AICPA's first pronouncement on accounting for pension plan costs was issued by the Committee on Accounting Procedure, in Accounting Research Bulletin (ARB) No. 36, published in 1948. In this bulletin the committee expressed the belief that costs of annuities based upon past service were generally incurred in contemplation of present and future services, not necessarily of the individual affected, but of the organization as a whole. Thus, the AICPA felt that such costs should be allocated to current and future services and not charged to retained earnings. It did not, however, specify how pension costs should be recognized in the accounts.

In September 1956, ARB No. 47 was issued. In this bulletin the committee specified how past service cost should be accounted for and also recognized the concept of vested benefits. The bulletin expressed the AICPA's preference for full accrual of pension costs over the remaining service lives of employees covered by a plan, generally on the basis of actuarial calculations. However, it regarded as being acceptable "for the present" minimum accruals whereby "the accounts and financial statements should reflect the accruals which equal the present worth, actuarially calculated, of pension commitments to employees to the extent that pension rights have vested in the employees. . . ." The committee stated that these accruals should not necessarily depend on funding arrangements, or on strict legal interpretations of a plan, and suggested that past service cost should be charged off over a reasonable period on a systematic and rational basis that would not distort the operating results of any one year.

Following the issuance of ARB No. 47, divergent accounting practices continued. In 1958, several companies that had previously followed the practice of accruing the full amount of current service costs (which coincided with contributions to the funds) either eliminated or drastically reduced pension costs charged to income. The supporters of these actions justified them on the grounds that funds provided in the past were sufficient to afford reasonable assurance of continuing pension payments, and more than sufficient to meet the company's liabilities for the then vested rights of employees. Thus, they felt the minimum requirements of ARB No. 47 were satisfied.

It was against this background that the Accounting Principles Board (APB), which succeeded the Committee on Accounting Procedure, decided that the subject needed further study and authorized an accounting research study. This study, published in 1965, detailed the accounting complexities of pension plans. In November 1966, after lengthy consideration, the APB promulgated its Opinion No. 8, "Accounting for the Cost of Pension Plans," primarily to eliminate inappropriate fluctuations in the amount of annual provisions for pension costs.

APB Opinion No. 8

Opinion No. 8 provided that, effective with fiscal periods beginning after December 31, 1966, costs charged to income should be determined in accordance with the following guidelines. The opinion states that the provision for pension cost should be based on an actuarial cost method that gives effect, in a consistent manner, to pension benefits, pension fund earnings, investment gains or losses (including unrealized gains and losses), and other assumptions regarding future events. The method selected should result in a systematic and rational allocation of the total cost of pensions among the employees' years of active service.

If the method selected includes past service cost as an integral part of normal cost, the provision for pension cost should be normal cost adjusted for the effect on pension fund earnings of differences between amounts accrued and amounts funded. If the actuarial cost method deals with past service cost separately from normal cost, the provision for pension cost should include normal cost, an amount for past service cost, and an adjustment for the effect on pension fund earnings of differences between amounts accrued and amounts funded. Provisions for pension cost should not necessarily be based on contributions to the pension fund, be limited to the amounts for which the company has a legal liability, or fluctuate widely as a result of pension fund investment gains or losses or other causes unrelated to the size and composition of the employee group.

Limits on the annual provision for pension costs were narrowed when Opinion No. 8:

increased the minimum required annual provision for pension costs to include a supplementary provision for vested benefits, if applicable;

required that actuarial gains and losses and unrealized appreciation and depreciation be recognized in the computation of the annual provision for pension cost, in a consistent manner that reflects the long-range nature of pension cost and avoids giving undue weight to short-term market fluctuations; and

eliminated pay-as-you-go and terminal funding as acceptable methods of computing the annual provision for pension costs, except in the rare instances where their application would not result in amounts differing materially from those obtained by the application of acceptable actuarial cost methods.

The APB concluded that all employees who can reasonably be expected to receive benefits under a pension plan should be included in the pension cost determination. It also concluded that any change made in the method of accounting for pension cost should not be applied retroactively. The opinion set forth disclosure requirements for accounting method changes as well as for other pertinent pension cost data.

APB Opinion No. 8 applies "both to written plans and to plans whose existence may be implied from a well-defined, although perhaps unwritten, company policy." Where a company has been providing its retired employees with benefits that can be determined or estimated in advance, there is generally a presumption that a pension plan exists within the meaning contemplated by the opinion.

FASB Statement No. 36

The Financial Accounting Standards Board (FASB), which replaced the Accounting Principles Board, is expected to issue, in 1984, a comprehensive Statement of Financial Accounting Standards on employer accounting and financial reporting for pension costs. A task force was appointed in 1979 to advise the FASB on these matters.

As an interim measure, in May 1980 the FASB issued Statement No. 36, "Disclosure of Pension Information," amending the disclosure requirements of APB Opinion No. 8.[1] This statement addressed the lack of comparable disclosures in employers' financial statements concerning their pension plans' financial status, and prescribed new *disclosures* to help correct this deficiency. It did not, however, modify any of the other provisions of Opinion No. 8. Although the exposure draft of the statement would have called for disclosures related to postretirement life insurance, medical, and other nonpension benefits, the board decided not to include those requirements in the final statement.

ANNUAL PROVISION FOR PENSION COST

The determination of the annual provision for pension cost requires consideration of the minimum and maximum provisions under Opinion No. 8.

Minimum Provision

Opinion No. 8 requires a minimum annual provision for pension cost equal to the total of (1) normal cost, (2) an amount equivalent to interest on *unfunded prior service cost,* and (3) a supplemental provision for *vested benefits,* if required.[2] The supplemental provision for vested benefits is required if the *un-*

---

[1] This statement is first effective for years beginning after December 15, 1979, and for a complete set of financial statements for interim periods beginning after December 15, 1979, and issued after June 30, 1980.

[2] The term *unfunded prior service cost,* as used herein, includes unfunded past service cost and unfunded increases in past service cost arising from plan amendments. Normal cost is generally funded on a current basis in conformance with past and present Internal Revenue Code requirements for qualified plans. In such cases, normal cost is not included in unfunded

funded or otherwise unprovided-for value of vested benefits at the end of the year is not at least 5% less than the comparable amount at the beginning of the year.[3] When the supplemental provision is required, it may be the lesser of:

1 an amount, if any, by which 5% of the value of unfunded vested benefits at the beginning of the year exceeds the reduction in the comparable value of unfunded vested benefits at the end of the year; or

2 an amount sufficient to make the aggregate annual provision for pension cost equal to the sum of (a) the normal cost, (b) amortization of prior service cost on a 40-year basis (including interest), and (c) interest equivalents on differences between provisions and amounts funded.

In comparing the value of unfunded vested benefits at the end of the year with the comparable amount at the beginning of the year, the amount at the end of the year should be measured exclusive of any net change resulting during the year from changes in benefits due to plan amendments.

Provision (1) described above is equal to 5% of the value of unfunded vested benefits at the beginning of the year to the extent that such 5% is not covered by a net reduction in such amounts due to plan experience during the year (e.g., contributions to the fund, fund earnings, and actuarial gains). The 5% is a declining-balance type of provision; assuming no change in unfunded vested benefits other than through the provision, it would take about 45 years to reduce the unfunded vested benefits to 10% of the original amount.

Within the general framework of these "minimum" provisions, a company may adopt, as a single accounting policy, one of three procedures regarding unfunded or otherwise unprovided-for prior service cost. It may provide for such cost on the basis of (1) the first method above, commonly referred to as the *interest only plus vesting* method, (2) the second method described above, commonly referred to as the *40-year amortization* method, or (3) the lower of the two determined on an annual basis, even though either method may call for a larger amount than the other in a particular year.

The 40-year amortization procedure has the practical advantage of avoiding the need for separately determining the annual change in unfunded vested benefits. The 40-year basis of amortization is computed as a level annual amount including the equivalent of interest. Thus, if a 4% interest factor is assumed in the actuarial calculations, the amortization rate would be approximately 5% and a 3.5% interest assumption would result in an amortization rate of about 4.7%.

---

prior service cost. *Vested benefits* are defined as benefits "that are not contingent on the employee's continuing in the employer's service."
[3] The term *unfunded or otherwise unprovided-for value of vested benefits* means an excess of the present value of vested benefits over the total of (a) the pension fund and (b) any balance sheet pension accruals, less (c) any balance sheet prepayments or deferred charges. For convenience, the term *unfunded vested benefits* will be used in this discussion in place of the longer term.

Maximum Provision

The maximum annual provision for pension cost is defined in Opinion No. 8 as the total of (1) normal cost, (2) 10% of *past service cost* at inception of the plan and of *increases or decreases in prior service cost* arising from plan amendments (in each case until fully amortized), and (3) interest equivalents on differences between provisions and amounts funded.[4] The 10% includes an interest factor and, assuming interest rates of between 4% and 6%, the maximum provision therefore requires from about 13 to slightly over 15 years to fully amortize such past service cost and increases or decreases in prior service cost.

Calculation of Annual Provision

The annual provision for pension expense must be within the range of the minimum and maximum limits established by APB Opinion No. 8. Illustrations of the calculation of the annual provision and comparison with the limits are provided in Figure 6-1. Assumptions are the same for both computations. In practice, computing both limits is usually not necessary because the determination is being made only for that limit which may be exceeded in the particular situation.

Valuing Vested Benefits

The *value of vested benefits* at a particular (valuation) date includes the value of the amounts of benefits payable or to become payable to retired employees and to ex-employees who have vested benefits and the value of benefits that would be creditable to employees in active service if they were to terminate service as of the valuation date.[5]

Vested benefits do not accrue ratably between valuation dates, but reflect the vesting percentage in effect for the individual employee on the valuation date. The valuation of vested benefits may be required for determining the annual pension expense provision, as discussed earlier, and/or for disclosure. The discussions in this section and in the following section on "Actuarial Factors" relate primarily to the determination of annual pension expense. The determination of benefit information for disclosure purposes as required by FASB Statement No. 36 is discussed under "Disclosures," later in this chapter.

As indicated in an interpretation of APB Opinion No. 8 published by the AICPA, the accrued benefit cost (unit credit) method of calculation should be used to determine the value of vested benefits, even though a different method may be used for other purposes. In the determination of the amount of un-

---

[4] *Past service cost* and *increases or decreases in prior service cost* as used in this paragraph refer to costs unreduced by amounts previously amortized.

[5] *Value of vested benefits* refers in this paragraph to the present value, at a particular actuarial valuation date, of future expected payments as determined actuarially.

FIGURE 6-1

Computation of limits of provision for annual pension expense as provided in APB Opinion No. 8

ASSUMPTIONS

Normal cost	$ 200,000
Employee contributions	25,000
Prior service cost:	
Unfunded at beginning of year	1,500,000
Funded in prior years	1,000,000
Amortization of actuarial gains	3,500
Amortization of unrealized appreciation	1,500
Unfunded pension accruals	50,000
Actuarial value of vested benefits:	
Beginning of year	5,000,000
End of year	5,300,000
Fund assets:	
Beginning of year	2,000,000
End of year	2,400,000
Interest rate	4%

OVERALL COMPUTATION

	Minimum		Maximum
	I	II	III
1. Normal cost	$200,000	$200,000	$200,000
2. Employee contributions, if not considered in arriving at normal cost	(25,000)	(25,000)	(25,000)
3. Interest on unfunded, unprovided-for prior service cost	58,000[1]		
4. Supplemental provision for vested benefits (see following computation)	47,500		
5. Amortization of prior service cost:			
(a) on a 40-year basis, including interest		126,250[2]	
(b) at 10% per year			250,000
6. Interest on excess of prior years' accounting provisions over amounts funded (or on excess of amounts funded over provisions)	2,000	2,000	2,000
7. Provision for actuarial (gains) or losses	(3,500)	(3,500)	(3,500)
8. Provision for unrealized (appreciation) or depreciation	(1,500)	(1,500)	(1,500)
9. Total	$277,500	$298,250	$422,000

Pension expense for the year must be an amount between Column III and the lesser (in any one year) of Columns I and II based upon an acceptable actuarial cost method consistently applied.

FIGURE 6-1 (continued)

1 Unfunded, unprovided-for prior service cost equals $1,500,000 less $50,000, or $1,450,000.
2 Level annual charge which will amortize total prior service cost of $2,500,000 (with interest) on a 40-year basis; amortization will cease when the unfunded amount of $1,500,000 has been amortized.

Computation of supplemental provision for vested benefits (Paragraph 17a of Opinion No. 8)

	At Date of Most Recent Valuation	At Date of Preceding Valuation
1. Actuarial value of vested benefits	$5,300,000	$5,000,000
2. Amount of pension fund (Note)	2,400,000	2,000,000
3. Unfunded amount (Item 1 minus Item 2)	2,900,000	3,000,000
4. Amount of balance sheet pension accruals less pension deferred charges (Note)	50,000	50,000
5. Actuarial value of unfunded or unprovided-for vested benefits (Item 3 minus Item 4)	$2,850,000	$2,950,000
6. 5% of Item 5 for the prior year	$147,500	
7. Excess of Item 5 for the prior year over Item 5 for the current year	100,000	
8. Excess of Item 6 over Item 7 (provision for vested benefits to Item 4, Overall Computation)	$ 47,500	

Note:

The dates for Items 2 and 4 may be the end of the company's fiscal year or the actuarial valuation date. Consistency is the primary consideration.

funded or unprovided-for value of vested benefits, the method of valuing the pension plan assets should preferably be consistent with that employed in periodic actuarial valuations in use for accounting purposes except that the use of full market value may not be desirable because its use might cause wide fluctuations in the unfunded vested benefit figure. Nonetheless, the use of full market value is acceptable pursuant to the aforementioned interpretation of APB Opinion No. 8, even where the full amount of appreciation has not been recognized in the cost provision.

ACTUARIAL FACTORS

The determination of the annual provision for pension cost involves the use of actuarial cost methods, actuarial assumptions, and methods of treating actuarial gains and losses.

Actuarial Cost Method

APB Opinion No. 8 defines five actuarial cost methods, discussed in Chapter 2, whose application would result in an appropriate annual provision for pension cost. Variations of those methods may also be used (e.g., the aggregate method with frozen, separately amortized, past service cost). For accounting purposes, many accountants prefer the entry-age normal cost (or entry-age level cost) method, the aggregate method, or the aggregate method variation referred to above. On the other hand, the accrued benefit method may initially result in lesser charges to income than the other methods.

Terminal Funding and Pay-as-You-Go

The opinion considers these accounting methods (the latter of which is not an actuarial cost method) unacceptable because they give no recognition to pension cost until the employees retire. However, in some circumstances the use of pay-as-you-go or terminal funding as a basis of accounting for a portion of total pension benefits would not have the effect of a material departure from the opinion. For example, if pay-as-you-go is used for employees already retired on the effective date of the opinion, its application would be limited to a diminishing class of employee and the difference between use of pay-as-you-go and an acceptable actuarial cost method might not be material. Similar considerations may be relevant with regard to supplementary pension benefits (other than payments pursuant to deferred compensation contracts, discussed later in this chapter) for a limited number of mature employees who are within five years of retirement age at the time a pension plan is adopted or amended.

Interest Component

Paragraph 23 of the opinion refers to the fact that "the equivalent of interest . . . may be stated separately or it may be included in the amortization." This statement pertains only to computation and should not be construed to allow any so-called interest component of pension cost to be classified in financial statements or treated as interest rather than pension cost for any other accounting purpose.

Actuarial Assumptions

Actuarial assumptions should be reasonable in relation to current and future conditions and consistently applied. They should ordinarily be based upon the current conditions of the pension plan. Although an uncommon practice, there may be instances where actuarial assumptions are not based on current plan conditions or provisions. For example, actuarial assumptions in some instances include a factor for anticipated increased benefit levels where they are reasonable in the light of either the company's past policy of bettering pension benefits or the company's reasonable expectation of increasing pension benefits in the future. When anticipated increased benefit levels are considered in the determination of normal cost, they should also be considered in the determination of prior service cost, where separately computed.

Actuarial Gains and Losses

Actuarial gains and losses arise from the need to use assumptions concerning future events. Under APB Opinion No. 8, adjustments required from time to time to reflect actual experience must be recognized in a consistent manner that reflects the long-range nature of pension cost. Except in specified circumstances relative to plant closings, acquisitions, and so forth, actuarial gains and losses are to be either spread or averaged rather than accorded immediate recognition. Immediate recognition is considered undesirable because of the possibility of wide fluctuations in annual pension expense. From 10 to 20 years is considered a reasonable period over which to spread actuarial gains and losses when spreading is accomplished by separate adjustment rather than by the routine application of the actuarial cost method used.

The averaging method of dealing with actuarial gains and losses involves determining an average annual amount of such gains or losses (e.g., a five-year moving average). Results under averaging may be appropriate for gains and losses which tend to be repetitive but may be inappropriate for unusual gains or losses. In certain instances, a combination of methods may be desirable. For example, spreading might be applied to gains or losses that are not expected to recur frequently, while averaging may be applied to recurring items.

When actuarial assumptions have been changed, past experience regarding actuarial gains and losses may not be an appropriate basis for averaging. The averaging method, when suitable, has the advantage of avoiding a possible cumulative effect that could result from use of the spread method. For example, if actuarial gains were to occur at the rate of $1,000 a year, spreading over 10 years would result in recognition of $100 in the first year, $200 in the second year (1/10 of the prior year's gain and 1/10 of the current year's gain), $300 in the third year, and so forth.

APB Opinion No. 8 recognized that "an effect similar to spreading or averaging may be obtained by applying net actuarial gains as a reduction of prior service cost in a manner that reduces the annual amount equivalent to interest on, or the annual amount of amortization of, such prior service cost and does not reduce the period of amortization." For example, the application of a $100,000 gain to prior service cost would, assuming a 4% rate, reduce the "interest" charge by $4,000 annually. As a period of 10 to 20 years is considered reasonable for spreading, the authors believe that net actuarial gains should not be applied to prior service cost if the remaining amortization period of such prior service cost is less than 10 years. While the opinion does not discuss applying a net actuarial loss to prior service, this would appear to be acceptable, provided prior service cost is being amortized over a remaining period of between 10 and 20 years, the period over which actuarial losses could otherwise be separately spread.

Unrealized Investment Appreciation and Depreciation

APB Opinion No. 8 requires recognition of unrealized appreciation or depreciation in the value of equity investments in the determination of pension cost on a rational and systematic basis that avoids giving undue weight to short-term market fluctuations. Appreciation and depreciation need not be recognized for debt securities expected to be held to maturity and redeemed at face value. Adopting a consistent method for according recognition to unrealized appreciation and depreciation is particularly important.

It should be noted that in certain cases (e.g., when investments are valued by the actuary at fair market value) unrealized appreciation or depreciation is recognized in the determination of actuarial gains and losses. In other cases (e.g., when investments are valued by the actuary at cost) unrealized appreciation or depreciation is not recognized in the determination of actuarial gains and losses and thus must be treated separately.

Actuarial Valuation Input Date

The actuary, in his valuation, will normally use employee census data as of the beginning of the year and will estimate the expense provision for the year. In the absence of any substantially changed conditions that would render obsolete the data on which the actuarial valuation was made (e.g., acquisition or disposal of a significant division, product line or segment of the business, or significant change in the level of benefits), a date within 12 months from the end of the year should be suitable for use in such determinations. Data as of an earlier date may also be suitable, but its use could present problems in some areas, such as the accumulated benefit information for disclosure purposes called for by Statement No. 36. (See later in this chapter and Chapter 8.)

Differences Between Funding and Accounting

As pointed out in Opinion No. 8, the actuarial cost method used for accounting need not be the same as the actuarial method used for funding. It follows that different actuarial assumptions may also be used for each of these two purposes even though the same general actuarial method may be used. Obviously, all relevant factors should be given proper recognition in the assumptions used for accounting. In most instances it is likely that the actuarial cost method and the actuarial assumptions used for funding purposes will also be appropriate for accounting use, but this will not always be so. Accordingly, actuarial methods and assumptions should be carefully considered from the standpoint of their appropriateness for accounting.

DEFINED CONTRIBUTION PLANS

As noted under "Pension Plans" in Chapter 1, some plans referred to as defined contribution plans provide a contemplated scale of benefits and thus may need to be treated for accounting purposes as defined benefit plans.

APB Opinion No. 8 states that the periodic cost of a defined contribution plan usually is appropriately measured by the amount of contribution determined by the formula specified in the plan. It would appear that where the employer's liability is limited to the amount of the pension fund, the amount of the defined contribution can be presumed to be the proper amount of the current charge to expense. This is often the case with bilateral plans negotiated between either an employer or a group of employers, such as an industry group, and a union or other employee representatives.

Where a plan provides both a formula for plan contributions and a scale for plan benefits, however, and the contributions are found to be inadequate or excessive for the purpose of funding the scale of benefits, subsequent adjustment of either the contributions or the benefits, or both, is necessary. If the plan history indicates that only the scale of benefits is adjusted, the plan presumably should be treated as a defined contribution plan. If, however, a company's liability for pension benefit levels is not limited by the amount of the pension fund or if the plan history indicates (and/or the current employer policy contemplates) the maintenance of benefit levels regardless of the amount of defined contribution or legal limitation of the employer's liability for such benefits, the plan should be treated as a defined benefit plan, with the current charge to expense computed actuarially.

Court Decisions

Caution is needed in determining whether collectively bargained fixed-contribution plans should be treated as defined contribution plans. Several court cases have dealt with the classification of this type of plan. In particular, the U.S. Court of Appeals in *Connolly* v. *Pension Benefit Guaranty Corporation,* in reversing a lower court decision, held that the plan in that case is not a defined contribution plan, but rather a defined benefit plan. The U.S. Supreme Court declined to review the appeals court decision.

The U.S. Court of Appeals held that to qualify as a defined contribution plan, *separate individual employee accounts* must be maintained and employee benefits must be based *solely* on amounts contributed for the individual, and the *Connolly* plan did not meet either requirement. The pension plan in *Connolly* was established by a collective-bargaining agreement and called for multiple employers' contributions to a union fund of a specified amount for each hour worked. The plan stated that the companies' obligation was limited to the defined contribution amount. Contributions, however, were not allocated to individual accounts and participants' benefits were defined and calculated on the basis of service, regardless of the adequacy of the amount contributed.

Employee Stock Ownership Plans

An employee stock ownership plan (ESOP) is one type of defined contribution plan. ESOPs are designed to invest primarily in the employer's stock, which is generally purchased from the company or its shareholders with outside financing, guaranteed by the company. ESOPs present special accounting and other problems which are discussed later in this chapter.

DISCLOSURES

APB Opinion No. 8, as amended by FASB Statement No. 36, calls for specific disclosures in financial statements, which are described in Figure 6-2.[6]

Accumulated Plan Benefits

As indicated in item 4 of Figure 6-2, companies are required to disclose the actuarial present value of vested and nonvested accumulated plan benefits and the net assets available for plan benefits for all defined benefit pension plans. If, however, these figures are not available, the company should disclose the reasons why such amounts are not provided and, as an alternative disclosure, provide the excess, if any, of the actuarially computed value of vested benefits over the total of the pension fund and any employer balance sheet pension accruals, less any employer balance sheet pension prepayments or deferred charges. The FASB anticipates that the only plans for which the information will not be available are those plans that do not report such information to the Department of Labor pursuant to ERISA. Such pension plans include those of foreign subsidiaries covering foreign employees and plans funded exclusively through insurance contracts which fully guarantee the amount of benefit payments.[7]

If an employer has more than one defined benefit pension plan, the required disclosures may be reported under Statement No. 36 in total for all plans, separately for each plan, or in such subaggregations as are considered most useful. A company may simultaneously maintain plans which have an actuarial present value of accumulated plan benefits in excess of net assets available for benefits and plans which have net assets available for benefits in excess of the actuarial present value of accumulated plan benefits. Statement No. 36 states that, in such cases, separate disclosures may be desirable if a significant number of participants in the "underfunded" plan are employed by a subsidiary or division that is unprofitable or experiencing a continuous decline in business. In the view of the authors, disclosure in those circumstances is usually desirable in

---

[6] As previously indicated, Statement No. 36 first became effective for annual financial statements for years ending on or after December 15, 1980.
[7] See Chapter 5 for a discussion of plans fully or partially exempted from the ERISA reporting and disclosure requirements.

FIGURE 6-2

Pension plan disclosure requirements under APB Opinion No. 8, as amended by FASB Statement No. 36

APB Opinion No. 8 (Paragraph 46), as amended by FASB Statement No. 36 (Paragraphs 7 and 8)

1   A statement that such plans exist, identifying or describing the employee groups covered.

2   A statement of the company's accounting and funding policies.

3   The provision for pension cost for the period.

4   The actuarial present value of vested accumulated plan benefits, the actuarial present value of nonvested plan benefits, and the plan's net assets available for benefits (including an employer's pension accruals as of the benefit information date to the extent such accruals exceed contributions receivable from the employer that are included in the plan's net assets available for benefits), all determined in accordance with the provisions of FASB Statement No. 35, "Accounting and Reporting by Defined Benefit Pension Plans."[1, 2] Where a company has more than one defined benefit plan, the disclosures may be reported in total for all plans, separately for each plan, or in such subaggregations as are considered most useful. In addition, the assumed rate of return used in determining the actuarial present values of vested and nonvested accumulated plan benefits and the benefit information date should be included. For plans for which this information is unavailable, disclosure should be made of the reason such amounts are not provided and the excess, if any, of the actuarially computed value of vested benefits over the total of plan assets and balance sheet pension accruals less any pension prepayments or deferred charges.

5   Nature and effect of significant matters affecting comparability for all periods presented, such as changes in accounting methods (actuarial cost method, amortization of past and prior service cost, treatment of actuarial gains and losses, etc.), changes in circumstances (actuarial assumptions, etc.), or adoption or amendment of a plan.

1 This disclosure is required under FASB Statement No. 36 and, accordingly, is initially effective for annual financial statements for years ending on or after December 15, 1980. Until the effective date of the statement, the following disclosure was required under APB Opinion No. 8: "The excess, if any, of the actuarially computed value of vested benefits over the total of the pension fund and any balance sheet pension accruals, less any pension prepayments or deferred charges."

2 Asset valuation method, and the actuarial cost method, and actuarial assumptions required by FASB Statement No. 35 are discussed in Chapter 8 under "Reporting Actuarial Benefit Information."

view of the fact that the law generally prohibits using the assets of one plan to pay benefits required under another plan.

FASB Statement No. 36 requires that the actuarially determined amounts to be disclosed be determined in accordance with the method described in FASB Statement No. 35 on accounting and reporting by defined benefit pension plans. Although not explicitly stated, the method described in Statement No. 35 results in an amount that would be computed using the accrued benefit cost method. However, although accumulated benefits are computed using that method, the employer company's provision for pension expense may continue to be determined in accordance with any one of several methods (including the accrued benefit cost method) under APB Opinion No 8. Accordingly, the method used for calculating the amounts for disclosures of accumulated plan benefits will often be different from that used to calculate the expense. In order to avoid any misunderstanding, disclosure of the actuarial methods used both for pension benefit disclosures and for pension expense calculations may be helpful to financial statement users.

Where analysis indicates that a defined contribution plan is in substance a defined benefit plan it should, as discussed earlier in this chapter, be accounted for as such. The benefit information called for by FASB Statement No. 36 should be disclosed. It should be noted, however, that where the relative position and undertakings of an employer associated with a multiemployer plan of this type are not determinable, information related to accumulated benefits (item 4, Figure 6-2) are not required. The particular circumstances, however, must be disclosed.

The actuarial present value of accumulated plan benefits and of vested plan benefits is to be disclosed as of the most recent date as of which the actuarial benefit information was determined. These same disclosures are also required for pension plan financial statements in accordance with FASB Statement No. 35, "Accounting and Reporting by Defined Benefit Pension Plans." As discussed in Chapter 8, these disclosures are to be based on actuarial calculations as of the end or beginning of the plan year.

In disclosing a plan's net assets available for benefits, the amount should include an employer's balance sheet pension accrual, to the extent that such accrual exceeds the plan contributions receivable from the employer.

SEC Requirements

Minimum disclosure requirements of the Securities and Exchange Commission were previously set forth in Rule 3-16 (g) of Regulation S-X. However, the SEC, in ASR No. 280, deleted Rule 3-16 (g) in its entirety, effective for years ending after December 15, 1980.

ACCOUNTING EFFECTS OF ERISA

There has been much publicity, discussion, and uncertainty regarding the accounting impact of ERISA on employers. As previously mentioned in this chapter, the Financial Accounting Standards Board has placed the overall subject of employer accounting for pension costs on its technical agenda and issued, pending completion of that project, Interpretation No. 3, "Accounting for the Cost of Pension Plans Subject to the Employee Retirement Income Security Act of 1974, an Interpretation of APB Opinion No. 8." The FASB subsequently issued Statement No. 36, "Disclosure of Pension Information, an Amendment of APB Opinion No. 8." The following discussion covers issues included in those pronouncements and other issues related to the impact of ERISA on accounting for pension costs.

Liability for Unfunded Prior Service Cost

APB Opinion No. 8, in paragraph 18, states: "If the company has a legal obligation for pension cost in excess of amounts paid or accrued, the excess should be shown in the balance sheet as both a liability and a deferred charge." An argument has been presented that since companies are now obligated by law to fund unfunded prior service cost (generally over a period of not more than 30 or 40 years), they have a legal obligation for pension cost, and thus should record a liability in the amount of unfunded prior service cost not already recorded.

FASB Interpretation No. 3 states that, based on an analysis of information presently available, the board does not believe that ERISA creates a legal obligation for unfunded pension costs that warrants accounting recognition as a liability pursuant to paragraph 18 of APB Opinion No. 8. The interpretation points out, however, that unless a waiver from the minimum funding requirements is obtained from the Secretary of the Treasury, the amount currently required to be funded should be recognized as a liability.

This accords with the view of some lawyers that although ERISA's funding requirements in one sense impose a legal obligation upon the company, the amount of the legal obligation at any point in time is only that portion of unfunded prior service cost required to be funded to date under the law.

Liability for Unfunded Vested Benefits

As indicated in Chapter 4 under "Plan Termination Insurance," if a plan is terminated with unfunded vested benefits, the Pension Benefit Guaranty Corporation (PBGC) will provide the beneficiaries with the prescribed benefits, up to the limits specified in ERISA, and will be able to place a priority lien on the employer's assets to the extent of 30% of the employer's net worth. The question has been raised as to whether unfunded vested benefits (up to the amount that potentially could become payable to the PBGC) should be recorded on the balance sheet as a liability, assuming the company does not purchase insurance coverage to protect against such liability.

The FASB interpretation indicates that a liability for unfunded vested benefits need not be recorded unless a plan is to be terminated. Without a plan termination, no benefits will be paid by the PBGC on behalf of the company and no liability to the PBGC will be created.

The interpretation states that when there is convincing evidence that a pension plan will be terminated (perhaps a formal commitment by management to terminate a plan) and the liability on termination will exceed fund assets and related prior accruals, the excess liability shall be accrued. The interpretation states further that if the amount of the excess liability cannot be reasonably determined, disclosure of the circumstances (including an estimate of the possible range of the liability) shall be made in the notes to the financial statements.

In some instances, circumstances may indicate that a plan termination is more than a remote possibility though the aforementioned "convincing evidence" is absent. Such circumstances would include a tentative decision by management to terminate a plan, or the possibility that the company may not be in a financial position to continue a plan. The latter instance may be indicated when the auditor deems it necessary to express an opinion containing what is commonly referred to as a "going concern" qualification. Although these types of situations are not discussed in the interpretation, it would appear that in such cases recording a liability is not necessary, but appropriate disclosure of the amount of the contingent liability should be made.

Pension Expense

Plan Compliance with ERISA

APB Opinion No. 8 generally speaks to computing pension cost in accordance with the plan's requirements. If the plan is not in compliance with ERISA, the provision for pension cost may be based on plan provisions that do not comply with ERISA. This will likely result in a loss contingency that may need to be reflected in the financial statements, depending upon the likelihood of incurring and reasonably estimating the amount of a liability. In this connection, the guidance in FASB Statement No. 5, "Accounting for Contingencies," although not directly applicable, may be helpful. To illustrate, consider a situation in which a plan instrument does not conform to ERISA's participation requirements. In that case, the provision for pension expense is computed excluding certain legally eligible participants, and the pension accrual will be inadequate. Thus, a determination should be made as to the likelihood (as defined by FASB Statement No. 5) that a liability will be incurred for the additional benefits, and for any fines and penalties that may be imposed for lack of compliance.[8]

Minimum and Maximum Pension Expense

APB Opinion No. 8 sets forth the minimum and maximum provisions for annual pension cost to be recorded in the financial statements. The minimum provision is to include, among other components, interest on unfunded prior service cost and, in certain instances a provision for unfunded vested benefits, but amortization of prior service cost as part of the provision is not required. The maximum provision should include, among other components, 10% of prior service cost. Questions have been raised in practice as to whether it is ac-

---

[8] ERISA specifies that certain penalties are levied against the plan or against the plan administrator. As discussed in Chapter 4, however, the employer company is often the plan administrator and, even if that is not the case, the employer may ultimately become liable for such penalties.

ceptable for accounting purposes to use ERISA's minimum and/or maximum funding standards instead of the minimum and maximum specified in APB Opinion No 8.

With respect to the minimum provision:

If a plan is fully funded under ERISA's minimum funding requirements and no funds are required to be paid to the plan in the current year, is it still necessary to include a provision for pension expense?

Can the minimum provision for pension cost continue to exclude an amount for amortization of prior service cost even though ERISA requires prior service cost to be funded?

In most cases, the answer to both these questions is yes. Funding and accounting for pension cost are largely independent concepts. Funding requirements are established by ERISA, whereas the annual pension provision for financial accounting purposes is determined in accordance with APB Opinion No. 8. This distinction between accounting and funding is supported by FASB Interpretation No. 3, in which the FASB reaffirmed that for financial accounting purposes the annual provision for pension cost is not necessarily determined by the funding of a pension plan and that the limits set forth in APB Opinion No. 8 are not changed as a result of ERISA.

As to the first question, while generally a provision would be required, there are unusual instances where it may not be necessary to provide for pension expense in a particular year. If, for example, plan assets have appreciated sufficiently in value whereby the amount of an actuarial gain is so large that the portion thereof spread or averaged (as described under "Actuarial Gains and Losses" earlier in this chapter) to the current year exceeds the normal and any other costs related to that year, there would be no provision for pension cost in that year. Disclosure should be made, however, of the current and future effect of that circumstance.

As to the second question, the authors' view differs somewhat from that set forth in the FASB interpretation. Although the annual pension cost to be charged to expense is not *necessarily* determined by a pension plan's funding, ERISA's funding requirements affect the rationale on which Opinion No. 8's minimum limit for the annual provision for pension cost is apparently based. The rationale for not requiring amortization of prior service cost appears to be based on the concept (described in paragraph 13 of APB Opinion No. 8) that in many cases a provision for normal cost plus an amount equivalent to interest on unfunded prior service cost will be adequate to meet, on a continuing basis, all benefit payments under the plan. The APB decided that so long as the provision is sufficient to amortize unfunded vested benefits over a reasonable period, no specific provision for unfunded prior service cost is required. The implication is that since unfunded prior service cost might never be paid, there is no need to charge such cost to expense.

It would appear, however, that since prior service cost must be funded under

ERISA, it is more difficult to argue that such cost need not be provided by charges to income. We believe it would be appropriate for the provision for pension cost to include, in addition to normal cost and interest on unfunded prior service cost, an amount sufficient to amortize the unfunded prior service cost, not already provided for, over a reasonable time (e.g., the funding period).[9] It appears that many companies which were previously not amortizing unfunded prior service cost as part of the provision are now doing so. By expensing unfunded prior service cost a company not only avoids building up an asset on its books that may never be recovered, but also is more likely to enter such cost into its product cost system and thus is more likely to recover that cost through reflection in the company's pricing structure.

Despite the arguments set forth above, we believe that auditors should not take exception where pension cost is accounted for in accordance with the principle set forth in the interpretation. The auditor may, however, encourage his clients to include as part of their annual provision for pension cost an amount sufficient to amortize the unfunded prior service cost not already provided for over a reasonable time period.

At any time, a change can be made in expense recognition from the minimum level under APB Opinion No 8 (where a provision for prior service cost is not included) to a provision which includes amortization of prior service cost. Such a change is considered a change in accounting method, which should be accounted for prospectively (see paragraph 47 of APB Opinion No. 8) and which would require a consistency exception in the auditor's report if the effect of the change is material.

With respect to whether ERISA affects the determination of pension expense in accordance with APB Opinion No. 8, a question regarding the *maximum* provision has also been raised in practice. The maximum provision under APB Opinion No. 8 includes, among other components, 10% of prior service cost. The issue is whether a higher percentage of prior service cost can now be included in the annual provision for pension expense as a result of ERISA.

Before ERISA, the maximum annual pension deduction allowable for income tax purposes was 10% of prior service cost, the same percentage as the maximum allowable for financial reporting purposes. ERISA increased that component of the allowable deduction to an amount representing amortization of prior service cost over 10 years, which is approximately 12 to 14% of prior service cost, depending upon the actuarial yield assumption. Although a charge to income based on the maximum tax deduction allowable under ERISA

---

[9] We believe that it is appropriate for the provision for pension cost to include amortization of unfunded prior service cost even when the full funding limitation applies (see "Full Funding Limitation" in Chapter 4). If, for example, plan assets appreciate sufficiently in value so that no contribution is required in a particular year, an actuarial gain will likely result. This gain, when determining the provision for pension cost, should be spread or averaged over time as described under "Actuarial Gains and Losses" earlier in this chapter. Thus, the benefit of the appreciation will be reflected in the provision in a consistent manner as anticipated by APB Opinion No. 8.

would appear to be consistent with the original intent of APB Opinion No. 8, and also would avoid the need to carry a deferred charge in the financial statements while resulting in a more conservative accounting treatment, it is not permitted. As previously pointed out, the FASB interpretation indicates the maximum limit for pension expense as set forth in APB Opinion No. 8 is not changed as a result of ERISA. However, a provision based on 10-year amortization will frequently not result in a significant difference from that based on 10% amortization. In such cases, there should be no objection to using the 10-year amortization.

Liability to Acquiring Company

Questions have been raised as to whether ERISA affects APB Opinion No. 16 requirements for reporting the results of business combinations. The opinion states (in a footnote to paragraph 88h) that, in a business combination accounted for under the purchase method, a liability should be recorded in the amount of the greater of (1) accrued pension cost computed in conformity with the accounting policies of the acquiring company for one or more of its pension plans or (2) the excess, if any, of the actuarially computed value of vested benefits over the amount of the pension fund.

One argument favors changed requirements for two reasons. Since APB Opinion No. 16 indicates that the acquiring company should record all liabilities related to the acquired company (including pension cost) whether or not shown in the financial statements of the acquired company, at the present value of amounts to be paid, and since ERISA indicates that unfunded prior service cost must now be funded, then unfunded prior service cost (rather than the greater of accrued cost computed in conformity with the policies of the acquiring company or unfunded vested benefits) is the amount that now represents the present value of amounts to be paid. APB Opinion No. 16, according to this view, should therefore be revised to require the recording of unfunded prior service cost as a liability in a purchase situation.

A counterargument states that since a liability for unfunded prior service cost is not normally required to be recorded, even in light of ERISA, such an amount should not be recorded in a purchase transaction. Some proponents of this argument believe that APB Opinion No. 16 should remain unchanged, while others believe that the requirement for recording unfunded vested benefits should be eliminated because no such liability need be recorded where an acquisition is not involved.

Still another argument cites the fact that ERISA requires an acquiring company to assume responsibility for unfunded vested benefits, as limited by ERISA, in the event of a plan termination. Because of this provision, it is argued, the term *vested benefits* referred to in APB Opinion No. 16 should be modified to read *vested benefits as limited by the termination insurance provisions of ERISA*.

The FASB will probably examine the current appropriateness of the APB

Opinion No. 16 requirements with respect to the amount of pension liability to be recorded in a combination accounted for under the purchase method. Until the FASB addresses this matter, however, one should proceed on the basis that ERISA has no direct impact on the present use or interpretation of the principles set forth in APB Opinion No. 16.

EMPLOYEE STOCK OWNERSHIP PLANS

Employee stock ownership plans (ESOPs) are a type of defined contribution plan and are not a new phenomenon. Recently, though, the increase in their use has drawn a good deal of attention from the financial community, including the accounting profession.

In the past, accounting for costs associated with an employee stock ownership plan (ESOP) was not well defined. APB Opinion No. 8 discusses defined contribution plans in general. Although other pronouncements discuss stock option plans, stock purchase plans, and stock appreciation rights, none directly discusses the accounting problems peculiar to ESOPs.[10] After the FASB's initial decision to decline consideration of the subject, the Accounting Standards Division of the AICPA issued a Statement of Position (SOP 76-3) entitled "Accounting Practices for Certain Employee Stock Ownership Plans." That SOP represents the first significant effort of the profession to define appropriate accounting by the employer for costs incurred in connection with an ESOP.

To illustrate the provisions of SOP 76-3, it is helpful to present a hypothetical set of facts which might apply to a typical ESOP. These assumptions provide a common frame of reference as the basis for subsequent discussion of ESOP-related accounting and reporting issues. The fact pattern is as follows.

A company forms a qualified ESOP (i.e., conforming to applicable provisions of the Internal Revenue Code).

The ESOP borrows money from an unrelated financial institution. The company is a party to the loan agreement and commits itself to make future contributions to the ESOP sufficient in amount to meet the debt service requirements. The commitment is frequently accompanied by a formal guarantee of the loan.

The ESOP uses the loan proceeds to buy common stock of the company from present stockholders and from the company.

The debt is collateralized by the company stock owned by the ESOP and is repaid in annual installments of principal plus interest.

---

[10] Chapter 13B of Accounting Research Bulletin No. 43, "Compensation Involved in Stock Option and Stock Purchase Plans," APB Opinion No. 25, "Accounting for Stock Issued to Employees," and FASB Interpretation No. 28, "Accounting for Stock Appreciation Rights and Other Variable Stock Option or Award Plans, an interpretation of APB Opinions No. 15 and 25."

Accounting for the Debt

In the past, ESOPs have been held out as a means of achieving *off balance sheet financing*—that is, obtaining financing without recording a liability. The main argument in support of that position is that the debt is legally that of the ESOP while the company merely has a commitment to contribute to the ESOP. Commitments, even guarantees, are normally not reported as direct obligations.

SOP 76-3 states that when either the ESOP's debt is guaranteed by the employer or the employer is committed to make future contributions to the ESOP sufficient to cover the debt service requirements, the debt should be recorded in the employer's financial statements. The employer should record a liability because in substance, the debt is the employer's debt; the employer has every intention, and is legally obligated, to make the contributions required for repayment of the loan. The SOP requires recording a liability regardless of whether the funds received from the ESOP for the sale of shares of employer stock are used to finance additional working capital (or fund other company needs) or to buy back its own shares. In addition to requiring the recording of the debt, the SOP requires that the related interest rate and other relevant terms of the debt be disclosed in the footnotes to the financial statements.

In reaching its conclusion, the Accounting Standards Division of the AICPA rejected the view that while the employer should record a liability when the ESOP purchases previously unissued shares, it should not record a liability when the ESOP purchases shares that are already outstanding. Rejection of that position is based on the premise that the purchase of outstanding shares is a transaction solely between two shareholders, and thus the employer company has neither received cash proceeds of a sale nor bought back its own shares. That premise is incorrect since the employer company, by guaranteeing the loan or committing to make future contributions, becomes a party to the transaction.

With respect to the offsetting debit to the recorded liability, the SOP requires that the debit be presented as a reduction of shareholders' equity, rather than as a deferred charge. The following premises underlie this conclusion.

When the company issues previously unissued shares to the ESOP, no real increase in equity capital results. Another event (i.e., repayment of the debt) must occur to trigger an expansion of equity capital. An analogy may be drawn to paragraph 14 of APB Opinion No. 25 which states that ". . . if stock is issued to a plan before some or all of the services are performed, part of the consideration recorded for stock issued is unearned compensation and should be shown as a separate reduction of stockholders' equity."

When the ESOP acquires shares from existing shareholders, a contraction of equity may be deemed to occur. Only when the related debt is liquidated can those shares acquired by the ESOP be considered outstanding.

The division rejected the view that the ESOP's purchase of already outstanding shares has no effect on the number of shares legally or substantively outstanding, such that the offsetting debit to the recorded liability should be recorded not as a reduction of shareholders' equity but rather as a deferred charge representing future employee services.

In a related issue, the SOP indicates that the recorded liability and offsetting charge to stockholders' equity should be reduced symmetrically as the ESOP liquidates the debt. This accounting treatment is consistent with the overall premise of the SOP, that the employer's liability is in substance a debt to the lender and, consequently, the liability is reduced not when funds are transferred to the ESOP through contributions, but rather when funds are transmitted by the ESOP to the lender.

Measuring Compensation Expense

Prior to the issuance of SOP 76-3, some accountants held the view that compensation expense should be recognized based on the fair market value of shares allocated to individual employees at the time such allocations are made (see paragraph 10 of APB Opinion No. 25). A similar but slightly different approach calls for recognition of compensation expense to occur as employees' rights to the shares vest. These treatments are based on the view that the period of allocation or vesting is the period in which the employee performs the services that "earn" the compensation. It was argued that this approach is consistent with paragraph 14 of APB Opinion No. 25 which states ". . . if stock is issued in a plan before some or all of the services are performed . . . the unearned compensation should be accounted for as an expense of the period or periods in which the employee performs services."

The SOP refutes these arguments in recommending that compensation expense should be measured by the amount contributed or committed to be contributed by the employer to an ESOP for a given year. The rationale supporting this accounting treatment is that such contributions are the proper measure of expense inasmuch as they represent expense irrevocably incurred regardless of whether the ESOP uses the funds to reduce the debt guaranteed by the employer. This treatment is consistent with accounting practice for discretionary contributions to profit-sharing plans.

The statement also provides that the portion of the contribution that in substance represents funding of the interest due on the recorded debt should be reported as interest expense in the income statement. In the fact pattern previously presented (in which the employer is committed to make contributions to the ESOP in amounts sufficient to cover debt service requirements), that portion of contributions representing principal liquidation would be identified and charged to compensation expense, while the interest element would be charged to interest expense. It should be noted, however, that "a significant minority within the Division" believes that the entire amount contributed to the ESOP should be reported as compensation expense.

Earnings Per Share and Dividends

The potential impact on earnings per share after an ESOP has acquired the employer's stock is a significant concern of management. This issue received considerable attention from the division and represents one of the few areas in which SOP 76-3 includes the expression of a minority viewpoint.

The majority view in the SOP reflects a conservative position resulting in maximum dilution of earnings per share. Specifically, the division stated that all shares held by an ESOP, whether acquired from the employer or from existing shareholders, should be treated as outstanding shares in the determination of earnings per share. In stating its conclusion, the division placed emphasis on the fact that an ESOP is a legal entity holding shares issued by the employer. Similarly, the SOP provides that dividends declared on shares held by an ESOP should be charged to retained earnings.

The minority viewpoint expressed in the SOP considers shares acquired by an ESOP from the employer as outstanding only to the extent that they become constructively unencumbered by repayments of debt principal. Consistent with this position, the minority believes that dividends on such shares should be charged to retained earnings only to the extent that the shares are constructively unencumbered. Any balance remaining would be reported as additional compensation expense. The minority apparently did not take exception to the majority's treatment for computing earnings per share or recording dividend payments when the ESOP acquires outstanding shares.[11]

The authors believe that the minority view on the computation of earnings per share and dividend accounting issues more closely reflects the economic substance of the transaction. When trust debt proceeds are transferred to the employer corporation, according to the minority view, the transaction is predominantly an incomplete capital transaction which will be completed only by liquidation of the related debt, and the shares acquired by the ESOP should thus be considered outstanding only to the extent that they are unencumbered. The majority viewpoint on this issue appears to be inconsistent with positions taken on other issues in the SOP; in concluding that the debt should be recorded in the employer's financial statements, the SOP emphasizes substance over form, but the legal form is central to the majority conclusion on calculating earnings per share and recording dividends.

Investment Tax Credit

The Internal Revenue Code permits taxpayers to elect an 11% investment credit (in lieu of the normal 10%), provided the taxpayer contributes to an

---

[11] In stating its position, the minority points out that "when trust debt proceeds are transferred to the employer corporation, a transaction of a predominantly financing nature has occurred." It appears that the minority position refers only to a case where the ESOP acquires shares from the employer rather than from existing shareholders.

ESOP an amount equivalent in value to the extra 1%. An employer may obtain an additional investment credit of up to ½ of 1% (raising the total to 11.5%) if the employer contributes an additional ½% to the ESOP and that amount is matched by employee contributions. SOP 76-3 indicates that the additional 1.5% investment tax credit should be reflected as a reduction of income tax expense in the same period that the related contribution is charged to compensation expense, regardless of the employer's normal method of accounting for investment tax credits.

Poolings of Interests and Tainted Shares

Although not covered by the SOP, questions have been raised as to whether acquisitions of employer company shares by an ESOP affect the determination of whether a business combination should be accounted for as a "purchase" or as a "pooling of interests."

APB Opinion No. 16, "Business Combinations," proscribes accounting for a business combination as a pooling of interests in certain circumstances. Paragraph 47(c) of the opinion states that in order to account for a business combination as a pooling of interests, there could have been neither distributions to stockholders nor retirement of securities by the parties to the combination in contemplation of effecting the combination. Paragraph 47(d) states that if a combination is to be accounted for as a pooling of interests, treasury shares may be reacquired only for purposes other than business combinations and no party to the combination may reacquire more than a normal number of shares between the dates the plan of combination is initiated and consummated. Purposes other than business combinations include acquisitions of shares "for option and compensation plans and other recurring distributions," provided that a systematic pattern of reacquisition is established at least two years before the plan of combination is initiated, or for less than two years if it coincides with the adoption of a new plan.

Although acquisitions of shares by an ESOP may in certain circumstances be deemed of a nature so as to preclude pooling of interests accounting, it appears that would ordinarily not be the case. Employer company stock is normally not acquired by an ESOP in contemplation of effecting a business combination; such shares are usually acquired by the ESOP for other purposes. Nonetheless, each case must be decided on its own merits.

SPECIAL SITUATIONS

Certain transactions and events require special consideration in accounting for employers' pension costs. These situations include plant closings, business combinations, changes in accounting, new labor agreements, and other situations.

Plant Closings

APB Opinion No. 8 states that actuarial gains or losses should be recognized immediately if they arise from a single occurrence not directly related to the operation of a pension plan and not in the ordinary course of an employer's business, such as a plant closing. An actuarial gain or loss on a plant closing can result from several factors. In some cases the terms of a labor agreement require that certain accrued but nonvested benefits automatically become vested when a plant closes, normally contributing to an actuarial loss. In many cases, the turnover assumption will prove to have been too low, contributing to an actuarial gain. Because the turnover assumption frequently has the greatest impact in a plant closing situation, it is not uncommon for a net actuarial gain to result.

In practice, difficulties have arisen in applying the guidance contained in APB Opinion No. 8 to plant closings. Those difficulties are perhaps best demonstrated by means of an example. Assume that before a plant closing, prior service cost related to the employees in that plant was $600, of which $200 was funded. Because of the plant closing, certain actuarial assumptions related to the pension costs associated with that plant prove to be incorrect and an actuarial gain of $150 results. The pertinent amounts before and after the plant closing are as follows:

	Before Plant Closing	After Plant Closing
Prior service costs	$600	$450
Portion provided for accounting purposes	200	200
Unprovided prior service costs[12]	$400	$250

Many actuaries take the position, with respect to paragraph 31 of APB Opinion No. 8, that the actuarial gain or loss resulting from the difference in prior service cost before and after the plant closing is the amount to be recognized. Under this interpretation, using the amounts in the example, the actuarial gain of $150 ($600 less $450) would be recognized immediately; the unprovided prior service cost of $400 (the remaining $250 plus the $150 taken into income) would be amortized in future periods. Although we have been advised that there is precedent for this treatment, the authors believe that it is inappropriate to immediately recognize the actuarial gain or loss as de-

---

[12] Note that the terms *prior service cost* and *vested benefits* would be synonymous when a plant closes.

scribed above and defer the unfunded vested benefits to future years. Reduction of an unbooked liability is not income and should not be recognized as such.

Another interpretation of paragraph 31 of APB Opinion No. 8 is to immediately recognize only an *accounting* gain or loss. The term *accounting* gain or loss as used here would represent the difference between the amount of prior service cost after the plant closing and the amount already provided. In the example, the amount of the charge under this approach would be $450 less $200, or the entire remaining unprovided prior service cost (vested benefits) of $250. Thus, any excess provision would be taken into income, whereas any remaining unfunded vested benefits would be expensed. The objective under this approach is to currently write off all unfunded costs related to the terminated employees so that there are no future charges related thereto. The only charges in future years would relate to differences in actual experience from that assumed (e.g., mortality, interest yield) as of the date of the plant closing, relating to the participants terminated as a result of the plant closing.

This accounting treatment is consistent with the advisory conclusion reached in an issues paper prepared by the Accounting Standards Division of the AICPA, "Accounting for Vested Pension Benefits Existing or Arising When a Plant Is Closed or a Business Segment Is Discontinued." The issues paper was forwarded to the FASB in 1980 for its consideration. The FASB, however, reported that it is including this issue in its comprehensive pension accounting project, so the Accounting Standards Division will take no further action with respect to this matter.

The authors believe that the accounting should in fact depend on the particular circumstances surrounding a plant closing. The impact of the closing on the trend of the company's levels of operations and employment is an important consideration. In some cases, a plant closing may be clearly regarded as an occurrence outside of the normal course of business because it results from a deliberate attempt or need to significantly reduce market share, operations, or the size of the work force. In other instances, however, a plant closing may, more appropriately, be considered as part of the normal course of the company's business. For example, a company may decide to close an older or less efficient plant in favor of expanding production at a more efficient location, the primary objective being to increase efficiency rather than to significantly reduce the work force or curtail production. It is, therefore, necessary to analyze the reasons for the closing and the impact of the closing on the company as a whole.

Using this principle, if in the earlier example the closing is considered an occurrence outside of the normal course of business, the remaining unfunded prior service costs of $250 related to the terminated employees would be expensed.

On the other hand, where a plant closing is more appropriately considered part of the normal course of the company's business, only any incremental prior service costs resulting from the plant closing (none in the example) should be expensed currently, and any remaining unfunded prior service costs ($250) continued to be amortized to future years in the normal way.

The discussion above does not address the accounting for the unfunded costs of those former plant employees whose retirement preceded the plant closing. Some believe the accounting for the liability to both groups should be the same. Others, however, believe the accounting recommended for the active employees should not extend to those former plant employees whose retirement preceded the closing, since the plant closing has no relevance to or impact on the pension costs of previously retired plant employees. This latter view represents the advisory conclusion reached by the AICPA's Accounting Standards Division in the issues paper.

The treatment for any differences between estimated plant closing costs and the actual costs subsequently incurred should also be considered. There is no existing literature on this matter, but it would seem that the accounting could be dependent on the circumstances. When adjustments to estimated pension costs related to a plant closing deal with normal activities of the plan, such as differences in mortality or interest yield, it would be appropriate to treat the adjustments as actuarial gains or losses to be recognized prospectively in accordance with APB Opinion No. 8. This treatment is consistent with the objectives of Opinion No. 8 and would avoid the possibility of recurring adjustments being separately classified in succeeding years' income statements. On the other hand, if an adjustment relates to a matter directly related to the closing, such as a higher than anticipated level of benefits due to a legal decision concerning the plan's provisions, it would be appropriate to apply the opinion and immediately recognize the adjustment and treat it in the same manner as the original item.

The difficulties in accounting for pension costs in plant closings as discussed in the preceding paragraphs may in certain circumstances be largely reduced if annual provisions for pension costs are based on calculations that reflect an assumption for future plant closings. Immediate recognition at the time of a plant closing of what could be large gains or losses would thus be avoided. Actuaries, however, generally do not include an assumption for plant closings in determining pension costs. In many instances, plant closings do not occur in the ordinary course of an employer's business, and it is difficult for an actuary or a company to estimate in advance whether and when plant closings will take place. There are instances, though, where a company has many plants or units, such as retail stores, and, based on past experience or other factors (e.g., anticipated changes in technology or product mix), the extent of future closings can be reasonably estimated. In such situations, it would be appropriate to use an assumption for future closings. Any difference between the pension costs estimated for expected closings and costs associated with actual closings would be an actuarial gain or loss to be spread or averaged over time as described previously in this chapter under "Actuarial Gains and Losses."

Business Combinations

For a business combination accounted for under the purchase method, APB Opinion No. 16 (paragraph 88h) states that liabilities for pension cost should be recorded at present values of amounts to be paid. Questions have been raised as to how to determine the amount to be recorded and, once recorded, how it is to be subsequently reduced.

Interest Rate

Alternatives to the interest rate to be used in present value calculations include the current interest rate and the interest rate used by the actuary.

The primary argument supporting use of the current interest rate is that the rate is indicated by APB Opinion No. 16 (paragraph 88h), which states that liabilities and accruals should be recorded "at present values of amounts to be paid determined at appropriate current interest rates." Another argument is that this treatment is supported by the statement in APB Opinion No. 16 (paragraph 94) that "the values assigned to assets acquired and liabilities assumed should be determined as of the date of acquisition."

Those favoring use of the rate used by the actuary argue that although paragraph 88h speaks to the current interest rate, the footnote to that paragraph that deals in some detail with pension costs should take precedence.[13] The references in that footnote to the "accounting policies of the acquiring corporation" and the "actuarially computed value of vested benefits" would seem to imply that the rate used by the actuary should be used in those calculations. A recalculation of the liability using a different rate is neither necessary nor very practicable, since a liability established pursuant to either method described in that footnote is already discounted by the actuary.

In the opinion of the authors, the rate used by the actuary is appropriate if that rate is based on current and anticipated conditions. The rate should be based on a number of factors, including the extent to which a plan is funded. For example, to the extent that plan assets are invested in long-term fixed-income securities, the interest rate should reflect the yield on those assets. To the extent that earnings on future contributions are to be used to fund the liability, the interest rate should reflect anticipated new money rates. The timing of contributions and benefit payments, portfolio turnover, and other pertinent factors should also be considered.

Discounting the Future Tax Effect

The estimated future tax effect relating to the pension liability recorded under the prescribed accounting for a business combination should be discounted to

---

[13] The footnote states that "an accrual for pension cost should be the greater of (1) accrued pension cost computed in conformity with the accounting policies of the acquiring corporation for one or more of its pension plans or (2) the excess, if any, of the actuarially computed value of vested benefits over the amount of the pension fund."

its present value. This is appropriate even though there are often uncertainties in practice that make it difficult to determine the timing of the tax consequences. Paragraph 89 of APB Opinion No. 16 states, "The impact of tax effects on amounts assigned to individual assets and liabilities depends on numerous factors, including imminence or delay of realization of the asset value and the possible timing of tax consequences."

Accruing Interest on the Liability

Possible alternative methods for accruing interest on the liability for pension cost recorded as a result of a business combination are the interest method (a level, effective interest rate on the liability) or the straight-line method (a level amount of interest). In the view of the authors, the interest method is appropriate. This is the method used by actuaries in computing interest charges on unfunded amounts; the actuary calculates an amount that represents a level payment comprising principal and interest required to fund the future obligation. It can be argued further that the principles set forth in paragraph 15 of APB Opinion No. 21, "Interest on Receivables and Payables," which calls for the use of the interest method, should apply. It should be noted that ordinarily the accrual amounts recommended by the actuary include interest on the recorded liability, in which case no separate interest accrual should be recorded.

Subsequent Reduction of the Liability

Alternatives for subsequently reducing the pension liability recorded upon acquisition in a business combination are (a) reducing the liability as it is funded, or (b) amortizing the liability over a reasonable period. In the view of the authors, the liability should be reduced as it is funded.

Under treatment (a), in periods subsequent to the acquisition, the provision for pension cost (with respect to the acquiree's plan) includes normal cost and interest on unfunded prior service cost. In addition, if the provision includes an amount for amortization of unfunded vested benefits or prior service cost, the amount provided should be exclusive of any portion of the pension cost accrued at acquisition. Funded amounts applicable to the pension cost accrued at acquisition should be charged against the liability. This treatment is consistent with the concept that the amount recorded at acquisition is a liability for future contributions to the pension plan and, as such, it should be reduced as those contributions are made.

Those in favor of amortizing the liability over a reasonable period of time argue that the pension cost accrued at acquisition might be considered more of a deferred income account than a liability and thus could be taken into income over a reasonable time period. Furthermore, approach (b) is much easier to apply because it eliminates the need for special actuarial calculations, which are often necessary in order to adhere to treatment (a). Nonetheless, APB Opinion No. 16 (paragraph 88h) indicates that the recording of pension cost is the accrual of a liability based on present values of amounts to be paid. Therefore, in the authors' view, alternative (a), reducing the liability as it is paid, is the appropriate treatment. If results using treatment (b) approximate the results of (a), treatment (b) would, of course, also be appropriate.

Changes in Accounting

There is some question about whether the effect of a change in accounting for pension expense should be treated as a cumulative effect adjustment in the year of change under APB Opinion No. 20, "Accounting Changes," or applied prospectively to the cost of the current year and future years under APB Opinion No. 8.

It seems clear that APB Opinion No. 8 takes precedence, since Opinion No. 20 states that it does not apply to the provisions of previous APB opinions that prescribe the manner of reporting accounting changes. Paragraph 47 of Opinion No. 8 states, ". . . pension cost provided under an acceptable method of accounting in prior periods should not be changed subsequently. Therefore, the effect on prior-year cost of a change in accounting method should be applied prospectively to the cost of the current year and future years, in a manner consistent with the conclusions of this opinion and not retroactively as an adjustment of retained earnings or otherwise." Disclosure of the change and its effect is required.

Changes in Actuarial Cost Methods

APB Opinion No. 20 indicates that ". . . in the preparation of financial statements there is a presumption that an accounting principle once adopted should not be changed in accounting for events and transactions of a similar type." The opinion further states that "The presumption that an entity should not change an accounting principle may be overcome only if the enterprise justifies the use of an alternative acceptable accounting principle on the basis that it is preferable." The question that is raised is what changes in actuarial cost methods are considered under APB Opinion No. 20 as changes to a preferable method.

The preferability of any change should be judged on its own merits while considering a number of factors including elements of business judgment and business planning. Changes in actuarial cost methods are made for any number of reasons. One reason that frequently forms the basis of a change in actuarial cost method is a change to conform to a change in the funding method, which latter change is to improve a company's cash flow. Although each situation must be judged independently, the rationale behind that type of change would normally be consistent with the concept of business judgment and business planning.

New Labor Agreements

Increased benefits resulting from a new labor agreement can create uncertainties as to the appropriate accounting. Consider, for example, a new multiyear (e.g., three-year) labor agreement providing for increased levels of benefits to participants retiring during the contract period and under which the benefits to be paid are based on the level in effect during the year in which retirement occurs. The question arises as to how to account for the increased benefits for individuals retiring during the contract period, individuals who will become eligible subsequent to the contract period and those individuals who are already retired, if affected by the contract provisions.

The following alternative methods of accounting for the additional pension cost for *individuals retiring during the contract period* are possible: (a) accounting for the cost on a pay-as-you-go basis, (b) reflecting in the current year's actuarial calculations only the increased benefit levels applicable to participants retiring in the current year, ignoring the additional increases for participants retiring in the subsequent contract years, and (c) taking into account in actuarial computations for the current year the fact that participants retiring in the subsequent contract years will receive the increased benefits.

The authors believe that method (c) should be followed.[14] Since a contract calling for higher benefits in the subsequent contract years is already in place, it is appropriate for the provision for pension costs to be based on the benefit levels agreed to. Since method (b) does not fully recognize the increases in benefits already contracted for, it is not appropriate. Method (a) is not appropriate inasmuch as APB Opinion No. 8 proscribes that method of accounting because it gives no recognition to pension costs until employees retire.

For those *employees who will become eligible for retirement benefits subsequent to the contract period,* there are also three alternative treatments. First, no increased benefits may be reflected for such participants. Second, the increased levels of benefits taking effect in each year of the contract period may be applied in each of those years to participants retiring after the end of the contract period. Or, third, the level of benefits effective at the end of the contract period can be applied to participants retiring after the contract period.

The third treatment is clearly preferable and should normally be used, since in most cases it would be unlikely for a labor agreement covering periods subsequent to the current agreement to prescribe a benefit level lower than that in effect during the last year of the contract. The second method is inappropriate, since that method only partially recognizes the higher benefit levels in the first two years. The first method is generally inappropriate. That method may be acceptable in unusual circumstances where, for example, there is evidence that benefit levels under a subsequent labor agreement will revert to the levels in place before the current agreement (e.g., where labor has indicated that it may trade off pension benefits for higher salary levels).

In connection with those *employees who retired before the new contract and are affected by the agreement,* a pay-as-you-go treatment would probably be

---

[14] Internal Revenue Service regulations prohibit a funding method from taking into account a benefit change that would become effective in a future year. This requirement could affect an employer's tax deduction since the cost of a future benefit provision would not currently be considered for tax deduction purposes. Accordingly, if method (c) is followed for financial statement purposes, differences between tax and financial reporting may result.

conservative; it would result in expensing the additional cost over a relatively short period. However, adding the additional cost to prior service cost and amortizing it over an appropriate number of years is consistent with APB Opinion No. 8 and is therefore preferable. There are some arguments for immediate expensing of the additional costs for retired individuals, but that is considered by many accountants to be an extreme treatment.

Other Situations

Regulated Companies

The applicability of APB Opinion No. 8 to financial statements of regulated companies is subject to the provisions of the Addendum to APB Opinion No. 2.[15] The addendum identifies regulated companies as "public utilities, common carriers, insurance companies, financial institutions, and the like that are subject to regulation by government, usually through commissions or other similar agencies." Paragraph 2 of the addendum states that where the regulated company is allowed to defer an expense which "in a nonregulated business would be written off currently," the deferment is appropriate "only when it is clear that the cost will be recoverable out of future revenues, and . . . not appropriate when there is doubt, because of economic conditions or for other reasons, that the cost will be so recoverable." Such deferment of pension expense would generally be indicated by appropriate accounting or rate orders having been obtained, or by substantially equivalent evidence and a reasonable expectation that costs will be recoverable from future revenues.

Nonprofit Organizations

Generally, statements of the Accounting Principles Board or of its predecessor, the Committee on Accounting Procedure, do not apply to nonprofit organizations (see Accounting Research Bulletin No. 43, Introduction, paragraph 5). There is no reason in principle, however, why the provisions of APB Opinion No. 8 should not apply to nonprofit organizations, particularly if their accounts are maintained on the accrual basis.

Government Contracts

Some companies perform work for the U.S. federal government under contracts that are subject to price adjustment pursuant to rules of the Cost Accounting Standards Board (CASB).[16] Certain of the standards issued by the CASB have provisions that are at variance with APB Opinion No. 8. For example:

[15] The FASB has a project on its agenda to reconsider the Addendum to APB Opinion No. 2 and determine the extent to which the rate-making process should affect the applicability of financial accounting standards. The board issued an exposure draft in 1982, and a final statement is expected in the fourth quarter of 1982.
[16] At the date of publication, a legislative proposal is pending to assign the functions of the CASB to the Office of Federal Procurement Policy within the Office of Management and Budget.

APB Opinion No. 8 generally calls for spreading or averaging actuarial gains and losses over 10 to 20 years as set forth earlier in this chapter under "Actuarial Gains and Losses," while CASB rules generally call for spreading over 15 years. Both provide for different treatments when certain actuarial cost methods are used.

APB Opinion No. 8 specifies that the provision should be between the stated minimum and maximum as set forth earlier in this chapter under "Annual Provision for Pension Cost." For cost accounting purposes the CASB rules limit the pension provision to amounts the plan is legally "compelled" to fund (e.g., under ERISA) or to amounts actually funded up to the amount of the provision for financial accounting purposes.

The above examples represent only two of the existing variances. Auditors engaged in an examination of financial statements of a company subject to CASB standards should be aware of these and other differences that may exist between APB Opinion No. 8 and the CASB standards. Auditors should also be aware that adjustments may be needed when financial statements prepared in accordance with generally accepted accounting principles are to be used for CASB purposes, as such differences may affect the company's position in the determination or redetermination of prices under its government contracts.

Deferred Compensation Contracts

Accounting for deferred compensation contracts is generally governed by the provisions of paragraphs 6, 7, and 8 of APB Opinion No. 12, which specifically relate to these contracts. APB Opinion No. 8, however, also refers to these contracts, indicating that its provisions are applicable thereto if the contracts taken together are equivalent to a pension plan, but does not specify the circumstances indicative of such equivalence.

This equivalence would most likely occur when a company's policy is to enter into deferred compensation contracts with an entire group or class of employees (such as officers of a certain level), instead of with only certain individuals in that group or class. The principal difference in the accounting methods called for under the two opinions is that APB Opinion No. 12 requires accrual of deferred compensation generally over the remaining service lives of individual employees, whereas APB Opinion No. 8 permits accrual of pension costs over varying time periods due to the alternative treatments allowed for providing for prior service cost.

Death and Disability Benefits

APB Opinion No. 8 states that the benefits to be considered in calculating the annual cost of a pension plan are ordinarily the retirement benefit, but they in many instances may also include death and disability payments unless provided for under separate arrangements. Generally, death and disability benefits should be considered as part of pension cost only if they are an integral part of the benefits provided by the pension plan.

CHAPTER SEVEN

Auditing Employer's Pension Costs

INTRODUCTION

The attention given to the auditing of pension costs increased greatly with the issuance of Opinion No. 8 of the Accounting Principles Board. The enactment of ERISA caused auditors to give still greater attention to pension costs.

While the broad applicability of APB Opinion No. 8 is basically unchanged, ERISA affects the auditing of the employer company in two general ways.

First, the effect of the law on the accounting for pension costs and related reporting, as discussed in Chapter 6, should be reflected in auditing procedures, and second, the potentially significant impact of noncompliance with ERISA on a company's financial statements requires that additional audit procedures be considered.

This chapter summarizes the principles of basic audit procedures allowing for the effects of ERISA.

BASIC OBJECTIVES AND AUDIT PROCEDURES

The audit of pension costs entails obtaining pertinent information regarding a company's pension plan as a basis for reaching a conclusion that the pension expense reported, when considered in relation to the financial statements taken as a whole, is stated in conformity with generally accepted accounting principles consistently applied, and that the appropriate related disclosures are made.

The materiality of pension costs, and the materiality of any possible understatement or overstatement of such costs to the fairness of presentation of the financial statements, should influence the selection of audit procedures and the extent and depth of the examination, just as materiality is considered in any other audit procedure.

Some of the information needed by the auditor can be obtained from the actuary's report, some is in the company's records, and some may be obtained by direct correspondence with (or through a supplementary report from) the actuary. Items of information related to pension plans that the auditor may need are summarized in Figure 7-1. This listing is furnished only for guidance and its inclusion herein should not be construed as a conclusion that all the items listed are needed in every case or, conversely, that in some cases additional information should not be sought.

Audit procedures employed to substantiate pension costs must be selected to meet the requirements of particular circumstances. The selection of appropriate audit procedures is a matter of judgment, applied to the facts of a particular situation. Procedures would normally include the following:

inquiry into the existence of pension plans or a practice of paying pensions which may constitute a plan under Opinion No. 8 (applies to all subsidiaries and divisions—foreign and domestic);

comparison of data relating to pension costs and of information disclosed in the financial statements with prior year's data for comparability;

review of the actuary's report and related information, and auditing of data used by the actuary in his calculations, as described in the following section;

determination that the provision for pension costs is within the limits established by APB Opinion No. 8; and

determination that the benefit disclosures are calculated in accordance with FASB Statement No. 36.

FIGURE 7-1

Information that may be needed for the audit of pension costs of employer companies

I.   General

1   Name of the plan.
2   Whether the plan is voluntary or negotiated.
3   Whether the plan is contributory.
4   Eligibility requirements.
5   Basis for determining benefit payments under the plan.
6   When employees are entitled to receive benefits, that is, normal retirement age, early retirement provisions, and so on.
7   Vesting rights provided under the plan.
8   Custodian or trustee of the plan assets.
9   Tax qualification status of the plan.
10 Qualifications of the actuary.

II.   Accounting and Funding Policies

1   Actuarial cost method used.
2   Basis of providing for prior service cost.
3   Actuarial assumptions.
4   Basis for recognizing unrealized appreciation and depreciation.
5   Method of dealing with actuarial gains and losses.

III.   Actuarial Valuations

1   Date as of which valuations are made.
2   Frequency of valuations.
3   Basis on which plan assets are stated.
4   Employee data on which the actuarial determinations are based.

IV.   Current Year's Transactions and Disclosures

1   Amount of the charge to expense, broken down by normal cost, amortization of prior service cost, provision for actuarial gains and losses, and interest equivalents.
2   Funding contribution, broken down by normal cost, amortization of prior service cost, amortization of actuarial gains and losses, interest equivalents, and other details of the funding standard account and alternative minimum funding standard account.
3   Changes during the year in actuarial cost methods or actuarial assumptions for accounting and funding purposes.
4   Amount of employees' contributions.
5   Actuarial present value of accumulated plan benefits.
6   Actuarial present value of vested plan benefits.
7   Amount of plan net assets available for benefits.
8   Value of unfunded prior service cost at beginning and end of the year.
9   Amount of actuarial gains and losses arising during the year.

Each pension plan that has a separate accountability under APB Opinion No. 8 should be considered independently in the audit of pension costs.

Actuarial Information

The Role of the Actuary

The actuary's role, which expanded with the issuance of APB Opinion No. 8, was further expanded by the enactment of ERISA and related regulations. In making the calculations needed to determine the amounts required for financial statement purposes, he needs to work closely with his client's accountant.

Suggested Audit Procedures

In considering the determinations made by the actuary in relation to the financial statements, the auditor needs to obtain and review sufficient competent evidential matter, normally by reviewing the actuary's report. Guidance to the auditor on using the work of a specialist in performing an examination of financial statements in accordance with generally accepted auditing standards is provided by the AICPA's Statement on Auditing Standards (SAS) No. 11, "Using the Work of a Specialist."

SAS No. 11 requires that auditors satisfy themselves as to the professional qualifications and reputation of the actuary. This can usually be done by determining that the actuary is a member of a recognized professional actuarial society (e.g., a Fellow of the Society of Actuaries or a member of the American Academy of Actuaries). Alternatively, the auditor might consider whether the actuary is an "enrolled actuary" under ERISA or the auditor might obtain competent professional advice on the actuary's qualifications from an actuary known by the auditor to be qualified.

The auditor may need to consult with the actuary when report items require clarification or explanation. The need for such consultation may be substantially reduced by making advance arrangements with the actuary to ascertain that the actuary's report will contain all the information required by the auditor. Also, where the auditor becomes aware of changes in conditions which he believes would affect the actuary's determinations, it would be appropriate, after discussing the matter with the client, for the auditor to advise the actuary.

Other audit procedures with respect to using the work of an actuary should be based on paragraphs 7 and 8 of SAS No. 11, which state:

7 An understanding should exist among the auditor, the client, and the specialist as to the nature of the work to be performed by the specialist. Preferably, the understanding should be documented and should cover the following:

a   The objectives and scope of the specialist's work.

b   The specialist's representations as to his relationship, if any, to the client.

c   The methods or assumptions to be used.

d   A comparison of the methods or assumptions to be used with those used in the preceding period.

e   The specialist's understanding of the auditor's corroborative use of the specialist's findings in relation to the representations in the financial statements.

f   The form and content of the specialist's report that would enable the auditor to make the evaluation in paragraph 8.

8   Although the appropriateness and reasonableness of methods or assumptions used and their application are the responsibility of the specialist, the auditor should obtain an understanding of the methods or assumptions used by the specialist to determine whether the findings are suitable for corroborating the representations in the financial statements. The auditor should consider whether the specialist's findings support the related representations in the financial statements and make appropriate tests of accounting data provided by the client to the specialist. Ordinarily, the auditor would use the work of the specialist unless his procedures lead him to believe that the findings are unreasonable in the circumstances.

As indicated above, the auditor should consider the relationship, if any, of the actuary to the client. SAS No. 11 states that work of a specialist unrelated to the client will usually provide the auditor with greater assurance of reliability because of the absence of a relationship that might impair objectivity. The SAS points out that if the specialist is related to the client (or, in the authors' view, if the auditor is not able to determine to his satisfaction that the actuary has no relationship with the client that might impair objectivity), the auditor should consider performing additional procedures with respect to some or all of the related specialist's assumptions, methods, or findings to determine that the findings are not unreasonable, or engage an outside specialist for that purpose.

Procedures which the auditor may find useful in implementing the requirements of SAS No. 11 are set forth in Figure 7-2. In following those procedures, the auditor should not expect to rely upon an actuary's conclusion as to the conformity of actuarially computed amounts with generally accepted accounting principles. Such a conclusion requires a skilled and experience-based knowledge of accounting principles, including the concept of materiality. Conversely, the auditor should refrain from making actuarial judgments.

Confirmation from Actuaries

As previously noted, SAS No. 11 indicates that the understanding among the auditor, client, and actuary regarding the actuary's representations as to his relationship to the client, if any, should preferably be documented. In this regard, the authors suggest that the actuary be requested to set forth in writing the circumstances of any relationship with the client. An illustrative letter of request, which should be modified to meet the needs of a particular engagement, is shown in Figure 7-3.

The auditor may want to ask the actuary to send a copy of the actuary's report as well as to confirm certain other information if it is not contained in the actuary's report. An illustrative letter requesting this information (which also requests information as to any relationship with the client that might impair

FIGURE 7-2

Suggested audit procedures for examining actuarially determined information

a Determine whether the actuary is familiar with the current terms of the pension plan and that he has accorded such terms proper recognition in his calculations. This may be accomplished by reviewing the actuary's report or, after discussing with the client, by contacting the actuary directly.

b Determine the professional reputation and qualifications of the actuary. Determine whether the actuary is unrelated to the client.

c Review and test the employee data given to the actuary, on which the actuarial calculations are based. Procedures outlined in (f) through (j) of Figure 9-1 should be used as a guide.

d Determine whether the actuarial methods used by the actuary to determine pension costs and accumulated plan benefits are appropriate and whether the same methods were used in the prior period.

e Determine whether the actuarial assumptions used to determine pension costs are not unreasonable on an overall basis.

f Determine that the value of pension fund assets used in actuarial calculations to determine pension costs is not unreasonable.

g Determine whether the effect of any changes in actuarial methods and assumptions has been disclosed.

h Determine whether the actuarially determined information contained in the financial statements agrees with the actuary's report.

i Review the period from the date of the actuarial valuation to the fiscal year-end (and beyond, to the extent known) to see whether any significant events have occurred which would materially affect amounts reflected in the financial statements (e.g., plant closings, changes in plan, changes in market value of equity securities). If such events have occurred, consult with the actuary and obtain an estimate of the dollar effect on such amounts.

the actuary's objectivity) has been extracted from a draft of the AICPA Audit Guide on Employee Benefit Plans and is presented in Appendix F.[1]

The authors do not consider it generally necessary to obtain from actuaries direct confirmation of information already in reports they have prepared and which have been submitted to the client. But it may, under certain circumstances, be desirable for the auditor to ask the actuary to confirm the date of the most recent actuarial valuation made by him. And as indicated in procedure (c) of Figure 7-2, where employee data used by the actuary in his calculations are not summarized in the actuary's report, such data should be confirmed directly with him.

[1] The Employee Benefit Plans and ERISA Committee of the AICPA is presently developing an AICPA Audit Guide, "Audits of Employee Benefit Plans." The scope and nature of this audit guide are discussed in Chapter 9.

FIGURE 7-3

Illustrative letter requesting actuary's representation as to any relationship that might impair the actuary's objectivity

[Client's Letterhead]

[Date]

[Name and Address of Actuary]

Gentlemen:

In connection with their examination of our financial statements for the period [period covered] our auditors, [name and address] have requested information regarding any relationship you now have or have had with [name of client] that might affect your capacity to [description of actuary's work]. They desire information as to whether during that period [and until you completed your work relating to that period] any partner or associate of [name of actuary]: has or had any direct financial interest or material indirect financial interest in [name of client] or in any of its affiliates; acts or has acted as an officer, director or employee of [name of client] or any of its affiliates; or has any other relationship with [name of client] or any of its affiliates.

In responding to this request, please report to our auditors the following information:

1 whether any relationship as described in the preceding paragraph exists or has existed;
2 the nature and extent of any such relationship; and
3 whether, in your opinion, any such relationship might affect your capacity to [description of actuary's work].

A return envelope is enclosed for your reply.

Very truly yours,
(Signature of Company Official)

Insured Plans

In the examination of insured pension plans, the auditor should obtain the applicable information listed in Figure 7-1. The audit procedures will vary substantially, however, from those discussed earlier in this chapter.

Normally, the insurance company's procedures in calculating premium charges will meet the requirements of APB Opinion No. 8 for determining normal cost. Similarly, the insurance company's procedures for arriving at dividends are normally satisfactory to meet the requirements of the opinion for accounting for investment gains. However, consideration should be given to spreading or averaging termination credits in accounting for gains related to turnover. In addition, consideration should be given to providing for the cost related to employees becoming covered under the pension plan where a mandatory waiting period has excluded employees from participation.

Auditing procedures normally involve examination of insurance company premium statements, review of amounts of dividends and termination credits in relation to those of prior years, and determination as to whether any provision is needed for employees expected to become covered under the plan. Such procedures would appear to give an auditor reasonable satisfaction that the provision for pension costs complies with paragraph 41 of Opinion No. 8. However, the enactment of ERISA and the time lapse since Opinion No. 8 was issued may give auditors reason to reevaluate such procedures and determine whether they are still sufficient. Auditors might now consider whether it would also be appropriate, for example, to review the method used by the insurance company in making its premium, dividend, and related calculations.

AUDIT PROCEDURES DIRECTLY RELATED TO ERISA

While basic procedures continue to follow past practice, some aspects of ERISA have introduced requirements which normally necessitate additional procedures, depending generally upon materiality of items affected by the law. As in other areas, however, materiality is not the sole consideration. For example, while the materiality of penalties is an important factor in ascertaining that the client is in compliance with ERISA, the auditor should nevertheless be alert to instances of noncompliance so as to be in a position to advise clients of a need to consider taking corrective action.

The auditor is concerned principally with the accounting and compliance aspects of ERISA.

Accounting Impact

Recorded Liability

As indicated in Chapter 6, a company should record as a liability the pension cost amount required to be funded to date under the law. The auditor should verify, by reference to the actuary's report, that the appropriate liability has been recorded.

Potential Plan Termination

Because of liabilities that may be involved in a plan termination, the auditor should be alert, when reading minutes of meetings of the company's board of directors and pertinent committees and when performing other audit procedures, to any evidence of a potential pension plan termination. Additionally, the auditor may wish to ask management about the possibility of any anticipated or potential plan termination. Where a plan termination is more than a remote possibility, the auditor should ensure that the financial statements contain appropriate entries or disclosures (see Chapter 6).

Minimum Provision

While the authors believe it would be appropriate for the minimum provision for pension cost to parallel the minimum amount to be funded under the law (see Chapter 6), a provision consistent with the minimum amount set forth in

APB Opinion No. 8 is in accordance with generally accepted accounting principles. The auditor should determine, as he has in the past, whether the provision is in accordance with the principles set forth in APB Opinion No. 8. Where the provision is based on the minimum required under APB Opinion No. 8, the auditor may recommend that the client make appropriate modification so that the provision is consistent with the minimum amount required to be funded under ERISA, but the auditor should take no further action if the recommendation is rejected.

Compliance with ERISA

Audit considerations related to determining whether a client is in compliance with ERISA fall into five main categories: (1) compliance of individual plan provisions with ERISA, (2) funding, (3) reporting and disclosure, (4) fiduciary responsibilities, and (5) record keeping. The following discussion includes for each category a description of the requirements and the penalties involved, including cross-references for further details, and suggested audit procedures to test compliance.

It is suggested that, in addition to the procedures described herein, the auditor obtain a representation from the client (in the letter of representation) that the client is in compliance with ERISA. The following sentence would be appropriate for inclusion in the representation letter: "The plan has complied with the provisions of ERISA and the regulations thereunder except as follows." Any instances of noncompliance, including breaches of fiduciary duties and engagement in prohibited transactions as defined in ERISA and regulations thereunder, should be specifically set forth in the representation letter.

Compliance of Individual Plan Provisions with ERISA

In order to conform to ERISA, plans must meet requirements with respect to participation, vesting, limits on benefits and contributions, back-loaded benefits, joint and survivor annuities, and so on. (Requirements are described under the same headings in Chapter 4.)

The auditor's concern with whether individual plan provisions comply with ERISA is based generally on the potential impact that noncompliance may have on the employer's financial statements. This impact may be in the form of an understatement of the provision for pension cost and of related actuarial disclosures such as present value of accumulated plan benefits. If, for example, the plan did not cover all employees required by ERISA to participate in the plan, the provision for pension cost and other actuarially calculated amounts would likely be understated. Noncompliance may also involve penalties (as discussed in Chapter 4), including disqualification of the plan and loss of its tax exempt status, both of which may need to be reflected in the financial statements.[2]

[2] Past experience has shown that a company whose plan instrument fails to comply with provisions of the Internal Revenue Code is normally allowed a period of time to take the neces-

By now, most plans have been amended to comply with ERISA, and the auditor has previously completed procedures to determine initial plan compliance. However, if a plan is initially established or amended in the current year and noncompliance with ERISA could have a material effect on the financial statements, the auditor should consider taking appropriate steps to redetermine plan compliance.

The auditor can normally satisfy himself that the provisions of the pension plan comply with ERISA in one of two ways. If the auditor can determine that the plan is a qualified plan under provisions of the Internal Revenue Code (which has been modified by ERISA to be virtually identical to the participation, vesting, and other provisions of ERISA described above), then he may conclude that the plan complies with the provisions of ERISA. The auditor may normally gain reasonable satisfaction that a plan is qualified under the code by examining a tax qualification letter, where such a letter has been issued by the Internal Revenue Service covering the current plan provisions.

The auditor can also satisfy himself that the provisions of the pension plan comply with ERISA by obtaining a letter from the client's legal counsel stating that the plan's provisions comply with either ERISA or the Internal Revenue Code.

These procedures for determining plan compliance with ERISA would be appropriate for the first year in which a plan has been amended or for new pension plans. If there are no plan amendments thereafter, in theory, little or no additional work related to plan compliance would be required in subsequent years. In practice, however, a tax qualification letter or other evidence of plan compliance normally carries less weight with the passage of time, inasmuch as the Internal Revenue Service is concerned not only with the plan provisions themselves but also with the manner in which the plan operates in accordance with those provisions. Therefore, in subsequent years the auditor should be alert to changes in the manner in which plan provisions are applied.

Any findings related to potential penalties which may need to be reflected in the financial statements, pursuant to the audit procedures described in this or the following sections of this chapter, should preferably be discussed with the client's legal counsel.

Funding

The funding requirements of ERISA and penalties which may be imposed for failure to comply therewith are summarized under "Funding" in Chapter 4. The auditor should satisfy himself that the funding provisions of ERISA have been complied with. This would likely include reviewing the entries in the funding standard account (and the alternative minimum funding standard ac-

---

sary steps so as to be in compliance and thereby avoid disqualification of the plan. But, although the IRS has permitted companies to retroactively correct deficient *plan instruments,* in those instances where disqualifying actions occur in the *operation* of otherwise qualified plans, retroactive steps may not be possible.

count if applicable) and agreeing entries with the actuary's report and cash disbursement records. Where the alternative minimum funding standard is used, the auditor should satisfy himself that its use is permitted.

Reporting and Disclosure

The reporting and disclosure requirements of ERISA and penalties which may be imposed for failure to comply therewith are described in Chapter 5.

The auditor should ascertain that the required pension plan reports, including the financial statements containing the appropriate disclosures, schedules, opinion of the independent qualified accountant, and actuary's report (where appropriate) have been filed with the Internal Revenue Service, and that the summary annual report has been furnished to participants and beneficiaries. Because the auditor will probably express an opinion on the employer company's financial statements well before the date on which the plan's financial statements are filed, he is not likely to be in a position, when auditing the employer's financial statements, to ascertain that the appropriate pension plan financial statements are filed for the current year. However, the auditor will be able to determine whether the prior year's financial statements were filed.

Fiduciary Responsibilities

The auditor should determine whether the employer company is, as will often be the case, considered to be a fiduciary (as well as a party in interest) under the law, in which case he will need to be alert during the audit for any breaches of fiduciary responsibility as established by ERISA. Fiduciary responsibilities and related penalties which may be imposed for failure to comply are summarized in Chapter 4.

While the auditor should inquire as to the occurrence of any prohibited transactions and should be alert for them during the course of the audit, few additional audit procedures for prohibited transactions should be needed because the auditor's normal audit work should familiarize him with significant transactions which might be prohibited under the law.

Record Keeping

ERISA requires employers to maintain such records as are sufficient to determine the benefits which are due, or may become due, to each employee (see Chapter 4). In most cases, such records must include data such as age, length of service, hours worked, salary, employee contributions, vesting percentage, and so forth. In multiemployer plans the necessary information is to be furnished by the employers to the plan administrator who is to maintain such records.

The auditor should consider whether the record-keeping requirements of ERISA are met. The auditor's regular audit work, particularly his review and testing of the client's payroll system, should normally enable him to make such a determination.

REPORTING CONSIDERATIONS

In expressing an opinion on a company's financial statements, the auditor needs to be concerned with comparability and consistency, and with conformity to APB Opinion No. 8, as amended by FASB Statement No. 36 and Interpretation No. 3.

Comparability and Consistency

The comparability of financial statements is affected by material changes in charges to pension expense which do not result from changes in volume of operations. Such material changes may result from changes either in accounting principles or in methods, thus requiring a comment as to consistency in the auditor's report, or from changes in conditions which, while requiring disclosure, would not require comment in the auditor's report (other than in reports accompanying financial statements to be filed with the Securities and Exchange Commission—see note to section 420.12 of the AICPA's Statement on Auditing Standards (SAS) No. 1).

Examples of material changes in pension expense which call for a comment as to consistency because they stem from a choice by management from among two or more accounting methods include:

adoption of a different actuarial cost method for pension costs from that previously used, for example, changing from the accrued benefit to a level cost method;

a change in period of amortization of prior service cost;

a change in the method of accounting for actuarial gains or losses and unrealized appreciation or depreciation, for example, from spreading to averaging or vice versa; and

a change in the method of valuing the pension fund, for example, changing from a valuation equal to 90% of market value to 75% of market value or vice versa, without a change in circumstances.

Examples of changes which do not involve consistency of accounting since they stem from altered conditions include:

changes in actuarial assumptions based on historical experience under a plan or current or prospective changes in employment conditions; and

adoption of a new plan or an amendment to an existing pension plan.

Material changes in charges to pension expense from such causes should be disclosed. If such a change has not materially affected the year's pension expense but will materially affect future years' expense, the nature of the change should be disclosed, with some indication of the effect, if determinable.

Although a company may adopt either a "minimum" or a "maximum" basis of determining pension expense under APB Opinion No. 8 (as discussed in Chapter 6), any change in the basis or method selected involves a change in accounting. All changes in methods of accounting for pension costs, whether to comply with the provisions of APB Opinion No. 8 or for other reasons, should be dealt with prospectively (see paragraphs 47 and 49 of the opinion).

Departures from the Opinion as Amended and Interpretation

Departures from APB Opinion No. 8 in determining pension expense constitute departures from generally accepted accounting principles. If such departures have a material effect upon the financial statements, they should be dealt with as called for in paragraphs 15 through 18 of the AICPA's Statement on Auditing Standards (SAS) No. 2.

Examples of departures from APB Opinion No. 8 (other than those relating to disclosure requirements) which, if material, may require qualification in the auditor's report are:

use of a terminal funding or pay-as-you-go basis of accounting;

failure to appropriately recognize actuarial gains or losses and unrealized appreciation or depreciation; and

use of a method resulting in a provision for pension cost which does not fall within the specified minimum and maximum limits.

Failure to observe the disclosure requirements of APB Opinion No. 8 as amended by FASB Statement No. 36 and of FASB Interpretation No. 3 also constitutes a departure from generally accepted accounting principles where pension costs or the related information is significant. If a client is unwilling to observe the aforementioned disclosure requirements, and the amount of pension costs, properly computed, is material in relation to income before extraordinary items or to net income, the auditor should consider whether a qualified opinion is necessary. Qualification of the auditor's opinion with regard to nondisclosure of required pension information should be dealt with as recommended in section 545 of the AICPA's Statement on Auditing Standards (SAS) No. 1.

As stated in Chapter 6, APB Opinion No. 8 regards as acceptable the determination of pension accruals within relatively broad limits, and allows for the choice of a number of actuarial cost methods, each of which in turn involves a number of actuarial assumptions. Thus, careful consideration and experienced judgment are required to determine whether a particular factor which appears to be at variance with the provisions of APB Opinion No. 8 results (when considered in relation to the overall effect of all pertinent factors) in pension expense being stated at an amount which materially departs from that which is acceptable under the opinion.

PART THREE

Pension Fund Accounting, Auditing, and Financial Reporting

CHAPTER EIGHT

Application of Generally Accepted Accounting Principles

INTRODUCTION

During the early years of the ERISA reporting requirements, accounting principles and financial reporting presentations applicable to plan financial statements were subject to initial uncertainties and differences of opinion. This was due largely to the limited financial reporting by pension plans prior to that time. As accounting principles and financial reporting presentations evolved, the range of options narrowed, and with the issuance of Statement of Financial Accounting Standards No. 35, "Accounting and Reporting by Defined Benefit Pension Plans," the alternatives have been significantly reduced.

This chapter describes generally accepted accounting principles and financial reporting applicable to pension plans.

HISTORICAL BACKGROUND

Relatively little attention was given to the preparation of pension plan financial statements until the ERISA requirements became effective. ERISA required the annual report to include, among other items, financial statements and certain supplemental schedules prepared in conformity with generally accepted accounting principles. At that time, however, there were no authoritative accounting pronouncements addressing accounting principles and financial reporting standards for pension plans, and the guidance provided by ERISA was often incomplete or nonexistent.

As indicated in Chapter 5, the Department of Labor (DOL) in 1976 issued temporary regulations which provided that a pension plan required to file an annual report could either report the information prescribed by ERISA or elect an alternative method of compliance. The alternative method of compliance required that assets and liabilities be stated at current value but, in contrast to requirements under ERISA, did not require financial statements to be prepared in accordance with generally accepted accounting principles. The temporary regulations also prescribed minimum disclosure for notes to the financial statements. The temporary regulations as issued in final form in 1978 furnished additional guidance on certain reporting matters.

FASB Statement No. 35

A project on accounting and reporting for employee benefit plans was placed on the FASB technical agenda in 1974 and in 1975 it issued a Discussion Memorandum on the subject. A draft of the proposed Statement of Financial Accounting Standards, "Accounting and Reporting by Defined Benefit Pension

Plans," was exposed by the FASB in 1977. As a result of over 700 comment letters received, significant changes were made in the initial document, resulting in the issuance of a revised exposure draft in 1979. The FASB's improvements on the document made the revised exposure draft more responsive to the needs of both plan financial statement users and preparers.

The Statement of Financial Accounting Standards No. 35, "Accounting and Reporting by Defined Benefit Pension Plans," was issued in March, 1980, in substantially the same form as the revised exposure draft. It represents the authoritative accounting pronouncement on accounting principles and financial reporting standards for defined benefit pension plans. These principles and reporting standards are discussed in this chapter. For purposes of accuracy and clarity, certain language used here is that of the FASB statement.

Statement No. 35 is effective for plan years beginning after December 15, 1980 with earlier application encouraged. Accordingly, to the extent the accounting and reporting requirements set forth in this chapter, as prescribed by FASB Statement No. 35, establish new principles or standards or eliminate acceptable alternatives, their application to plan financial statements for plan years beginning on or before December 15, 1980, is not required. But when presented together with financial statements for plan years beginning after December 15, 1980, Statement No. 35 requires that financial statements of prior plan years be restated.

The statement applies to plans that are covered by ERISA as well as those that are not. Its scope is limited to accounting and reporting by defined benefit pension plans. Although the statement does not cover defined contribution pension plans, it should provide useful guidance with respect to accounting and financial reporting by such plans.[1] The scope of the statement also excludes interim financial statements because few, if any, plans publish such statements and because consideration of issues related thereto would have delayed issuance of the statement.

METHODS OF ACCOUNTING

Although many pension plans maintain their accounts on a cash basis or a modified cash basis, generally accepted accounting principles call for financial reporting under the accrual method of accounting. Financial statements contained in annual reports providing information prescribed by ERISA are to be in accordance with generally accepted accounting principles and are prepared, therefore, on the accrual basis. Financial statements contained in filings reporting information prescribed by DOL regulations governing the alternative

---

[1] As this book goes to press, the AICPA Audit Guide, "Audits of Employee Benefit Plans," moves along the approval process and is likely to be published shortly. The draft Guide contains guidance on accounting for defined contribution plans which is consistent with the guidance set forth in this chapter for defined benefit plans. We understand that the FASB intends to amend its Statement No. 32 to designate the accounting principles and practices in the Guide as preferable for the purpose of applying APB Opinion No. 20, *Accounting Changes.*

method of compliance, however, need *not* conform to generally accepted accounting principles, and may be prepared on either the cash, modified accrual, or accrual basis. Footnotes to those financial statements, though, are to set forth any variances from generally accepted accounting principles. This chapter provides guidance in accounting and reporting by plans in accordance with generally accepted accounting principles.

As indicated in the preceding section, accounting changes adopted to conform to the provisions of FASB Statement No. 35 are to be made retroactively by restating prior period financial statements. Since the statement prescribes accrual basis accounting, a change from the cash basis to the accrual basis of accounting for financial reporting should be accounted for retroactively.

FINANCIAL STATEMENTS

The primary objective of a pension plan's financial statements, as set forth by the FASB in Statement No. 35, is to provide financial information that is useful in assessing the plan's present and future ability to pay benefits when due. This objective recognizes that the content of plan financial statements should focus on the needs of plan participants because pension plans exist primarily for their benefit. Providing information useful in assessing the performance of plan administrators and other fiduciaries in managing the plan assets they control is inherent in providing information useful in assessing benefit security.

To accomplish this objective, a plan's annual financial statements should include:

1   a statement of net assets available for benefits as of the end of the plan year;
2   a statement of changes in net assets available for benefits for the plan year;
3   information regarding the actuarial present value of accumulated plan benefits as of either the beginning or end of the plan year; and
4   information regarding the effects, if significant, of certain factors affecting the change in the actuarial present value of accumulated plan benefits.

The *statement of net assets available for benefits* should be presented in enough detail to allow for identification of the plan's resources that are available for benefits. Requirements for reporting plan assets are discussed in a later section.

The *statement of changes in net assets available for benefits* should be presented in sufficient detail to identify significant changes and at a minimum should include:

the net appreciation (depreciation) in fair value for each significant class of investments, including gains and losses on investments bought and sold during the year, segregated between investments whose fair values have been measured by quoted prices in an active market and those whose fair values have been otherwise determined;

investment income exclusive of appreciation or depreciation;

contributions from the employer(s), segregated between cash and noncash contributions;

contributions from participants;

contributions from other identified sources (for example, state subsidies or federal grants);

benefits paid to participants;

payments to insurance companies to purchase contracts that are excluded from plan assets, against which amount related dividend income may be netted;[2]

administrative expenses.

The *actuarial present value of accumulated plan benefits* should be segmented into at least the following categories:

vested benefits of participants currently receiving payments;

other vested benefits; and

nonvested benefits.

This segmentation was adopted by the FASB since it concluded it would be useful in assessing a plan's short-term versus long-term liquidity requirements. It might also provide some indication of the relative degree of objectivity or subjectivity inherent in determining the benefit information. Present employees' accumulated contributions, as of the benefit valuation date (including interest, if any), must also be disclosed.

The method of presentation of the accumulated benefit information may vary. The alternatives include a separate statement, inclusion in the net assets statement as a liability or as an equity interest (assuming the benefit information is as of the same date as the net assets statement), or in notes to financial statements. However, the three categories of benefit information set forth above must be presented in the same location.

In many cases the actuarial benefit calculations as of the end of the most recent plan year will not be completed by the time the financial statements are prepared and, accordingly, the actuarial present value of accumulated plan benefits is presented as of the beginning of the year. Under these circumstances, a statement of net assets available for benefits as of the beginning of the year, a statement of changes in net assets available for benefits for the preceding plan year, and information regarding changes in the actuarial present value of accumulated plan benefits must also be presented. This additional in-

[2] Guidelines for the inclusion or exclusion of contracts with insurance companies in plan assets are set forth subsequently in this chapter under "Contracts with Insurance Companies."

formation is necessary to satisfy the basic objective of a plan's financial statements.

The method of presenting information regarding the effects of certain factors affecting the *change in the actuarial present value of accumulated plan benefits* also allows for flexibility. This information may be presented in notes to the financial statements, in a separate statement or in a combined statement with changes in net asset information assuming all of the change information covers the same period. Effects of plan amendments, changes in the nature of a plan (e.g., merger with another plan), and changes in actuarial assumptions, if significant, are required to be presented.[3] The significant effects of other individual factors such as benefits accumulated, the increase (for interest) resulting from the decrease in the discount period, and benefits paid may but are not required to be identified. If a statement format is used and only the required information is disclosed, an additional "other" category will be needed to balance the statement. If a footnote format is used, the actuarial present value of accumulated plan benefits as of the preceding benefit information date should also be disclosed. Inasmuch as changes in actuarial assumptions are changes in estimates, the effects of those changes should be accounted for prospectively in the years affected and should not be accounted for by restating amounts reported in financial statements for prior years.

Illustrative financial statements, including footnote disclosures, are included at the end of this chapter.

Use of Averages or Approximations

The use of averages or other methods of approximation in pension plan financial reporting is appropriate as long as the approximations provide reasonable results. In this regard, the board explicitly states that it recognizes that literal application of certain of the requirements of Statement No. 35 could require a degree of detail in record keeping and computation that might be unduly burdensome. Accordingly, the use of averages or other methods of approximation is appropriate, provided the results obtained are substantially the same as the results contemplated by the statement. Thus, for example, rolling back to the beginning of the year or projecting to the end of the year detailed employee service-related data as of a date within the year may be acceptable in approximating beginning- or end-of-year *benefit information.* The use of averages and other methods of approximation consistent with recommended actuarial practice may be useful in conjunction with other provisions of this statement, particularly when applied to plans sponsored by small employers. If participants' individual historical salary data for plan years before the effective date of

---

[3] Plans that determine the actuarial present value of accumulated plan benefits using insurance company rates (discussed later in this chapter under "Assumptions Used in Determining the Actuarial Present Value of Accumulated Plan Benefits") should, if practicable, disclose the effect of changes in actuarial assumptions reflected in changes in those rates.

this statement are not available, reasonable approximations thereof are acceptable.

PLAN ASSETS

Principal pension plan assets are contributions receivable and investments held directly or through a bank or an insurance company. The following sections discuss their treatment under generally accepted accounting principles.

Contributions Receivable

Contributions receivable are the amounts due to the plan as of the plan year-end from the employer(s), and employees and other sources of funding, where applicable. Amounts due include those pursuant to formal commitments as well as legal or contractual requirements. With respect to an employer's contributions, evidence of a formal commitment may include a resolution by the board of directors of the employer, a consistent pattern of making payments after the plan's year-end pursuant to an established funding policy where the payments are attributable to the preceding plan year, a deduction of a contribution for federal income tax purposes for periods ending on or before the reporting date or the employer's recognition as of the plan year-end of a contribution payable to the plan. The existence of accrued pension costs in employer company financial statements does not, by itself, provide sufficient support for recognition of a contribution receivable. An adequate allowance should be provided for estimated uncollectible amounts.

A clear determination of contributions receivable can generally be made based on this definition. However, there are circumstances where this guidance may not be adequate. Consider, for example, the situation where an employer company takes advantage, for federal income tax purposes, of the opportunity to attribute to the current tax year (year one) contributions that would otherwise apply to the subsequent year (year two). This opportunity exists when unfunded prior service cost has not been amortized at its maximum allowable rate under the Internal Revenue Code, and year two contributions have been at least partially funded prior to the due date of the income tax return (including extensions).

Under this approach, contributions made in year two up to the due date of the income tax return for normal cost, amortization of prior service cost, and any other factors considered by the actuary as applying to year two may be attributed (up to deduction limits specified in the Internal Revenue Code) to amortization of prior service cost for year one. One might take the position that this accelerated tax deduction may be included in receivables since deduction for federal tax purposes of a contribution made for a period ending on or before the financial statement reporting date provides evidence of a formal commitment to the plan. It is questionable, however, whether the FASB intended that the definition of contributions receivable should include such amounts.

Investments

Since investments are in virtually all instances a pension plan's largest asset, their valuation is particularly important. All plan investments, including equity and debt securities, real estate, and bank common or commingled trust funds, but not contracts with insurance companies, should be stated at fair value as of the date of the financial statements.[4] The FASB considered various alternatives to fair value, including historical cost, moving-average-value, and different methods for different types of investments (e.g., equity securities at fair value and debt securities at cost).[5] The FASB rejected these alternatives, concluding that fair value provides the most relevant information with respect to a plan's investments consistent with the primary objective of a pension plan's financial statements.

As previously indicated in this chapter, the scope of Statement No. 35 does not include defined contribution pension plans. Although consideration should be given to applying the guidance contained in the statement (stating investments other than contracts with insurance companies at fair value) to defined contribution plans, the use of alternatives is not proscribed.[6] Present practice indicates, however, that most defined contribution plans value investments at fair value. Defined contribution plans reporting ERISA required financial information in accordance with the alternative method of compliance are required to state investments at fair value.

Where investments are valued at cost and fair value is substantially lower than cost, consideration should be given to whether the securities should be written down to their fair values. In making such determination, the plan administrator can be guided by the considerations outlined in the AICPA's auditing interpretation on "Evidential matter for the carrying amount of marketable securities" issued in 1975.

Determining Fair Value

The fair value of an investment is the amount a pension plan could reasonably expect to receive for it in a sale between a willing buyer and a willing seller; that is, in other than a forced sale. The relative difficulty of determining fair value depends upon the nature of the investments held. For securities traded in an active market, published market quotations should be used as the basis for the determination. The closing price on the financial statement date will usually be the fair value unless the security was not traded that day, in which

---

[4] The terms *market value, fair market value, current market value,* and *fair value* are often used interchangeably. Some accountants restrict use of the terms *market value, fair market value,* and *current market value* to the value of investments regularly traded on a securities market (where market quotations are readily available), and the term *fair value* to investments not regularly traded on a securities market and thus valued in good faith by the plan's board of trustees or administrative committee. In this chapter the term *fair value* is used as an all-inclusive term covering all of the above.

[5] The term *historical cost* when applied to bonds generally means original cost, plus or minus amortized discount or premium.

[6] See footnote 1 in this chapter.

case the price will be either the appropriate closing bid or the average of bid and asked prices. Where a plan's investments include restricted securities which cannot be offered to the public without first being registered, the board of trustees or the administrative committee must give appropriate consideration to the effect of the restriction on determining the fair value of the restricted securities. Fair value should be adjusted to reflect brokerage commissions and other selling expenses, where significant.

In the case of other investments without readily determinable values, such as securities of closely held corporations or real estate, various special procedures may be required to determine fair value. If there is not an active market for an investment but there is such a market for similar investments, selling prices in that market may be helpful in estimating fair value. If a market price is not available, expected cash flows discounted at an appropriate interest rate may aid in estimating fair value. The use of independent experts qualified to estimate fair value may be necessary for certain investments.

For considering fair value determinations, the AICPA's Industry Audit Guide, "Audits of Investment Companies," excerpted in Figure 8-1, may be found useful.

Effective Date of Transactions

In order to prepare financial statements on the accrual basis, purchases and sales of securities should be reflected on a trade-date basis. Thus, where the plan's books are maintained on a settlement-date basis, the accounts should be adjusted to a trade-date basis to reflect year-end transactions unless the effect of such adjustment would not be material to the financial statements taken as a whole.

Similarly, dividend income should be recorded on the ex-dividend date, rather than on the record or payment date. Income from other investments such as interest and rent should be recorded as earned and appropriate accruals made.

Disposition of Securities

For defined contribution plans carrying investments at historical cost,[7] the cost of securities sold must be determined to calculate gain or loss on disposition. Any of the following methods, when consistently applied, should be acceptable: (1) average, (2) identified (e.g., specific blocks of stock at their actual cost), (3) first-in, first-out, or (4) last-in, first-out.

Contracts with Insurance Companies

Insurance contracts should be recognized and measured under generally accepted accounting principles in the same manner as that reported by the pension plan in the annual report under ERISA, or which would have been reported were the plan subject to the reporting requirements of ERISA.

The recognition of insurance contracts in item 13 of Form 5500 is dependent

[7] See footnote 1 in this chapter.

FIGURE 8-1

Recommendations for valuing securities, as stated in AICPA Industry Audit Guide, "Audits of Investment Companies"

Securities Traded on a National Securities Exchange

Ordinarily, little difficulty should be experienced in valuing securities listed or traded on one or more security exchanges, since quotations of completed transactions are published daily. If a security was traded on the valuation date, the last quoted sales price generally is used. In the case of securities listed on more than one national securities exchange, the last quoted sales price up to the time of valuation on the exchange on which the security is principally traded should be used or, if there were no sales on that exchange on the valuation date, the last quoted sale price up to the time of valuation on the other exchanges should be substituted. Registered companies value their portfolio at the time of the close of trading on the New York Stock Exchange.[1]

If there were no sales on the valuation date but published closing bid and asked prices are available, the valuation in such circumstances should be within the range of these quoted prices. Some companies, as a matter of general policy, use the bid price, others use the mean of the bid and asked prices, and still others use a valuation within the range considered best to represent value in the circumstances. Each of these policies is considered to be acceptable if consistently applied. Normally, it is not considered to be acceptable to use the asked price alone. Where, on the valuation date, only a bid price or an asked price is quoted or the spread between bid and asked price is substantial, quotations for several days should be reviewed. If sales have been infrequent or there is a thin market in the security, further consideration should be given to whether "market quotations are readily available" as a practical matter. If it is decided that they are not readily available, the alternative method of valuation, that is, "fair value as determined in good faith by the board of directors" should be used.

Over-the-Counter Securities

Quotations are available from various sources for most unlisted securities traded regularly in the over-the-counter market. These sources include tabulations in the financial press, various quotation publications and financial reporting services, and individual broker-dealers. A company may adopt a policy of using a mean of the bid prices, or of the bid and asked prices, or of the prices of a representative selection of broker-dealers quoting on a particular security; or it may use a valuation within the range of bid and asked prices considered best to represent value in the circumstances. Any one of these policies is considered to be acceptable if consistently applied. Normally, the use of the asked prices alone is not acceptable.

Ordinarily, quotations for an over-the-counter security should be obtained from more than one broker-dealer unless available from an established marketmaker for that security, and quotations for several days should be reviewed. In all cases, the quotations should be from unaffiliated persons. NASDAQ may be the most convenient source of such quotations. Where quotations appear questionable, consideration should be given to valuing the security at "fair value as determined in good faith by the board of directors."

United States Treasury bonds and notes usually bear longer term maturities than those classified under "Short-Term Investments" below and are often purchased, at least partially, for their capital appreciation potential. Such securities are valued at quoted market.

Securities Valued "In Good Faith"

It is incumbent upon the board of directors to satisfy themselves that all appropriate factors relevant to the value of securities for which market quotations are not readily available have been considered and to determine the method of arriving at the fair value of each such security. To the ex-

162

FIGURE 8-1 (continued)

tent considered necessary, the board may appoint persons to assist it in the determination of such value, and to make the actual calculations pursuant to the board's direction. Consistent with this responsibility, the board also must review continuously the appropriateness of the method used in valuing each issue of securities in the company's portfolio. The directors must recognize their responsibilities in this matter and whenever technical assistance is requested from individuals who are not directors, the findings of such individuals must be carefully reviewed by the directors in order to satisfy themselves that the resulting valuations are fair.

As Accounting Series Release No. 118 states, no single standard for determining fair value in good faith can be laid down, since fair value depends upon the circumstances of each individual case. As a general principle, the current "fair value" of an issue of securities being valued by the board of directors would appear to be the amount which the owner might reasonably expect to receive from them upon their current sale, although there usually is no intention to make a current sale. Current sale should be interpreted to mean realization in an orderly disposition over a reasonable period of time. Methods which are in accord with this principle may, for example, be based on a multiple of earnings, or a discount (or less frequently a premium) from market of a similar, freely traded security, or a yield to maturity with respect to debt issues, or a combination of these and other methods. Some of the general factors which the directors should consider in determining a valuation method for an individual issue of securities include (1) the fundamental analytical data relating to the investment; (2) the nature and duration of restrictions on disposition of

the securities; and (3) an evaluation of the forces which influence the market in which these securities are purchased and sold. In the case of investments made in several securities of the same issuer, such as those made by many SBICs and venture capital companies, the valuation of the "package" as a whole may be appropriate. Among the more specific factors which must be considered are the type of security (debt or equity), financial standing of the issuer, availability of current financial statements, cost at date of purchase, size and period of holding, discount from market value of unrestricted securities of the same class at the time of purchase, special reports prepared by analysts, information as to any transactions or offers with respect to the security, existence of merger proposals or tender offers affecting the securities, reported prices and extent of public trading in similar securities of the issuer or comparable companies, maintenance of investee's business and financial plan, use of new funds to achieve planned results, changes in economic conditions including those in the company or industry, and other relevant matters.[2] This guide does not purport to delineate all factors which may be considered. The directors should take into consideration all indications of value available to them in determining the "fair value" assigned to a particular security. The information so considered and, insofar as practicable, the basis for the board's decision, should be documented in the minutes of the directors' meeting and the supporting data retained for the inspection of the company's independent auditor.

1 Rule 22c-1(b) of the 1940 act.
2 Accounting Series Release Nos. 113 and 118.

upon their classification. As indicated in Chapter 3, pension plans may enter into various types of insurance contracts. These contracts can generally be classified dependent on whether the related payment to the insurance company is currently allocated to purchase immediate or deferred annuity contracts for individual participants (allocated contracts) or the payment is accumulated in an unallocated fund (unallocated contracts) used to directly meet benefit payments when they come due or to purchase annuities for individual participants upon retirement (or earlier termination of service where the participant's benefits are partially or fully vested).

Under an allocated contract, plan benefits are fully guaranteed upon payment of the premiums to the insurance company. Examples of allocated contracts include individual life insurance or annuity contracts, group permanent insurance contracts, and deferred group annuity contracts. Under unallocated contracts, plan benefits are guaranteed only to the extent funds are available. Deposit administration group annuity contracts (DA) and immediate participation guarantee contracts (IPG) are examples of unallocated contracts.

The applicable instructions to item 13 of Form 5500 indicate that unallocated insurance contracts should be recognized in item 13 and allocated contracts fully guaranteeing the amount of benefit payments should be excluded. Under generally accepted accounting principles, plan financial statements should follow the same treatment. The exclusion of allocated contracts from plan financial statements is based on the view that when an insurance company has fully guaranteed the pension benefits, it incurs, and removes from the plan, the obligation to pay those benefits. The plan has met its obligation to provide these benefits by making payments to the insurance company to purchase the annuity contracts and no longer has the assets that will be used to pay the benefits. In relation to the primary objective of plan financial statements to provide information useful in assessing the plan's ability to pay benefits when due, a participant would look toward the financial stability of the insurance company rather than to those of the plan. The instructions to Form 5500 appear to call for inclusion of retired life funds and exclusion of participation rights. The FASB concluded that, although it might have some conceptual difficulties with such treatment, it chose the practical solution of conforming to the ERISA reporting rules. Another area where there might be some conceptual difficulties, perhaps requiring more definitive guidance, involves whole life policies on the lives of individual participants. Such policies may be considered allocated contracts, in which case they would be excluded from plan assets for Form 5500 reporting purposes and therefore excluded for financial statement purposes. It can be argued that excluding whole life contracts from plan assets would be appropriate in cases where the payment of the face value or of cash surrender value of the policies is to be made directly to plan participants or their beneficiaries, inasmuch as the individual would look to the insurance company for payment of benefits. However, when proceeds of the contract are to be paid to the plan and would become part of the plan's general funds, the contracts might be more appropriately included as assets of the plan.

With respect to *measurement* of insurance contracts, the instructions to Form 5500 call for investments in separate accounts to be carried at fair value but permit other contracts to be valued at either fair value or amounts determined by the insurance company in accordance with the terms of the contract, referred to as contract value. Contract value will almost invariably be used in plan reporting, since insurance companies do not normally report fair value to the plan. Stating insurance contracts at contract value, however, is inconsistent with stating all other plan investments at fair value. The FASB, in its consideration of this inconsistency, indicated in Statement No. 35 that a fair value approach for insurance contracts would necessitate extra calculations which, according to information the board received, might be extremely complex. The FASB concluded that it did not have sufficient information at the time the statement was issued to enable it to reach definitive conclusions concerning the feasibility of determining a contract's value and decided to adopt a practical solution to measurement of contracts so that issuance of the statement would not be further delayed.

Commingled and Master Trust Funds

Bank common or commingled trust funds (commingled funds), insurance company pooled separate accounts, and master trusts contain assets which are pooled for investment purposes. Commingled funds and pooled separate accounts contain assets of plans sponsored by two or more employers. For this definition a controlled group of corporations is considered a single employer. Master trusts hold assets only of plans maintained by a single employer or members of a controlled group of corporations.

With respect to commingled funds, a pension plan acquires units of such funds, generally referred to as *units of participation*. Pooled separate accounts are similar to commingled funds. A plan's share of pooled separate accounts is also determined on a participation unit basis. Periodically, such as each month or quarter, the unit value is determined based on the fair values of the underlying assets. The amount of equity a pension plan has in a commingled fund or pooled separate account is determined by multiplying the unit value by the number of units.

Although commingled funds and pooled separate accounts are conceptually very similar, there is a difference in form. Assets invested in a commingled fund are held in trust for the plan, while assets invested in a pooled separate account are the property of the insurance company, with the plan having specified rights thereto. With respect to master trusts, each plan has an undivided interest in the assets of such a trust and ownership is represented by the proportionate dollar interest or by units of participation.

The accounting and financial reporting for plan investments in commingled funds, pooled accounts, and master trusts is not addressed in FASB Statement No. 35. But, the Department of Labor reporting and disclosure regulations do prescribe regulatory accounting for these funds for plans subject to ERISA reporting requirements.

The authors believe that investments in commingled funds and pooled separate accounts should be reported as one separate line item in the statement of net assets available for benefits, and the change in value should be similarly reported in the statement of changes in net assets available for benefits. The plan's financial statements should not otherwise report its proportionate share of the underlying investments and transactions of these funds and accounts.

Investments in master trusts should preferably be reported in the same manner as commingled funds and pooled separate accounts provided that significant details of the assets of the trust are disclosed. This suggested accounting treatment for commingled funds and pooled separate accounts is consistent with DOL reporting and disclosure regulations. With respect to master trusts, the DOL, in contrast to the view of the authors and other observers, had mandated that plans include their allocable portion of the trust's assets and liabilities and transactions in Form 5500, items 13 and 14.[8] In 1982, the DOL reversed its position, and now calls for the reporting of only the one line item in item 13 and item 14. Therefore, if plans follow the author's preferred treatment for presenting the financial statements, those statements and items 13 and 14 would be presented in a consistent manner.

Financial Statement Presentation

Investments should be presented in the statement of net assets available for benefits in enough detail to identify the types of investments. Separate line items will usually be provided for each major class of plan investments such as U.S. government securities, corporate bonds and debentures, equity securities, common or commingled funds, contracts with insurance companies, mortgages, and real estate investments. Further, the financial statements should indicate the basis of determining fair value of assets, that is, quoted market prices or other basis.

Other Financial Statement Disclosures

Footnote disclosures to the plan financial statements should, where applicable, include the following with respect to investments:

a description of the method(s) and significant assumptions used to determine the fair value of investments and the reported value of contracts with insurance companies;

the accounting policy regarding the purchase of contracts with insurance companies that are excluded from plan assets and the plan's divided income for the year that is related to excluded contracts;

identification of individual investments that represent 5% or more of the net assets available for benefits; and

significant investment transactions in which the plan is jointly involved with the plan sponsor, the employer company, or the employee organization; this disclosure is generally most relevant to real estate transactions.

Disclosure of the historical cost of investments is not required by FASB Statement No. 35 since the FASB was not convinced that such disclosure would enhance the ability of a user of the financial statements to assess the plan's ability to pay benefits when due.

[8] Items 13 and 14 are a schedule of plan assets and liabilities and a schedule of plan income, expenses, and changes in net assets, respectively.

Pension plans not within the scope of FASB Statement No. 35 that prepare financial statements stating investments at other than fair value should normally disclose:

the fair value of major classes of investments,
the method followed for determining the cost of securities sold.

Operating Assets

Plan assets used in plan operations (e.g., building, equipment, furniture and fixtures, and leasehold improvements) should be presented at cost less accumulated depreciation or amortization under generally accepted accounting principles. This is in conflict with the DOL regulations concerning ERISA annual reports prepared under the alternative method of compliance, since the regulations make no differentiation between operating and other assets, and require assets to be stated at current value. Practice in ERISA filings under the alternative method, however, has been to state these assets at cost less accumulated depreciation.

REPORTING ACTUARIAL BENEFIT INFORMATION

Pension plans have heretofore generally not included amounts for pension payments related to future periods as a liability in the financial statements, and a number of plans have not even disclosed any form of actuarially determined obligation for pension benefits. FASB Statement No. 35, however, *does require* defined benefit pension plans reporting under generally accepted accounting principles to report specified actuarial benefit information. The FASB concluded that in order for plan financial statements to provide financial information that is useful in assessing the plan's present and future ability to pay benefits when due, it is essential that the financial statements present information about both the net assets available for benefits and the benefits to be paid.

The FASB considered several alternatives for the benefit information to be included in financial statements, including vested benefit information and unfunded prior service cost. Vested benefit information alone was rejected, since it generally understates the benefits reasonably expected to become payable as a result of service rendered. Prior service cost was rejected since the amount can vary significantly depending on actuarial cost method used. This would detract from the usefulness of plan financial statements since comparability is impaired.

The FASB concluded that the benefit information to be presented should be the actuarial present value of accumulated plan benefits. Accumulated plan benefits are those future benefit payments that are attributable, under the plan's provisions, to participants' service rendered prior to the benefit information date.[9] Accumulated plan benefits comprise benefits expected to be paid to retired or terminated employees or their beneficiaries, beneficiaries of deceased employees, and present employees or their beneficiaries. They include non-vested benefits as well as vested benefits. Accumulated plan benefits should be adjusted to their actuarial present value.

Accumulated plan benefits should be reported only to the extent that related assets are included in the financial statements. Thus, in the case of plans where benefits are fully guaranteed by an insurance company and the related assets are not reflected in the plan's financial statements, the actuarial present value of accumulated plan benefits should exclude the fully insured benefits.

Assumptions Used in Determining the Actuarial Present Value of Accumulated Plan Benefits

Plan administrators will find it necessary to use actuarial expertise in determining benefit information. The assumptions to be included by the actuary in the accumulated benefit calculations are prescribed by FASB Statement No. 35. Figure 8-2, excerpted from FASB Statement No. 35, sets forth the specific guidelines for determining accumulated plan benefits.

The actuarial present value of accumulated plan benefits is determined by applying actuarial assumptions to the accumulated plan benefit amounts determined pursuant to Figure 8-2. The actuarial assumptions are used to adjust those amounts to reflect the time value of money (discounts for interest) and the probability of payment (decrements such as mortality, disability, withdrawal, and early retirement) between the benefit information date and the expected date of payment. The actuarial assumptions should presume an ongoing plan and should reflect the best estimate of the plan's future experience solely with respect to each individual assumption (explicit approach).[10]

Salary Increase Assumption

Although other assumptions of future experience are reflected, the FASB decided that future salary increases should not be recognized in measuring benefits. Rather, the impact of salary increases should not have an effect until the increase in compensation occurs. The FASB put forth several arguments in support of this view. One argument is that the total increase in a participant's accumulated plan benefit attributable to an increase in compensation in a given year is properly considered to have been earned in that year, not in an

---

[9] The benefit information date is the date as of which the benefit information is presented. As indicated earlier in the chapter, benefit information can be presented either as of the end or beginning of the plan year and, if the information regarding changes in the accumulated benefits is not presented in statement form, it should also be presented as of the prior plan year-end.

[10] The alternative to the explicit approach is the implicit approach whereby two or more assumptions may not individually represent the best estimate of the plan's future experience but the aggregate effect approximates the results of an explicit approach.

FIGURE 8-2

Measuring accumulated plan benefits

To the extent possible, plan provisions shall apply in measuring accumulated plan benefits. In some plans, benefits are a specified amount for each year of service. Even if a plan does not specify a benefit for each year of service, another of its provisions (e.g., a provision applicable to terminated employees or to termination of the plan— if independent of funding patterns) may indicate how to measure accumulated plan benefits. If the benefit for each year of service is not stated by or clearly determinable from the provisions of the plan, the benefit shall be considered to accumulate in proportion to (a) the ratio of the number of years of service completed prior to the benefit valuation date to the number that will have been completed when the benefit will first be fully vested, if the type of benefit is includable in vested benefits (e.g., a supplemental early retirement benefit that is a vested benefit after a stated number of years of service), or (b) to the ratio of completed years of service to projected years of service upon anticipated separation from covered employment, if the type of benefit is not includable in vested benefits (e.g., a death or disability benefit that is payable only if death or disability occurs during active service).

In measuring accumulated plan benefits, the following shall apply.

1   Except as indicated in (2) and (3) below, accumulated plan benefits should be based on participants' history of pay and service and other appropriate factors as of the benefit information date.

2   Projected years of service should be a factor only in determining participants' expected eligibility for particular benefits, such as:

  (a)   increased benefits that are granted provided a specified number of years of service are rendered, such as a pension benefit that is increased from $9 per month to $10 per month for each year of service if 20 or more years of service are rendered;

  (b)   early retirement benefits;

  (c)   death benefits;

  (d)   disability benefits.

3   Automatic benefit increases specified by the plan (e.g., automatic cost-of-living increases) that are expected to occur after the benefit information date should be recognized.

4   Benefits to be provided by means of contracts excluded from plan assets for which payments to the insurance company have been made should be excluded.

5   Plan amendments adopted after the benefit information date should not be recognized.

6   If it is necessary to take future compensation into account in the determination of Social Security benefits, participants' compensation as of the benefit information date shall be assumed to remain unchanged during their assumed future service. Increases in the wage base or benefit level pursuant to either the existing Social Security law or possible future amendments of the law should not be recognized.

earlier year. Another argument is that future salary increases are not unlike certain other future price changes, the accounting effects of which are recognized in the periods in which the price changes occur. This view considers it inappropriate to reflect future salary increases resulting either from changing levels of productivity or from changing wage levels (due either to general price level changes or changes in supply and demand factors) for constant levels of productivity until the economic conditions giving rise to these changes are present.

In the view of the authors, however, since Statement No. 35 states that the actuarial present value of accumulated plan benefits represents the future benefit payments attributable under the plan to employee service rendered to date, the effect of future salary increases should have been required to be reflected. The increased benefits resulting from participants' service performed to the benefit valuation date have already been earned. If one is calculating anticipated benefit payments based on already performed service, it makes little sense not to apply to that service the salary level that will in fact be applied. The failure to recognize future salary increases, while recognizing other factors (e.g., turnover and mortality) expected to occur in the future that will affect benefits to be paid, is inconsistent. Although there are situations, such as in connection with some career-average type plans, where including a factor for salary increases would not significantly affect accumulated plan benefits, in many other cases, particularly in final-pay type plans, there would be a significant effect.

Interest Assumption

As previously indicated, accumulated plan benefits should be adjusted for the time value of money. The benefits should be discounted at assumed rates of return reflecting the expected rates of return during the periods for which payment of benefits has been deferred. The assumed rates should be consistent with the returns realistically achievable on the types of assets held by the plan, the plan's investment policy, and the rates of inflation assumed in estimating automatic cost-of-living adjustments. Assumed rates of return reflect expected rates on existing assets and those available in the marketplace, expected rates from the reinvestment of actual returns from those investments, and investments expected to be held in the future. Thus, accumulated plan benefits generally will not be discounted solely at rates of return on existing investments. However, to the extent that assumed rates of return are based on values of existing plan assets those expected rates should be based on the values presented in the plan's financial statements. The rate of return may be adjusted to account for plan administrative expenses.[11]

The importance of the determination of the assumed rates of return cannot be stressed enough. It is not unusual to find that a small increase or decrease in an assumed rate of return can decrease or increase the actuarial present value of accumulated plan benefits by a very significant amount. This is of great concern, evidenced by the number of comments received by the FASB on this point. Many said that year-to-year changes in accumulated plan benefits as a result of changes in assumed rates should be avoided as much as possible. Averaging techniques were suggested, whereby assumed rates are changed only when it is apparent that the long-term rate trend has changed. Many actuaries support this viewpoint. The FASB, however, in rejecting this view, stated that although long-term rates must be considered in determining appro-

---

[11] Alternatively, these expenses can be assigned to future periods and discounted to the benefit valuation date.

priate assumed rates of return, apparent material changes in long-term rates should not be ignored on an annual basis solely to avoid annually adjusting assumed rates of return.

Alternative

In selecting certain assumptions to be used in determining the actuarial present value of accumulated plan benefits, an acceptable alternative to that discussed in preceding paragraphs is to use those assumptions that are inherent in determining the estimated cost that would be incurred at the benefit valuation date to obtain a contract with an insurance company to provide participants with their accumulated plan benefits. However, other assumptions that are necessary but are not inherent in that estimated cost must be selected pursuant to the above requirements.

Disclosures

The financial statement footnote disclosures should include description of the method(s) and significant assumptions (e.g., assumed rate of return) used to calculate the actuarial present value of accumulated plan benefits. If administrative expenses expected to be paid by the plan are reflected by adjusting the assumed rate of return, this method should be disclosed. Changes in the method or assumptions, if any, should also be disclosed.

ADDITIONAL FINANCIAL STATEMENT DISCLOSURES

FASB Statement No. 35 requires the following disclosures in addition to the footnote disclosures related to investments and actuarial benefit information set forth previously in this chapter:

a brief general description of the plan agreement, including vesting and benefit provisions;[12]

a description of significant plan amendments adopted during the year ending on the latest benefit information date; if amendments were adopted between the latest benefit information date and the date of the financial statements, it should be disclosed that the actuarial present value of accumulated plan benefits does not reflect those amendments;

---

[12] If material providing this information is otherwise published and made available, these disclosures may be omitted provided that reference to such other source is made and disclosure similar to the following is made in the financial statements: "Should the plan terminate at some future time, its net assets generally will not be available on a pro rata basis to provide participants' benefits. Whether a particular participant's accumulated plan benefits will be paid depends on both the priority of those benefits and the level of benefits guaranteed by the PBGC at that time. Some benefits may be fully or partially provided for by the then existing assets and the PBGC guaranty while other benefits may not be provided for at all."

a brief description of the priority order of participants' claims to the assets of the plan upon plan termination and, for plans subject to ERISA, benefits guaranteed by the Pension Benefit Guaranty Corporation (PBGC), including a discussion of the application of the PBGC guaranty to any recent plan amendment;[13]

funding policy and any changes in such policy; if a plan is contributory, the method of determining participants' contributions should be disclosed; a description of noncash contributions, if any, from the employer should be included; if any significant costs of plan administration are absorbed by the employer, that fact should be disclosed; plans subject to ERISA should disclose whether the minimum funding requirements of ERISA have been met; if a minimum funding waiver has been granted by the Internal Revenue Service or if a request for a waiver is pending before the IRS, that fact should be disclosed;

the federal income tax status of the plan, if a favorable letter of determination has not been obtained or maintained;

plan administrative expenses;

significant transactions in which the plan is jointly involved with the plan sponsor, the employer company, or the employee organization;

unusual or infrequent events or transactions occurring after the latest benefit information date but before issuance of the financial statements that might significantly affect the usefulness of the financial statements in an assessment of the plan's present and future ability to pay benefits; an example of an event that would require disclosure is a plan amendment adopted after the latest benefit information date that significantly increases future benefits that are attributable to participants' service rendered before that date; if reasonably determinable, the effects of such events or transactions should be disclosed; if such effects are not quantified, the reasons why they are not reasonably determinable should be disclosed.

Notes to plan financial statements prepared pursuant to the ERISA reporting and disclosure requirements that should be "considered" when filing under the act, but "shall" be included when filing under the alternative method of compliance, include some of the disclosures required under FASB Statement No. 35 and certain additional disclosures.[14] Those disclosures required by ERISA that are not specifically prescribed by FASB Statement No. 35 are:

---

[13] See previous footnote.

[14] The ERISA reporting and disclosure requirements do not specifically require all the footnote disclosures required for defined benefit plans by FASB Statement No. 35. However, financial statements contained in annual reports filed reporting information prescribed by the act are to be in accordance with generally accepted accounting principles, and those contained in filings reporting information prescribed by the alternative method of compliance are to set forth in footnotes to the financial statements any variances from generally accepted accounting principles.

a description of material lease commitments and other commitments and contingent liabilities;

a description of any agreements and transactions with persons known to be parties in interest;

the federal income tax status of the plan (FASB Statement No. 35 requires the disclosure only when a favorable letter of determination has not been obtained or maintained); and

any other information required for a fair presentation.

The alternative method of compliance also calls for a description of any variances between generally accepted accounting principles and the principles followed in the financial statements, and an explanation of any differences between the financial statements and items 13 and 14 of Form 5500. In the view of the authors, different categorization of amounts with identical totals would probably not be considered a difference requiring explanation. Thus, for example, if total assets are the same, no explanation is needed even though the categories of assets presented are different. On the other hand, differences that need to be explained would include, for example, instances where items 13 and 14 are prepared on the cash basis of accounting, while the accrual basis is used for the financial statements.

The footnote disclosure requirements described in the two preceding paragraphs for financial statements prepared pursuant to ERISA reporting and disclosure requirements are applicable to both defined contribution and defined benefit pension plans. If the plan administrator of a defined contribution plan follows the guidance contained in FASB Statement No. 35, certain modifications to the statement's suggested disclosures, as previously set forth, would be appropriate. Those disclosures that relate to the actuarial present value of accumulated plan benefits, minimum funding requirements, and PBGC plan termination provisions would not apply.

The illustrative financial statements at the end of this chapter include illustrative footnote disclosures.

INTERNAL CONTROL

Internal control for pension plans has some special characteristics. Although detailed discussion is not feasible in the scope of this chapter, those special features of internal control methods and procedures for pension plans which were identified by the AICPA's Health, Welfare, and Pension Fund Task Force in a draft position paper are summarized below. The language, with certain modifications, is that of the position paper.

Contributions to Multiemployer Plans

Contributions from employers, on a self-assessed basis, will represent the majority of the plan receipts. Contributions are generally determined by the number of hours or days worked or gross earnings of the participant at a standard contribution rate.

Employers commonly report contributions on standard preprinted forms that are supplied by the plan. These forms generally show the employer's name, participant's name, social security number, and bases upon which the contributions are made. The plan should have a procedure for establishing initial accountability over the reporting forms immediately upon receipt (e.g., by document number or dollar or other control total), and the forms should be controlled throughout the processing operations, from the time of receipt of contributions to final postings to the participants' eligibility records and employers' contribution records.

The plan's internal control procedures should be adequate for disclosing and following up missing or delinquent employer reports and contributions as well as for detecting and following up employer overpayments or underpayments. Such internal control procedures may include the auditing of employers' records on a systematic or exception basis, the mailing of periodic statements requesting participants to report any discrepancies in hours worked and/or contributions reported on their behalf by employers, or a reconciliation of employee status reports furnished by the union to employer contribution reports.

Contributions are generally mailed directly to a bank for credit to the plan's account or received at the plan's office, in which latter case prenumbered receipt forms should be used. The numerical sequence of the forms and subsequent depositing of the cash in the bank should be subjected to internal review and checking. Contributions received should be deposited intact on a timely basis, and not be used for payment of plan expenses.

A method which generally provides for good internal control over the receipt and deposit of contributions is the adoption of a "lock box" system, under which employers mail the remittances and contribution reports to a bank. The bank deposits all receipts, prepares a record of the deposit, and forwards the deposit record and related contribution reports to the plan for further processing.

When an office has been established to serve more than one plan, proper controls are necessary to insure that remittances are deposited to the proper accounts. The controls established should include an audit trail which can be traced through to the general ledger postings.

The plan should maintain a cumulative record of employers' contributions, because the plan is required to report annually on contributions made by employers. The totals of contributions recorded in the cumulative record should be periodically reconciled with records of participants' eligibility and with the cash receipts book.

Investments

The plan's investment policy and the responsibility for custody of its securities should be established by the board of trustees. The trustees should abide by any restrictions that may be imposed by the trust agreement or by governmental regulations.

Where the plan administrator is directly responsible for making the investment decisions, significant transactions should be approved by the board of trustees or by an appropriate committee. Where the investment decisions are made by a custodian who also acts as trustee, the plan's agreement with the custodian/trustee should be approved by such board or committee. The board or committee should also monitor investment performance.

Benefits

Applications for the commencement of benefit payments should be carefully processed. An individual not involved in the original processing procedures should review the applicant's eligibility and determine that the retirement benefits have been properly determined in conformity with the participant's payroll and personnel records and with the plan documents. The board of trustees (multiemployer plan) or the administrative committee or its designee (single-employer plan) should approve all applications for benefits.

Controls should be established to ensure that individuals receiving benefits are eligible for the continuation of such benefits. Procedures might include periodic comparison, by an individual not involved in processing benefit applications, of endorsements on paid checks with signatures in personnel records or on benefit applications; sending of greeting cards to pensioners, returnable to the plan in the event of nondelivery; reviewing obituary notices; and visiting pensioners.

Bonding Requirements

ERISA specifies minimum amounts of fidelity bond coverage (with certain exceptions) for every fiduciary of a pension plan and every person who handles funds or other property of such a plan.

Multiemployer pension plans may require employers to provide, at their own expense, a performance bond or other security to cover the payment of contributions in the event of insolvency. Performance bonds or other security should be periodically reviewed for adequacy.

Administrative Expenses of Multiemployer Plans

Although the trustees are responsible for the approval of all administrative expenses, responsibility for approving routine expenses is usually delegated to the administrator or other responsible employees of the plan. Because of their fiduciary responsibility, the trustees should make certain that the internal control procedures for administrative expenses are adequate. The board of trustees will generally also retain the authority to approve any such expenditures over a stated amount.

Contract or professional administrators are paid according to various criteria, for example, the number of participants covered by the plan, employer's reports processed, and so forth. Therefore, it is important that the plan's records provide the information necessary to determine the reasonableness of such payments.

ILLUSTRATIVE FINANCIAL STATEMENTS

In Figure 8-3, the illustrative financial statements for a defined benefit pension plan are those presented in FASB Statement No. 35. They are presented as single-year statements and include only those footnotes required by generally accepted accounting principles. Accordingly, they do not contain certain additional footnote disclosures (see the "Additional Financial Statement Disclosures" section of this chapter) and supplemental schedules[15] required by the DOL, nor *comparative* statements of net assets available for plan benefits which are required when filing under the alternative method of compliance.

The formats presented and the wording of accompanying notes are illustrative only and do not necessarily reflect a preference of the board. Further, the circumstances assumed for the hypothetical C&H Company Pension Plan are designed to facilitate illustration of many of the Statement No. 35 requirements. Therefore, the notes to the illustrative financial statements are probably more extensive than would be expected for a typical plan.

---

[15] These schedules are not required under generally accepted accounting principles. The schedule requirements are discussed in Chapter 5.

FIGURE 8-3

Illustrative financial statements,
single-employer plan (defined benefit plan)

Contents

FIGURE 8-3 (continued)

C&H Company Pension Plan
Statement of Net Assets Available for Benefits

	December 31 1981
Assets	
Investments, at fair value (Notes B(1) and E)	
United States government securities	$ 350,000
Corporate bonds and debentures	3,500,000
Common stock	
C&H Company	690,000
Other	2,250,000
Mortgages	480,000
Real estate	270,000
	7,540,000
Deposit administration contract, at contract value (Notes B(1) and F)	1,000,000
Total investments	8,540,000
Receivables	
Employees' contributions	40,000
Securities sold	310,000
Accrued interest and dividends	77,000
	427,000
Cash	200,000
Total assets	9,167,000
Liabilities	
Accounts payable	70,000
Accrued expenses	85,000
Total liabilities	155,000
Net assets available for benefits	$9,012,000

The accompanying notes are an integral part of the financial statements.

FIGURE 8-3 (continued)

C&H Company Pension Plan
Statement of Changes in Net Assets Available for Benefits

	Year Ended December 31 1981
Investment income	
Net appreciation in fair value of investments (Note E)	$ 207,000
Interest	345,000
Dividends	130,000
Rents	55,000
	737,000
Less investment expenses	39,000
	698,000
Contributions (Note C)	
Employer	780,000
Employees	450,000
	1,230,000
Total additions	1,928,000
Benefits paid directly to participants	740,000
Purchases of annuity contracts (Note F)	257,000
	997,000
Administrative expenses	65,000
Total deductions	1,062,000
Net increase	866,000
Net assets available for benefits	
Beginning of year	8,146,000
End of year	$9,012,000

The accompanying notes are an integral part of the financial statements.

FIGURE 8-3 (continued)

C&H Company Pension Plan
Statement of Accumulated Plan Benefits

	December 31 1981
Actuarial present value of accumulated plan benefits (Notes B(2) and C)	
Vested benefits	
Participants currently receiving payments	$ 3,040,000
Other participants	8,120,000
	11,160,000
Nonvested benefits	2,720,000
Total actuarial present value of accumulated plan benefits	$13,880,000

The accompanying notes are an integral part of the financial statements.

FIGURE 8-3 (continued)

C&H Company Pension Plan
Statement of Changes in Accumulated Plan Benefits

	Year Ended December 31 1981
Actuarial present value of accumulated plan benefits at beginning of year	$11,880,000
Increase (decrease) during the year attributable to:	
Plan amendment (Note G)	2,410,000
Change in actuarial assumptions (Note B(2))	(1,050,500)
Benefits accumulated	895,000
Increase for interest due to the decrease in the discount period (Note B(2))	742,500
Benefits paid	(997,000)
Net increase	2,000,000
Actuarial present value of accumulated plan benefits at end of year	$13,880,000

The accompanying notes are an integral part of the financial statements.

FIGURE 8-3 (continued)

C&H Company Pension Plan
Statement of Accumulated Plan Benefits
and Net Assets Available for Benefits
[An alternative for pages 178 and 180]

	December 31 1981
Accumulated Plan Benefits (Notes B(2) and C)	
Actuarial present value of vested benefits	
Participants currently receiving payments	$ 3,040,000
Other participants	8,120,000
	11,160,000
Actuarial present value of nonvested benefits	2,720,000
Total actuarial present value of accumulated plan benefits	13,880,000
Net Assets Available for Benefits	
Investments, at fair value (Note B(1) and E)	
United States government securities	350,000
Corporate bonds and debentures	3,500,000
Common stock	
C&H Company	690,000
Other	2,250,000
Mortgages	480,000
Real estate	270,000
	7,540,000
Deposit administration contract, at contract value (Notes B(1) and F)	1,000,000
Total investments	8,540,000
Receivables	
Employees' contributions	40,000
Securities sold	310,000
Accrued interest and dividends	77,000
	427,000
Cash	200,000
Total assets	9,167,000
Accounts payable	70,000
Accrued expenses	85,000
Total liabilities	155,000
Net assets available for benefits	9,012,000
Excess of actuarial present value of accumulated plan benefits over net assets available for benefits	$ 4,868,000

The accompanying notes are an integral part of the financial statements.

FIGURE 8-3 (continued)

C&H Company Pension Plan
Statement of Changes in Accumulated Plan
Benefits and Net Assets Available for Benefits
[An alternative for pages 179 and 181]

	Year Ended December 31 1981
Net Increase in Actuarial Present Value of Accumulated Plan Benefits	
Increase (decrease) during the year attributable to:	
Plan amendment (Note G)	$ 2,410,000
Change in actuarial assumptions (Note B(2))	(1,050,500)
Benefits accumulated	895,000
Increase for interest due to the decrease in the discount period (Note B(2))	742,500
Benefits paid	(997,000)
Net increase	2,000,000
Net Increase in Net Assets Available for Benefits	
Investment income	
Net appreciation in fair value of investments (Note E)	207,000
Interest	345,000
Dividends	130,000
Rents	55,000
	737,000
Less investment expenses	39,000
	698,000
Contributions (Note C)	
Employer	780,000
Employees	450,000
	1,230,000
Total additions	1,928,000
Benefits paid directly to participants	740,000
Purchases of annuity contracts (Note F)	257,000
	997,000
Administrative expenses	65,000
Total deductions	1,062,000
Net increase	866,000
Increase in excess of actuarial present value of accumulated plan benefits over net assets available for benefits	1,134,000
Excess of actuarial present value of accumulated plan benefits over net assets available for benefits	
Beginning of year	3,734,000
End of year	$ 4,868,000

The accompanying notes are an integral part of the financial statements.

FIGURE 8-3 (continued)

C&H Company Pension Plan
Statement of Net Assets Available for Benefits
[If a beginning-of-year benefit information date is selected]

	December 31	
	1981	1980
Assets		
Investments, at fair value		
(Notes B(1) and E)		
United States government securities	$ 350,000	$ 270,000
Corporate bonds and debentures	3,500,000	3,670,000
Common stock		
C&H Company	690,000	880,000
Other	2,250,000	1,860,000
Mortgages	480,000	460,000
Real estate	270,000	240,000
	7,540,000	7,380,000
Deposit administration contract,		
at contract value (Notes B(1) and F)	1,000,000	890,000
Total investments	8,540,000	8,270,000
Receivables		
Employees' contributions	40,000	35,000
Securities sold	310,000	175,000
Accrued interest and dividends	77,000	76,000
	427,000	286,000
Cash	200,000	90,000
Total assets	9,167,000	8,646,000
Liabilities		
Accounts payable		
Securities purchased	—	400,000
Other	70,000	60,000
	70,000	460,000
Accrued expenses	85,000	40,000
Total liabilities	155,000	500,000
Net assets available for benefits	$9,012,000	$8,146,000

The accompanying notes are an integral part of the financial statements.

FIGURE 8-3 (continued)

C&H Company Pension Plan
Statement of Changes in Net Assets
Available for Benefits
[If a beginning-of-year benefit information date is selected]

	Year Ended December 31	
	1981	1980
Investment income		
Net appreciation (depreciation) in		
fair value of investments (Note E)	$ 207,000	$ (72,000)
Interest	345,000	320,000
Dividends	130,000	110,000
Rents	55,000	43,000
	737,000	401,000
Less investment expenses	39,000	35,000
	698,000	366,000
Contributions (Note C)		
Employer	780,000	710,000
Employees	450,000	430,000
	1,230,000	1,140,000
Total additions	1,928,000	1,506,000
Benefits paid directly to participants	740,000	561,000
Purchases of annuity contracts (Note F)	257,000	185,000
	997,000	746,000
Administrative expenses	65,000	58,000
Total deductions	1,062,000	804,000
Net increase	866,000	702,000
Net assets available for benefits		
Beginning of year	8,146,000	7,444,000
End of year	$9,012,000	$8,146,000

The accompanying notes are an integral part of the financial statements.

FIGURE 8-3 (continued)

C&H Company Pension Plan
Statement of Accumulated Plan Benefits
[If a beginning-of-year benefit information date is selected]

	December 31 1980
Actuarial present value of accumulated plan benefits (Notes B(2) and C)	
Vested benefits	
Participants currently receiving payments	$ 2,950,000
Other participants	6,530,000
	9,480,000
Nonvested benefits	2,400,000
Total actuarial present value of accumulated plan benefits	$11,880,000

At December 31, 1979, the total actuarial present value of accumulated plan benefits was $10,544,000. During 1980, the actuarial present value of accumulated plan benefits increased $700,000 as a result of a change in actuarial assumptions (Note B(2)). Also see Note G.

The accompanying notes are an integral part of the financial statements.

FIGURE 8-3 (continued)

C&H Company Pension Plan
Notes to Financial Statements*

A. Description of Plan. The following brief description of the C&H Company Pension Plan (*Plan*) is provided for general information purposes only. Participants should refer to the Plan agreement for more complete information.

1 *General.* The Plan is a defined benefit pension plan covering substantially all employees of C&H Company (*Company*). It is subject to the provisions of the Employee Retirement Income Security Act of 1973 (ERISA).

2 *Pension Benefits.* Employees with 10 or more years of service are entitled to annual pension benefits beginning at normal retirement age (65) equal to 1½% of their final 5-year average annual compensation for each year of service. The Plan permits early retirement at ages 55–64. Employees may elect to receive their pension benefits in the form of a joint and survivor annuity. If employees terminate before rendering 10 years of service, they forfeit the right to receive the portion of their accumulated plan benefits attributable to the Company's contributions. Employees may elect to receive the value of their accumulated plan benefits as a lump-sum distribution upon retirement or termination, or they may elect to receive their benefits as a life annuity payable monthly from retirement. For each employee electing a life annuity, payments will not be less than the greater of (a) the employee's accumulated contributions plus interest or (b) an annuity for five years.

3 *Death and Disability Benefits.* If an active employee dies at age 55 or older, a death benefit equal to the value of the employee's accumulated pension benefits is paid to the employee's beneficiary. Active employees who become totally disabled receive annual disability benefits that are equal to the normal retirement benefits they have accumulated as of the time they become disabled. Disability benefits are paid until normal retirement age at which time disabled participants begin receiving normal retirement benefits computed as though they had been employed to normal retirement age with their annual compensation remaining the same as at the time they became disabled.

B. Summary of Accounting Policies. The following are the significant accounting policies followed by the Plan:

1 *Valuation of Investments.* If available, quoted market prices are used to value investments. The amounts shown in Note E for securities that have no quoted market price represent estimated fair value. Many factors are considered in arriving at that fair value. In general, however, corporate bonds are valued based on yields currently available on comparable securities of issuers with similar credit ratings. Investments in certain restricted common stocks are valued at the quoted market price of the issuer's unrestricted common stock less an appropriate discount. If a quoted market price for unrestricted common stock of the issuer is not available, restricted common stocks are valued at a multiple of current earnings less an appropriate discount. The multiple chosen is consistent with multiples of similar companies based on current market prices.

Mortgages have been valued on the basis of their future principal and interest payments discounted at prevailing interest rates for similar instruments. The fair value of real estate investments, principally rental property subject to long-term net leases, has been estimated on the basis of future rental receipts and estimated residual values discounted at interest rates commensurate with the risks involved.

* The notes are for the accompanying illustrative financial statements that use an end-of-year benefit information date. Modifications necessary to accompany the illustrative financial statements that use a beginning-of-year benefit information date are presented in brackets.

FIGURE 8-3 (continued)

The Plan's deposit administration contract with the National Insurance Company (*National*) (Note F) is valued at contract value. Contract value represents contributions made under the contract, plus interest at the contract rate, less funds used to purchase annuities and pay administration expenses charged by National. Funds under the contract that have been allocated and applied to purchase annuities (that is, National is obligated to pay the related pension benefits) are excluded from the Plan's assets.

2 *Actuarial Present Value of Accumulated Plan Benefits.* Accumulated plan benefits are those future periodic payments, including lump-sum distributions, that are attributable under the Plan's provisions to the service employees have rendered. Accumulated plan benefits include benefits expected to be paid to (a) retired or terminated employees or their beneficiaries, (b) beneficiaries of employees who have died, and (c) present employees or their beneficiaries. Benefits under the Plan are based on employees' compensation during their last five years of credited service. The accumulated plan benefits for active employees are based on their average compensation during the five years ending on the date as of which the benefit information is presented (the *valuation date*). Benefits payable under all circumstances—retirement, death, disability, and termination of employment—are included, to the extent they are deemed attributable to employee service rendered to the valuation date. Benefits to be provided via annuity contracts excluded from plan assets are excluded from accumulated plan benefits.

The actuarial present value of accumulated plan benefits is determined by an actuary from the AAA Company and is that amount that results from applying actuarial assumptions to adjust the accumulated plan benefits to reflect the time value of money (through discounts for interest) and the probability of payment (by means of decrements such as for death, disability, withdrawal, or retirement) between the valuation date and the expected date of payment. The significant actuarial assumptions used in the valuations as of December 31, 1981 [1980] and December 31, 1980 [1979] were (a) life expectancy of participants (the 1971 Group Annuity Mortality Table was used), (b) retirement age assumptions (the assumed average retirement age was 60), and (c) investment return. The 1981 [1980] and 1980 [1979] valuations included assumed average rates of return of 7% [6.25%] and 6.25% [6.75%], respectively, including a reduction of .2% to reflect anticipated administrative expenses associated with providing benefits. The foregoing actuarial assumptions are based on the presumption that the Plan will continue. Were the Plan to terminate, different actuarial assumptions and other factors might be applicable in determining the actuarial present value of accumulated plan benefits.

C. Funding Policy. As a condition of participation, employees are required to contribute 3% of their salary to the Plan. Present employees' accumulated contributions at December 31, 1981 [1980] were $2,575,000 [$2,325,000], including interest credited at an interest rate of 5% compounded annually. The Company's funding policy is to make annual contributions to the Plan in amounts that are estimated to remain a constant percentage of employees' compensation each year (approximately 5% for 1981 [and 1980]), such that, when combined with employees' contributions, all employees' benefits will be fully provided for by the time they retire. Beginning in 1982, the Company's contribution is expected to increase to approximately 6% to provide for the increase in benefits attributable to the Plan amendment effective July 1, 1981 (Note G). The Company's contributions for 1981 [and 1980] exceeded the minimum funding requirements of ERISA.

Although it has not expressed any intention to do so, the Company has the right under the Plan to discontinue its contributions at any time and to terminate the Plan subject to the provisions set forth in ERISA.

D. Plan Termination. In the event the Plan terminates, the net assets of the Plan will be allocated, as prescribed by ERISA and its related regulations, generally to provide the following benefits in the order indicated:

FIGURE 8-3 (continued)

(a) Benefits attributable to employee contributions, taking into account those paid out before termination.

(b) Annuity benefits former employees or their beneficiaries have been receiving for at least three years, or that employees eligible to retire for that three-year period would have been receiving if they had retired with benefits in the normal form of annuity under the Plan. The priority amount is limited to the lowest benefit that was payable (or would have been payable) during those three years. The amount is further limited to the lowest benefit that would be payable under plan provisions in effect at any time during the five years preceding plan termination.

(c) Other vested benefits insured by the Pension Benefit Guaranty Corporation (*PBGC*) (a U.S. governmental agency) up to the applicable limitations (discussed below).

(d) All other vested benefits (that is, vested benefits not insured by the PBGC).

(e) All nonvested benefits.

Benefits to be provided via contracts under which National (Note F) is obligated to pay the benefits would be excluded for allocation purposes.

Certain benefits under the Plan are insured by the PBGC if the Plan terminates. Generally, the PBGC guarantees most vested normal age retirement benefits, early retirement benefits, and certain disability and survivor's pensions. However, the PBGC does not guarantee all types of benefits under the Plan, and the amount of benefit protection is subject to certain limitations. Vested benefits under the Plan are guaranteed at the level in effect on the date of the Plan's termination. However, there is a statutory ceiling on the amount of an individual's monthly benefit that the PBGC guarantees. For plan terminations occurring during 1981 and 1980, that ceiling which is adjusted periodically was $X,XXX.XX and $1,159.09 per month, respectively. That ceiling applies to those pensioners who elect to receive their benefits in the form of a single-life annuity and are at least 65 years old at the time of retirement or plan termination (whichever comes later). For younger annuitants or for those who elect to receive their benefits in some form more valuable than a single-life annuity, the corresponding ceilings are actuarially adjusted downward. Benefit improvements attributable to the Plan amendment effective July 1, 1981 (Note G), may not be fully guaranteed even though total benefit entitlements fall below the aforementioned ceilings. For example, none of the improvement would be guaranteed if the plan were to terminate before July 1, 1982. After that date, the PBGC would guarantee 20% of any benefit improvements that resulted in benefits below the ceiling, with an additional 20% guaranteed each year the plan continued beyond July 1, 1982. If the amount of the benefit increase below the ceiling is also less than $100, $20 of the increase (rather than 20%) becomes guaranteed by the PBGC each year following the effective date of the amendment. As a result, only the primary ceiling would be applicable after July 1, 1986.

Whether all participants receive their benefits should the Plan terminate at some future time will depend on the sufficiency, at that time, of the Plan's net assets to provide those benefits and may also depend on the level of benefits guaranteed by the PBGC.

E. Investments Other Than Contract with Insurance Company. Except for its deposit administration contract (Note F), the Plan's investments are held by a bank-administered trust fund. The following table presents the fair values of those investments. Investments that represent 5% or more of the Plan's net assets are separately identified.

FIGURE 8-3 (continued)

	December 31, 1981		December 31, 1980	
	Number of Shares or Principal Amount	Fair Value	Number of Shares or Principal Amount	Fair Value
Investments at Fair Value as Determined by Quoted Market Price				
United States government securities		$ 350,000		$ 270,000
Corporate bonds and debentures				
National Locomotive 6% series C bonds due 1990	$600,000	480,000	$600,000	492,000
General Design Corp. 5½% convertible debentures due 1993	$700,000	520,000	$350,000	250,000
Other		2,260,000		2,618,000
Common stocks				
C&H Company	25,000	690,000	25,000	880,000
Reliable Manufacturing Corp.	12,125	625,000	9,100	390,000
American Automotive, Inc.	5,800	475,000	6,800	510,000
Other		680,000		500,000
		6,080,000		5,910,000
Investments at Estimated Fair Value				
Corporate bonds and debentures		240,000		310,000
Common stocks		470,000		460,000
Mortgages		480,000		460,000
Real estate		270,000		240,000
		1,460,000		1,470,000
		$7,540,000		$7,380,000

FIGURE 8-3 (continued)

During 1981 [and 1980], the Plan's investments (including investments bought, sold, as well as held during the year) appreciated [(depreciated)] in value by $207,000 [and ($72,000), respectively], as follows:

Net Appreciation (Depreciation) in Fair Value

	Year Ended December 31 1981	Year Ended December 31 1980
Investments at Fair Value as Determined by Quoted Market Price		
United States government securities	$ (10,000)	$ 8,000
Corporate bonds and debentures	(125,000)	50,000
Common stocks	228,000	(104,000)
	93,000	(46,000)
Investments at Estimated Fair Value		
Corporate bonds and debentures	(11,000)	9,000
Common stocks	100,000	(49,000)
Mortgages	(5,000)	4,000
Real estate	30,000	10,000
	114,000	(26,000)
	$ 207,000	$ (72,000)

F. Contract with Insurance Company. In 1978, the Company entered into a deposit administration contract with the National Insurance Company under which the Plan deposits a minimum of $100,000 a year. National maintains the contributions in an unallocated fund to which it adds interest at a rate of 8%. The interest rate is guaranteed through 1983 but is subject to change for each succeeding five-year period. When changed, the new rate applies only to funds deposited from the date of change. At the direction of the Plan's administrator, a single premium to buy an annuity for a retiring employee is withdrawn by National from the unallocated fund. Purchased annuities are contracts under which National is obligated to pay benefits to named employees or their beneficiaries. The premium rates for such annuities to be purchased in the future and maximum administration expense charges against the fund are also guaranteed by National on a five-year basis. The annuity contracts provide for periodic dividends at National's discretion on the basis of its experience under the contracts. Such dividends received by the Plan for the year[s] ended December 31, 1981 [and 1980] were $25,000 [and $24,000, respectively]. In reporting changes in net assets, those dividends have been netted against amounts paid to National for the purchase of annuity contracts.

G. Plan Amendment. Effective July 1, 1981, the Plan was amended to increase future annual pension benefits from 1¼% to 1½% of final 5-year average annual compensation for each year of service, including service rendered before the effective date. The retroactive effect of the Plan amendment, an increase in the actuarial present value of accumulated plan benefits of $2,410,000, was accounted for in the year ended December 31, 1981. [The actuarial present values of accumulated plan benefits at December 31, 1980 and December 31, 1979 do not reflect the effect of that Plan amendment. The Plan's actuary estimates that the

FIGURE 8-3 (continued)

amendment's retroactive effect on the actuarial present value of accumulated plan benefits at December 31, 1980 was an increase of approximately $1,750,000, of which approximately $1,300,000 represents an increase in vested benefits.]

H. Accounting Changes. In 1981, the Plan changed its method of accounting and reporting to comply with the provisions of Statement of Financial Accounting Standards No. 35 issued by the Financial Accounting Standards Board. Previously reported financial information pertaining to 1980 [and 1979] has been restated to present that information on a comparable basis.

CHAPTER NINE

Auditing Financial Statements of Pension Plans

INTRODUCTION

Pension plan financial statements were not commonly prepared prior to the ERISA financial reporting requirements as discussed in Chapter 8. Similarly, examinations of pension plan financial statements by independent accountants were not commonly performed prior to the ERISA requirement, generally effective for plan years ending on or after December 31, 1975. As a result, accountants had little practical experience in auditing plan financial statements, and authoritative literature on the subject was virtually nonexistent.

Pension plan audits were complicated by the lack of authoritative pronouncements addressing accounting and financial reporting for pension plans. Accordingly, accounting and reporting practices varied widely. The issuance of FASB Statement No. 35, however, has served to establish consistent accounting practices for defined benefit plans. The accounting and reporting requirements of that statement are discussed in Chapter 8.

ERISA requires that examinations of plan financial statements be conducted in accordance with generally accepted auditing standards (GAAS). In practice, however, differences of opinion existed among auditors regarding the application of GAAS to pension plan audits. Department of Labor (DOL) reporting and disclosure regulations, issued in temporary form in 1976 and in final form in 1978, provided guidance with respect to some of the uncertainties relating to the audit procedures to be applied, but at the same time the regulations created other ambiguities.

For example, the DOL regulations lessened uncertainties regarding procedures required to be applied to investments held by a bank or similar institution or insurance carrier (*institution*), by providing for a limitation on the scope of an auditor's examination with respect to such investments. An auditing interpretation issued in 1977 by the staff of the AICPA's Auditing Standards Division provides guidance with respect to the auditor's report in such circumstances (see "Limited Scope Examination Pursuant to DOL Regulations" in Chapter 10). These DOL regulations, however, did not address audit procedures for investments held by an institution where a standard auditor's report is to be issued, and left many other audit issues unanswered.

The Employee Benefit Plans and ERISA Committee of the AICPA is developing an AICPA audit guide, "Audits of Employee Benefit Plans." An exposure draft of the guide was published in June, 1980. When issued in final form, this audit guide will be the first authoritative pronouncement to thoroughly discuss audits of pension plans. As such, it should resolve many problems and uncertainties relating to the unique aspects of pension plan audits. The audit guide will cover both defined benefit and defined contribution plans and will apply to plans subject to the financial reporting requirements of ERISA as well as those that are not.

This chapter reviews what the authors view as generally accepted auditing standards and indicates how they apply to pension plan audits. The audit standards and procedures discussed in this chapter are consistent with those contained in the exposure draft of the forthcoming AICPA audit guide.

The auditing procedures suggested here are not intended to be complete but are to serve instead as a guide to the unusual features likely to be encountered in examining the financial statements of pension plans. Many of the audit procedures outlined in this chapter (e.g., ascertaining that the terms of the plan comply with the requirements of ERISA, reviewing the actuary's report and employer payroll and other pertinent records) will already have been performed in those instances where the auditor also serves as auditor of the employer company, in which case such steps need not be repeated.

The applicability of auditing procedures discussed herein to specific situations will vary with the circumstances, and thus the procedures to be performed on a particular audit engagement must necessarily be designed to meet the circumstances of that engagement. The results of the auditor's review, testing, and evaluation of the plan's system of internal control will largely determine the nature, extent, and timing of the substantive audit procedures to be performed. Internal control systems for pension plans have some special characteristics, which were discussed in Chapter 8 under "Internal Control."

INDEPENDENCE

Before accepting an engagement, the auditor should consider any relationship he may have with a plan to satisfy himself that he is in compliance with the AICPA's standards regarding independence. The AICPA's independence standards are consistent with the Department of Labor independence guidelines, set forth in Chapter 5. Accordingly, auditors who are independent under the AICPA standards will be independent for purposes of auditing financial statements filed under ERISA's requirements.

The auditor, in accordance with AICPA Ethics Rulings and Department of Labor regulations, may engage in related activities which will not affect the recognition of his independence. For example, the plan auditor may audit and provide other professional services, such as actuarial services, to the employer company or, in the case of a union plan, to the union and one or more of the contributing employer companies. Also, it is appropriate for the auditing firm to provide actuarial services to the plan. In such cases all significant matters of judgment must be determined or approved by client personnel who are in a position to have an informed judgment on the results. The auditor of the plan could not, however, act in a capacity of plan trustee or administrator.

CONTRIBUTIONS

In auditing contributions, consideration must be given to evidence of employers' formal commitments, as well as legal or contractual requirements. Audit procedures needed for considering the correctness of the information the plan uses in determining contributions for the year and contributions receivable depend upon whether the plan is a single-employer plan or a multiemployer plan. Audit procedures that may be applied to single-employer plans include those shown in Figure 9-1.

Multiemployer Plans

Determining contribution amounts in multiemployer plans has a complexity and uncertainty not present with single-employer plans, and thus the auditor may need special procedures to obtain the required degree of confidence in the amount of contributions the plan reports for the year. In testing the reported amount, the auditor should determine that the plan is maintaining adequate records of the contributions of the various employers and of the cumulative benefit credits of the individual plan participants of those employers.

This normally requires a review of the employers' contribution reports which usually accompany each periodic payment under the terms of the plan, for the purpose of checking the total hours worked and dollars earned (or whatever basis is used for determining contributions) and for allocating benefit credits to individual plan participants. If significant participants' data is missing or incomplete, the auditor should inquire about the methods used by the plan administrator to give effect to the missing data.

The auditing procedures to be used might include those shown in Figure 9-2. Note that these procedures are directed at noncontributory plans. Where a multiemployer fund is based on a contributory plan, the auditor should consider, in addition to the procedures shown therein, certain of the procedures provided in the section on single-employer plans (e.g., confirming contributions directly with participants).

Employer Records

The examination of employer records is necessary to enable the auditor to gain assurance of the correctness of contributions reported. This is because, in the case of a defined contribution plan, the employer records are the source of hours worked, pay rates, or other data which form the basis of contribution amounts. Similarly, in a defined benefit plan, employer records also are the source of pertinent data used by the actuary in determining contribution amounts. In both cases the reliability of the information used in the determination of contributions is an audit responsibility.

Thus, the auditor should examine employer records even when a plan administrator omits disclosure of actuarial information in the financial statements and requests the auditor not to perform audit procedures on such information

FIGURE 9-1

Suggested audit procedures for examining contributions received and receivable in financial statements of single-employer pension plans

Contribution Records

(a) Tracing of contributions recorded in the plan's general ledger to the cash receipts book and to deposits shown by bank statements.

(b) Review of amounts received subsequent to the statement date to ascertain whether reported contributions receivable are consistent therewith.

(c) Review of the adequacy of the allowance for doubtful accounts.

Confirmations

(d) Confirmation of contributions recorded as received and receivable by direct correspondence with the employer company or by comparison to employer company records.

(e) In contributory plans, confirmation of employee contributions directly with participants where deemed appropriate, on a sample basis. Exceptions reported in the confirmation replies should be investigated.

Employer Records[1]

(f) Reconciliation of total gross earnings shown by the employees' earnings records with total wages shown by the general ledger and the payroll tax reports.

(g) Comparison of payroll data (e.g., salary, hours worked, hiring date, sex, birth date) for a selected group of employees to the employee earnings records, time records, and personnel files.

(h) Comparison of payroll data with the participants' data furnished to the actuary.

(i) Testing to ascertain the reliability and completeness of the basic data used by the actuary in his calculations (e.g., work force size, hours worked, sex), including tracing key data from the actuary's report if shown therein, or confirming such data with the actuary. This test would normally include a selection of individuals as well as summary totals. If contributions are not based on actuarial determinations, as with most defined contributions plans, test the data (e.g., hours worked) used in the calculation of contributions.

(j) Determine whether contributions received and accrued comply with the applicable provisions of the plan instrument and, where applicable, with the collective-bargaining agreement.

Actuary's Report

(k) For defined benefit plans, review of the actuary's report to determine that the year's reported amount of contributions is consistent therewith.

(l) The guidance contained in the AICPA's Statement on Auditing Standards No. 11, "Using the Work of a Specialist," set forth in Chapter 7 under "Actuarial Information," should be followed when relying on the work of an actuary.

Compliance

(m) Review of the criteria used by the plan in accruing employer company contributions to determine that such criteria have been consistently applied and that contribution amounts comply with generally accepted accounting principles and the provisions of ERISA.

1 For alternative procedures to use when the auditor is unable to examine employer records, see "Alternative Procedures for Employer Records" later in this chapter.

FIGURE 9-2

Suggested audit procedures for examining contributions received and receivable in financial statements of multiemployer pension plans

Contribution Records

(a) Reconciliation of total cash receipts shown by cash receipts book for a selected period to (1) the total amount credited to the general ledger contribution accounts, (2) the total amount posted to the employers' contribution records, and (3) deposits shown by the bank statements.

(b) Testing of amounts transferred to other bank accounts when employer contributions are deposited in a central bank account.

(c) Comparison of selected individual employer contribution payments as shown by the cash receipts book to (1) the amount shown on the employer's contribution reports and (2) the amount posted to the individual employer contribution record, accompanied by the tracing of selected postings from the employer contribution record to the cash receipts book and to the employer's contribution report.

(d) Testing the arithmetical accuracy of a selected number of contribution reports and ascertaining whether the correct contribution rate was used.

(e) Review of employer's contribution reports to test the accuracy of the postings to participants' records, and tracing entries on the participants' records to the contribution reports on a test basis. For defined contribution plans, determine that the contribution allocation to individual accounts conforms with the plan instrument.

(f) Reconciliation of total participant's credits posted to the records for a selected period to the total credits shown by employers' contribution reports.

(g) Determination of the reasonableness of contributions receivable at the statement date by comparing to collections received subsequent to the statement date, with an accompanying test review of the related employers' contribution reports to ascertain that such receipts apply to the year under examination. If the plan's books are held open after the year-end, ascertain that amounts received in the new year that pertain to the year under examination have been properly recorded as accounts receivable.

(h) Employing such tests as may be deemed appropriate in the circumstances to ascertain the nature and amount of any delinquent or unreported contributions.

(i) Review of the adequacy of the allowance for doubtful accounts.

Confirmations

(j) Confirmation of contributions recorded as received and receivable during the period under examination on a test basis, by direct correspondence with selected employers. The extent of confirmation procedures and the type of request (positive or negative) to be used are a matter of judgment. The auditor should select the accounts to be confirmed and control the preparation and mailing of the requests. All exceptions reported in the confirmation replies should be investigated. When positive confirmations have been used and no reply received (to either a first or second request), the auditor should use alternate auditing procedures to provide evidence as to the validity of significant nonresponding accounts.

Employer Records[1]

(k) Audit procedures from (f) through (j) in Figure 9-1.

1 For alternative procedures to use when the auditor is unable to examine employer records, see "Alternative Procedures for Employer Records" later in this chapter.

FIGURE 9-2 (continued)

(l) Comparison of employers' contribution report data for a selected number of participants with the data shown on the employees' earnings records, and tracing of a selected group of employees' earnings records to the employers' contribution reports to ascertain that they have been properly included in or excluded from the reports.

Actuary's Report

(m) For defined benefit plans, review of the actuary's report to determine that the amount of contributions is consistent therewith.

(n) The guidance contained in the AICPA's Statement on Auditing Standards No. 11, "Using the Work of a Specialist," set forth in Chapter 7 under "Actuarial Information," should be followed when relying on the work of an actuary.

Compliance

(o) Review of the criteria used in accruing employer company contributions to determine that such criteria have been consistently applied and that contribution amounts comply with generally accepted accounting principles. For defined benefit plans (other than certain tax-qualified or insured plans), money-purchase plans and target benefit plans, determination that the plan is maintaining the (memorandum) funding standard account(s) and that the contributions required to be made are in accordance with the provisions of ERISA.

(see "Actuarial Information" later in this chapter). The examination of employer records remains necessary even under these circumstances, because the auditor is still responsible for reviewing data used by the actuary in his calculations affecting amounts reflected in the plan financial statements for contributions and contributions receivable.

Alternative Procedures for Employer Records

It is important to note that, in some circumstances, the auditor may be unable to examine employer records, in which case he should attempt to perform appropriate alternative auditing procedures to satisfy himself that the information on which contributions and other actuarially determined amounts are based is reasonable. In the case of a single-employer plan, the auditor should attempt to obtain a report from the employer's auditor stating that the appropriate auditing procedures have been performed.

In the case of a multiemployer plan, the auditor may likewise attempt to obtain reports from the auditors of selected employers stating that appropriate auditing procedures have been performed. Alternatively, if the plan or related union maintains a complete record of participants available for work, the auditor may deem it appropriate to test the data on which contributions and other actuarially determined amounts are based by corresponding directly with participants. Such correspondence, which should call for confirmation by the participant of employer, hours, pay rates, and so on, may be administered by the auditor or by the plan or union under the auditor's control.

Other alternative procedures might be appropriate depending on the particular circumstances. For example, if the plan administrator, as part of normal plan procedures, periodically visits employers to verify data submitted to the plan, the auditor may deem it appropriate to review and test the plan's procedures.

When reports are obtained from the employer's auditor or from the auditors of selected employers, the auditor should, in addition to reviewing such reports, satisfy himself as to the independence and professional reputation of the other auditors and perform such other procedures as he considers appropriate in the circumstances, as described in section 543.04 of the AICPA's Statement on Auditing Standards (SAS) No. 1.

The auditor may sometimes be unable to satisfy himself using the alternative procedures. (See "Scope Limitations" later in this chapter for further discussion of employer records.)

INVESTMENTS

While the audit procedures related to investments will parallel those used for other entities whose principal assets are investments, various adaptations are necessary because of the nature of pension plan operations and the requirements of ERISA.

Trusteed Investments

Physical Accountability

The auditor should perform procedures to satisfy himself that investments reported as held at the statement date actually exist, are the property of the plan, and no liens, pledges, or other security interests exist. The auditor can verify the existence of securities either by inspecting and counting them or by obtaining a confirmation from the custodian. In order to rely on a confirmation, the auditor must be satisfied with the custodian's legal responsibility for assets held in trust, reputation, and financial resources. (See "Custodial Relationships" later in this chapter for further discussion.)

The auditor should inspect deeds, title policies, and leases covering real property. Loan and mortgage instruments should be examined, and the balances and terms should be confirmed, with appropriate consideration of collectibility.

Fair Value

Investments other than contracts with insurance companies are generally stated at fair value in pension plan financial statements. FASB Statement No. 35, as well as ERISA (which calls for application of generally accepted accounting principles for defined benefit plans covered by Statement No. 35) and the DOL regulations governing the alternative method of compliance, all prescribe fair value accounting for investments. However, defined contribution plans reporting financial information under ERISA and (until Statement No. 35 became effective) defined benefit plans filing under ERISA may state investments at cost.[1]

For a plan with investments stated at fair value the auditor should substantiate the fair value of investments and test the computation of the net change in their fair value.

Determining the fair value of publicly traded securities as of the statement date presents little difficulty because trading prices are usually published. Substantiating the reported fair value of investments without a readily determinable value, however, can present some difficulties. The most common such investments are real estate, investments in closely held corporations, and investments with restricted marketability (e.g., unregistered securities).

The fair value of investments for which market quotations cannot be readily obtained should be determined by the plan's administrative committee for single-employer plans or board of trustees for multiemployer plans. The auditor must remember that he does not function as an appraiser and is not expected to substitute his judgment for that of management; he should only ascertain whether the procedures followed and results obtained by management appear to be reasonable and adequate. He is justified in expecting that the plan's administrative committee or board of trustees will have developed a body of information and documentation as the basis for their judgment of fair value and in expecting that information and documentation to be available for his consideration.

For considering securities valuations, see Figure 8-1 in Chapter 8. The auditor may also find it useful to refer to Accounting Series Releases No. 113 and 118 of the Securities and Exchange Commission.

The auditor should review and test the various reports, analyses, computations, appraisals, and other material used in determining the fair value as of the statement date. Written representations from specialists qualified in the area of the particular assets under consideration may be used as the basis for considering the reasonableness of values reported by the plan. When using a specialist, the auditor should apply the procedures contained in the AICPA's Statement on Auditing Standards No. 11, "Using the Work of a Specialist." These procedures are set forth in Chapter 7 under "Actuarial Information."

When the auditor is unable to satisfy himself as to the reasonableness of the amounts at which a significant amount of investments without a readily determinable value are stated, appropriate qualification of the auditor's opinion should normally be made. In such instances, the "subject to" form of qualified opinion has generally been rendered when the auditor is satisfied that the procedures followed and the information obtained by the plan with respect to the valuation of such investments are adequate to enable the plan to value the se-

[1] See footnote 1 in Chapter 8.

curities.[2] Recently, however, some auditors have advocated an "except for" type of report when unable to gain satisfaction as to the reasonableness of stated amounts of investments. The reasoning put forth is that if the auditor's procedures are not sufficient to gain satisfaction as to the reasonableness of the amounts, a scope limitation exists. The Auditing Standards Board is considering this matter. Until it is fully resolved, most auditors will likely follow the traditional approach of using the "subject to" language.

The draft audit guide states that if the auditor determines that the plan's valuation procedures are inadequate or unreasonable, or if the underlying documentation does not appear to support the valuation, the auditor should appropriately qualify his opinion, with an "except for" introduction, with respect to the securities carried at fair value.[3] The exception would relate to lack of conformity with generally accepted accounting principles.

Where circumstances warrant, an adverse opinion or possibly a disclaimer of opinion may be appropriate. See AICPA Statement on Auditing Standards (SAS) No. 2 for further discussion.

Cost

As previously indicated, most plans will state investments other than contracts with insurance companies at fair value. However, where investments are stated at cost, the auditor should substantiate the cost of investments and the amount of realized gains and losses by comparing reported cost as reflected in investment records (tested in prior or current year's examination) to cash records and by examining brokers' advices and other relevant documents, such as notes, mortgages, and closing statements. Also, the auditor may want to determine the fair value of investments stated at cost to determine if that value is less than cost. Where marketable securities are carried at cost and market value is substantially lower than cost, the auditor should consider the implications of the AICPA's auditing interpretation on "Evidential matter for the carrying amount of marketable securities" in determining whether such investments should be written down to their market values and/or other disclosures made in the financial statements and in selecting the type of opinion to be expressed.

Investment Restrictions and Limitations

The auditor should test whether the plan's investments violate any restrictions or limitations on types of investments imposed by the plan instrument or plan policy. In addition, the auditor should inquire whether the plan's investments violate applicable laws or regulations. Where approval of investment transactions by the board of trustees or administrative committee is required, the auditor should examine evidence of approvals.

---

[2] Where the range of possible values of such securities would not have a significant effect on the fairness of presentation of the financial statements, the auditor normally has expressed an unqualified opinion.

[3] An example of the "except for" form of opinion is provided under "Departures from the Standard Report" in Chapter 10.

Income

The auditor should test amounts of interest and dividend income received and receivable by computation, reference to appropriate published sources, or review of cash receipts and related documentation. Such procedures should include tests for unrecorded amounts.

Custodial Relationships

Trust arrangements range from directed trusts to discretionary trusts. In a directed trust the trustee acts as custodian of the plan's investments and is responsible for collecting the investment income while the plan directs the trustee as to investment transactions. With such a trust, the plan usually maintains the investment records together with the supporting evidential matter. Accordingly, the auditor may perform his normal auditing procedures.

In a discretionary trust the trustee has discretionary authority over investment decisions. With discretionary trusts, generally the trustee issues periodic reports to the plan but retains the related documentation supporting those transactions. Although the plan may have internal accounting controls over the accuracy of such reports and/or maintain its own records of the transactions, the plan's lack of supporting evidential matter, such as brokers' advices, will normally require the auditor to alter his normal procedures.

Many auditors believe an acceptable procedure in auditing discretionary trusts is to obtain a report (often referred to as a "single-auditor" report) from the independent auditor of the bank's trust department stating that he has performed a review of pertinent internal controls of the trust department's accounting system. Ordinarily, the plan auditor would not review the trust department auditor's single-audit working papers, but would satisfy himself as to the independence and professional reputation of the trust department auditor in accordance with Section 543.10 of SAS No. 1, "Part of Examination Made by Other Independent Auditors." The single-auditor report allows the auditor to place reliance on the trust department's reports of plan transactions, and is considered an acceptable approach under the audit guide.

Some auditors believe that a report on internal control might not provide the plan auditor with sufficient assurance of the reliability of the periodic reports of the plan's transactions as prepared by the trust department. They maintain that reports of the trust department's independent auditor should state that substantive tests, including examination of brokers' advices, were performed with respect to the particular plan's transactions. If unable to obtain such a report, those plan auditors would make appropriate examination of pertinent books and records at the bank. As previously indicated, these additional testing procedures are not considered necessary by the audit guide where a single-auditor report is available.

The audit guide specifies that, where a single-auditor report cannot be obtained, the plan auditor, in order to express an unqualified opinion on the plan's financial statements, would need to visit the bank to make a study and evaluation of the relevant internal accounting controls of the bank's trust department. But even if the plan auditor were to use the work of the bank's independent auditor or internal auditor, it would normally not be practical for the plan auditor to make a study and evaluation of the bank trust department's internal control system. Accordingly, under the guide, where the plan auditor is unable to obtain a single-auditor report on the trust department's system of internal controls, a scope limitation would normally result (see "Scope Limitations" later in this chapter for a further discussion).

It should be noted that a number of auditors follow the practice of obtaining a confirmation from the bank, not a single-auditor report, and of issuing an unqualified opinion on the plan's financial statements. This practice, when coupled with other normal audit procedures, including testing the plan's internal procedures for testing the accuracy of the trust department's reports of plan transactions, would be considered acceptable until the audit guide is issued in final form.

In a number of situations, securities are held by a third-party depository for the account of a plan's custodian. A procedure which has sometimes been followed in such cases is for the plan's auditor to:

> obtain a report issued by the depository's independent auditor indicating that he has counted the securities held by the depository and has confirmed such counts with the depository's clients, for example, the custodian; and
>
> obtain a report from the custodian's independent auditor indicating that he has confirmed with the depository security holdings as shown on the custodian's records and performed appropriate tests of the custodian's records, and that such records indicate the securities listed in an attached schedule are being held at the depository for the account of the plan. When the securities listing is as of a date differing from the plan's fiscal year-end, the report of the custodian's auditor would indicate that he has reviewed the system of internal control and/or performed the stated audit procedures at various times throughout the year. This would enable the plan auditor to rely on such a report in reconciling to the plan's year-end balances.

Generally, however, in such situations the plan's auditor will attempt to obtain, directly from the custodian, a confirmation which lists the securities and indicates that although they are in the physical possession of a depository, the custodian is nevertheless financially and legally responsible for such securities. To rely on such a confirmation, the auditor would usually want to be satisfied with the reputation and financial resources of the custodian.

Commingled Funds

A plan may use a bank common or commingled trust fund (commingled funds) to invest some or all of a plan's assets.[4] Where a plan holds investments in such funds, the auditor normally should apply the following procedures:

verify, by physical examination or confirmation with the trustee, the number of units of participation in the fund held by the plan;

examine supporting documents for selected plan transactions in units of participation; and

review the financial statements of the commingled fund and relate the per unit information reported therein to amounts reported by the plan, including fair value, purchase and redemption values, and income amounts; if the fund's financial statements have been examined by an independent accountant, the plan auditor should obtain a copy of the report of the fund auditor; the plan auditor should be satisfied as to the independence and professional reputation of the auditor of the commingled fund in accordance with Section 543.10 of SAS No. 1; if the financial statements of the commingled fund are not examined by an independent accountant, the plan auditor should obtain a copy of a single-auditor report relating to the commingled fund's activities and internal accounting controls, if available, or apply appropriate audit procedures at the bank, including a study and evaluation of the internal accounting controls relating to the income amounts and unit values of the commingled fund; where the plan auditor is unable to apply these procedures, a scope limitation will result (see "Scope Limitations" later in this chapter for a further discussion).

Master Trusts

A company or a group of companies under common control sponsoring more than one pension plan may use a master trust to invest assets relating to some or all of the plans.[5] Where the same auditor examines the individual plans whose assets are in a master trust, it will normally be more efficient for the auditor first to apply auditing procedures to the master trust, and then to examine how ownership is attributed to the individual plans.[6] The auditor should review the trust agreement to satisfy himself that the accounting for the individual plan's interests is consistent with the allocation method set forth in the agreement. Where the accounting is not specified in the agreement, the auditor

---

[4] For a discussion of the features of commingled funds and master trusts, see "Commingled and Master Trust Funds" in Chapter 8.

[5] See footnote 4.

[6] Where the master trust is audited by another independent accountant, the plan auditor should obtain the financial statements of the trust and the auditor's report thereon. Procedures for reviewing the financial statements and relying on the other auditor's report, consistent with those for commingled funds set forth in the previous section of this chapter, should be applied.

should determine that all administrators of the plans participating in the master trust agree with the method of allocation.

Contracts with Insurance Companies

A plan may invest some or all of the plan's assets with an insurance company pursuant to any one of several types of contracts. The monies invested may be held in separate accounts by the insurance company or commingled with the insurance company's general assets (often referred to as *general accounts*). Separate accounts generally pool the funds of several plans (*pooled separate accounts*) although they may be established separately for one plan (*individual separate accounts*).[7]

As indicated in Chapter 8, contracts with insurance companies can generally be classified dependent on whether the related payment to the insurance company is currently allocated to purchase immediate or deferred annuity contracts for individual participants (allocated contracts) or the payment is accumulated in an unallocated fund (unallocated contracts) used to directly meet benefit payments when they become due or to purchase annuities for individual participants upon retirement (or upon earlier termination of service where the participant's benefits are partially or fully vested). Deposit administration group annuity contracts (DA) and immediate participation guarantee contracts (IPG) are examples of unallocated contracts.

Contributions under DA contracts or under IPG contracts are deposited with the insurance company and credited to an unallocated account. When an employee retires, the amount required to purchase an immediate annuity to provide for the retiree's pension is charged to the account. Under one form of IPG contract, pension payments are made directly from the account. DA contracts provide interest on the account at a guaranteed rate, and dividends or rate credits (generally net of contract expenses) are determined solely at the discretion of the insurance company. IPG contracts provide interest based on the insurance company's actual investment income, so that there is an "immediate participation" in the insurance company's investment performance. Expenses under an IPG contract are charged directly to the account. A more complete description of these contracts is included in Chapter 3.

As indicated in Chapter 8, in accordance with generally accepted accounting principles and with ERISA reporting and disclosure requirements, allocated insurance contracts legally guaranteeing the amount of benefit payments should be excluded from plan assets, and unallocated contracts should be included in plan assets. Accordingly, the auditor will need to carefully review insurance contracts to determine if they should be reported as assets in plan financial statements.[8]

[7] For a description of the features of pooled separate accounts, see "Commingled and Master Trust Funds" in Chapter 8.

[8] Plans providing benefits *exclusively* through allocated insurance contracts are exempt from the ERISA requirement to prepare financial statements and to have the statements examined by an independent accountant (see Chapter 5).

FIGURE 9-3

Suggested information for confirmation with insurance companies which hold pension plan assets

(a) The contract value of the funds in the general account or the fair value of the funds in the separate account at the plan's year-end and the basis for determining such values.

(b) Contributions (premium payments) made during the year, including the dates received by the insurance company.

(c) Interest and dividends, and changes in their value, and whether such amounts have been earned or credited during the year on an estimated or actual basis.

(d) Refunds and credits paid or payable by insurance company during year due to termination of plan members.

(e) Dividend or rate credit given by insurance company.

(f) Annuities purchased and/or benefits paid or payable during the year from unallocated insurance contracts.

(g) Amount of asset management fees, commissions, sales fees, premium taxes, and other expenses (sometimes collectively referred to as "retention") charged or chargeable by insurance company during the year.

(h) Amounts of transfers between various funds and accounts.

(i) Special conditions applicable upon termination of contract.

For contracts includable in the plan's financial statements, audit procedures are needed to establish the existence of the assets, substantiate their reported value, determine whether the terms of the contract are being complied with, and ascertain that the changes in such assets during the period are fairly presented. The auditor should, of course, read the contract between the plan and the insurance company, and should correspond directly with the insurance company to confirm information such as that summarized in Figure 9-3. Additional procedures depend on the type of contract, as discussed in the following sections.

Separate Accounts

An individual separate account is operated similar to a bank discretionary trust fund. Such accounts are sometimes audited by independent accountants, in which case the plan auditor may review the other auditor's report. Otherwise, the audit procedures are similar to those for discretionary trust funds discussed earlier in this chapter. They include obtaining a copy of a "single-auditor" report relating to the insurance company's separate account internal accounting controls or applying appropriate auditing procedures at the insurance company.

Pooled separate accounts are similar to bank commingled funds and the additional audit procedures are similar to those discussed previously in this chapter under "Commingled Funds." Those procedures include auditing the balance of and transactions in the plan's units of participation in the pooled account, and obtaining the report of an independent accountant on the financial statements of the pooled separate account, obtaining a copy of a single-

FIGURE 9-4
Some representative procedures for auditing benefit payments

(a)   Review, on a test basis, the approved applications for benefits and ascertain that the current benefit amounts have been properly approved.

(b)   Check, on a test basis, employees' eligibility for the payment of benefits and the continuation of benefits.

(c)   Check, on a test basis, the benefit payment calculation, and ascertain whether a responsible individual has reviewed the calculation independently.

(d)   Compare data (including endorsements) on paid benefit checks with payment records, and ascertain that long outstanding checks are investigated.

(e)   On a test basis, examine canceled checks for, or confirm by direct correspondence with selected participants or beneficiaries, benefits recorded as paid during the period under review. Compare signatures with the application for plan benefits or with other appropriate plan documents.

(f)   Ascertain that payments made to participants or beneficiaries over an unusually long number of years are still appropriate.

(g)   For defined contribution plans, trace the amount paid to the individual participants' account records.

auditor report relating to the separate account's internal accounting controls, or applying appropriate auditing procedures at the insurance company.

Where the plan auditor is unable to apply these procedures, a scope limitation will result (see the "Scope Limitations" section of this chapter for a further discussion).

Deposit Administration Group Annuity Contracts and Immediate Participation Guarantee Contracts

The following auditing procedures, in addition to those previously set forth for contracts with insurance companies in general, should be applied where plan assets are invested pursuant to a DA or IPG contract.

For DA contracts, evaluate the reasonableness of the interest credited to the contract in relation to the guaranteed rate stipulated in the contract.

For IPG contracts, consider the plan administrator's conclusion regarding the reasonableness of the investment income credited to the contract. Reference should be made to insurance yield data furnished by the insurance company to the plan. Generally, this evaluation would sufficiently satisfy the auditor as to the aggregate investment yield. If, however, the amount credited does not appear to be reasonable, the auditor should apply additional procedures, such as inquiring of the insurance company regarding its compliance with the method of computing investment yield under the terms of the contract. If still not satisfied with the reasonableness of the investment return credited to the plan, the auditor should consider requesting the plan administrator to contact the insurance company to arrange for the insurer's independent auditor to perform agreed-upon procedures and issue a report thereon. Those procedures would be applied to the insurer's determination of investment return in accordance with the terms of the contract.

Determine that benefit payments were made to eligible beneficiaries and in the correct amounts when the benefits are paid directly from the fund. The auditor should consider applying the representative procedures for auditing benefit payments set forth in Figure 9-4. Where annuities are purchased for employees upon retirement, determine that the purchases were made based on rates stipulated in the contract and on benefit levels set forth in the plan document.

Determine whether expenses charged to the fund are in accordance with the insurance contract or otherwise authorized by the plan.

Read the insurance company's financial statements.

BENEFIT PAYMENTS

Audit procedures related to benefit payments are aimed at determining that recipients of payments were eligible beneficiaries, that payments were made in the correct amounts, and that persons no longer eligible for benefit payments are being removed from the benefit rolls. Some representative procedures the auditor may wish to use are shown in Figure 9-4.

ADMINISTRATIVE EXPENSES

In reviewing a pension plan's administrative expenses, the auditor should ascertain whether they were authorized and supported by appropriate documentation and whether amounts were properly classified in the financial statements. For this purpose the auditor may review the terms of the plan agreement and minutes of the meetings of the board of trustees or administrative committee to determine whether administrative expenses were properly authorized, and he may examine contracts, invoices, and other supporting documentation.

Where the plan uses a contract administrator, the propriety and reasonableness of the payments should be evaluated by testing the basis of the contract payment.

Where one office functions as a service organization for several plans, the auditor should review how the organization allocates administrative expenses not directly associated with a specific plan, in order to ascertain that the allocation is based on an equitable method. He should also determine that the method selected was approved by the board of trustees.

SUBSEQUENT EVENTS

The plan auditor should consider events subsequent to the date of the financial statements through the date of the auditor's report to determine whether adjustment of or disclosure in the financial statements is required. Auditing procedures to be used might include, but are not necessarily limited to, those shown in Figure 9-5. These have been excerpted from a draft of the forthcoming AICPA audit guide.

Since investments normally represent the major portion of a pension plan's assets, the auditor should be alert for material changes in the market value of securities subsequent to the statement date, particularly where his opinion is dated near the end of the filing period permitted by ERISA. This does not mean that the auditor should verify a recent portfolio valuation, but rather that he should be alert for major declines in securities markets having a very significant effect on the plan's asset values.

Where the auditor becomes aware of any such material changes, he should consider whether there is adequate disclosure in the financial statements (see Sections 560.05 and 560.07 of SAS No.1). Such disclosure, if deemed appropriate, should normally refer to the portfolio as a whole. There may be exceptions, however, as in the case of a material change in the market value in a substantial holding of the employer company's stock, where disclosure relating only to that stock might be made. Such disclosure might be as follows:

> The market value of the Able Corporation common stock has declined from $11.25 per share at June 30, 1980 to $7.875 per share at January 16, 1981. Based upon the 31,-128 shares held at June 30, 1980, this represents an aggregate decrease in market value from $350,190 to $245,133. The market value at January 16, 1981 of the other common stocks held at June 30, 1980 was approximately the same as the market value at June 30, 1980.

FIGURE 9-5
Suggested audit procedures for reviewing subsequent events

(a) Review minutes of board of trustees or administrative committee meetings held through the completion of field work.

(b) If available, obtain interim financial statements of the plan for a period subsequent to the audit date and compare with the financial statements being examined and investigate any unusual fluctuations.

(c) Discuss and inquire of the plan administrator concerning:

abnormal disposal or purchase of investments since year-end;

amendments to plan and trust instruments, and insurance contracts;

any matters involving unusual terminations of participants, such as terminations arising from a sale of a division or layoffs;

changes in commitments or contingent liabilities of the plan.

(d) If there is a significant period of time between the date of the response of the plan's legal counsel and the date of completion of field work, the auditor should obtain supplemental legal representations.

ACTUARIAL INFORMATION

As indicated in Chapter 8, defined benefit pension plans are required to disclose the actuarial present value of accumulated plan benefits segmented into the following categories:

vested benefits of participants currently receiving payments;

other vested benefits; and

nonvested benefits.[9]

While disclosure of the actuarial present value of accumulated plan benefits would not be relevant to defined contribution plans, such plans may disclose the present value of vested benefits. Such amounts, however, generally would not involve actuarial calculations.

In considering the reasonableness of the actuarially determined information, the auditor should follow the procedures discussed under "Suggested Audit Procedures" in Chapter 7. In addition, the plan auditor should determine that the actuary has reviewed the relevant portions of the plan financial statements and agrees with the reference to his work in the financial statements.

If the plan administrator omits disclosure of actuarial information in the financial statements he would create a departure from generally accepted accounting principles, and would preclude the expression of an unqualified opinion.

SCOPE LIMITATIONS

The scope of the auditor's examination may be affected by conditions that preclude the application of one or more auditing procedures that the auditor considers necessary in the circumstances. Such scope limitations, whether imposed by the plan administrator or by circumstances beyond his control, will preclude the auditor from expressing an unqualified opinion on the financial statements.

Guidance on the auditor's opinion to be expressed where a scope limitation exists is provided by SAS No. 2. Where the scope limitation restricts an important aspect of the audit procedures to be performed (e.g., examination of employer records or obtaining a required single-auditor report) and appropriate alternative procedures cannot be performed, it may be necessary for the auditor to disclaim an opinion. In the less pervasive circumstances, however, a qualified opinion may be appropriate. Guidance and illustrative auditor's re-

---

[9] Such disclosures would be made only to the extent that assets related to the actuarial benefits are included in the financial statements. Thus, in the case of plans where benefits are legally guaranteed by an insurance company and the related assets are not reflected in the plan's financial statements, the actuarial present value of accumulated plan benefits should not reflect such insured benefits.

ports for certain types of scope limitations are set forth in Chapter 10 under "Departures from the Standard Report."

If the auditor's report on plan financial statements is to be included in annual reports filed under ERISA and a scope limitation exists that will preclude the auditor from expressing an unqualified opinion, the auditor may wish to advise the plan administrator that although such action is not anticipated, the Secretary of Labor has the right to reject any annual report containing a qualified opinion.

AUDIT REQUIREMENTS DUE TO ERISA

Some features of ERISA require the modification of audit procedures, or the development of additional procedures, to allow for matters which could have significant effects on the financial statements.

Principal areas where this will be required, other than those discussed earlier in this chapter, are plan compliance with ERISA, transactions prohibited by ERISA, and reporting and disclosure requirements of ERISA.

Plan Compliance with ERISA

Although penalties for failure to comply with requirements of ERISA are generally not likely to affect the pension plan directly (as discussed in Chapter 4), the auditor should normally be satisfied that the participation, vesting, joint and survivorship coverage, and certain other plan provisions comply with ERISA's requirements for two reasons:

1 With respect to a qualified pension plan, failure to comply with ERISA's requirements could result in disqualification of the plan and loss of tax-exempt status of the plan. In such an event it would be necessary to provide for income taxes with respect to investment income (including net realized gains) of the plan.
2 With respect to either a qualified or nonqualified plan, failure to meet ERISA's requirements could result in misstatement of contributions receivable and, for defined benefit plans, misstatement of the actuarial present value of accumulated plan benefits.

The procedures to be followed by the auditor to determine that the terms of the plan comply with pertinent requirements of ERISA should normally parallel those discussed under "Compliance of Individual Plan Provisions with ERISA" in Chapter 7. Where the auditor of the plan also audits the financial statements of the employer, he need not duplicate his efforts. Where the plan's auditor does not audit the employer, an alternative procedure to those mentioned in Chapter 7 would be to obtain a report from the employer's independent auditor indicating the procedures he followed and his findings with respect to plan compliance with ERISA. Such a report can be relied upon only where the plan's auditor satisfies himself as to the independence and professional reputation of the employer's auditor and performs such procedures as he considers appropriate, as described in Section 543.04 of SAS No. 1. As indicated in connection with these procedures in Chapter 7, by now the provisions of most plans have been amended to comply with the requirements of ERISA and the related appropriate auditing procedures have been applied in prior years. Where there have been no subsequent amendments, minimal work related to plan compliance would be required in subsequent years.

Transactions Prohibited by ERISA

Transactions prohibited by ERISA could give rise to significant receivables because a plan fiduciary is liable to make good any losses to the plan resulting from a breach of fiduciary duties and to restore to the plan any profits which he made through the use of the plan's assets. Accordingly, the auditor should apply procedures to ascertain whether there has been a breach of fiduciary duties as listed in Figure 4-1 or whether prohibited transactions such as those listed in Figure 4-2 have occurred and, if so, whether a receivable and/or other disclosure should be reflected in the financial statements.[10]

Such procedures might include:

1 inquiring whether any activities or transactions which might be prohibited have occurred;
2 obtaining from the plan administrator a list of all parties in interest (to use as a reference point during the course of the auditor's examination), reviewing the administrator's procedures for identifying parties in interest, and examining related documentation to determine whether the list appears to be complete; and
3 ascertaining whether any prohibited transactions have been disclosed as a result of past Internal Revenue Service or other governmental examinations.

Because the auditor should, as a result of his regular audit work, be familiar with significant transactions which might be prohibited, it is anticipated that few, if any, additional procedures will be deemed necessary in most instances.

Reporting and Disclosure Requirements of ERISA

As part of his examination, the auditor should determine whether the financial statements and supplemental schedules have been prepared in conformity with

[10] Individual and class exemptions from certain of these prohibited transaction rules have been granted in accordance with ERISA regulations. These exemptions are not discussed in Chapter 4.

ERISA and the related DOL reporting and disclosure regulations (see "Accountants" in Chapter 5). He normally need not be unduly concerned, however, as to whether the other reporting and disclosure requirements of ERISA (see the relevant items in Table 5-1[11]) have been complied with, because any penalties imposed for noncompliance are not likely to have an impact on the plan (see the discussion under "Enforcement" in Chapter 4). The auditor should nonetheless be alert to instances of noncompliance with respect to such items so as to be in a position to advise his client of a need to consider taking corrective action.

Supplemental Schedules

The auditor's normal audit procedures should be sufficient to permit him to report on most of the information included in the supplemental schedules. To satisfy himself as to the completeness and correctness of the information in certain of the schedules, however (such as the schedule of 3% reportable transactions), the auditor may have to perform some additional procedures.

It is important to note that the schedule of party-in-interest transactions need not include any transactions exempted from prohibited transaction rules. Thus, only prohibited transactions need to be reported on that schedule, the related auditing procedures for which are described above. However, the footnotes to the financial statements should nonetheless include a description of agreements and transactions with parties in interest. SAS No. 6, "Related Party Transactions," and, more recently, SFAS No. 52, "Related Party Disclosures," offer useful guidance in this regard, but note that the definition of parties in interest is somewhat broader than the definition of related parties.

Another schedule (or additional statement) which might require additional audit consideration is that relating to plan assets held by banks, insurance carriers, and so on, which are not regulated, supervised, or subject to periodic examination by a state or federal agency. Since virtually all banks and insurance carriers are regulated, supervised, and subject to periodic examination by a state or federal agency, however, the need for additional audit procedures with respect to plan assets held by such organizations should be rare.

OTHER AUDIT CONSIDERATIONS

Bonding

The auditor should determine whether the fund maintains at least the required minimum amount of fidelity insurance in accordance with provisions of ERISA.

---

[11] Reviewing the actuarial statement (described in Table 5-1) is of course important for audit purposes, as discussed in other sections, but determining the statement's compliance with ERISA is not a matter of specific concern because any penalties arising from noncompliance are not likely to have an impact on the plan.

Taxes and Other Reports

The auditor should review tax returns and other reports filed pursuant to government regulations, and should ascertain whether a tax ruling or determination letter has been obtained.

Transaction Approval

The auditor should acquaint himself with the collective-bargaining agreement, the declaration of trust, the insurance contract, and other plan documents, and be alert to any transactions that require the approval of the board of trustees (multiemployer plan) or administrative committee (single-employer plan).

Potential Plan Termination

The auditor should be alert to any evidence of a potential pension plan termination when reading minutes of meetings of the board of trustees and administrative committee and when performing other audit procedures. In addition, the auditor may wish to inquire of the employer's management as to the possibility of a plan termination. Where a plan termination is more than a remote possibility, the auditor should ensure that the situation is appropriately reflected or disclosed in the financial statements.

Letter of Representation

Immediately prior to the completion of the field work, it is desirable that the auditor obtain a letter of representation, signed by the appropriate official(s) and worded to fit the individual circumstances of the engagement. The letter should normally include, in addition to those representations obtained in accordance with SAS No. 19, "Client Representations," representations related to compliance with ERISA, any potential plan termination, changes in plan provisions, party-in-interest transactions, value of investments including those stated at fair value as determined by the board of trustees or administrative committee, and other pertinent matters. The management representation letter should be signed by officials of the plan, generally the plan administrator and the individual equivalent to the chief financial officer. If the sponsoring employer company is the plan administrator, one or more company officials responsible for administration of and accounting for the plan should sign the letter. The plan auditor should generally not request bank officials to sign the letter. Where in the auditor's judgment an affirmative statement from a trustee bank regarding certain of the items covered in the letter of representation is necessary, the auditor should have the plan administrator request that the bank provide the auditor with the appropriate statement. The request, however, should be limited to the required information and not include the letter of representation in its entirety.

An illustrative letter of representation is presented in Figure 9-6 for use as a guide and should be modified to meet the needs of a particular engagement.

FIGURE 9-6

Illustrative letter of representation

(Date of auditor's report)

(Name and Address of Auditors)

Gentlemen:

In connection with your examination of the financial statements of (name of plan) as of (date) and for the (period of examination) for the purpose of expressing an opinion as to whether such financial statements present fairly the financial position and results of operations of (name of plan) in conformity with generally accepted accounting principles (other comprehensive basis of accounting), we confirm, to the best of our knowledge and belief, the following representations made to you during your examination. (The plan may specify the materiality limits agreed upon as follows: Certain representations in this letter are described as being limited to those matters which may have a "material" effect on the financial statements. As used herein, the term *material* means any item or similar group of items involving potential amounts of more than $_____ [or_____ % of assets, liabilities, net assets available for plan benefits, or net additions].)

1 We are responsible for the fair presentation in the financial statements of financial position and results of operations in conformity with generally accepted accounting principles or other comprehensive basis of accounting.
2 We have made available to you all:
   (a) financial records and related data;
   (b) minutes of the meetings of the board of trustees (or administrative committee), or summaries of actions of recent meetings for which minutes have not yet been prepared.
3 There have been no:
   (a) irregularities involving management or employees who have significant roles in the system of internal accounting control;
   (b) irregularities involving other employees that could have a material effect on the financial statements; (We understand the term *irregularities* to mean those' matters described in Statement on Auditing Standards No. 16, a copy of which you have furnished to us.)
   (c) communications from regulatory agencies concerning noncompliance with or deficiencies in financial reporting practices or other matters that could have a material effect on the financial statements.
4 We have no plans or intentions that may materially affect the carrying value or classification of assets and liabilities.
5 The following have been properly recorded or disclosed in the financial statements and/or supplemental schedules:
   (a) transactions with parties in interest, as defined in ERISA Section 3 (14) and regulations thereunder, including related party transactions (and related amounts receivable or payable, sales, purchases, loans, transfers, leasing arrangements, and guarantees) as described in Statement of Financial Accounting Standards No. 57, a copy of which you have furnished to us;
   (b) investments in default or considered to be uncollectible;
   (c) reportable transactions (as defined in ERISA Section 103(b)(3)(H) and regulations thereunder);
   (d) arrangements with financial institutions involving compensating balances or other arrangements involving restrictions on cash balances or similar arrangements;
   (e) agreements to repurchase assets previously sold;
   (f) amounts representing the obligation for pension benefits (actuarial present value of accumulated plan benefits);

FIGURE 9-6 (continued)

(g) changes made in the actuarial assumptions or methods between (prior actuarial valuation date), (current actuarial valuation date), and (statement date);

(h) changes made in plan provisions between the actuarial valuation date and the date of this letter.

6 There are no:

(a) violations or possible violations of laws or regulations whose effects should be considered for disclosure in the financial statements or as a basis for recording a loss contingency.

(b) other material liabilities or gain or loss contingencies that are required to be accrued or disclosed by Statement of Financial Accounting Standards No. 5. (We understand the term *contingencies* to mean those matters described in Statement of Financial Accounting Standards No. 5, a copy of which you have furnished to us.)

7 There are no unasserted claims or assessments that our lawyer has advised us are probable of assertion and must be disclosed in accordance with Statement of Financial Accounting Standards No. 5.

8 There are no material transactions that have not been properly recorded in the accounting records underlying the financial statements.

9 The plan has satisfactory title to all owned assets, and there are no liens or encumbrances on such assets nor has any asset been pledged.

10 Provision has been made for any material loss to be sustained in the fulfillment of, or from inability to fulfill, any investment-related or other purchase or sales commitments.

11 We have complied with all aspects of contractual agreements that would have a material effect on the financial statements in the event of noncompliance.

12 We intend to finance on a long-term basis short-term notes payable amounting to $_____ with borrowings available under the financing agreement dated _____.

13 There were no omissions from the employee data provided the plan's actuarial consultants for the purpose of determining the actuarial present value of accumulated plan benefits, and other amounts reflected in the financial statements.

14 The plan administrator agrees with the actuarial cost method and assumptions used by the actuary for funding purposes and for determining accumulated plan benefits and has no knowledge or belief that would make such methods or assumptions inappropriate under the circumstances.

15 The plan is a qualified trust under Section 401(a) of the Internal Revenue Code, and intends to continue as a qualified trust.

16 The plan has complied with the provisions of the Employee Retirement Income Security Act of 1974 (ERISA) and the regulations thereunder, except as follows:
(We understand this listing to include all instances of noncompliance, including breaches of fiduciary duties and engaging in prohibited transactions as defined in ERISA Sections 404 and 406, respectively, and regulations thereunder.)

17 There is no present intent to terminate the plan.

18 No events have occurred subsequent to the statement date that would require adjustment to, or disclosure in, the financial statements.

_____
(Name of plan)

_____
(Plan administrator or an employer
company officer if the company
is the plan administrator)

_____
(Name and title of the individual
equivalent to the chief financial
officer of the plan)

CHAPTER TEN

Auditor's Reports on Pension Plan Financial Statements

INTRODUCTION

An auditor's report on pension plan financial statements will be included for most plans as part of the annual report required to be filed under ERISA's reporting and disclosure requirements. This chapter discusses the appropriateness of the standard report as well as departures that may be required.

Illustrative standard reports and examples of certain departures therefrom are provided. The wording, however, may need to be modified to meet the particular circumstances of the engagement. These illustrative auditor's reports are consistent with the guidance contained in a draft of the AICPA's proposed audit guide, "Audits of Employee Benefit Plans" (audit guide), and the general form of many of the illustrative reports herein is from the audit guide.

STANDARD REPORT

When the auditor has examined a pension plan's financial statements in accordance with generally accepted auditing standards and concludes that they have been prepared in conformity with generally accepted accounting principles, and that such principles have been applied on a basis consistent with the preceding period, a standard (unqualified) report is appropriate.

Illustrative standard auditor's reports covering defined benefit pension plan financial statements prepared in accordance with FASB Statement No. 35, "Accounting and Reporting by Defined Benefit Pension Plans" are provided in Figures 10-1 and 10-2.[1] In these illustrations it is assumed that the required information regarding the actuarial present value of accumulated plan benefits and the changes therein are presented in separate financial statements, rather than in the financial statement footnotes. Figure 10-1 assumes the actuarial benefit information is presented as of the end of the plan year and Figure 10-2 assumes the actuarial benefit information is presented as of the beginning of the plan year. If the information is included in the notes to the financial statements, the language in the first sentence of the scope paragraph in Figure 10-1 might read:

We have examined the statement of net assets available for benefits of [name of plan] as of December 31, 19X2, and the related statement of changes in net assets available for benefits for the year then ended.

The illustrative auditor's reports in Figures 10-5 and 10-9 relate to situations where the accumulated benefit information is not presented in statement format.

The illustrative auditor's report in Figure 10-1 addresses financial statements covering one year. However, two-year comparative statements will frequently be presented, for any of several reasons.

For example, under generally accepted accounting principles, if information regarding the actuarial present value of accumulated plan benefits is presented as of the beginning, rather than the end, of the year, prior year statements of net assets available for benefits and of changes in net assets available for benefits are required.

As another example, under the alternative method of complying with ERISA's reporting and disclosure requirements, plans must present comparative statements of assets and liabilities. In such cases, the auditor's report will need to be modified, as provided by AICPA's Statement on Auditing Standards (SAS) No. 15. The illustrative auditor's report in Figure 10-2 assumes that the stated prior year financial information is presented.

---

[1] The accounting principles and financial reporting standards set forth in FASB Statement No. 35 are discussed in Chapter 8.

FIGURE 10-1

**Illustrative unqualified auditor's report
where actuarial benefit information is presented
in separate statements, based on an end-of-year
actuarial benefit information date**

We have examined the statements of net assets available for benefits and of accumulated plan benefits of [name of plan] as of December 31, 19X2, and the related statements of changes in net assets available for benefits and of changes in accumulated plan benefits for the year then ended. Our examination was made in accordance with generally accepted auditing standards and, accordingly, included such tests of the accounting records and such other auditing procedures as we considered necessary in the circumstances.

In our opinion, the financial statements referred to above present fairly the financial status of the plan as of December 31, 19X2, and the changes in its financial status for the year then ended, in conformity with generally accepted accounting principles applied on a basis consistent with that of the preceding year.

FIGURE 10-2

**Illustrative unqualified auditor's report
where actuarial benefit information is presented
in separate statements, based on a beginning-of-year
actuarial benefit information date**

We have examined the statements of net assets available for benefits of [name of plan] as of December 31, 19X2 and 19X1, and the related statements of changes in net assets available for benefits for the years then ended and the statement of accumulated plan benefits as of December 31, 19X1, and the related statement of changes in accumulated plan benefits for the year then ended. Our examinations were made in accordance with generally accepted auditing standards and, accordingly, included such tests of the accounting records and such other auditing procedures as we considered necessary in the circumstances.

In our opinion, the financial statements referred to above present fairly the financial status of the plan at December 31, 19X1 and the changes in its financial status for the year then ended, and information regarding net assets available for benefits and changes therein at and for the year ended December 31, 19X2, in conformity with generally accepted accounting principles applied on a consistent basis.

Reporting on ERISA-Required Supplemental Schedules

As indicated in Chapter 5, annual reports filed pursuant to ERISA requirements are required to contain certain supplemental schedules which are required to be covered by the auditor's report. SAS No. 29, "Reporting on Information Accompanying the Basic Financial Statements in Auditor-Submitted Documents," provides reporting guidelines when the auditor submits to his client or to others a document that contains information in addition to the basic financial statements. The following guidelines are set forth in the SAS.

The report should state that the examination has been made for the purpose of forming an opinion on the basic financial statements taken as a whole.

The report should identify the accompanying information. Identification may be by descriptive title or page number of the document.

The report should indicate that the accompanying information is presented for purposes of additional analysis and is not a required part of the basic financial statements. The report may refer to those regulatory agency requirements applicable to the information.

The report should express an opinion on whether the accompanying information is fairly stated in all material respects in relation to the basic financial statements taken as a whole or disclaim an opinion on the information, depending on whether the information has been subjected to the auditing procedures applied in the examination of the basic financial statements. The auditor may express an opinion on a portion of the accompanying information and disclaim an opinion on the remainder.

The report on the accompanying information may be added to the auditor's standard report on the basic financial statements or may appear separately in the auditor-submitted document.

An illustrative separate paragraph where the auditor's report covers additional information and the auditor has applied auditing procedures and is expressing an unqualified opinion on the additional information is as follows:

Our examination was made for the purpose of forming an opinion on the basic financial statements taken as a whole. The supplemental schedules of [identify] are presented for purposes of complying with the Department of Labor's Rules and Regulations for Reporting and Disclosure under the Employee Retirement Income Security Act of 1974 and are not a required part of the basic financial statements. The supplemental schedules have been subjected to the auditing procedures applied in the examination of the basic financial statements and, in our opinion, are stated fairly in all material respects in relation to the basic financial statements taken as a whole.

When additional information is presented on which the auditor expresses a qualified or adverse opinion or disclaims an opinion the above paragraph should be modified in accordance with SAS No. 29.

Reference to Confirmation of Investments

As indicated under "Investments—Physical Accountability" in Chapter 9, investments held as of the plan year-end may be confirmed with the custodian rather than inspected and counted. Where the securities are confirmed, some auditors make reference to this fact in the scope paragraph of the auditor's report. Those auditors, for example, might add language such as the following as the last sentence of the scope paragraph:

Investments owned at December 31, 19X2, were confirmed to us by the custodian.

While such addition to the scope paragraph has been considered acceptable, the draft audit guide does not address this issue and such wording is not included in the examples of auditor's reports contained therein.

Reference to Actuaries in Auditor's Report

In accordance with SAS No. 11, the auditor should not make reference to the work or findings of an actuary when expressing an unqualified opinion on financial statements. Such a reference in an unqualified opinion might be misunderstood to be a qualification of the auditor's report or a division of responsibility, neither of which is intended. If the auditor expresses a qualified or adverse opinion or disclaims an opinion as a result of the report or findings of an actuary, reference to the actuary may be made in the auditor's report when the auditor believes the reference will facilitate an understanding of the reason for the opinion modification.

Reference to Other Auditors in Auditor's Report

As indicated under "Custodial Relationships" in Chapter 9, there may be instances in which the auditor of a pension plan will obtain a report from another independent auditor. For example, the plan auditor may obtain a report of an independent auditor of a commingled fund or of a pooled separate account, where plan assets are invested in such funds or accounts, or he may obtain a single-auditor report on the trustee's system of internal accounting controls, where plan assets are held in a discretionary trust. Although the amount of the plan's assets covered by the other auditor's report may be material to the net assets of the plan, the plan auditor would ordinarily be the principal auditor. Since the plan auditor applies procedures with respect to investments, contributions, benefit payments, actuarial information, and other elements of the financial statements, the plan auditor ordinarily is the only auditor in a position to express an opinion on the plan's financial statements.

The work of the other auditor generally is used as competent evidential matter regarding the value of certain investments, and the plan auditor ordinarily need not refer to the other auditor in his report. Although the plan auditor may use reports by other auditors, the other auditors are not responsible for auditing a portion of the plan's financial statements as of any specific date or for any specific period. Thus there cannot be a meaningful indication of a division of responsibility for the plan's financial statements.

DEPARTURES FROM THE STANDARD REPORT

Under some circumstances, the standard report will be inappropriate and the auditor will have to express other than an unqualified opinion. Some of the situations likely to lead to a departure from an unqualified opinion involve scope limitations imposed by the plan administrator pursuant to Department of Labor (DOL) regulations or by an inability to examine employer records, problems related to investment valuation or internal control, and financial statements prepared on a cash or modified cash basis.

Limited Scope Examination Pursuant to DOL Regulations

Common practice indicates that many plan administrators limit the scope of the auditor's examination to exclude financial information prepared by a bank, a similar institution, or an insurance carrier (*institution*). As indicated in Chapter 5, this is permitted under DOL reporting and disclosure regulations where the institution is regulated and supervised and subject to periodic examination by a state or federal agency and as long as the information is certified as complete and accurate by the institution.

Where the scope of the auditor's examination has been restricted in this way, the plan auditor should nonetheless compare information covered by the certification of the institution to the related information in the financial statements and supplemental schedules and determine that it is presented in compliance with the DOL reporting and disclosure regulations. Also, where the certified data are based on information supplied by the plan administrator, the auditor should be satisfied that amounts reported by the institution as received from or disbursed at the discretion of the plan administrator are properly determined in accordance with the terms of the plan.

Figures 10-3, 10-4, and 10-5 provide illustrative auditor's reports where the plan administrator restricts the auditor's examination with respect to financial information prepared and certified to by a bank, similar institution, or insurance carrier. The example in Figure 10-3 relates to an examination of current year financial statements only. The example in Figure 10-4 relates to an examination of comparative statements of net assets available for benefits and of accumulated plan benefits for two years, and statements of changes in net assets available for benefits and changes in accumulated benefits, and supplemental schedules, as of or for the current year only. In that example the plan administrator does not restrict the scope of the auditor's examination in the current year, but did restrict the examination in the prior year with respect to financial information prepared and certified by an institution.

The example in Figure 10-5 relates to an examination of comparative two-year statements of net assets available for benefits and a single-year statement of changes in net assets available for benefits, and assumes information regarding accumulated plan benefits. Changes therein are included in the notes to the financial statements. In that example the plan administrator restricts the scope of the examination in the current year but did not restrict the prior year examination.

Guidance on reporting on prior year financial statements is provided in SAS No. 15. The SAS calls for dating the auditor's report as of the completion of the

FIGURE 10-3

**Illustrative auditor's report where the plan administrator
restricts the auditor's examination with respect to information
prepared and certified by a bank, similar institution, or insurance carrier**

We have examined the financial statements and schedules of [name of plan] as of December 31, 19XX, and for the year then ended as listed in the accompanying index. Except as stated in the following paragraph, our examination was made in accordance with generally accepted auditing standards and, accordingly, included such tests of the accounting records and such other auditing procedures as we considered necessary in the circumstances.

As permitted by Section 2520.103-8 of the Department of Labor Rules and Regulations for Reporting and Disclosure under the Employee Retirement Income Security Act of 1974, the plan administrator instructed us not to perform, and we did not perform, any auditing procedures with respect to the information summarized in Note X, which was certified by [name of bank], the trustee of the plan, except for comparing the information to the related information included in the 19XX financial statements and supplemental schedules. We have been informed by the plan administrator that the trustee holds the plan's investment assets and executes investment transactions. The plan administrator has obtained a certification from the trustee as of and for the year ended December 31, 19XX, that the information provided to the plan administrator by the trustee is complete and accurate.

Because of the significance of the information that we did not audit, we are unable to, and do not, express an opinion on the accompanying financial statements and schedules taken as a whole. The form and content of the information included in the financial statements and schedules, other than that derived from the information certified by the trustee, has been examined by us and, in our opinion, is presented in compliance with the Department of Labor Rules and Regulations for Reporting and Disclosure under the Employee Retirement Income Security Act of 1974.

FIGURE 10-4

**Illustrative auditor's report on comparative financial statements
where the plan administrator does not restrict the auditor's examination
in the current year, but did restrict the examination in the prior year
with respect to financial information prepared and certified
by a bank, similar institution, or insurance carrier**

We have examined the statements of net assets available for benefits of [name of plan] as of December 31, 19X2 and 19X1, the related statement of changes in net assets available for benefits for the year ended December 31, 19X2, and the statements of accumulated plan benefits as of December 31, 19X2 and 19X1, and the related statement of changes in accumulated plan benefits for the year ended December 31, 19X2. Except as explained in the following paragraph, our examinations were made in accordance with generally accepted auditing standards and, accordingly, included such tests of the accounting records and such other auditing procedures as we considered necessary in the circumstances.

As permitted by Section 2520.103-8 of the Department of Labor Rules and Regulations for Reporting and Disclosure under the Employee Retirement Income Security Act of 1974, investment assets held by [name of bank], the trustee of the plan, and transactions in those assets were excluded from the scope of our examination of the plan's 19X1 financial statements, except for comparing the information provided by the trustee, which is summarized in Note X, to the related information included in the financial statements.

225

FIGURE 10-4 (continued)

Because of the significance of the information that we did not audit, we are unable to, and do not, express an opinion on the plan's financial statements at or for the year ended December 31, 19X1. The form and content of the information included in the 19X1 financial statements, other than that derived from the information certified by the trustee, has been examined by us and, in our opinion, is presented in compliance with the Department of Labor's Rules and Regulations for Reporting and Disclosure under the Employee Retirement Income Security Act of 1974.

In our opinion, the financial statements referred to above of [name of plan] at December 31, 19X2, and for the year then ended, present fairly the financial status of [name of plan] at December 31, 19X2, and the changes in its financial status for the year then ended, in conformity with generally accepted accounting principles applied on a basis consistent with that of the preceding year.

Our examinations were made for the purpose of forming an opinion on the financial statements taken as a whole. The supplemental schedules of (1) assets held for investment, (2) transactions in excess of 3% of the current value of plan assets, and (3) investments in loans and fixed-income obligations in default or classified as uncollectible as of or for the year ended December 31, 19X2, are presented for purposes of complying with the Department of Labor Rules and Regulations for Reporting and Disclosure under the Employee Retirement Income Security Act of 1974 and are not a required part of the basic financial statements. The supplemental schedules have been subjected to the auditing procedures applied in the examination of the basic financial statements as of and for the year ended December 31, 19X2, and, in our opinion, are stated fairly in all material respects in relation to the basic financial statements taken as a whole.

most recent examination. However, the procedures performed in an examination that has been restricted as permitted by DOL reporting and disclosure regulations generally are not sufficient to enable the auditor to update his report on the prior year financial statements. Accordingly, the auditor should consider dual dating his report. In such circumstances the auditor's report in Figure 10-5 may be dated as follows:

May —, 19X3, except for the fourth paragraph, the date of which is November —, 19X2.

Scope Limitation—Employer Records

Where a scope limitation exists because the auditor is unable to examine employer records or to perform appropriate alternative audit procedures, as discussed in Chapter 9, the auditor should be guided by the considerations outlined in paragraphs 10–12 of SAS No. 2. For a discussion of the type of opinion to be expressed, see "Scope Limitations" in Chapter 9. Figure 10-6 provides an illustrative auditor's report under these circumstances.

Investment Valuation

Where investments which a plan values "in good faith" involve a significant amount of securities without a readily determinable fair value, the auditor may find it inappropriate to express an unqualified opinion. (See discussion in

FIGURE 10-5

**Illustrative auditor's report on comparative financial statements
where the plan administrator restricts the auditor's examination
in the current year with respect to financial information
prepared and certified by a bank, similar institution or insurance carrier
but did not restrict the examination in the prior year**

We have examined the statements of net assets available for benefits of [name of plan] as of December 31, 19X2 and 19X1, and the related statement of changes in net assets available for plan benefits for the year ended December 31, 19X2, and the supplemental schedules of (1) assets held for investment, (2) transactions in excess of 3% of the current value of plan assets, and (3) investments in loans and fixed-income obligations in default or classified as uncollectible as of or for the year ended December 31, 19X2. Except as explained in the following paragraph with respect to the 19X2 financial statements and supplemental schedules, our examinations were made in accordance with generally accepted auditing standards and, accordingly, included such tests of the accounting records and such other auditing procedures as we considered necessary in the circumstances.

As permitted by Section 2520.103-8 of the Department of Labor Rules and Regulations for Reporting and Disclosure under the Employee Retirement Income Security Act of 1974, the plan administrator instructed us not to perform, and we did not perform, any auditing procedures with respect to the information summarized in Note X, which was certified by the [name of bank], the trustee of the plan, except for comparing the information to the related information included in the 19X2 financial statements and supplemental schedules. We have been informed by the plan administrator that the trustee holds the plan's investment assets and executes investment transactions. The plan administrator has obtained a certification from the trustee as of and for the year ended December 31, 19X2, that the information provided to the plan administrator by the trustee is complete and accurate.

Because of the significance of the information in the plan's 19X2 financial statements that we did not audit, we are unable to, and do not, express an opinion on the accompanying financial statements and supplemental schedules at or for the year ended December 31, 19X2. The form and content of the information included in the financial statements and supplemental schedules, other than that derived from the information certified by the trustee, has been examined by us, and in our opinion, is presented in compliance with the Department of Labor's Rules and Regulations for Reporting and Disclosure under the Employee Retirement Income Security Act of 1974.

In our opinion, the statement of net assets available for benefits of [name of plan] as of December 31, 19X1, presents fairly the financial status of [name of plan] at December 31, 19X1, in conformity with generally accepted accounting principles applied on a basis consistent with that of the preceding year.

Chapter 9 under "Fair Value.") Figure 10-7 provides illustrative explanatory and opinion paragraphs which are appropriate when the plan's procedures do not appear to be adequate to determine the fair value of investments.

Where circumstances warrant, an adverse opinion or a disclaimer of opinion may be appropriate, in which instances the auditor should be guided by the considerations outlined in paragraphs 41 to 47 of SAS No. 2.

Most pension plans will state investments other than insurance contracts at fair value due to the requirements of FASB Statement No. 35 for defined benefit plans and the DOL reporting and disclosure regulations governing the alternative method of compliance. However, where marketable securities are carried at cost and market value is substantially lower than cost, the auditor

FIGURE 10-6

**Illustrative auditor's report where the auditor has been unable
to apply all the procedures the auditor considers necessary
with regard to participants' data maintained
by the sponsoring employer companies**

We have examined the statements of [identify] of the [name of plan] as of December 31, 19X2 and 19X1, and for the years then ended. Except as explained in the following paragraph, our examinations were made in accordance with generally accepted auditing standards and, accordingly, included such tests of the accounting records and such other auditing procedures as we considered necessary in the circumstances.

The plan's records and procedures are not adequate to assure the completeness of participants' data on which contributions and benefit payments are determined, and the board of trustees did not engage us to perform, and we did not perform, any other auditing procedures with respect to participants' data maintained by the sponsor companies or individual participants.

Because of the significance of the information that we did not audit, we are unable to, and do not, express an opinion on the accompanying financial statements.

FIGURE 10-7

**Illustrative explanatory and opinion paragraphs of auditor's report
where the plan financial statements contain a significant amount
of investments without a readily determinable fair value
and the plan's valuation procedures do not appear
adequate to support the valuation**

As discussed in Note X, investments amounting to $——————— (xx% of net assets available for benefits) as of December 31, 19X2, have been valued at fair value as determined by the board of trustees. We have reviewed the procedures applied by the trustees in valuing the investments and have inspected the underlying documentation. In our opinion, those procedures do not appear to be adequate to determine the fair value of the investments.[1]

In our opinion, except for the effects, if any, on the financial statements of the procedures used by the board of trustees to determine the valuation of investments as described in the preceding paragraph, the financial statements referred to above present fairly the financial status of [name of plan] at December 31, 19X2, and the changes in its financial status for the year then ended, in conformity with generally accepted accounting principles applied on a basis consistent with that of the preceding year.

Our examination was made for the purpose of forming an opinion on the basic financial statements taken as a whole. The additional information presented in supplemental schedules of (1) assets held for investment, (2) transactions in excess of 3% of the current value of plan assets, and (3) investments in loans and fixed-income obligations in default or classified as uncollectible as of or for the year ended December 31, 19X2, is presented for purposes of complying with the Department of Labor Rules and Regulations for Reporting and Disclosure under the Employee Retirement Income Security Act of 1974 and is not a required part of the basic financial statements. That additional information has been subjected to the auditing procedures applied in the examination of the basic financial statements for the year ended December 31, 19X2, and, in our opinion, except for the effects, if any, of the valuation of investments as described above, the additional information in the supplemental schedules is fairly stated in all material respects in relation to the basic financial statements taken as a whole.

1 If the note to the financial statements does not discuss the effect of the departure from generally accepted accounting principles, a sentence such as the following should be added at the end of this paragraph: "The effect, if any, on the financial statements and supplemental schedules of not applying adequate procedures to determine the fair value of the securities is not determinable."

should be guided by the considerations outlined in the AICPA's auditing interpretation on "Evidential matter for the carrying amount of marketable securities" in determining which type of opinion to express.

Internal Control Deficiency

In a typical multiemployer plan, employers generally determine their liability to the plan and submit reports and contributions to the plan on a self-assessment basis. It is the responsibility of the board of trustees to ascertain whether the employers' contributions are being determined and made in accordance with the provisions of the applicable agreement.

Since employer contributions are normally the principal source of revenue, an important aspect of the plan's system of internal control involves the establishment of procedures (e.g., examination of employer payroll records and confirmation with participants) to determine the correctness of employer contributions. The inadequacy or absence of such procedures may prevent the auditor from satisfying himself that contributions receivable and contribution revenue are fairly presented in the financial statements. In instances where there is an inadequacy or absence of such internal procedures, and where alternative audit procedures either do not result in the necessary assurance, are impractical, or have been limited by the client, the auditor should generally disclaim an opinion on the financial statements. An illustration of the wording of a disclaimer of opinion in one such instance is shown in Figure 10-8.

Non-GAAP Basis

Although financial statements reporting financial information prescribed by ERISA itself must conform to generally accepted accounting principles (GAAP), as indicated in Chapter 5, financial statements reporting information prescribed by DOL regulations governing the alternative method of compliance may be at variance from GAAP. Accordingly, it is not uncommon for auditors to be asked to report on non-GAAP financial statements, such as those prepared on a cash or modified cash basis. In such cases, the standard report is not appropriate.

SAS No. 14 provides guidance on auditor's reports of examinations of financial statements that are prepared in accordance with a comprehensive basis of accounting other than GAAP, including cash basis statements and modifications thereof having substantial support. Cash basis financial statements that adjust plan investments to fair value in accordance with the alternative method of compliance are considered to be prepared on a modified cash basis of accounting. Figure 10-9 provides an illustrative auditor's report on plan financial statements prepared on such basis.

If financial statements prepared on a modified cash basis or other basis not in conformity with GAAP do not disclose information regarding accumulated plan benefits, the auditor should comment in his report on the lack of such disclosure and should express a qualified or an adverse opinion.

FIGURE 10-8

Illustrative auditor's report disclaiming an opinion
where the auditor finds internal control procedures to be inadequate
or absent and alternative audit procedures are impractical

We have examined the financial statements of [name of plan] as listed in the accompanying index on [page number]. Except as set forth in the following paragraph, our examination was made in accordance with generally accepted auditing standards and, accordingly, included such tests of the accounting records and such other auditing procedures as we considered necessary in the circumstances.

The internal control procedures adopted by the plan are not adequate to assure the completeness of employer contributions to the plan and the plan's records do not permit the application of adequate alternative procedures regarding employer contributions.

Since the internal control procedures adopted by the plan are not adequate to assure the completeness of employer contributions to the plan and we were unable to apply adequate alternative procedures regarding employer contributions, as noted in the preceding paragraph, the scope of our work was not sufficient to enable us to express, and we do not express, an opinion on the financial statements listed on [page number].

FIGURE 10-9

Illustrative auditor's report on pension plan financial statements
prepared on the modified cash basis

We have examined the statements of net assets available for plan benefits (modified cash basis) of [name of plan] as of December 31, 19X2 and 19X1, and the related statement of changes in net assets available for plan benefits (modified cash basis) for the year ended December 31, 19X2. Our examinations were made in accordance with generally accepted auditing standards and, accordingly, included such tests of the accounting records and such other auditing procedures as we considered necessary in the circumstances.

As described in Note X, the plan's policy is to prepare its financial statements and supplemental schedules on a modified cash basis of accounting, which differs from generally accepted accounting principles. Accordingly, the accompanying financial statements and schedules are not intended to be presented in conformity with generally accepted accounting principles.

In our opinion, the financial statements referred to above present fairly the net assets available for plan benefits of [name of plan] at December 31, 19X2 and 19X1, and the changes in net assets available for plan benefits for the year ended December 31, 19X2, on the basis of accounting described in Note X, which basis has been applied in a consistent manner.

Our examinations were made for the purpose of forming an opinion on the financial statements taken as a whole. The supplemental schedules (modified cash basis) of (1) assets held for investment, (2) transactions in excess of 3% of the current value of plan assets, and (3) investments in loans and fixed-income obligations in default or classified as uncollectible as of or for the year ended December 31, 19X2, are presented for purposes of complying with the Department of Labor Rules and Regulations for Reporting and Disclosure under the Employee Retirement Income Security Act of 1974 and are not a required part of the basic financial statements. The supplemental schedules have been subjected to the auditing procedures applied in the examination of the basic financial statements as of and for the year ended December 31, 19X2, and, in our opinion, are fairly stated in all material respects in relation to the basic financial statements taken as a whole.

APPENDIXES

APPENDIX A

Analysis of the ERISA Minimum Participation Standards

INTRODUCTION

This is a detailed analysis of ERISA's minimum standards for plan participation as described in final regulations issued by the Internal Revenue Service.[1]

The regulations generally describe the conditions employers may impose

---

[1] Code Reg. Sections 1.410 (a)-1 through 1.410 (d)-1, 1.413-1 (b), 1.413-2 (b).

upon employees in order to become eligible for plan participation. Specifically, they detail the permissible minimum age and service requirements, allowable maximum age limitations, and mandatory coverage rules found in Section 202 of ERISA and Section 410 of the Internal Revenue Code.

APPLICABILITY

ERISA's standards for plan participation generally apply to all defined benefit (pension) plans and defined contribution (profit-sharing, stock bonus, and money-purchase) plans.[2] For a complete list of plans not subject to the minimum participation standards, see the list of excluded plans provided in Appendix C.

MINIMUM AGE AND SERVICE
REQUIREMENTS FOR PLAN ELIGIBILITY

An employer may generally require employees to complete up to one "year of service" and to attain the age of 25 in order to be eligible to begin to accrue plan benefits.[3]

If a plan provides for full vesting after three years of service or less, the commencement of plan participation may be delayed until the completion of not more than three years of service. The regulations emphasize that three consecutive years of service cannot be required, although plans may require the completion of three years without an intervening "break in service."

In addition, a plan maintained exclusively for employees of an educational institution[4] by a tax-exempt employer can exclude employees from plan participation until they attain age 30 and complete one year of service, provided that participants are fully vested in employer-derived benefits after the completion of not more than one year.

A plan may also exclude certain categories of employees, provided that it meets one of the coverage tests explained in more detail at the end of this section, which require a certain percentage or nondiscriminatory classification of all employees to be included as participants.

A plan must comply with these guidelines even if it merely implies, rather than explicitly specifies, an age or service requirement. For example, if a plan requires employees to work in a certain department in order to participate in the plan, and under the company's policy employees must complete at least five years of service to work in that department, the plan is implicitly imposing

---

[2] DOL Reg. Section 2530.201-2.
[3] Code Reg. Section 1.410 (a)-3. For an explanation of a "year of service" for eligibility purposes, see Appendix C.
[4] As defined in Code Section 170 (b) (1) (A) (ii).

a five-year eligibility requirement, which is clearly prohibited. Satisfying the minimum *coverage* tests would not correct this type of violation.

Supplemental benefits such as cost-of-living increases to retirees are not subject to the minimum age and service requirements. Thus, a cost-of-living increase to retirees does not violate the minimum participation standards even though employees must wait longer than one year and be older than 25 years of age to be eligible for this ancillary benefit.

These guidelines also state that plans which at some point freeze entry into the plan, allowing for no new participants, are not in violation of these minimum participation rules.

Uncovered Job Categories

As previously indicated, the plan may exclude employees in certain job categories from plan participation. Nevertheless, years of service completed in such a job category, or with a nonparticipating employer who is in the same "controlled group" as the participating employer, must still be taken into account for eligibility purposes.[5] For example, if an employee working in an uncovered job category transfers to "covered" status, his service in the prior job category would count toward the satisfaction of the service requirement for initial plan eligibility. Therefore, this type of employee might be able to enter the plan immediately, instead of being treated like a new employee.

Break in Service Rules[6]

One-Year Waiting Period

A plan may require any employee who incurs a break in service to complete a year of service upon his return in order to again be considered a plan participant.

If an employee was vested[7] when his break occurred, he must be retroactively credited with a year of plan participation upon the completion of that one-year "waiting period." In effect, such employee's service completed before his break, for eligibility purposes, is reinstated at such time. If the one-year waiting period is not imposed, the eligibility service that the employee completed before his break must be taken into account; and the employee must be immediately considered a participant upon rehire.

The same rule for retroactive credit applies, where the waiting period is imposed, to a nonvested employee whose break for eligibility purposes was shorter than the length of his prebreak eligibility service. However, a nonvested

---

[5] For this purpose, the "controlled group" includes the participating employer and other companies with which it is connected through a common "controlling interest." A controlling interest is considered to be 80%. See also DOL Reg. Section 2530.210.

[6] For a complete discussion of the break in service rules, see Appendix C.

[7] *Vested* for this purpose means having a nonforfeitable right to an employer-derived benefit. This rule governs even partially vested employees.

employee can be treated as a new employee obliged to complete the service requirement for plan admission, with no retroactive credit, if his "break" was equal to or longer than his length of prebreak eligibility service (the "parity rule").

Certain plans may avoid granting an employee who returns to work, but remains for less than a year, additional benefit accrual with respect to such short period of service by imposing the one-year waiting period that delays participatory status. The advantage of imposing a one-year waiting period for purposes of reinstating the employee to participant status may be diminished, however, in the case of plans using the "general method" of computing service since both defined contribution plans and defined benefit plans may disregard *any* year of service for benefit accrual purposes during which an employee fails to complete 1,000 hours of service.[8]

Finally, any entitlement within the scope of ERISA contingent upon an employee's status as a "participant" may be affected by the imposition of the waiting period. A person failing to complete a year of service upon his return may not be considered a participant eligible, for example, to elect a preretirement joint and survivor annuity derived from any prebreak benefit accruals.[9]

Special Rule for Certain Plans

Plans requiring more than one year of service (providing for immediate full vesting upon the completion of at least three years of service) can disregard service completed before a break in service if an employee had not, as of his break, completed the total number of years required for plan admission. Thus, such an employee can be required to satisfy the full service requirement upon his return to work, receiving no credit for prior years.

PLAN ENTRY DATES

Employees who satisfy their plan's age and service requirements must actually become plan participants, if they are otherwise eligible, no later than the earlier of:

first day of the first plan year beginning after the employee satisfies the eligibility requirements; or

six months after he completes the eligibility requirements.

In other words, no full-time employee hired after his 24th birthday can be kept out of the plan longer than 18 months from his date of hire, provided he is otherwise eligible. Thus, a plan must have at least two entry dates, six months apart, one such date being the plan's anniversary date, if it incorporates the one year/age 25 condition for plan participation.

[8] DOL Reg. Section 2530.204-2.
[9] Code Reg. Section 1.401 (a)-11.

Plans using a single annual entry date for all employees can require employees to complete no more than six months of service and to be no older than age 24½. Thus, these employees would not be precluded from plan entry for more than 18 months—six months for eligibility service plus a period of time up to one year until the next entry date occurs.

Absence Occurring on an Entry Date

These regulations state that employees who are "separated" from service on the date they would have entered the plan must be permitted to participate in the plan immediately upon return to work, provided that no break in service had occurred. No retroactive credit to the original entry date need be granted. The term *separated* is not defined, but we assume that it denotes a quit, discharge, or retirement as opposed to an absence due to such reasons as illness or layoff. This definition is consistent with both the conference reports on ERISA and final IRS regulations on elapsed time.[10]

On the other hand, the regulations state that a person who is "absent" on his entry date must commence participation *retroactively* to his original entry date upon his return to active service if his plan determines service on the elapsed time basis. Although it is not defined, the term *absence* apparently means an absence due to illness, layoff, or similar circumstances in keeping with associated elapsed time regulations and the implications of the conference reports on the subject.

Although the IRS only discusses retroactive plan admission with respect to elapsed time plans, we assume that all "absent" employees should be similarly treated regardless of the service computation method used. The conference report on the issue, aimed only at general method plans, implies the need for such retroactive treatment by emphasizing the distinction between a *separation* and an *absence*.

MAXIMUM AGE LIMITATIONS: DEFINED BENEFIT PLANS AND TARGET BENEFIT PLANS

Defined benefit plans and target benefit[11] plans are permitted to exclude employees who are hired up to five years before "normal retirement age." "Normal retirement age" is the earlier of:

---

[10] See also Appendix C, memorandum concerning service computation methods.

[11] Target benefit plans are defined contribution plans under which a specified nondiscretionary amount of contributions is made by the employer on the basis of the amount necessary to provide a "target" level of retirement income for each participant. Unlike a defined benefit plan, the employer has no obligation to actually provide the full amount of income "targeted" by the plan if the plan's specified level of funding proves insufficient.

the age specified by the plan, or if not specified, the age beyond which an employee will not accrue a larger benefit because of increased age or service, or

the date the participant attains age 65, or the tenth anniversary of the date the participant entered the plan, if later.

Defined contribution plans, except for target benefit plans, may not exclude any employee from participation on the basis of a maximum age limitation upon hire or rehire.

Defined benefit plans which had a maximum age for plan admission before these standards came into effect may not continue to exclude employees if the previous maximum is now too restrictive. Affected employees must be able to enter the plan as of ERISA's effective date.

Example: Before ERISA came into effect, a plan with a normal retirement age of 65 precluded employees from commencing participation if they were hired on or after age 55. In compliance with ERISA, the plan increases its maximum age limitation for plan entry to age 60. A certain employee hired at age 58 is age 61 when ERISA becomes effective. This employee must be able to enter the plan as of the ERISA effective date, although his years of service completed before plan entry need not be counted for benefit accrual purposes. However, all service from date of hire would generally have to be recognized for purposes of vesting and eligibility.

Note that defined benefit plans using a normal retirement age based on the later of age 65 or the tenth anniversary of the employee's plan participation may not incorporate a maximum age limitation for plan entry because no employee would be within five years of normal retirement age when first employed.

Age upon Rehire

Under a defined benefit plan, if an employee is rehired within five years of normal retirement age and if his pretermination years of eligibility service are disregarded by reason of the "parity rule," such an employee can be excluded from plan participation. In all other cases, age upon rehire is not a valid reason for exclusion.

COVERAGE TESTS

In order to be considered qualified by the IRS, retirement plans, except those benefiting an owner-employee[12] (which are subject to stricter requirements

[12] As defined under Section 401 (c) (3) of the code.

in years beginning before 1984), and those which benefit air pilots covered by collectively bargained agreements (for which a special rule applies), must meet one of the following coverage tests.

Percentage Test

Part A

At least 70% of all employees must be participants. The term *all employees* includes the total number of employees within the controlled group of the employer adopting the plan, less:

those not satisfying the age and service requirements for plan eligibility,

employees subject to a collectively bargained agreement under which a pension plan was the subject of good-faith bargaining (even if no pension plan for such employees was adopted as a result of such negotiation), and

nonresident aliens who receive no earned income from U.S. sources.

If the plan fails this part of the percentage test, Part B must be passed.

Part B

If 70% or more of *all* employees are eligible to participate (whether or not they currently are participating), 80% of the eligibles must be actual participants; Part B is only applicable to those plans in which participation is optional.

When determining the number of eligible employees, those on temporary leave of absence must be counted.

Example: Employer A who maintains Plan X employs a total of 1,600 persons. The following calculation is made to reflect the "statutory exclusions":

Employees under the minimum age (25) for eligibility for participation in Plan X	150
Employees with less than the minimum length of service (one year) for eligibility for participation in Plan X	200
Employees excluded from Plan X because they are covered by a collectively bargained agreement, under which a pension plan was the subject of good-faith bargaining	300
Nonresident alien employees	50
Total excluded	700
All employees (1,600 − 700)	900

Plan X does not cover hourly paid employees and requires employees to contribute to the plan in order to participate. The following calculation is made to determine the number of participants:

Hourly paid employees	200
Employees not electing to participate	100
Total nonparticipating employees	300
Total number of participants (all employees, 900 − 300)	600

Part A:

$$\frac{600 \text{ (total participants)}}{900 \text{ (all employees)}} = 66\%$$

Since only 66% of all employees are covered by Plan X, Part A is not passed.

Part B: There are 700 employees "eligible" to participate (600 already covered plus 100 who are eligible but declined to participate):

$$\frac{700 \text{ (total eligible)}}{900 \text{ (all employees)}} = 77\%$$

$$\frac{600 \text{ (total participants)}}{700 \text{ (total eligible)}} = 85\%$$

Since more than 70% of *all* employees are eligible and 85% of those eligible are participating, Part B is passed; and the plan meets the minimum coverage requirements.

Classification Test

A plan will have to pass this test if the percentage test is failed.

Under this test, it must be demonstrated that the plan benefits a classification of employees found by the IRS not to be discriminatory in favor of officers, shareholders, or highly compensated individuals. The classification of an employee as "highly compensated" is made on the basis of the facts and circumstances of each case. The fact that a plan is integrated with social security does not make the plan discriminatory.

IRS Forms 5300 and 5301, the applications for a letter of determination as to a plan's qualified status, direct plan sponsors to submit a specific schedule in demonstration of this classification test if the plan fails the percentage test.

The format of the schedule requires employers to show the numbers of eligible and ineligible employees, the number of participants, and those who are officers or shareholders, according to compensation brackets reflecting the pay pattern of the employer.

This schedule must reflect all employees of the "controlled group," *including* those who have not yet satisfied the minimum age and service requirements but excluding the union employees and nonresident aliens referenced above.

The IRS regulations[13] require employers seeking to pass the classification

---

[13] Code Reg. Section 1.410 (b)-1 (d) (2).

test to demonstrate that there is only a "reasonable difference" between the percentage of all highly compensated employees covered by the plan and the covered percentage of all rank-and-file workers. Demonstrating nondiscrimination under this criterion may be difficult for many employers, particularly where a plan includes almost all of the highly compensated employees but covers a significantly smaller percentage of the total rank-and-file group.

It should be noted that the question of acceptable coverage is a continuing requirement, and the IRS stresses that coverage should be reviewed when the annual return/report is due. Plans must satisfy coverage requirements on at least one day each quarter during the plan year. Plans must continue to operate in a nondiscriminatory manner regardless of the results of either of these tests.

MULTIPLE PLANS

An employer may combine the data from more than one plan, designating that the multiple plans constitute a single plan for this purpose, in order to demonstrate the satisfaction of the coverage requirements.

Certain owner-employee plans and employee stock ownership plans may not be combined with any other plan for this purpose.

SPECIAL RULE FOR CASH OR DEFERRED ARRANGEMENTS

The regulations indicate that an employee who exercises his option under a plan to immediately receive his share of an employer contribution instead of having his share paid to the plan for later distribution will not be considered "covered" by the plan. This is because a qualified profit-sharing plan must primarily provide deferred compensation. This rule could have resulted in the failure of a "cash or deferred" plan to satisfy the minimum coverage tests if a substantial number of employees under the plan had elected immediate payment. However, the Revenue Act of 1978 allows all of the employees eligible to benefit under a plan, not just those deferring income, to be considered "covered employees" for the purpose of satisfying either the percentage or classification coverage test. In addition, the cash or deferred plan must satisfy other requirements in order to be qualified, such as compliance with special nondiscrimination rules which limit the percentage of employer contributions that can be deferred by highly compensated employees. A highly compensated employee is defined for cash or deferred plans as an employee who is paid more than two-thirds of all other eligible employees.

APPENDIX B

ERISA's Vesting Standards

INTRODUCTION

This is an analysis of ERISA's minimum vesting standards, intended for use as a reference source. To facilitate further research, footnoted citations have been included.

BACKGROUND

The requirements with respect to an employee's nonforfeitable right to an accrued benefit under a qualified retirement plan are contained in Title I of ERISA as well as Title II of ERISA, which adds Section 411 to the Internal Revenue Code making compliance with the requirements necessary for favorable tax treatment. Final IRS regulations Section 1.411 (a)-1 through 9, issued on August 22, 1977, provide guidelines for the implementation of these vesting requirements. Beginning in 1984, certain "top-heavy" plans will be subject to accelerated vesting requirements. See Appendix H for a discussion of top-heavy plan rules.

APPLICABILITY

ERISA's minimum vesting standards generally apply to all defined benefit (pension) plans and defined contribution (profit-sharing, stock bonus, and money-purchase) plans. For a complete list of plans not subject to the minimum vesting standards, see the list of excluded plans provided in Appendix C.

AFFECTED EMPLOYEES

The vesting rules apply only to employees who are employed by a company on or after the date these rules take effect. They do not apply to benefits payable to an employee who separated from service before that date and who never returns to service after the effective date of these rules.[1]

EMPLOYEE-DERIVED BENEFITS

An employee must have a nonforfeitable right at all times to any benefit derived solely from his contributions. Thus, the balance of an employee's account comprised only of his contributions and any interest attributable thereto or any defined benefit attributable to his contributions must be completely vested at all times.[2]

However, there is one exception to this rule. If an employee dies after benefit commencement but before receiving pension payments amounting to the total sum he contributed to his plan, his plan is not required to distribute the balance of such sum to his beneficiary. This exception applies to both mandatory contributions (i.e., contributions made as a requisite to plan participation) and completely voluntary contributions.

---

[1] IRS Reg. Section 1.411 (a)-2(f).
[2] IRS Reg. Sections 1.411 (a)-1(a) (2) and 1.411 (a)-4 (b) (1) (ii).

FULL VESTING UPON NORMAL RETIREMENT AGE

Types of Benefits Affected

ERISA requires that *normal retirement benefits* attributable to employer contributions must be fully vested upon and after normal retirement age.[3]

The normal retirement benefit under a defined benefit plan is the benefit payable at normal retirement age or, *if greater,* after "early retirement age."[4] Clearly *ancillary* benefits from pension plans, such as medical benefits or certain disability benefits, are not considered a part of the defined normal retirement benefits. Thus, it may be necessary to consider the employee's accrued benefit for each year after early retirement age in order to determine the exact level to which he is entitled upon retirement.

For example, assume that an employee's salary decreases after early retirement age, age 60, and that benefit determinations for each year after age 59 yield the following amounts:

	Final Average Earnings	×	Benefit %	×	Actuarial Reduction for Early Receipt	=	Annual Benefit
Age 60	$50,000		30%		.80		$12,000
61	46,600		31		.84		12,135
62	43,200		32		.88		12,165
63	39,800		33		.92		12,083
64	36,400		34		.96		11,881
65	33,000		35		1.00		11,550

In this case, the normal retirement benefit is $12,165, the highest benefit determination for the period between early and normal retirement ages.

Note, however, that a pension benefit payable to an active employee from an integrated plan may decrease during the "protected period" on account of social security increases.[5] In addition, actuarial subsidies need not be considered in determining the normal retirement benefit.

[3] IRS Reg. Section 1.411 (a)-1 (a).
[4] IRS Reg. Section 1.411 (a)-7 (c).
[5] Social security increases may decrease benefits while the participant is employed, but not after he has terminated service. See IRC Section 401 (a) (15).

Determination of Normal Retirement Age

The term *normal retirement age* for purposes of determining full vesting usually means the age specified in the plan when a plan participant is entitled to full benefits.[6] The age may be less than age 65.[7] However, the later of:

the date the participant attains age 65, or

the tenth anniversary of the date the participant commenced participation,

will be considered the normal retirement age for this purpose, if the normal retirement age specified in a plan extends beyond this date.

Many plans provide for normal retirement benefits upon attainment of age 65 and 10 years of service. However, under certain circumstances, an individual, age 65, may reach his tenth anniversary of participation prior to attaining 10 years of service. In such a case, the participant could retire with a nonforfeitable right to his benefits accrued to that date.

If no normal retirement age is specified in a plan, the date beyond which benefits do not increase because of increased age or service would be considered the normal retirement age specified by the plan. If the plan uses the tenth anniversary of participation for the normal retirement age, all years of service which may be disregarded for eligibility purposes due to a break in service need not be taken into account when determining the anniversary of plan admission. Furthermore, the first day of the *year*—the eligibility computation period—in which participation commenced would be considered the starting point for measuring anniversaries.

It should be recognized that the phrase *normal retirement age* is defined in terms of a person reaching a certain age while in *participant* status. It is unclear whether an employee who is still in service and who reaches the specified age or date for normal retirement age but who is not then accruing a benefit—in *participant* status—must be fully vested in a previously accrued benefit. The problem is not addressed in either the statute or the regulations.[8]

---

[6] IRS Reg. Section 1.411 (a)-7 (b).

[7] Revenue Ruling 78-120.

[8] It appears that Congress's intention in requiring full vesting at this age was to protect employees who are hired late in life from losing out on a retirement benefit because of their plan's lengthy vesting service requirement. It may not have been the legislators' intention to require full vesting at this age for those employees who accrued a retirement benefit earlier in their careers, but who are not active participants upon reaching normal retirement age because of the category of job they hold at that time. In any event, it is fairly certain that any action to circumvent ERISA's rules, such as relegating rank-and-file employees to uncovered job categories shortly before reaching normal retirement age, would violate the IRS' rules for nondiscrimination. On the other hand, for purposes of vesting, ERISA generally requires a plan to give credit for years of service with an employer in an uncovered job classification. Thus, for example, an hourly employee who changes to salaried would receive vesting credit under his employer's salaried-only plan for the prior years of service he was paid for.

VESTING SCHEDULES

ERISA prescribes certain minimum levels of vesting with respect to the employer-derived normal retirement benefit that has accrued for a participant as of the date of his separation from service. Any one of the following three alternative schedules must be satisfied with respect to an employee's *total* accrued benefit (noting that the plan may satisfy different schedules for different classes of employees):[9]

Ten-year vesting. Full vesting upon the completion of 10 "years of service."

Five to 15-year vesting. According to the following table:

Completed "Years of Service"	Nonforfeitable Percentage of Accrued Benefit
5	25%
6	30
7	35
8	40
9	45
10	50
11	60
12	70
13	80
14	90
15	100

"Rule of 45." The greater of two percentages as determined under either of the following schedules, whichever is applicable:

1.

Completed "Years of Service"	Sum of Age (on Last Birthday) and Service	Nonforfeitable Percentage of Accrued Benefit
5	45 or 46	50%
6	47 or 48	60
7	49 or 50	70
8	51 or 52	80
9	53 or 54	90
10	55 or more	100

[9] IRS Reg. Section 1.411 (a)-3.

2.

Completed "Years of Service"	Nonforfeitable Percentage of Accrued Benefit
10	50%
11	60
12	70
13	80
14	90
15	100

We emphasize that the minimum vesting rates apply to benefits accrued *both before and after* the advent of ERISA. A plan could not, for example, incorporate one of these schedules into the plan for only future benefit accruals.

Plans are not required to adopt one of the three schedules exactly as they appear above but must maintain at least the level of vesting provided under one particular schedule, with respect to *each year of service completed by each employee.* A plan could not incorporate different schedules for different groups of employees, even if those schedules are those prescribed by ERISA, if such classification evades the purpose of ERISA; for example, different schedules for groups categorized on the basis of their age and service would be prohibited. Finally, a plan may, of course, provide a more liberal schedule of vesting than any of those shown above.

Example: Plan A has this vesting schedule:

Completed "Years of Service"	Nonforfeitable Percentage of Accrued Benefit
2	0%
3	30
4	35
5	40
6	45
7	50
8	55
9	60
10	65
11	70
12	75
13	80
14	85
15	100

This schedule is consistent with or is more liberal than the 5- to 15-year vesting schedule for all years of service except year 14, which falls below the prescribed level by 5%. Therefore, the schedule is not permitted.

Discrimination in Favor of the Prohibited Group: "4-40" Vesting

Section 411 (d) (1) of the code provides that if there has been a pattern of abuse (such as the dismissal of employees before they become vested) or potential for abuse leading to discrimination in favor of employees who are officers, shareholders, or highly compensated (the "prohibited group"), a plan will be in violation of the law even if all other necessary conditions are met, including compliance with an ERISA vesting schedule.

Moreover, the conference report on ERISA stipulates that a faster rate of vesting may be imposed upon plans if the likely rate of employee turnover for the "prohibited group" is substantially less than the rate of turnover for rank-and-file employees. The reason for this is that such a turnover pattern could result in more plan funds being paid to highly compensated employees than to short-term, lowly paid individuals.

This is the faster rate of vesting—"4-40" vesting—discussed in the conference report:

Completed "Years of Service[10]"	Nonforfeitable Percentage
0–3	0%
4	40
5	45
6	50
7	60
8	70
9	80
10	90
11	100

A rate of vesting more rapid than "4-40" will not be required unless there is actual plan abuse, such as a pattern of firing employees to avoid vesting.

In compliance with Congress' intent for faster vesting, the IRS issued Revenue Procedure 76-11 (amplifying Revenue Procedure 75-49) which delineates the procedures to be followed when applying for a letter of determination to demonstrate nondiscrimination for this purpose.[11]

---

[10] Includes all service that must be taken into account without regard to exclusions for (1) pre-age 22 service, and (2) years of service in which the employee failed to make mandatory contributions.

[11] The IRS procedures are merely an interim approach to the problem of coordinating the vesting and discrimination requirements. See proposed IRS Reg. Section 1.411 (d)-1.

In addition to complying with one of ERISA's three vesting schedules, the IRS maintains that a plan, in order to avoid the need to adopt the faster "4-40" vesting, must either:

maintain or improve upon the vesting schedule on which its previous letter of determination was based; or

satisfy the *key employee* test, by demonstrating that the number of key employees in the plan does not exceed a specified percentage of the number of prohibited group participants; or

satisfy the *turnover* test, by showing that the turnover rate for rank-and-file members is not substantially greater than that of prohibited group members; or

demonstrate in some other way to the satisfaction of the IRS that the plan is not discriminatory.

The IRS has issued proposed regulations which would continue the facts and circumstances tests to determine if a pattern of abuse is present in the plan's operations or if there is discriminatory vesting. As originally proposed, the regulations set forth two safe harbors which required vesting more rapid than 4-40. The safe harbor provision has been withdrawn, but some doubt remains as to whether 4-40 vesting should be considered as a safe harbor. Congress has enacted a joint resolution prohibiting the IRS from using funds to disqualify a plan or issue an unfavorable determination letter with respect to a plan with vesting requirements equal to or more stringent than 4-40.

For years beginning after 1983, the Tax Equity and Fiscal Responsibility Act of 1982 (TEFRA) requires vesting more rapid than 4-40 in certain "top-heavy" plans. (See Appendix H.)

Periods To Be Included in Vesting Service

Generally, all "years of service,"[12] regardless of job category or status, with an employer maintaining a plan must be taken into account for the purpose of determining vesting.

In addition, the following periods of service are to be considered.

Service with commonly controlled employers.[13]   Any service with a member of the *controlled group* of companies of which the participating employer is a part must be taken into account. This refers to all businesses, domestic or

---

[12] *Years of service* are specifically defined by law for this purpose. For those plans using a method of computing lengths of service based on hours of service, a year of service is generally a 12-month period during which 1,000 hours of service are completed. The rules for computing lengths of service as a function of a prescribed hour of service are very specific and detailed.

[13] IRS Reg. Section 1.411 (a)-5 (b) (3) (iv) (B) and DOL Reg. Part 2530.

foreign, which are at least 80% controlled by a group member. Thus, employees shifting to and from affiliated companies or subsidiaries are considered to have a continuous span of vesting service with respect to any benefit accrued under a plan maintained by any member of the controlled group.

Employment with a predecessor employer.[14]   If a predecessor employer previously maintained the plan of a current employer, service with the predecessor employer must be considered vesting service under the current employer's plan. In some cases, service with a predecessor employer will have to be considered service under the current employer's plan even if the predecessor employer had not maintained that plan. Regulations are to be issued on this subject.[15] The conference report on ERISA specifies that a plan granting past service credits for benefit accrual purposes in recognition of service with a predecessor employer must also recognize this service for vesting purposes. This provision found its way into Title I of ERISA [Section 204 (b)] but for whatever reason was *not* added to the code.

Covered employment under a predecessor plan.[16]   When a plan is adopted by an employer as a successor to a previously maintained plan, employment covered under the former plan must sometimes be recognized as service under the new—successor—plan. This service must be recognized when:

as of the date the successor plan is established, or former plan was terminated, whichever is later, the employee covered under the former plan completed a greater number of *years of service*[17] under that plan compared to his number of years of breaks in service, if any, occurring after that time;

the former plan was or will be terminated after the effective date of these vesting rules; and

the successor plan is a qualified retirement plan established within five years following or preceding the termination of the former plan.

Service with other participating employers.[18]   Years of service with any employer who maintains a particular plan must be considered vesting service for purposes of that plan (while the employers are maintaining the plan). This applies to both collectively bargained multiemployer plans and other plans involving a number of employers.

Excludable Periods

Specific periods of time may be disregarded when determining the extent to which an employee is vested:

[14] IRS Reg. Section 1.411 (a)-5 (b) (3) (iv) (A) and DOL Reg. Part 2530.
[15] Code Section 414 (a) (2).
[16] IRS Reg. Section 1.411 (a)-5 (b) (3) (v).
[17] Years of service and breaks in service as defined for other vesting purposes, but without regard to employees' extent of vesting. Disregard years between plan termination and successor establishment.
[18] IRS Reg. Section 411 (a)-5 (b) (3) (iv) (B).

Service before age 22.[19]   Plans using the *elapsed time* method for determining vesting may disregard all service before the attainment of age 22.

Plans using computation periods may disregard all computation periods before the period in which an employee turns age 22.

Plans complying with the "rule of 45" may disregard pre-age 22 years of service only to the extent that the employee did not enter the plan at any time during such a year.

Certain periods under contributory plans.[20]   If a plan requires an employee to make contributions as a condition of employment, as a condition of his participation in the plan, or as a condition of obtaining benefits or additional benefits attributable to employer contributions, service during which an employee fails to contribute when eligible to do so may be disregarded for vesting purposes. Plans may disregard only those computation periods during which no contributions whatsoever were made.

The determining factor for the exclusion of these periods of service is the employee's failure to contribute *when he is otherwise eligible to do so.* Therefore, periods of service before an employee became eligible to contribute to the plan and those periods during which an employee is employed in a job category not covered by the plan may not be disregarded.

However, a plan may not ignore a year of service when the employee withdraws the contribution he made with respect to that year, even if he never restores them to the plan.

Service before the plan was maintained:[21]

Years of service during which the employer did not maintain the plan— years before the effective date of the plan or before the date an individual employer has adopted the plan, regardless of when other employers had adopted it—may generally be disregarded. Thus, vesting service does not have to include service before the plan came into existence, although many plans will nevertheless recognize such periods of time.

When two or more plans maintained by different employers are merged, only service from the respective effective date of each component plan must be considered in determining vesting for the employees covered by each of those component plans.

Years subsequent to a plan's termination date usually may be ignored. However, in the case of a "frozen plan," if contributions continue to be made to fund previously accrued benefits, years after the "termination date" must be recognized for vesting purposes even though benefits do not continue to accrue.

---

[19] IRS Reg. Section 411 (a)-5 (b) (1).
[20] IRS Reg. Section 411 (a)-5 (b) (2).
[21] IRS Reg. Section 1.411 (a)-5 (b) (3).

Service permitted to be disregarded under the break in service rules.[22]   Appendix C discusses the break in service rules in terms of each method of calculating service.

Service before January 1, 1971.[23]   If an employee fails to complete at least three years of service, whether or not consecutive, after December 31, 1970, his pre-January 1, 1971, service may be ignored for vesting purposes. In counting those three years, the exceptions listed under this section of our analysis may not be utilized.

Service completed before ERISA effective date.[24]   Service completed before the effective date of ERISA's vesting requirements which would have been disregarded under the *break in service rules* of the pre-ERISA plan may now be disregarded for vesting purposes.

A pre-ERISA break in service rule is one which governs the loss of prior vesting or benefit accruals, or which denies an employee eligibility to participate by reason of separation or failure to complete a required period of service within a specified period of time. Thus, former rules governing plan participation on the basis of job category or location may not qualify as a break in service rule for this purpose, although a pre-ERISA, five-year service requirement for initial plan eligibility most likely would.

Note that service permitted to be disregarded under the cash-out rules contained in the IRS regulations relate only to service taken into account for *benefit accrual purposes;* those cash-out rules do not provide for the cancellation of vesting service.[25]

Full Vesting upon Plan Termination or Partial Termination

Upon the termination or *partial termination* of a plan, the rights of each affected employee to benefits accrued to date, to the extent funded, must be fully vested.[26]

Partial termination is not a clearly defined term within the law but is determined with regard to all the facts and circumstances of each case. Regulations indicate, however, that the following events are taken into consideration when determining whether or not a partial termination occurs:[27]

exclusion of a covered group of employees from plan participation, whether by reason of discharge or plan amendment;

[22] IRS Reg. Section 1.411 (a)-5 (b) (4).
[23] IRS Reg. Section 1.411 (a)-5 (b) (5).
[24] IRS Reg. Section 1.411 (a)-5 (b) (6).
[25] IRS Reg. Section 1.411 (a)-7 (d) (4).
[26] IRS Reg. Section 1.411 (d)-2 (a).
[27] IRS Reg. Section 1.411 (d)-2 (b) (1).

amendment to the plan that adversely affects the rights of employees to vest in plan benefits.

The *complete discontinuance* of employer contributions to a profit-sharing plan will require full vesting of account balances. Complete discontinuance is determined on a case-by-case basis, but the IRS considers these factors when it is distinguishing between a complete discontinuance and a temporary suspension of benefits:

whether the employer may be calling the cessation of contributions a mere "suspension" to avoid the full vesting requirement;

whether contributions have been recurring and substantial;

whether it is likely that the employer will not be making contributions in the future.

If a defined benefit plan no longer grants *future* benefit accruals, or decreases them, a partial termination occurs if such a cessation of accruals results in the reversion of plan assets to the employer. Otherwise, a decrease in future benefit accruals would generally not require the full vesting of benefits.[28]

EVENTS RESULTING IN THE LOSS OF BENEFITS

Vested rights to accrued benefits must always be unconditional to the extent that they do not become vested sooner than the law requires. Thus, forfeiture clauses otherwise prohibited by law may be enforced when they affect only benefits that become vested under plan provisions that are more liberal than necessary.[29]

For example, under most circumstances the law would prohibit a plan provision which cancels an employee's benefits if the employee begins working for a competitor. However, such a clause may be enforced if it applies only to benefits that have become fully vested *prior* to the completion of 10 years of service. But after 10 years of service, ERISA's vesting schedules would take over, barring this type of forfeiture.

The IRS regulations also clarify these points:

Excess actuarial reductions.   A benefit adjustment in excess of a reasonable actuarial reduction can result in a benefit *forfeiture* which violates the vesting rules.

Integrated benefits.   The rules on nonforfeitability are not violated merely because plan benefit levels are reduced to take social security benefits into account.

[28] IRS Reg. Section 1.411 (d)-2 (b) (2).
[29] IRS Reg. Section 1.411 (a)-4 (a).

Sufficiency of assets. A plan may provide that vested benefits are contingent upon the sufficiency of plan assets. For example, a defined benefit plan may provide that, even though a certain level of retirement income is *vested,* payment of such benefit is nevertheless contingent upon the adequacy of funding. For example, an employee may not receive the entire amount of his fully vested pension if the plan, upon termination, does not have sufficient assets to cover his particular benefits. (And even though PBGC guarantees may come into play, they will not always match the benefit level promised by the plan.)

The following events are recognized as conditions which may properly result in the loss of an otherwise *vested* accrued benefit:

Death.[30] No employer-derived benefit, even if *vested,* has to be paid to any beneficiary solely because an employee dies in active employment. Of course, plans must still comply with ERISA's rules on the availability of preretirement survivor annuities.

Suspension of benefits upon rehire.[31] Under most circumstances, benefits may be suspended when a retiree is rehired by the employer or continues to work after normal retirement age.

Collectively bargained multiemployer plans.[32] Under certain circumstances, a benefit payable from a multiemployer plan attributable to service with an employer before that employer was required to contribute to the plan may be forfeited when the employee's current employer withdraws from the plan.[33]

Missing beneficiaries and participants.[34] If the person entitled to a benefit cannot be found, his benefit may be forfeited. However, the benefit must be reinstated if it is later claimed by that person.

Benefits may be lost, however, by reason of state excheat laws.

Withdrawal of mandatory contributions.[35] Under certain conditions, benefits which are not yet 50% vested may be forfeited when the employee withdraws his mandatory contributions associated with them.

Retroactive plan amendments.[36] Forfeiture of benefits due to a retroactive plan amendment are permitted under limited circumstances, if approved by the Department of Labor. These amendments are the subject of Section 412

---

[30] IRS Reg. Section 1.411 (a)-4 (b) (1).
[31] IRS Reg. Section 1.411 (a)-4 (b) (2) and DOL Reg. Section 2530.203-3 (b) (1).
[32] IRS Reg. Section 1.411 (a)-4 (b) (5).
[33] IRS Reg. Section 1.414 (f)-1 (b) (2) defines the extent to which benefits may be disregarded as a result of an employer's withdrawal from the plan.
[34] IRS Reg. Section 1.411 (a)-4 (b) (6).
[35] IRS Reg. Section 1.411 (a)-7 (d) (2) and (3).
[36] IRS Reg. Section 1.411 (a)-4 (b) (3).

(c) (8) of the Internal Revenue Code. See the following section, however, on prohibited benefit cutbacks.

Prohibited Benefit Cutbacks

As a general rule, a plan amendment may not decrease previously accrued benefits. Final IRS regulations indicate that plan provisions which indirectly affect accrued benefits as a result of the amendment would also be subject to scrutiny. Examples of such provisions include those relating to years of service and breaks in service as well as to actuarial factors used in computing optional or early retirement benefits.

SPECIAL RULES FOR CLASS-YEAR PLANS

Vesting

Class-year plans are profit-sharing, stock bonus, and money-purchase plans which identify each year's contribution as an individual *class.* Each class of contributions becomes vested within a specified number of years so that a participant may have many classes of contributions vested in varying degrees at a particular point in time. For example, a plan may state that each class of contributions will become fully vested within four years, provided that the participant is still an employee on that date. Thus, contributions made on an employee's behalf in 1980 would become fully vested in 1984, and those made in 1981 would become fully vested in 1985.

The IRS requires qualified class-year plans to provide full vesting for each class no later than five plan years after the plan year for which the contribution is made.[37] Note that a class-year plan may not require an employee to complete a certain number of years of service to become fully vested in any contribution, the common method of measuring vesting under other types of defined contribution plans. Instead, vesting must be predicated upon the number of years that have elapsed from the year of contribution. However, this kind of plan is allowed to cancel any nonvested contribution when an employee merely separates from service before the year in which full vesting is to occur and is not rehired during the plan year of separation.[38] This is an obvious departure from the stringent break in service rule imposed upon other types of plans.

[37] IRS Reg. Section 1.411 (d) (3) (a). Note that the regulation speaks in terms of an *employee's* right to full vesting. The employee need not be a plan participant when the time for vesting occurs.

[38] *Separation from service* is not defined in the regulation. We assume it denotes a quit, discharge, or retirement as opposed to absence due to leaves, illness, layoffs, and so on, as described for other purposes in DOL regulations and conference reports on ERISA.

Example

Plan A provides that each class of employer contributions will become fully vested at the end of the fourth plan year after the contribution year, and no vesting will be credited before that time. The plan year is a calendar year. The plan incorporates the *separation from service* rule. John, a Plan A participant, is credited with contributions for 1980, 1981, and 1982. These contributions would become vested at the end of 1984, 1985, and 1986, respectively (the vesting years). John separates from service on December 1, 1983, and returns to work on January 2, 1984. Since John separated from service in 1983 and returned the following plan year, none of the classes of contributions listed above will ever become payable to him because his separation occurred before each of the vesting years.

The Effect of Withdrawals on Vesting

When counting the number of years that have elapsed in order to determine the vesting of a particular class, plans are not required to recognize any year for which there was a withdrawal and no repayment of contributions related to that class nor any subsequent year during which the employee made no repayment of those funds.[39]

IMPORTANT FACTORS
FOR PLAN DESIGN

Vesting is a key element in the design of any defined contribution or defined benefit plan. It should therefore be analyzed in light of an employer's costs and benefit objectives as well as statutory requirements. In the latter regard, the following points should be carefully considered in order to identify circumstances that might involve specific vesting requirements.

the level provided by a current vesting schedule in comparison with a new one;

service under a *predecessor* plan;

employees within the *controlled group* of the employer;

classes of covered employees, frequency of transfers between classes and locations;

[39] IRS Reg. Section 1.411 (d)-3 (a) (2) (ii). The regulation does not distinguish between mandatory employee contributions or employer contributions but the former would most likely be the only type of contribution permitted to be withdrawn before a class becomes vested. Note that the cancellation of an employer-derived *benefit*, but *not vesting service*, associated with withdrawn mandatory contributions is permitted in some cases, under Reg. Section 1.411 (a)-7 (d) (2) and (3). Such regulation is applied to each class separately in succeeding order of time.

the correctness and practicality of the plan's *break in service* rules;

the method used for computing vesting service and the coordination of service counted for other purposes;

employee contributions;

in-service distributions and withdrawals;

the plan's *normal retirement age;*

employer's policy on rehiring terminated employees, granting leaves of absence, frequency of layoffs, and so forth;

discrimination in favor of the *prohibited group;* and

turnover rates for different classes of employees.

APPENDIX C

An Analysis of the ERISA Minimum Standards Regulations Relating to Hours of Service

INTRODUCTION

The standards imposed by ERISA with respect to the periods of service which must be recognized under defined benefit and defined contribution plans have caused almost every employer to reassess plan coverage, employment practices, record-keeping systems, and general plan administration.

The minimum standards of ERISA relating to participation, vesting, and benefit accrual are based on a common element, the year of service. As defined in ERISA, a *year of service* means a 12-month period designated by the plan during which the participant has completed 1,000 hours of service. The term *hour of service* and the rules regarding the permissible 12-month periods that could be designated by the plan were left to the Department of Labor (DOL) to be developed in regulations.

This is a detailed analysis of the minimum standards regulations issued by the DOL which provide guidelines with respect to permissible methods of computing service under retirement plans.[1] The analysis has been designed as a reference source for use by persons involved in the design and administration of retirement plans. It is divided into four major sections:

Method I—The General Method: Counting Hours of Service and the Equivalencies;

Method II—The Elapsed Time Method;

Additional Service Rules; and

Factors To Be Considered When Adopting Service Computation Method.

Within each section, the applicable service computation rules are outlined and analyzed. In addition, footnoted citations have been provided throughout.

BACKGROUND CONCERNING THE REGULATIONS

On September 8, 1975, the DOL issued proposed and temporary rules which prescribed minimum standards for retirement plans relating to the crediting of periods of service. A hearing was subsequently held regarding alternatives to the *year of service* definition and related provisions.

While the proposed and temporary regulations were in the process of revision, the DOL issued four ERISA Technical Releases in June 1976, describing the forthcoming changes in an effort to provide immediate guidance to the public engaged in amending their pension plans.

Final regulations were issued on December 28, 1976. One of the most important changes incorporated in these regulations is the creation of the *elapsed time* method, in response to public comment, published as a temporary rule effective immediately. The elapsed time rules were finalized in an IRS regulation issued June 16, 1980.

PLANS SUBJECT TO THE MINIMUM STANDARDS AND EXCEPTIONS

The minimum standards requirements relating to periods of service for the purposes of eligibility, vesting, and benefit accrual apply generally to all de-

---

[1] Regulations under Chapter XXV, Subchapter C, Part 2530.

fined benefit (pension) and defined contribution (profit-sharing, money-purchase, stock bonus, etc.) plans. Excepted from coverage are:[2]

unfunded deferred compensation plans for a select group of management or highly compensated employees;

plans maintained by organizations exempt from taxation under Section 501 (c) (8) or (9) of the Internal Revenue Code and which do not provide for any employer contributions;

plans maintained by labor organizations exempt from taxation under Section 501 (c) (5) of the code and which do not provide for any employer contributions after ERISA's enactment date (September 2, 1974);

a trust that is exempt from taxation under Section 501 (c) (18) of the code;

individual retirement accounts, annuities, or retirement bonds;

excess benefit plans (plans providing benefits in excess of the maximum contribution and benefit limitations under Section 415 of the code);

government plans;

church plans (unless they elect ERISA coverage);

plans maintained to comply with applicable workmen's compensation, unemployment compensation, or disability insurance laws;

agreements providing payments to retired partners or to deceased partners' successors in interest as described in Section 736 of the code; and

plans maintained outside the United States primarily for the benefit of persons substantially all of whom are nonresident aliens.

METHOD I—THE GENERAL METHOD: COUNTING HOURS OF SERVICE AND THE EQUIVALENCIES

As previously indicated, an employee completing at least 1,000 hours of service during a 12-month computation period must generally be credited with one year of service. Any hour, as described below, for which the employee is paid (or is entitled to payment) by his employer, whether or not he actually works during such period, must be counted. *Unpaid periods of time under this method need not be recognized for any purpose.*

Definition of Hour of Service

An hour of service[3] must include the following *paid* periods of time:

hours of service for which an employee is paid, or entitled to payment, *for the performance of duties* for the employer,

---

[2] DOL Reg. Section 2530.201-2.
[3] DOL Reg. Section 2530.200b-2 (a)—must be explicitly incorporated in plan [Section 2530.200b-2 (f)].

hours of service for which an employee is paid or entitled to payment by the employer on account of a period of time *during which no duties are performed* (even if the employment relationship has terminated) due to vacation, holiday, illness, incapacity (i.e., a condition preventing the performance of duties such as pregnancy), disability, layoff, jury duty, military duty, or leave of absence, and, in this regard,

> only 501 hours of service need be credited to the employee for a single continuous period of absence whether or not such period occurs in one computation period,

> these unworked hours must be credited[4] to the computation period in which the first unit of unworked, but paid, time relates. If the absence extends into more than one computation period, the plan may allocate the recognized hours proportionately over two (but not more than two) computation periods. However, if the absence is for no longer than 31 days, the recognized hours may (if done on a consistent basis) be wholly allocated to the first, or the second, computation period, and

> no credit is required for periods of time for which the employee receives payments under a plan maintained solely for the purpose of complying with workmen's compensation laws, or unemployment compensation or disability insurance laws, or under a program under which he is reimbursed solely for medical or medically related expenses, and

hours of service for which back pay is either awarded or agreed to by the employer, and, in this regard,

> these hours need not be credited if they are already counted under the hours of service described above, for duties performed or not performed,

> the 501-hour limit also applies when the back pay is for periods during which no work is performed, and

> these hours of service should be credited to the computation period for which the back pay was awarded, which may differ from the computation period in which the back pay was actually received by the employee.

Calculating Hours for Nonservice Time

There are two prescribed ways to derive a number of hours from the dollar amount of payment received for nonservice time depending on whether payments are made on the basis of units of time.[5]

Units of Time

If the payment is based on units of time, that is, hours, days, weeks, or months, the number of hours should be calculated on the basis of the regularly sched-

---

[4] DOL Reg. Section 2530.200b-2 (c)—may be incorporated in plan by reference [Section 2530.200b-2 (f)].

[5] DOL Reg. Section 2530.200b-2 (b)—may be incorporated in plan by reference [Section 2530.200b-2 (f)].

uled working hours included in the applicable unit of time, or any reasonable basis reflecting the average hours worked by the employee. The method must be consistently applied with respect to all similarly situated employees.

For example, if an employee is paid for two weeks vacation and is scheduled to work 40 hours per week, he must be credited with 80 hours of service (two weeks times 40 hours).

Suppose that another employee, who has no regular work schedule, received three weeks of vacation pay. His plan provides that such payments are to be based on a 40-hour work week, regardless of actual hours usually worked. Thus, the employee would be credited with 120 hours of service (three weeks times 40 hours).

Units Other Than Time

If the payment for a period of nonservice is not based on units of time, but is, for example, made on account of a period of disability, the number of hours must be based on the employee's most recent hourly rate of compensation. For example, if an hourly employee paid at a rate of $5 per hour receives $500 on account of a disability, he will be credited with 100 hours of service ($500 divided by $5).

For a nonhourly employee, hours of service are calculated by dividing the payment by an hourly rate determined by dividing his most recent rate of compensation for a specific unit of time by his number of regularly scheduled hours included in the applicable unit of time. If a salaried employee who receives $320 per week received the same amount for a disability, he would be credited with 62½ hours of service, provided he was scheduled to work 40 hours per week. ($320 ÷ 40 hours = $8 per hour. $500 ÷ $8 = 62½ hours.)

If an employee has no regular work schedule, hours of service are to be based upon a reasonable factor which reflects the average hours worked by the employee over a representative period of time, consistently used.

Avoiding Double Credit

Plans are not required to give *double credit* for a single period of service. For example, if an employee is paid two extra weeks' salary for unused vacation time, no additional hours of service need be credited to him with respect to the additional compensation (vacation pay) he received. Moreover, plans are not required to credit an employee with more hours of service for a period of time during which no work was performed than the number of working hours regularly scheduled for him.

For example, if an hourly paid worker whose rate of pay is $3.50 per hour receives a lump-sum payment of $600 on account of his disability which lasted two weeks, he need not be credited with 171 hours of service ($600 divided by $3.50) if he would have been scheduled to work only 80 hours during those two weeks.

Additional Examples

The following examples will further clarify these hour of service rules.

Employee A worked 880 hours in the beginning of the computation period, then quit and was at that time paid for four weeks vacation which he had not taken earlier that year. He was scheduled to work for 40 hours a week. Thus, he was credited with 160 hours of service for his vacation (40 hours multiplied by four weeks) plus 880 hours of service for the entire computation period. Note that he was credited with 160 hours for the period of time for which he received his vacation pay even though his employment relationship was severed.

Employee B who normally works 37½ hours a week received sick pay from his employer for 10 weeks. At the end of such time, he began to receive disability payments from the disability plan to which he contributes for the remainder of the computation period. The employer does not contribute to this disability plan. Employee B is credited with 375 hours of service under his pension plan for the entire computation period. Because the employer does not contribute to the disability plan, no credit is given to the employee beyond the 10 weeks (375 hours).

Minimum Numbers of Hours of Service for Different Plan Purposes and Appropriate Computation Periods

The chart on the following page briefly outlines how many hours of service are needed to complete a year of service for different plan purposes and the computation period(s) prescribed for each such year.

Computation Periods

The following examples illustrate how computation periods work for different plan purposes.

Under Plan A, an employee must complete 1,000 hours of service in the first year of employment, or anniversaries thereof, in order to be eligible to participate. Thus, an employee who fails to complete 1,000 hours in his first year of employment must complete 1,000 hours in the second, or some subsequent, anniversary year in order to satisfy the one-year eligibility requirement. The plan year is a calendar year.

The time line on page 268 shows that an employee commences employment on 6/1/77. He completes one year of service for eligibility purposes as of 5/31/79, the end of the year in which he completed 1,100 hours of service (700 hours from 6/1/78 to 1/1/79 and 400 hours from 1/1/79 to 6/1/79). The first year of employment is disregarded because he only earned 700 hours (350 hours from 6/1/77 to 1/1/78 and 350 hours from 1/1/78 to 6/1/78).

Plan Purpose	Prescribed Computation Period	Number of Hours of Service in Computation Period
Eligibility to Participate	*Initially:* The 12-month period beginning with the employee's first day of employment[6] *Subsequently:* Either: The 12-month period beginning with an anniversary of the employee's first day of employment,[6] *or* The plan year in which falls an anniversary of the employee's first day of employment[6]	1,000 equals a full year of eligibility service.
Vesting in Employer-Derived Benefits	Any designated 12-month period[7]	1,000 equals a full year of vesting service.
Benefit Accrual	Any designated 12-month period[8]	*Defined Benefit Plans:* Plans must credit a participant who completes 1,000 or more hours of service with *at least a*

[6] DOL Reg. Section 2530.202-2—must be explicitly incorporated in plan [Section 2530.200b-1 (a)]. If the first day of employment cannot be ascertained (e.g., records in terms of payroll periods rather than actual days or hours worked), the plan can use the beginning of the 31-day (or less) period during which an employee began work as the starting date of the initial computation period. The computation period should end on the anniversary of the last day of this period. Analogous principles apply to subsequent computation periods, if based upon employment anniversaries [thus creating 31-day (or less) overlaps]. If subsequent computation periods are based upon plan years, the rule must be with regard to the anniversary of the starting date of the initial computation period, rather than with regard to the last day of that period. A similar rule applies for the purpose of determining an employee's commencement of participation. DOL Reg. Section 2530.202-2 (e).

[7] DOL Reg. Section 2530.203-2—must be explicitly incorporated in plan [Section 2530.200b-1 (a)]. A plan may be amended to change the vesting computation period. However, no employee can receive less vesting credit with the new period in force than he would have received if not for the amendment. This requirement is satisfied if a year of vesting is given for the old computation period as well as for the new one, where the required hours are completed in each of those 12-month periods. See DOL Reg. Section 2530.203-2 (c). See DOL Reg. Section 2530.200b-4 (b) (2) for similar rules for vesting computation periods beginning on the employee's first day of employment, and subsequent periods beginning after a break.

[8] DOL Reg. Section 2530.204-2—must be explicitly incorporated in plan [Section 2530.200b-1 (a)]. A plan may be amended to change the accrual computation period. However, the resulting shortened period immediately preceding the first new period must use a ratably shortened service requirement in lieu of the usual 1,000-hour requirement. DOL Reg. Section 2530.204-2 (e).

Plan Purpose	Prescribed Computation Period	Number of Hours of Service in Computation Period
		partial year of benefit accrual service. However, the benefit accrual service need only reflect the hours completed as a participant. A plan is allowed to count only *hours worked* when determining the partial accrual for a participant who was credited with 1,000 or more hours of service as long as prohibited discrimination does not result.
		Hours needed to complete a *full year* of benefit accrual service can not exceed the customary work year, *i.e.,* 2,080 for most industries. For further explanation, see below, "Special Rules for General Method."
		Defined Contribution Plans: Usually 1,000 participant hours must equal a year of benefit accrual. For exceptions, see below, "Special Rules for General Method."
Break in Service	*For purposes of eligibility to participate:* The eligibility computation period used subsequent to the initial period[9] *For purposes of vesting:* The vesting computation period[10]	Less than 501 hours can be considered a one-year break in service.

[9] DOL Reg. Section 2530.200b-4 (a) (2).
[10] DOL Reg. Section 2530.200b-4 (a) (3).

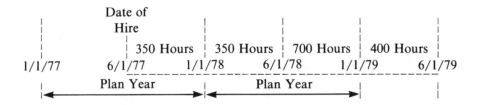

This plan could have designated the first year of employment as the initial eligibility computation period and the plan year for subsequent computation periods. Thus, the employee described above would have satisfied his one-year eligibility requirement as of the last day of the 1978 plan year which is the plan year that began within his first year of employment, because the employee completed 1,050 hours of service in that plan year (350 hours from 1/1/78 to 6/1/78 and 700 hours from 6/1/78 to 1/1/79).

Note how there is an overlap in determining the starting point of computation periods after the initial one. If an employee completes 1,000 hours of service in both the initial and the first subsequent computation periods (when this is the plan year), *two* years of service must be credited for eligibility purposes. For example, the line below indicates that an employee completes 1,000 hours in his first year of employment and 1,000 hours in the overlapping plan (calendar) year. He has thus accumulated *two* years for eligibility purposes.

Thus, for full-time employees who would meet the 1,000 hours of service test in any computation period, this overlap has special significance where a plan requires up to three years of service for eligibility to participate or where a plan provides that prebreak service will be disregarded if the length of break in service is equal to or greater than prebreak service. The most dramatic effect of

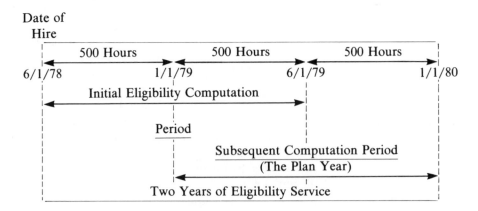

the rule would occur in the case of a full-time employee hired on the last day of a calendar plan year; one year and one day later, this employee would be credited with *two* years of service.

Returning now to our original example (where all eligibility computation periods are based on an employee's employment commencement date), Plan A provides that participation begins as soon as the eligibility conditions are met, accrual computation periods are calendar plan years, and that a full year of benefit accrual is credited for 2,000 hours of service. Only hours of service while in participant status are used for benefit accrual purposes.

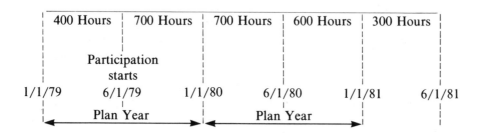

The above time line is a continuation of the one shown previously for our employee under Plan A; the service condition for eligibility was met as of 6/1/79. Thus, for the 1979 plan year, he is credited with 700/2000 or 35% of a benefit accrual year—only the hours of service completed as a *participant* in 1979 are taken into account for the 1979 benefit accrual year. For the 1980 plan year, he is credited with 1300/2000 or 65% of a benefit accrual year.

Break in Service Rules

ERISA's break in service rules govern the extent to which an employee's service completed prior to a break in service may be disregarded. These rules:

apply to employees who terminate their employment *after* the date that ERISA became effective for their plan (in 1976 for most plans), and

do not apply to service completed by an employee prior to termination of employment which occurred before this date. However, if he is rehired after ERISA is in effect, the rules *would apply* to such pre-ERISA service, at least to a minor extent, as will be seen later.

Some employers will be more liberal than necessary just to avoid the administration of these often complex break in service rules. For example, rehired employees are often granted credit for previously completed service even though it is not required under ERISA's break in service rules. This approach is often appropriate for employers who rarely rehire employees or who want to use a liberal reinstatement policy as an incentive to bring back former employees.

Parity Rule

For employees who are completely nonvested as to employer provided benefits, years of service completed before a break in service are not required to be considered for the purpose of eligibility to participate, or for vesting, if the number of consecutive one-year breaks in service, as determined for either purpose, equals or exceeds the number of years of service for that purpose. Thus, the number of consecutive years of break in service must be compared to the former years of service as determined for the same purpose. For either eligibility or vesting, years of service disregarded because of the parity rule may be disregarded in making the relevant comparison under a subsequent application of the rule.[11]

When service for *either* eligibility *or* vesting is disregarded because of the parity rule, such service may also be disregarded for the purpose of benefit accrual.[12]

The parity rule is not applicable for employees who have *any degree* of vesting in employer-provided benefits.

Example: Employee A works for two years and nine months and then incurs four consecutive years of break in service. His plan provides for full vesting upon the completion of 10 years of service (none before) and for entry into the plan upon the completion of one year of service within the first year of employment or the plan year, regardless of age. The vesting computation period is the calendar plan year. The plan incorporates the parity rule for both eligibility and vesting purposes.

Because Employee A worked at least 1,000 hours in the year he terminated,

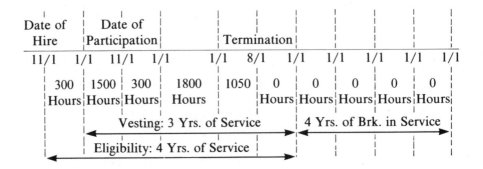

[11] Code Reg. Sections 1.410 (a)-5 (c) (4) and 1.411 (a)-6 (c) (1) (iii).
[12] DOL Reg. Section 2530.204-1 (b).

Employee A is credited with a year of benefit accrual, eligibility, and vesting service with respect to that year. Because of the overlap treatment, he picks up an additional year for eligibility purposes at the beginning of his work span. Therefore, although he worked less than three calendar years preceding his four-year break, we count four prebreak eligibility years for this employee. And when we compare this number to the number of his one-year breaks—four in all—we find that his service can be canceled under the parity rule. Likewise, it is clear that prebreak vesting service can also be canceled. The plan could also have provided for the cancellation of prebreak benefit accrual service.

Break in Service Computation Periods

Since different computation periods are assigned for different plan purposes, it is possible for an employee to incur a break in service for one purpose, but not for another. Thus, the type of computation period must be identified in order to determine if an employee incurs a break for a specific plan purpose.

A break in service for the purpose of eligibility to participate is determined by using the computation periods used to determine eligibility after the initial year. Therefore, if a plan uses the plan year for the "secondary" eligibility computation period, it must use the plan year to measure a break in service for eligibility. The computation period within which a break in service is determined for *vesting* purposes is always the *vesting* computation period; for example, the plan year.

Plans with Immediate Vesting after Three Years of Service

In the case of a plan that requires the completion of up to three years of service for plan eligibility, if an employee incurs a break in service before satisfying that service requirement, prebreak service may be completely disregarded for eligibility purposes so that a rehired employee can be required to satisfy the full three-year service requirement after his break.[13]

Plans which impose this three-year service rule must provide that employees will become fully vested upon completion of no more than three years of service.

One-Year Waiting Period

Years of service completed before a break in service are not required to be reinstated for the purpose of eligibility or vesting until a year of service (1,000 hours) is completed after a break.[14] The initial computation period used in measuring this one-year waiting period must begin on the reemployment commencement date; where a plan uses the plan year for the secondary eligibility

---

[13] Code Reg. Section 1.410 (a)-5 (c) (2).
[14] Code Reg. Sections 1.410 (a)-5 (c) (3) and 1.411 (a)-6 (c) (1) (i).

computation period, it must also use the plan year for measuring the one-year waiting period when the waiting period is not completed within the initial computation period. After the completion of the one-year waiting period, prebreak participation and vesting must be reinstated. The waiting period must also be considered like any other period of service in the determination of eligibility, vesting, and benefit accrual service under the applicable rules of the plan.

In general, contributory plans would most likely reinstate returning participants promptly (i.e., to ignore the waiting period rule) in order to require their immediate contributions.

Special Rule for Defined Contribution Plans

Under a defined contribution plan, service completed subsequent to a break in service does not have to increase the vesting percentage of a prebreak account balance.[15]

Pre-ERISA Service

To the extent a plan has to determine hours of service completed before the effective date of ERISA, a plan may use whatever resources are reasonably accessible. Plans may estimate the hours worked if the data on hand is insufficient for an exact count.[16]

The techniques used to determine pre-ERISA service should take into account the extent to which service has to be measured. For example, pre-ERISA vesting service which would have been canceled by virtue of the plan's pre-ERISA break in service rules is allowed to remain canceled (for vesting purposes) even after the effective date of ERISA. Thus, the popular "continuous service" requirement that considered every employee a new employee when he returned to work after a termination would enable a plan to completely ignore pre-ERISA service *for vesting purposes* for all employees not on the payroll on the effective date of ERISA.[17] Such a plan would also be able to ignore pre-ERISA service for *purposes of benefit accrual.*[18] Thus, the plan would have to consider pre-ERISA service for employees who quit before ERISA's effective date and return afterward for only the limited purpose of determining the date the returning employee must be eligible to participate.

Equivalency Methods

Recognizing that many employers do not keep records that would enable them to count each hour for which an employee is paid and because a large segment

---

[15] Code Reg. Section 1.411 (a)-6 (c) (1) (ii).
[16] DOL Reg. Section 2530.200b-3 (b).
[17] Code Reg. Section 1.411 (a)-5 (b) (6).
[18] DOL Reg. Section 2530.204-2 (b).

of the work force does not work on an hourly basis, the Department of Labor established certain alternative methods which are intended to eliminate the need for detailed record keeping.[19] The equivalency rules do not, however, completely eliminate the need to count hours.

The equivalency methods basically fall into three categories:

1 equivalency based on periods of employment;
2 equivalency based on modified hours of service; and
3 equivalency based on earnings.

Method[20]		Employment Periods Equivalent to a Year of Service[21]
Credit these numbers of hours whenever the employee completes one hour of service in the chosen period of time:		
(a) *Day:*	10	100 days = 1 year of service $\left(\text{i.e., } \dfrac{1000 \text{ hours}}{10} \right)$ 50 days = maximum days for a break in service $\left(\text{i.e., } \dfrac{500}{10} \right)$
(b) *Week:*	45	23 weeks = 1 year of service 11 weeks = maximum weeks for a break in service
(c) *Semimonthly Payroll Period:*	95	11 semimonthly payroll periods = 1 year of service 5 periods = maximum periods for a break in service
(d) *Month:*	190	6 months = 1 year of service 2 months = maximum months for a break in service
(e) *Shift:*	Number of Hours in Shift	Assuming 8 hours in shift: 125 shifts = 1 year of service 62 shifts = maximum shifts for a break in service

[19] DOL Reg. Section 2530.200b-3 (c).
[20] DOL Reg. Section 2530.200b-3 (e)—time periods of shifts used as periods of employment must be set forth in document (such as collective-bargaining agreement) referred to in plan.
[21] Where employment periods overlap two different computation periods, hours of service may be credited to the overlapping periods on any consistent basis. DOL Reg. Section 2530.200b-3 (e) (6).

In addition, a combination of the first two categories may be used. The equivalency used to calculate service must be set forth in the plan document.[22]

Equivalencies Based on Periods of Employment

The preceding table shows the number of employment periods that will be considered a year of service if this equivalency method is used.

Note that using days of service will probably be the most liberal period to use since only 100 days are needed to complete a year of service as compared to weeks of service which would require, when converted back to days, about 115 working days (five working days in each week), and months which would require approximately 120 days (on the basis that there are about 20 working days in each month). On the other hand, by using smaller units of time less unworked time will be credited. For example, if an hour is completed during one month, the whole month must be credited. If the plan uses the weekly basis, only the particular week will be credited. Also note that the above rules are superceded by the rule for hours of service for paid periods of nonworking time, where the payments are not based on units of time.[23]

Equivalencies Based on Modified Hours of Service[24]

Method	Hours Equivalent to a Year of Service
(a) If only *hours worked* are counted (including hours for which back pay is received):	870 hours = 1 year of service 435 hours = maximum hours for a break in service
(b) If only *regular time* (exclusive of overtime[25]) hours are counted:	750 hours = 1 year of service 375 hours = maximum hours for a break in service

As indicated on the chart above, if a plan does not wish to track every paid hour during a given period of time, that plan will be forced, in accordance with the particular modified hours equivalency chosen, to recognize less than 1,000 hours as a year of service to compensate for the possibility that an employee may have actually completed more hours during a particular period than were recorded under that method.

With respect to the *hours worked* equivalency, the smaller number reflects the omission of hours of service for which no duties are performed.

---

[22] DOL Reg. Section 2530.200b-3 (c) (1).
[23] DOL Reg. Section 2530.200b-3 (e) (4).
[24] DOL Reg. Section 2530.200b-3 (d).
[25] Overtime for which a premium rate is paid either under Section 7(a) of the Fair Labor Act of 1938 or because the overtime hours are in excess of bona fide standard hours.

With respect to the *regular time hours* equivalency, a smaller number of hours would constitute a year of service in order to account for overtime hours that are not included in the calculation.

Combination of Equivalencies Based on Periods of Employment and Modified Hours of Service

The alternative method of calculating service based on periods of employment can be combined with the hours worked or regular time hours equivalency.[26] For example, a plan may provide that an employee who completes one hour of *worked* time during a week will be credited with 45 hours of service; however, only 870 hours will be needed to accrue a full year of service, instead of 1,000. Similarly, if a plan combines the use of the *regular time* equivalency with one of the methods based on a period of employment, only 750 hours will be needed to complete a year of service. The reduced number of hours of service (435 and 375, respectively) for purposes of determining a break in service are also in effect in such cases.

Equivalencies Based on Earnings

The last type of equivalency is one based on an employee's earnings during the computation period.[27] Actually, this method is more of a means of deriving a number of hours from payroll data than it is an equivalency in the sense of the previously explained methods.

An *hourly paid* employee may be credited with a number of hours in a computation period based on his earnings if:

the number of hours of service are equal to the total of earnings paid from time to time during the computation period divided by the employee's hourly rate as in effect at such times (including the overtime rate, at the option of the plan) during the period, or they are equal to the employee's earnings while working during the computation period, divided by the employee's lowest hourly rate of earnings during the computation period, or by the lowest rate of such a similarly situated employee; and if

870 hours are treated as equivalent to the 1,000-hour year of service, 435 hours being equivalent to the 500-hour break in service.

A *nonhourly* employee may be credited with a number of hours of service in a computation period based on his earnings if the following conditions are met:

the number of hours of service credited are at least equal to the employee's total earnings for *hours worked* during the computation period divided by the employee's *lowest hourly rate* of compensation during the computation period. The lowest hourly rate is determined by the employee's rate of com-

[26] DOL Reg. Section 2530.200b-3 (e) (7).
[27] DOL Reg. Section 2530.200b-3 (f).

pensation for the applicable period (e.g., one week) divided by the number of hours regularly worked. The plan may use a basis of a 40-hour week or any other reasonable factor for those employees who do not have a regular schedule. It may use the lowest hourly rate for similarly situated employees in the case of an employee who does not have a fixed rate of pay for a specific period of time;[28] and

750 hours are treated as equivalent to the 1,000-hour year of service, 375 hours being equivalent to the 500-hour break in service.

Since overtime may not be reflected in this calculation, 750 hours or the equivalent imposed under the regular time method is required to be used under this method.

Examples of Equivalency Methods

1 Employee A's pension plan uses the *weekly* equivalency method. In one computation period, Employee A works each Monday and only during that day for 40 weeks. He then takes a three-week vacation during which he is paid his usual salary. He quits after his vacation is completed. Employee A must be credited with 45 hours for each of the 40 weeks, yielding 1,800 hours of service, plus 135 hours representing his paid vacation, for a total of 1,935 hours of service.

2 Employee B's pension plan counts only *regular hours* as opposed to all hours including overtime hours. Employee B worked 900 hours regular time and 100 hours overtime. Under this method, though he would be credited with only 900 hours of service, he would nevertheless have well over the 750 hours needed for a year of service.

3 Employee C's pension plan counts only *hours worked* and counts hours on a *monthly* basis. Employee C works sporadically each month, but always works at least one hour per month. During the computation period in question, he worked for two consecutive months, then became disabled for four months and received payments from his employer's disability plan. Employee C would be credited with 380 hours, the period he worked. The 435 hours needed to avoid a break in service would not be reached.

METHOD II—THE ELAPSED TIME METHOD

The elapsed time method as described in the final IRS regulations provides an alternative to the hours of service concept and its equivalency variations.[29] Under a plan that uses the elapsed time method, service is determined by the

---

[28] The IRS Alert Guidelines mention that the use of this rate must not discriminate in favor of highly paid employees.
[29] Code Reg. Section 1.410 (a)-7.

length of time that has elapsed between two dates of reference. By completely eliminating the task of counting hours, this method reduces the record keeping involved in maintaining a plan. However, elapsed time plans are required to give credit for certain *unpaid* absences and short-term service. In addition, interrupted periods of service would generally have to be aggregated in a manner which keeps track of fractional portions of a year.

General Rules

Service for Determining Eligibility To Participate and Vesting

Under the elapsed time method, generally all service from an employee's first date of service to the end of his period of continuous service must be taken into account for eligibility and vesting. The period of continuous service is not considered to terminate until the earlier of:

the date on which the employee quits, dies, retires, or is discharged (a "hard" absence), or

the date which is one year after the day he leaves and remains absent for some other reason (or combination of reasons), such as disability, vacation, leave of absence, holiday, sickness, layoff (a "soft" absence).

Therefore, soft absences (paid or unpaid) up to 12 months in length would have to be included in the employee's span of continuous service. Furthermore, the regulations include a special rule on absences known as the "service spanning rule." This rule provides that:

If an employee quits, retires, or is discharged while on a "soft absence" and returns to work within 12 months after he originally left, his continuous service must not be considered to have been interrupted, that is, eligibility and vesting service must continue to be credited throughout the period.

Similarly, if an employee quits, retires, or is discharged and returns to work within 12 months, his absence must also be treated as continuous service for vesting and eligibility purposes.

If an employee quits during a soft absence, the plan must take into account only the period of time from the first day of that absence to the anniversary of such date, or until the date he quits, if that occurs before the anniversary date. For example, assume that an employee is laid off for 13 months and is then called back to work. He informs his employer at that point that he is terminating employment. However, he does return to work 10 months after being recalled. Continuous service would have to be credited for the first 12 months of the layoff, but no credit would have to be granted for the absence following this 12-month period; the elapsed time rules never require a plan to recognize more than 12 consecutive months of unworked time. As discussed in detail later, even though the 11-month absence is not considered continuous service, the employee would not incur a break in service for purposes of determining whether past service can be canceled.

Service To Be Taken into Account for Benefit Accrual Purposes

Generally, all service from the employee's date of plan admission to the date on which his continuous service terminates must be counted. However, any period of time after the employee is discharged, quits, or retires and prior to re-employment, need *not* be counted as part of continuous service for benefit accrual purposes, even though such period *may* have to be recognized for vesting and eligibility purposes. On the other hand, periods of time up to 12 months during which an employee is absent for any other reason (a soft absence) which must be taken into account for vesting and eligibility purposes must also be counted for benefit accrual purposes.

Examples:

1   Employee A begins to work on 1/1/77 and becomes a participant in a defined benefit pension plan immediately. He quits on 6/12/78. Employee A returns to work for the employer on 5/12/79, and again becomes a participant immediately. His span of continuous service, as it differs for various purposes, is shown on the time line below:

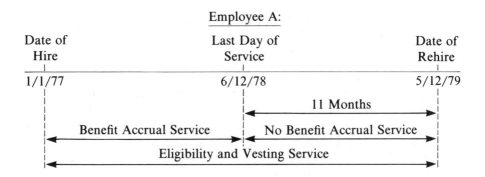

Employee A:

Date of Hire	Last Day of Service	Date of Rehire
1/1/77	6/12/78	5/12/79

Since Employee A was absent for less than 12 months (11 months) his continuous service for certain purposes includes the period of absence. Thus, his eligibility and vesting service must include all time from 1/1/77 to 5/12/79. However, only the period of time before he left, between 1/1/77 and 6/12/78, has to be taken into account for benefit accrual purposes; this is because Employee A's absence was not a "soft absence." This example shows that the service spanning rule applies for eligibility and vesting purposes, but not for benefit accrual purposes.

2   Employee B begins to work on 6/1/77. On 6/1/78 he becomes a participant in a retirement plan upon completing the one-year eligibility requirement. He takes a two-year leave of absence beginning on 12/1/79 and does not

return upon the expiration date of his leave. The employer wants to recognize leaves of any length until the date of their expiration for all plan purposes (which would exceed the minimum requirements imposed by the regulation), but only if the employee returns to work when the leave expires. Thus, the employer's generous policy will not apply to Employee B although he must be given the benefit of the regulation's minimum requirements.

As the time line below illustrates, Employee B's continuous service for all purposes terminates on 12/1/80, which is the earlier of his termination (the expiration date of the leave) and the first anniversary of his last day of active service. Employee B returns to work on 3/1/82. The period between 12/1/80 and 3/1/82 is not recognized for any plan purpose; it is analogous to a break in service under the general method, as will be explained later.

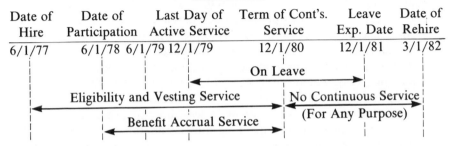

Employee B:

3   Employee C begins his employment on 3/1/78 and becomes a participant in a defined benefit pension plan immediately. He works for three years until 3/1/81 when he is laid off by his employer. On 8/1/81 he is called back to work but he informs his employer that he does not wish to return. On 3/5/82, however, he does go back to work for the employer.

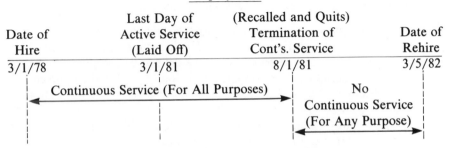

Employee C:

Employee C must be credited with continuous service for all plan purposes from 3/1/78, his date of hire, to 8/1/81. The period between 8/1/81 and 3/5/82 can be disregarded since Employee C returned more than 12 months after his last day of active service, 3/1/81. However, as will be explained later, the period disregarded is *not* analogous to a break in service.

Break in Service Rules

The break in service rules for the elapsed time method are generally similar to the rules explained for the general method.

Under the elapsed time method, a break in service is simply *a period of absence of one year or longer.* A period of absence, in turn, is a period during which there is no continuous service. As indicated earlier, since certain periods of nonemployment are considered part of "continuous service," these periods would *not* be considered "periods of absence" for the purpose of determining whether or not a break in service occurred.

Therefore, if a nonworking period is a soft absence, a break in service will be delayed or may not occur at all. For example, a 25-month leave of absence could be classified as a 13-month "period of absence" for break in service purposes (since the first 12 months must be considered continuous service). Thus, the break in service would not begin until 12 months after the employee actually stops working. On the other hand, a 23-month leave could lead to only an 11-month interruption and no break in service would occur at all.

Note that the special service spanning rule has no impact on breaks in service. This is because the spanning rule only comes into play for nonemployment periods shorter than a year in length.

The break in service rules for elapsed time plans generally work in the same way as those for the general method—the length of the break is compared to the length of prior service in order to determine whether prebreak service can be disregarded. There is one possible difference, however. Under the general method, whenever vesting service can be disregarded under the rule of parity, prior benefit accrual service may be also disregarded. *However, under the elapsed time method, benefit accrual service can be cancelled only when service for eligibility purposes can be disregarded under the rule of parity.*

Example 1:   Employee A, after completing five years of service, is not vested to any extent in employer-derived benefits. He then quits and his period of absence lasts four years. The retirement plan is a defined benefit plan which contains the rule of parity but has no "waiting period" for rehired employees.

Employee A's five years of continuous service completed before his termination must be aggregated with any postabsence period of employment for eligibility, vesting, and benefit accrual purposes, because his four-year break in service was shorter than the length of his previous service.

Let us now suppose that the plan had been a defined contribution plan with 10-year *cliff vesting.* Upon his termination, Employee A received no distribu-

Employee A:

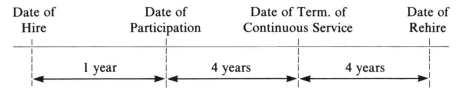

Date of Hire | Date of Participation | Date of Term. of Continuous Service | Date of Rehire

1 year | 4 years | 4 years

tion because he was not vested; his account balance was forfeited. In this case, prebreak employment must enable him to participate immediately upon rehire. Prebreak vesting service must also count toward the vesting of future additions to his plan account. However, the postbreak employment does not have to vest Employee A in the account balance that he forfeited because of the special rule for defined contribution plans.

Example 2: Employee B worked for six years and was not vested to any extent in employer-derived benefits. He then quit and his period of absence lasted four years. The plan is a contributory defined benefit plan and Employee B began participation in the plan when he became 25, after working for three years. He contributed for only one year; the plan provides that no vesting service is given for periods during which no contributions were made when the employee was required to do so.

Employee B:

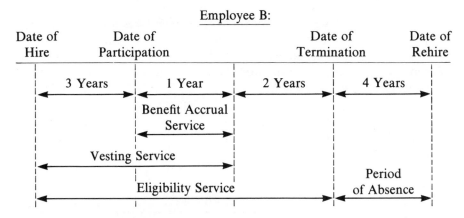

Date of Hire | Date of Participation | Date of Termination | Date of Rehire

3 Years | 1 Year | 2 Years | 4 Years

Benefit Accrual Service

Vesting Service

Period of Absence

Eligibility Service

First, since Employee B's four-year break in service was equal in length to his period of vesting service, his service completed before his termination can be disregarded for the purpose of determining his nonforfeitable percentage of employer-derived benefits.

Secondly, his prior service, for purposes of satisfying the one-year eligibility requirement, *cannot* be disregarded because his prior six-year period of eligibility service is no longer than his four-year break in service. Thus, Employee B must not be required to satisfy the one-year eligibility requirement again unless the plan imposes the waiting period; in that event, the service from date of rehire must then be recognized retroactively when the one-year waiting period is completed.

Finally, Employee B's one year of benefit accrual service (when he contributed as a participant) can not be disregarded because his vesting service was canceled. Therefore, Employee B returns as an immediately eligible participant, with no previous vesting service but with one year of service for benefit accruals.

Periods of Suspension

As previously explained, a break in service is a period of absence at least 12 months long. A break in service allows the plan to apply the rules of cancellation or reinstatement of previously completed service.

As a result of the special service spanning rules which require certain nonemployment periods to be counted as continuous service, it should be noted that there may occur certain "periods of suspension"—nonemployment periods which are *not* included in continuous service but do not trigger a break in service. This period of suspension is analogous to a year under the general method of calculating service during which an employee completes more than 500 hours of service, thereby avoiding a break in service, but by completing less than the required 1,000 hours of service falls short of attaining credit for a year of service.

Example: An employee works for three years, then takes a leave of absence on 4/1/78, intending to return in one year. He was not vested to any extent when he left; the pension plan has a 10-year cliff vesting provision. The pension plan incorporates the parity rule and the employee quits on 6/1/78 but returns to work on the following 3/1/79.

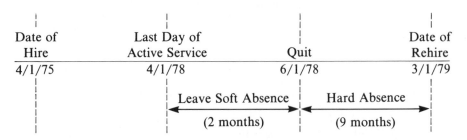

The employee must be credited with eligibility, vesting, and benefit accrual service from the last day of active service to the date he quit. In addition, the time between 6/1/78 and 3/1/79, a total of nine months, must be considered continuous service and will count for eligibility and vesting purposes (but not benefit accrual purposes) because he returned within 12 months from his last day of active service. No break in service occurred since the whole span of time was considered continuous service.

Let us suppose now that this employee returned on 5/1/79 instead of 3/1/79:

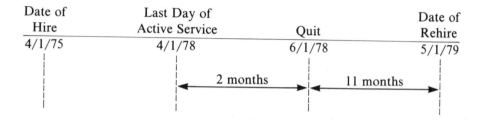

Date of Hire	Last Day of Active Service	Quit	Date of Rehire
4/1/75	4/1/78	6/1/78	5/1/79

2 months   11 months

The employee still has not incurred a break in service because he returned before the end of the 12-month period beginning with his termination of continuous service, 6/1/78. Since he did not return within 12 months from the last day of his active service, however, the absence beginning 6/1/78 and ending 5/1/79 is not considered continuous service, although the two-month period from 4/1/78 to 6/1/78 remains intact, recognized as credit for all plan purposes.

Thus, no break in service occurs, yet the period between 6/1/78 and 5/1/79—the period of suspension—is not recognized for any plan purpose.

ADDITIONAL SERVICE RULES

As previously mentioned, there are additional applicable regulations, in particular those issued by the IRS, which provide rules concerning eligibility, vesting, and benefit accrual for employee benefit plans. At this point we will briefly highlight certain aspects of the regulations which require special consideration for service calculation methods.

Eligibility To Participate: In General

As already noted, certain periods of eligibility service which occur before a break in service may be disregarded. Furthermore, even after an employee has satisfied the service condition for eligibility to participate, actual participation may be denied him if he does not meet a job classification requirement or may be delayed until he meets an age requirement. Additionally, an employee covered under the plan after satisfying the minimum age and service requirements may have his participation in the plan (i.e., his entry date) delayed further, but not later than the earlier of the first day of the plan year beginning after the satisfaction of the requirements or the date six months after such satisfaction.[30] If, however, the employee is separated from service on the date his participa-

[30] Code Reg. Section 1.410 (a)-4 (b).

tion would have commenced, the entry date may be further delayed until his return.[31]

In determining eligibility to participate, any service completed by an employee with a member of a *controlled group*[32] that includes the employer maintaining the plan, must be recognized as service for purposes of eligibility. Similarly, any service with the employer, regardless of age or job classification, must also be taken into account. For example, an individual who has been a union employee for one year and who then transfers into a nonunion position must be credited with the year of union employment for purposes of eligibility in the nonunion plan, provided all other conditions are met. Thus, although requirements based on age or job classification may prevent actual plan participation, they cannot also be used to prevent the running of the time period associated with eligibility service.

Special Rules for Elapsed Time Method

The regulations again make the distinction between hard and soft absences for elapsed time plans with respect to the entry dates prescribed by ERISA.[33]

If an employee is absent from work on his appropriate entry date in the plan because of a soft absence, he must be considered to have begun participation in the plan as of that entry date when he returns, if otherwise eligible. On the other hand, if he had quit, the plan must allow him to immediately become a participant when he returns, if otherwise eligible, but no retroactive credit back to the entry date on which he was absent must be given.[34]

Vesting: In General

In addition to those periods of employment that may be disregarded under the break in service rules, the following periods of time may also be disregarded in determining an employee's vesting service:[35]

> years of service completed before the employee reaches age 22 (unless the plan's vesting provisions qualify *only* under the "rule of 45"),
>
> years of service during which the employee failed to make any portion of the mandatory contributions to a plan when required to do so,

---

[31] Code Reg. Section 1.410 (a)-4 (b) (1). Note that the regulations do not define *separated from service.*

[32] DOL Reg. Section 2530.210. For example, a company is considered "controlled" for this purpose if 80% or more of its stock is owned by another entity. The "controlled group" consists of all companies under common control, whether domestic or foreign.

[33] Code Reg. Section 1.410 (a)-7 (c).

[34] Note that Code Reg. Section 1.410 (a)-4 (b) (1) does not clearly make the distinction between *absences* and *separations.* If absence in the code regulation includes both soft and hard absence (rather than only soft absence), then the IRS would be calling for retroactive credit whatever the cause of the absence—a more stringent requirement than that of the DOL.

[35] Code Reg. Section 1.411 (a)-5 (b).

periods of time before the employer established the plan or a predecessor plan,

years of service completed prior to January 1, 1971, unless the employee completes at least three years of vesting service after December 31, 1970, and

periods of service completed prior to the effective date of ERISA's vesting rules which were disregarded under the break in service rules of the pre-ERISA plan.

Service with a controlled group member and service in any job category whether it is a *covered* job category or not must be taken into account for vesting purposes, if not excludable for one of the above reasons.

Special Rules for Elapsed Time Method

The excludable segments of time described above may be disregarded under the elapsed time method although they would generally not be measured in terms of any computation period.

Vesting may be counted in whole years only.[36] However, when aggregating nonconsecutive periods of vesting service, plans must combine periods of less than one year. For example, an employee completes five years and seven months of service, quits, and returns to complete six years and eight months of service. He must be credited with at least 12 years of vesting service upon his second termination—five years plus six years plus one year (seven months plus eight months, dropping the three months remaining). The periods of time, including fractions, must be aggregated to yield the combined number of whole years only.

Benefit Accrual: In General

As previously indicated, certain periods of time may be excluded from benefit accrual service because of the break in service rules. In addition, periods during which an employee fails to make mandatory contributions to a plan when required to do so and, of course, other periods during which the employee is not a participant (such as the period preceding the entry date after the satisfaction of the eligibility requirements of the plan and any period while in an uncovered job category) may be excluded. Finally, it should be noted that in a defined benefit plan, participation may be subject to a requirement that there be at least two continuous years of service.[37]

A defined contribution plan may provide that a participant will not be credited with an allocation, if he is not actively employed, regardless of the reason for the absence, on the date of allocation which is generally the last day of the

---

[36] Code Reg. Section 1.410 (a)-7 (d) (i) and (iv).
[37] Code Reg. Section 1.411 (b)-1 (d) (1). The regulation provides that the interruption of continuity would only come about if there is a break in service.

plan year. However, such a policy must not discriminate in favor of the so-called prohibited group.[38]

When an employee is "cashed out" of his account in a defined contribution plan, or of his accrued retirement benefit in a defined benefit plan upon termination of employment, the service with respect to which he received the distribution can sometimes be disregarded for purposes of calculating his future retirement benefit (an important consideration if the employee resumes employment at a later date).[39] In addition, an employee's employer-derived benefit (as opposed to service) can sometimes be canceled as a result of the withdrawal of mandatory employee contributions.

Special Rules for General Method

As noted earlier, both defined benefit and defined contribution plans that use the general method of calculating service are allowed to disregard any accrual computation period during which an employee fails to complete 1,000 hours of service; otherwise, such a plan must generally credit an employee with at least a fraction of a year of benefit accrual. Even if the employee is not a participant during the whole of a given accrual computation period, the plan must nevertheless consider all the hours of service completed by the employee during that computation period for the purpose of determining his completion of the minimum 1,000 hours of service.

For example, suppose that an employee completes 600 hours in the first six months of an accrual computation period and at that point enters the plan. During the last six months of the period, he completes 800 hours of service. All of the hours of service (1,400) completed by the employee during the accrual computation period must be considered when deciding whether or not the employee satisfied the minimum 1,000-hour requirement, even though only 800 hours were completed as a participant. However, the plan is not obligated to credit the employee with more than 800 hours in that year for benefit accrual purposes. Therefore, a plan basing full benefit accrual on 2,000 hours per year would credit this employee with 2/5 (800 hours/2,000 hours) of a year of benefit accrual.

Defined benefit plans using the general method of computing service are not permitted to reduce an employee's benefit by both crediting him with less than full-time service and less than full-time compensation. A "double prorate" is not allowed.[40] The following examples illustrate various solutions to this problem in a defined benefit plan.

Example 1:   Employee X's defined benefit plan formula provides for a *career-average* benefit, equal to 2% of compensation for each year of participation. A full *year of participation* equals 2,000 hours of service. Employees are credited

---

[38] DOL Reg. Section 2530.200b-1 (b) and Revenue Ruling 76-250.
[39] Code Reg. Section 1.411 (a)-7 (d).
[40] DOL Reg. Section 2530.204-2 (d).

with a prorata portion of benefit accrual service for years in which at least 1,000 hours of service but less than 2,000 are completed.

Employee X works 1,000 hours each year for 20 years. As a part-time employee, he earned $8,000 each year. By prorating his years of credited service to reflect less than full-time work, his retirement benefit is calculated as follows:

2% × $8,000 × 10 years of credited service (i.e., 20 years × 1,000/2,000 hours) = $1,600 per year.

This is not permissible. The employee's benefit is reduced because he is a part-time employee earning a part-time level of earnings and is again reduced because he is only credited with a ratable portion of service.

To correct the situation, the plan may either:

grant full years of benefit accrual for any accrual computation period in which 1,000 hours of service is completed, *or*

annualize the employee's income to reflect what he would have earned had he worked for a full year (2,000 hours).

Under the first alternative, Employee X's benefit would be:

2% × $8,000 × 20 years = $3,200 = his annual benefit.

Under the second alternative:

2% × $16,000 ($8,000 doubled to reflect a full year's compensation) × 10 years = $3,200 = annual benefit.

Using either alternative, the result happens to be the same in our example. This would not necessarily be the case in actual practice.

Example 2: Employee Y's defined benefit plan is a *final average* type of plan. The benefit formula is 2% of the average of the employee's compensation for his last five years of service, multiplied by the number of years of benefit accrual service. One full year of benefit accrual service is based on 2,000 hours of service; if less than 2,000 hours are completed in a benefit accrual computation period, the employee is credited with a fractional part of a year.

Employee Y was a full-time employee for 10 years, completing 2,000 hours in each year and earning $10,000 per year. For the next 10 years he worked part time, completing 1,000 hours per year. His earnings for the last five years before his termination of employment at age 45 were:

Age 41 - $5,000	Age 43 - $6,500	Age 45 - $8,000
Age 42 - $6,000	Age 44 - $7,000	

In order to avoid *double proration,* the plan must annualize the above compensation so that the last five years' compensation would be:

Age 41 - $10,000   Age 43 - $13,000   Age 45 - $16,000
Age 42 - $12,000   Age 44 - $14,000

yielding an average of $13,000.

Thus, employee Y's retirement benefit would be calculated as follows:

2% × $13,000 × 15 years of benefit accrual service (i.e., 10 part-time years × 1,000/2,000 hours + 10 full-time years) = $3,900 per year.

In this type of plan, if the part-time years were recognized as full years for benefit accrual purposes, but with salaries not being annualized, the benefit would be smaller than the benefit that results from the method shown above. (This is because his part-time level of salary would be imputed to all years, even his full-time years.) IRS regulations make it clear, however, that annualized compensation would have to be used in the calculation of this benefit.[41]

A defined benefit pension plan may provide for benefit accruals on a basis that does not take into account computation periods.[42] For example:

benefit accruals under a career average plan might be based on compensation earned during a participant's entire period of participation in the plan, and

benefit accruals under a final pay plan or a non-salary-related plan might be based on hours of service (or hours actually worked or regular time hours actually worked) during a participant's entire period of participation in the plan.

Special Rules for Elapsed Time Method

Since the fundamental concept behind the elapsed time method is the recognition of certain time spans within which an employee completes even one hour of service, the proration of credited service in defined benefit plans for less than full-time employment is inappropriate and not permitted. Thus, the rules described for the general method with respect to proration of service are generally inapplicable.

Note, however, that certain periods of absence under the elapsed time method can be disregarded for benefit accrual purposes. For example, if an employee works only five hours each week for a year as a participant, he must nevertheless be credited with a full year of participation. On the other hand, if an employee worked this schedule for five months, quit (as opposed to being temporarily on leave, layoff, etc.), and returns two months later, the two

[41] Code Reg. Section 1.411 (a)-7 (c) (5).
[42] DOL Reg. Section 2530.204-3 (a).

months may be disregarded and the employee may be credited with only 10 months of benefit accrual service with respect to that year. However, when determining the year's benefit accrual for such employee (i.e., under a career average plan), his compensation must be adjusted to reflect the fact that he worked only 10 months out of the year; crediting such employee with only 10 months of service while basing his benefit for such year's service on only 10 months' compensation would have the effect of double proration. Alternatively, of course, the benefit formula could use actual compensation, but with no regard to scaling down for only fractional periods of participation.

The regulations clearly indicate that any plan which uses the elapsed time method for the purpose of benefit accrual may *not* disregard for such purpose any 12-month period during which the employee worked but did not complete 1,000 hours of service. Such an exclusion is permitted only under the general method of calculating service (unless, as noted, the special variation which ignores computation periods is used).

Military Service

The Supreme Court's decision in the case of *Alabama Power Co.* v. *Davis* necessitates the recognition of absences due to military service. It is clear that employees who are rehired by their employers upon the completion of military service must be credited with benefit accrual service for their time spent in the military, as if they had continuously worked for the employer during the absence in question. This requirement presently applies to defined benefit plans only, as the Supreme Court decision does not address itself to defined contribution plans.

The decision raises several questions concerning the calculation of benefits derived from military leave (particularly, if the plan is of the career-average type or is contributory). Unfortunately, the minimum standards regulations do not provide answers to these questions; they merely include a general provision to the effect that they do not supercede provisions of other federal laws.[43]

It should be noted that not all military service is protected under the law and need not be so credited in retirement plans. The eligibility requirements for this protection are:

the employee must have left a position to enter the military that was other than a temporary position, and

the employee must have satisfactorily served for a period of time not exceeding the time limits specified under the law and must make a timely application (usually within 90 days of his release from military service) to return to work.

---

[43] DOL Reg. Section 2530.200b-2 (d).

Using Different Methods for Different Classes of Employees or Different Plan Purposes

The DOL and IRS regulations both indicate that different methods of calculating service can be used in one plan. The combination can be used in either of two ways.[44]

First, the regulations provide that different methods may be used for different *plan purposes* provided they are consistently applied and are reasonable. Thus, the general method of calculating service may be used in conjunction with either an equivalency or the elapsed time method. For example, a plan could incorporate the use of the general method for eligibility purposes with the use of the elapsed time method for purposes of vesting and participation. This approach would preclude less-than-1,000-hour employees from entering the plan initially but would not prevent them from advancing on the vesting schedule. Furthermore, once an employee commenced participation (because he had a 1,000-hour-or-more year), he would thereafter also accrue full benefits whether or not he completed 1,000 hours in subsequent years.

Secondly, the regulations provide that plans may use different methods for different *classifications of employees* provided the classifications are reasonable and consistently applied. However, the use of different methods for different classifications is not "reasonable" if the intent of the distinction is to preclude less-than-full-time workers from obtaining basic entitlement with respect to eligibility, vesting, or benefit accrual. Thus, designating the general method for hourly personnel and the elapsed time method for salaried personnel appears legitimate if it is not done with the intention of preventing a category of employees from receiving plan benefits. On the other hand, establishing part-time versus full-time categories may not be so valid; the regulations indicate that the effect of relegating the less-than-1,000-hour worker to part-time status, and thus imposing the general method of crediting service upon him under which he would be ineligible for participation, is not reasonable.

Finally, it should be noted that different methods of crediting service may be used for the pre-ERISA period than for the post-ERISA period.[45]

Transfers Between Methods of Crediting Service

Transfer Within One Plan[46]

If an employee remains a participant in the same pension plan but transfers to a different job classification so that his service is no longer credited on the basis of the general method but instead on the elapsed time method, he must receive credit for the period of service consisting of:

---

[44] DOL Reg. Section 2530.200b-3 (c) (2) and (3) and Code Reg. Section 1.410 (a)-7 (a) (5).
[45] DOL Reg. Section 2530.200b-3 (b) (last sentence).
[46] Code Reg. Section 1.410 (a)-7 (f) (1) must be explicitly incorporated in plan.

the number of years of service credited to him before the computation period in which the transfer occurs, and

the period of time beginning on the first day of the computation period during which he transfers and ending on the date of the transfer, or the service that is taken into account for the computation period in which his transfer occurred if this period of service will result in more service being credited.

His service count must start under the elapsed time method as of the date of the transfer, or alternatively, if the employee receives credit for the entire computation period in which his transfer occurred, as described above, his service must begin under the elapsed time method with the day after the end of that computation period.

If an employee switches from the elapsed time method to the general method for computing service, a similar rule is in effect to protect the employee from losing any credit due to the transfer. Such an individual must receive credit under his plan for:

the number of years of service (ignoring any fraction) credited to the employee as of the transfer, and

a number of hours of service determined under one of the equivalencies for any fractional part of a year completed as of the date of the transfer. These hours are to be credited to the computation period in which the transfer occurs. The equivalencies to be used can be any of those previously described which are based on periods of employment (days, weeks, months, etc.), must apply to all similarly situated employees, and must be specified in the plan document.

In this type of transfer, service during the computation period in which the transfer occurs and before the actual date of the transfer could very well be double-counted. This would occur where such service would have the effect of increasing the number of whole years under the elapsed time method by one.

Transfer to a Different Plan[47]

When an employee transfers to a plan under which he will receive credit for his service while a participant of a former plan, that service must be redetermined using the method prescribed in the new plan.

Plan Amendment to Change Methods

If a plan is amended to change the method of crediting service for any purpose or class of employees from or to the elapsed time method, the rules relating to transfers within one plan must be applied to every affected employee.[48]

---

[47] Code Reg. Section 1.410 (a)-7 (f) (2).
[48] Code Reg. Section 1.410 (a)-7 (g) must be explicitly incorporated in plan amendment.

FACTORS TO BE CONSIDERED WHEN ADOPTING
SERVICE COMPUTATION METHOD

Since a plan's service requirements to a great extent constitute the foundation of a retirement plan, the method of computing service must be chosen with care. The following paragraphs analyze the relationship between each method and various benefit factors, employment practices, and administrative procedures.

Inclusion of Part-Time Personnel: In General

Since each computation method will treat temporary, part-time, salaried, hourly, and full-time employees somewhat differently, the employee population to be covered must be carefully examined. In addition to the cost of providing less-than-full-time workers with benefits, their inclusion undoubtedly will cause extra record keeping and administrative problems for what may be an unstable and short-term work force.

All part-timers, regardless of how sporadically or little they work, are likely to be eligible for participation in elapsed time plans. Furthermore, the elapsed time method requires that a full year of vesting be granted any employee who completes even one hour of service within a 12-month period, as opposed to the 1,000-hour minimum set forth under the general method.

By using the general method, employees working less than 1,000 hours per year may be completely excluded. In addition, employers can mitigate the impact of including other part-time workers (i.e., those working more than 1,000 hours but less than full-time) by prorating less-than-full-time years for benefit accrual purposes. As a general rule, *hours worked* and *regular time* equivalencies are convenient methods for work forces with a great deal of nonservice time and overtime, respectively. On the other hand, periods of employment equivalencies are useful for workers who do not work regularly scheduled hours, if they are hourly workers. Shift equivalencies may facilitate a large plan's record keeping.

Benefit Accrual

General method career-average plans, under which an employee is credited with retirement benefits based on each year's compensation, will generally not be adversely affected by the inclusion of less-than-full-time personnel. Of course they must avoid "double proration" by either reflecting full-time compensation when they prorate years of credited service for less-than-full-time employees or by not prorating and reflecting only the part-time compensation earned.

If a career-average plan adopts the elapsed time method, credited service may not be prorated. Nevertheless, the part-time employee's benefit will reflect only the actual part-time compensation earned over the span of his career.

Thus, the results may be similar to those under the general method for part-timers who work at least 1,000 hours a year. The significant difference comes about in the need to accrue small benefits for the less-than-1,000-hour employees.

Final average plans which use the elapsed time method may face special problems if they include part-time employees who may at some time in their careers become full-time. In such circumstances, retirement benefits may reflect the average of their highest years' compensation instead of their actual history of part-time employment. These elapsed time plans must credit all employees, regardless of their full- or part-time status, with complete years of benefit accrual; benefits may not be reduced by prorating their years of credited service, a recourse available only to general method plans.

Unless less-than-1,000-hour employees are excluded from entering a defined contribution plan which uses the elapsed time method, benefit allocations will generally have to be made for all employees, even if they work few hours and their compensation for the year is very minimal. This is analogous to the problem under career-average defined benefit plans.

Contributory elapsed time plans may avoid the problem of having to pay benefits to part-time or temporary personnel since there is a good chance that lowly paid or intermittent workers will not elect to make the required contributions. However, such plans must be careful to include enough employees to meet the Internal Revenue Code's minimum coverage requirements. On the other hand, contributory plans using the general method for crediting service must face the problem of what to do with employee contributions made in a year that turns out to include less than 1,000 hours of service.

Periods of Absence

Each method will obviously have different implications for plan design depending upon the employment practices of the company. For example, frequent leaves of absence, recurrent layoffs, changes in employee status or job category, transfers between subsidiaries or between union and management, and the reemployment of former employees are all occurrences which will be treated differently under either service measurement technique. The following shows how the treatment of employees' absences differs under the two methods.

Plan Purpose for Which Absence Must Be Recognized

Type of Absence	General Method	Elapsed Time Method
Leaves, layoffs, illness, disability, or other soft absences (*unpaid*)	None	Eligibility, vesting, benefit accrual (up to 12 months)

Type of Absence	General Method	Elapsed Time Method
Absence between quit, discharge, or retirement and rehire (*unpaid*)	None	Eligibility, vesting (if total absence—including other types of absence that are contiguous—is less than 12 months)
Absence due to cause specified in DOL Reg. Section 2530.200b-2(a) (2) (*paid*)	Up to 501 hours	As for unpaid, depending on whether hard or soft absence and duration
Absence due to cause not specified in DOL Reg. Section 2530.200b-2(a) (2) (*paid*)	None	As for unpaid, depending on whether hard or soft absence and duration

Validity of Elapsed Time Method

When considering the elapsed time approach, employers should realize that this method is not sanctioned by ERISA itself. It represents a modification and interpretation of the prescribed 1,000-hour standard in response to the public demand for a simpler method of calculating service.

As such, it is possible that the method conflicts with ERISA by interfering with an employee's statutory entitlements based upon his completion of a certain number of hours of service. For example, an employee subject to the elapsed time method who would have completed enough service to become fully vested had his plan used the general method of counting service, but who failed to work the required span of time under his "elapsed time" plan, may be denied a nonforfeitable right to a plan benefit. Various groups of pension rights advocates are voicing their opposition to the elapsed time method on this basis.

Plan Amendment Costs

Since the elapsed time regulations are final, employers may now wish to weigh the cost of amending their plans to adopt this method against potential administrative cost savings.

Record-Keeping Systems

A primary advantage of the elapsed time method is that no records need be kept on the hours worked by employees. This is especially attractive for those employers who never kept such records during pre-ERISA years or whose plans substantially cover full-time salaried personnel. On the other hand, payroll data maintained for certain hourly groups of employees can sometimes be easily utilized for plan purposes, so that the general method or an equivalency can be tailored to the needs of this type of group.

Communication to Employees

Plans are sometimes intricately designed to comply with the absolute minimum prescribed standards with provisions which exactly satisfy the demands of the employer but which are awkward to administer and, most importantly, too complicated to communicate to participants. Since the summary plan description requirements demand clear nontechnical explanations of plan benefits, an employer must critically consider the practicality of the technique he intends to use to measure service. Elapsed time plans usually lend themselves to easy explanation. Hourly based "years of service," corresponding computation periods, and equivalencies are often difficult to communicate and may appear inappropriate for salaried employees. Stringent break in service rules are cumbersome to explain regardless of the method used to compute service.

Considering the effort required to comply with the strictures of the law and the cost of providing employees with retirement benefits, most employers will want to devise workable plans that will be clearly understood by employees.

Qualified Joint and Survivor Annuities Under ERISA

INTRODUCTION

Most employers maintaining qualified pension plans have found it necessary to modify their methods of distributing retirement income in light of ERISA's requirement for spouses' coverage. This analysis provides a comprehensive explanation of the IRS regulations relating to this coverage for use as a reference source. The appropriate sections of the regulations are cited for easy reference.

BACKGROUND

On October 3, 1975, the IRS issued temporary and proposed regulations concerning "qualified joint and survivor annuities" that certain pension and profit-sharing plans must offer for the purpose of providing financial protection to plan participants' surviving spouses. The final regulations issued in January 1977 vary significantly from those temporary rules.[1]

Certain provisions of the final joint and survivor regulations were challenged in court and, as a result, have been invalidated. The IRS has announced that it will no longer follow the invalidated parts, but will amend the regulations. Pending the adoption of the amended regulations, the IRS has issued a summary of the changes expected to be made. These changes are discussed later.[2]

This analysis is divided into two major sections: the pre- and postretirement joint and survivor annuity rules as they relate to (1) defined benefit plans, and (2) defined contribution plans.

DEFINED BENEFIT PLANS

Absent an employee's election to the contrary, the spouse of a plan participant who is to receive a life annuity as the normal form of benefit under the plan or

---

[1] Code Reg. Section 1.401 (a)-11.
[2] IRS Notice 82-4.

who has selected a life annuity as an optional form must automatically receive retirement income from a plan if the participant dies:

after retirement that occurred on or after either normal retirement age or *early retirement age;* or

during employment after normal retirement age.

This coverage is referred to as the *postretirement* automatic qualified joint and survivor annuity.

Early retirement age is obviously a key definition. Wherever it appears in this appendix, it means the latest of the following dates:

the early retirement date provided by the plan; this refers to the earliest date a participant can elect to receive *retirement* (other than disability) benefits without regard to requirements for approval;

the date which is 10 years before the participant's normal retirement date; or

the first day of plan participation.

In addition to the postretirement coverage, most plan participants must have the right to elect financial protection for their spouses in the event they die in employment after reaching early retirement age but before reaching normal retirement age. This is known as preretirement survivor annuity coverage.

In both cases, plan participants must be provided with certain information concerning spouses' coverage. The IRS provides further guidelines as to the percentage of benefits payable to spouses and the circumstances under which this protection must be afforded.

POSTRETIREMENT QUALIFIED JOINT AND SURVIVOR ANNUITY

Types of Benefits Subject to Automatic Payment

The final regulations originally required that plans offering retirement benefits in the form of a life annuity must provide for the automatic payment of a qualified joint and survivor annuity benefiting spouses. This provision has been invalidated by the courts, and the IRS has announced it will amend the final regulations to delete this requirement. Under the guidelines issued by the IRS, which may be relied upon pending adoption of the amended regulations, plans will no longer be required to provide for automatic payment of a qualified joint and survivor annuity benefiting spouses because the plan offers a life annuity as a benefit option. However, if a plan provides any form of benefit payment in the form of a life annuity, a life annuity may not be paid unless an election has been made not to take the qualified joint and survivor annuity. The early survivor requirements and the other joint and survivor requirements remain unchanged.

Examples of life annuities[3] would be:

a *straight* life annuity under which payments are made only for the lifetime of the participant;

a 10-year temporary life annuity under which monthly payments continue to be made until 10 years have elapsed or the death of the participant, whichever occurs first.

Temporary annuities which provide benefits for a fixed period of time do not have to be treated in this manner.

The following types of benefits which are *not* considered *retirement* benefits do *not* have to comply with these rules.

Disability benefits from a retirement plan in the form of *temporary* life annuities. These benefits are not considered *retirement* benefits, even though they may provide regular income to the disabled plan member after he terminates employment. For further discussion concerning disability benefits paid from a pension plan, see the section headed "Who Must Be Covered and When."

Medical benefits.

Social security supplements. These are benefits not in excess of the social security benefit amount which are paid to a retiree from a plan for the period of time before he begins to collect social security.

Other ancillary benefits not directly related to retirement benefits such as incidental death benefits.

Providing for the automatic payment of lump-sum distributions no greater than $1,750, representing the present value of a participant's nonforfeitable benefit derived from employer contributions, does not violate the joint and survivor annuity rules. These lump-sum amounts do not have to be converted into qualified joint and survivor annuities.[4]

Nature of Qualified Joint
and Survivor Annuity

A *qualified* joint and survivor annuity is one that meets the following conditions.

---

[3] Code Reg. Section 1.401 (a)-11 (b) (1).
[4] Code Reg. Section 1.401 (a)-11 (a) (2).

The contingent annuitant (the survivor) is the participant's spouse.

The survivor annuity for the spouse must not be less than 50% or more than 100% of the annuity payable during the joint lives of the participant and his spouse.

The joint and survivor annuity must be at least the *actuarial equivalent* of the normal form of payment or any greater optional form. In other words, the conversion of the normal form of payment to the qualified joint and survivor form should serve only to rearrange the manner and timing of the participant's pension under the plan and should not diminish its value.

The surviving spouse's benefit cannot be reduced or terminated due to remarriage.[5]

Who Must Be Covered and When

Unless a participant elects otherwise, the categories of married plan participants for whom benefits become payable in the form of a life annuity listed below must automatically receive their retirement pensions subject to the qualified joint and survivor rules.

Normal retirees.[6] Those beginning to receive benefits upon reaching normal retirement age.

Late retirees.[7] Those retiring *after* reaching normal retirement age, *or* those dying after attaining normal retirement age while actively employed by the company maintaining the plan.

Early retirees.[8] Those retiring on or after early retirement age whether they begin to collect benefits immediately or defer them to a future date. This includes individuals who retire at that time because of disability; any disability benefit payable as a life annuity is then considered a retirement benefit.

Thus, a surviving spouse must be entitled to coverage after the participant, as described above, dies. In the case of an *early* retiree or *late* retiree, coverage would be in effect even if the participant's benefits had not yet commenced.

The provision concerning early retirees represents a marked departure from the traditional operation of a joint and survivor annuity under which survivor benefits would normally have been triggered only after the participant's benefits had commenced or the participant had attained normal retirement age. The cost of this extra "insurance" may be passed on to the participant (e.g., by cov-

---

[5] Code Reg. Section 1.401 (a)-11 (b) (2).

[6] Code Reg. Section 1.401 (a)-11 (a) (1) (i) (A). *Normal retirement age* is defined under Section 411 (a) (8) of the code. Briefly, it is the age specified by the plan or the later of age 65 or the 10th anniversary of the commencement of plan participation.

[7] Code Reg. Section 1.401 (a)-11 (a) (1) (i) (A), (B), and (D).

[8] Code Reg. Section 1.401 (a)-11 (a) (1) (i) (C) and (D).

erage charges similar in nature to those described later for the preretirement survivor annuity), provided a form of payment is available under which no out-of-pocket expenses are required.[9]

Because this special protection is required only with respect to the qualified automatic form, many plans do not provide the same coverage under optional forms of payment. Where this is the case, the spouse of a participant who retired early, deferred receipt of his income, elected a qualified joint and survivor annuity and died before his benefits began, is entitled to pension benefits under the automatic qualified form. But if the participant had elected an optional form instead, no payments would be made to the spouse. Where this difference in benefit forms exists, the employer should be careful to explain the precise circumstances under which surviving spouses will be financially protected. In these cases, participants may want to delay the election of options until just before beginning to receive benefits.

Note that the qualified joint and survivor annuity rules apply only to persons actively participating—that is, currently accruing benefits—in plans on or after the ERISA compliance date. Participants who began to receive annuity benefits (whether retirement or disability) before the compliance date are not covered by these rules.[10]

The following types of married participants need *not* be covered.

Deferred vested participants. Those who terminate employment before reaching early retirement age. Thus, a *deferred vested* participant's spouse would not be automatically entitled to retirement income if the participant dies before beginning to collect benefits. However, where the participant's benefits commence on or after early retirement age, joint and survivor coverage would be in effect (unless, of course, termination from employment occurred before the ERISA compliance date) for the spouse.

Participants receiving benefits before early retirement age. Those who begin to receive retirement benefits from their pension plans under lifetime annuities *before* reaching early retirement age (that is, before the later of the earliest date on which the participant could elect to receive retirement benefits or the start of the 10-year period preceding normal retirement age). These plans are neither required to initially pay benefits in the automatic form nor to offer that form to the retiree at a later date.

Marriage Requirements

The automatic form need only apply to participants who have been married to the same spouse for at least one year as of their *benefit commencement date.*[11] Of course, many plans will not impose any requirement as to length of marriage.

---

[9] Code Reg. Section 1.401 (a)-11 (e).
[10] Code Reg. Section 1.401 (a)-11 (f).
[11] Code Reg. Section 1.401 (a)-11 (d) (3) (i).

The regulations do not address the question of common law marriage; some plans may specifically state what constitutes a marriage for this purpose.

Claims for Benefits

Plans may require participants to submit written claims for plan benefits before payments can commence. However, if a plan member submits a claim that includes all of the information necessary for the payment of benefits but does not indicate the form of payment he prefers, the plan is required to pay benefits subject to the qualified joint and survivor annuity rules, where applicable.[12]

Examples

Normal Retirees

The XYZ Plan has a normal retirement age of 65. Employee A retires at age 65. He is married. The normal form of benefit from this plan is a straight life annuity, having no survivor protection. The plan may not pay the straight life annuity to Employee A unless A has elected not to take the qualified joint and survivor annuity.

Late Retirees

Employee B, who is married, dies while actively employed at age 68. She did not elect not to take the qualified joint and survivor annuity. Therefore, the plan may not pay benefits in the form of a life annuity.

Early Retirees

The XYZ Plan also provides for early retirement at age 55 with 10 years of service. Early retirees may elect to begin to receive their pensions immediately or to defer them. Employee C, at age 55, is eligible for early retirement benefits. He is married. At this time, he terminates his employment, elects no option, and decides to collect his pension immediately. Employee C dies at age 57. His spouse then begins to receive the retirement benefits payable under the automatic qualified joint and survivor annuity.

Employee D retires at age 55, but elects no options, and decides to defer his pension until age 60. He dies at age 57. His spouse will be eligible for retirement income under the automatic qualified joint and survivor annuity in the amount that would be payable to her if he had begun to collect benefits just before his death.

Employee E also retires at age 55. She immediately elects out of the automatic form in favor of an annuity providing a guaranteed number of payments and defers the receipt of her pension until age 62. Employee E dies at age 60. In accordance with the terms of the XYZ Plan, Employee E's optional form of annuity (and the survivor income protection it provides) does

---

[12] Code Reg. Section 1.401 (a)-11 (d) (2). Also see Code Reg. Section 1.401 (a)-14.

not go into effect until benefits commence. Since Employee E elected out of the automatic form, which would have covered her spouse in this event, no pension benefits are payable to her spouse upon her death.

Employee F is a member of the ABC Plan. Early retirement benefits in the form of a lifetime annuity are payable when participants reach age 50, after having completed 10 years of service. Normal retirement age is 65. Employee F retires upon reaching his early retirement age—age 50. He immediately begins to collect benefits. The plan is not obligated to automatically provide the qualified annuity or offer it at any time thereafter because benefits are paid *before* the early retirement age defined by the IRS for this purpose.

If Employee F's pension had commenced upon age 55 or later, the automatic form of annuity would have been in effect since benefits would have started on or after the defined early retirement age, that is, 10 years before normal retirement age.

Deferred Vested Participants

Employee G is a member of the DEF Plan. He is fully vested when he terminates his employment at age 40. The DEF Plan provides that Employee G can elect to receive benefits at age 55 or anytime thereafter. Employee G elects no option and decides to collect benefits beginning at age 57. He dies at age 56. His spouse will not be paid benefits under the automatic qualified joint and survivor annuity form because Employee G did not remain in service until early retirement age and did not begin to collect benefits after reaching that age.

Disabled Retirees

The GHI Plan provides for lifetime benefits to be paid on account of disability if the participant had attained age 55 and had completed 15 years of service. Early retirement benefits can start as early as age 60, if the participant had completed 10 years of service. Employee H becomes disabled at age 55 and begins to collect disability benefits. The plan is not obligated to pay these benefits in the automatic form since the age at which this income is payable pertains to disability benefits, is not otherwise applicable to retirement benefits, and therefore does not qualify as the early retirement age. Had Employee H deferred the commencement of benefits until age 60 or later, her benefits would have to be paid in the automatic form (subject to an election to the contrary) because benefits would have started on the defined *early retirement age*.

Electing Out of the
Postretirement Automatic Form

Under the final regulations, participants entitled to the automatic form of payment must have the opportunity to *elect out* of it and to choose an alternative form of retirement income.[13] This election must be in writing and must be revocable during the *election period* described below so that a participant can switch back to the automatic form if he so desires. If the automatic form is revoked, however, the election period for the basic election continues to run. However, this rule will no longer be applicable under the forthcoming amended regulations, which will no longer require an automatic joint and survivor annuity upon retirement. An election not to take a qualified joint and survivor will be required before the plan can pay a life annuity.

A plan may require the written approval of the participant's spouse when the participant rejects the automatic form of payment.[14]

The Election Period

In general, the election period must:

be at least 90 days in length;

begin *after* the necessary information concerning forms of payment (described later) is provided the participant;

end no earlier than 90 days before the commencement of benefits.

Any participant who separated from service after these rules went into effect, but who was not given the option of electing out of the automatic payment, must be given the choice of receiving the balance of his benefits in an elected form of payment. This participant must have 90 days in which to make the election, starting after he is notified of this right, and must be supplied with the information concerning forms of payment. If this participant has died, the right of election must be granted his personal representative.[15]

If a benefit amount cannot be ascertained within the time frame established under these rules, the payment may be delayed. But benefits must be paid retroactively to the date otherwise due.[16]

In addition to the general rules described above, there are prescribed *beginning and end points* of election periods for each plan participant. Considering the complications involved, many employers allow for election periods that start sooner and/or end later than necessary. Table I identifies the *minimum* requirements for election periods and dates for disclosure of information pertaining to the postretirement coverage.[17]

---

[13] Plans that provide *only* the qualified automatic form are obviously not required to offer an election out.
[14] Code Reg. Section 1.401 (a)-11 (c) (1) (i) (B).
[15] Code Reg. Section 1.401 (a)-11 (c) (1) (ii) (B).
[16] Code Reg. Section 1.401 (a)-14 (d).
[17] Code Reg. Section 1.401 (a)-11 (d) (1) (ii) and (3) (ii).

Table I

Timetable for Postretirement Qualified
Joint and Survivor Annuities

Event	Deadline for Individual Participant
1. Provide required explanatory information.	If there is no early retirement age: Nine months before normal retirement age. If the preretirement survivor annuity is automatic: Nine months before early retirement age. If the preretirement survivor annuity is elective: Six months before early retirement age. If the plan provides for a waiting period during which the preretirement survivor annuity is not effective, the six months must be extended back to a date which is six months plus the length of the waiting period.
2. Start election period.	After issuance of above information—no later than 180 days before benefit commencement date.
3. End election period.	No fewer than 90 days after start; period must not end before 90 days ahead of benefit commencement date. If the participant requests additional information, extend the period by at least 90 days after information is received. (It must be received no later than 30 days after request.) If the initial information was mailed or personally delivered (not posted), the plan may require that requests for additional information be made within a certain number of days (not less than 60) after receipt of the initial information; then the election period only has to be extended by 60 days.

Required Explanatory Information

The following items of information must be provided to affected participants:[18]

a general description of the annuity and the circumstances under which it is paid;

the availability of the *election out;*

an explanation of the financial effect of making this election illustrated in terms of:

an arithmetic or percentage reduction from a single life annuity, or

a table showing the difference in dollars between the single life annuity and joint and survivor annuity for a hypothetical plan benefit;

a notice that participants may request more information in terms of his particular benefit, as described below, including directions on how this information can be obtained.

Employers may use the following methods of communicating this information:[19]

by mail or personal delivery;

permanent posting (which will remain available throughout the election periods);

repeated publication in a company periodical read by employees.

The additional information to be made available on request includes a written explanation in nontechnical language of the terms of the automatic form and the financial effect upon the *individual's benefit* of electing out of the automatic form. The dollar differences between forms must be shown. No more than one request has to be honored and that answer must be furnished by mail or personal delivery.

If the plan allows the spouse of a deceased participant to *elect out* of the survivor annuity, the spouse must be furnished, within a reasonable time after request, with a written explanation in nontechnical language of the survivor annuity and any other benefits which may be selected in its place. The explanation must contain a comparison of the various benefits that can be elected in dollar terms. Only one such request must be honored.

When Options Out Are Effective

Many plans will stipulate that an election out of the automatic form in favor of an optional one or a revocation of that election will be recognized immediately.

[18] Code Reg. Section 1.401 (a)-11 (c) (3) (i).
[19] Code Reg. Section 1.401 (a)-11 (c) (3) (ii).

However, some plans provide that the effectiveness of such an election will be conditioned on the participant's remaining alive for a certain period of time after the election is actually submitted. The IRS states that "waiting periods" of up to two years are acceptable.[20] However, if a participant dies from accidental causes *after* he had revoked a prior election out of the qualified annuity, reclaiming the automatic form, the revocation must be honored so that the spouse will be covered even if his death occurred during the waiting period.

Plans which use waiting periods may have to start benefit payments *without* regard to an option out, that is, in the automatic joint and survivor form when the benefit commencement date occurs before the waiting period has lapsed. Then, upon the expiration of the waiting period, the plan would distribute benefits in accordance with the elected option. This is obviously a complicated type of distribution.

The regulations do *not* specify that election periods must begin on a date which is early enough to include a plan's entire waiting period, before the commencement of benefits. Employers wishing to mitigate this problem should establish an election period that is at least as long as the plan's waiting period.

PRERETIREMENT SURVIVOR ANNUITY

The preretirement survivor annuity provides a spouse's benefit similar to that provided by the postretirement joint and survivor annuity. But instead of protecting spouses *after* participants retire or reach normal retirement age, this benefit covers spouses in the event of the participant's death *during employment, after early retirement age,* and *before normal retirement age.* Unlike the postretirement joint and survivor annuity, the benefit does not have to be automatic, but plans must allow eligible plan members to positively elect this special coverage. Participants may then be charged for this benefit. This requirement will not be changed in the upcoming amendment of the final regulations.

Level of Income Provided

If a participant elects to have his spouse covered by a preretirement survivor annuity, the amount of benefits payable to the spouse upon the participant's death must be at least equal to the amount which would have been payable to the spouse had the participant started to receive early retirement benefits in the form of a qualified joint and survivor annuity just before his death. Of course, plans may also provide benefits that are greater than this amount.[21]

[20] Code Reg. Section 1.401 (a)-11 (d) (4).
[21] Code Reg. Section 1.401 (a)-11 (b) (3).

Example

Employee X elected the coverage provided by the preretirement survivor annuity. He died while employed, before reaching normal retirement age. His accrued benefit under his plan, payable upon normal retirement age, equaled $300 per month for his lifetime only. However, if he had begun to receive retirement benefits just before his death, he would have been entitled to receive a reduced early retirement benefit of $210 per month for his lifetime. But under the qualified 50% joint and survivor annuity, he would have received $170 per month for his lifetime, while his spouse would have been entitled to half of this, or $85 per month after his death. Therefore, his spouse will be entitled to $85 per month for her lifetime under the preretirement survivor annuity.

Eligible Participants

Each active *participant*[22] who:

reaches early retirement age,[23] but not normal retirement age, and
is employed by the employer maintaining the plan,

must be given the right to elect a preretirement survivor annuity benefiting his spouse. The election must be in writing and must be revocable.[24]
   Breaks in service after early retirement age must neither invalidate a period election nor prevent a participant from making an election or revoking it.

When Survivor Benefits Are Payable

Upon a valid election for this survivor annuity, an individual's surviving spouse must be entitled to benefits upon the individual's death if:

death occurred while the individual was employed by the employer maintaining the plan and before his normal retirement age, and
the employee had reached early retirement age.

If participants have the chance to elect this coverage *before* they reach early retirement age (for example, as soon as they have received the information concerning this annuity), employers should carefully point out that elections will nevertheless become effective only after early retirement age is attained.
   Of course, no elections are required if a plan automatically provides that the

---

[22] *Active participant* means a person for whom benefits are being *currently* accrued under a plan (after December 31, 1975) and would not include other persons currently employed, even those with vested benefits.
[23] Again, this refers to the later of 10 years before normal retirement age, the plan's early retirement age (for other than disability benefits), or the date participation began.
[24] Code Reg. Section 1.401 (a)-11 (c) (2).

survivor annuity benefiting a participant's spouse is the sole form of benefit paid with respect to these *eligible* participants.

Delayed Effective Dates

Some plans state that elections are not effective for up to two years after they are made, regardless of when the election takes place. That is, if the participant dies within two years (or other shorter period of time) after the election is made, his surviving spouse will not be covered. Plans which impose waiting periods must provide that an election will nevertheless cover the surviving spouse if the employee's death occurs during the waiting period from accidental causes.[25]

Marriage Requirements

Plans may provide that a participant electing preretirement coverage must be married to his spouse for at least one year upon the date of his death in order for survivor benefits to be paid.

The Election Period

The election period for survivor coverage must start after the required explanatory information is issued and must end at normal retirement age, or when service is terminated before that time. Eligible persons who were actively participating when these rules came into effect, on the first day of the plan year starting in 1976, may have shorter election periods than those described by this regulation.

Although the election periods pertaining to the preretirement and postretirement qualified annuities do not have to be the same, it may be easier to administer and explain plan provisions if these two types of election periods are coordinated.

Table II indicates the *minimum* requirements for election periods and dates for disclosure of information relating to the preretirement survivor annuity.[26]

Required Explanatory Information

Prior to the start of the election period, eligible participants must be given a general description of the preretirement survivor annuity, election information, and a description of the circumstances under which it will be paid if elected, in addition to a general explanation of the relative financial effect of the election on the participant's benefit.

[25] Code Reg. Section 1.401 (a)-11 (d) (4).
[26] Code Reg. Section 1.401 (a)-11 (c) (2) (ii) and (3) (ii).

Table II

Timetable for Preretirement Survivor Annuity

Without Waiting Periods

Event	Deadline for Individual Participant
1. Provide required explanatory information.	Six months before early retirement age.
2. Start election period.	Three months before early retirement age.
3. End election period.	At normal retirement date or termination of service if earlier.

With Waiting Periods

Event	Deadline for Individual Participant
1. Provide required explanatory information.	Six months plus the length of the waiting period before early retirement age.
2. Start election period.	Three months plus the length of the waiting period before early retirement age. (For example, if the waiting period is two years, the election period must begin two years and three months before early retirement date.)
3. End election period.	At normal retirement date or termination of service if earlier.

The regulations are not clear as to whether it is necessary to offer additional information concerning an individual participant's preretirement coverage. In any case, the general information initially distributed to eligible employees will normally provide enough information since it will include a description of coverage charges and the financial effect of the election.

The methods of communicating this information are the same as those described for the postretirement automatic form. Due dates for disclosure are shown in Table II.

If a plan participant dies after these rules came into effect, but before this election was made available to him, the plan must provide the participant's spouse, or if dead, the spouse's personal representative with the option of electing the survivor annuity. Payments under the annuity may be reduced to reflect any benefits already paid. The survivor must have at least 90 days after receiving the appropriate information in which to elect the coverage.

Charges for Coverage

Since this preretirement coverage protects surviving spouses while participants are still employed and not retired, some pension plans charge participants or survivors for the protection by reducing their benefit payments.

The first method involves the reduction of the *participant's* ultimate retirement benefit. If the spouse collects the preretirement annuity, no charge is imposed.

A second and very common method is to charge either the participant, his contingent annuitant, or beneficiary, whichever begins to receive benefits first, for the time during which the coverage was in effect. For example, benefits paid to a participant's spouse upon the death of the participant, which occurred either during active employment or after he has retired but before benefit commencement, would be reduced on account of this coverage.

Example

Employee Y is a participant in the ABC Plan. Early retirement benefits are payable in the form of a life annuity under the ABC Plan when age 55 is reached and 10 years of service have been completed. Employee Y was hired at age 50 and immediately started to participate. He is married.

The ABC Plan provides that the preretirement survivor annuity will become effective immediately upon election (or at early retirement age, if later). The plan provides Employee Y with an explanation of this benefit six months before his 60th birthday, his early retirement date. The election period starts immediately upon his receipt of this information. Retirement benefits, whether they are paid to the participant or his survivor, are reduced for each month of coverage.

Employee Y elects this coverage as soon as he receives the information and is told it will go into effect on his 60th birthday. Employee Y retires at age 65, his normal retirement age. His benefit, regardless of the form of annuity in which it is received, will reflect the reduction for 60 months of coverage.

Now assume that Employee Y had died at age 62, while employed. His spouse would then have been entitled to receive monthly retirement income under the preretirement survivor annuity which would reflect the coverage charge.

If Employee Y had retired at age 62 and died at age 63 after having deferred benefit commencement to age 65, his spouse would have been covered by the postretirement joint and survivor annuity, absent an election to the contrary. Then the spouse's benefit would reflect the preretirement coverage charges in addition to any charge imposed for the postretirement coverage, in this case, from age 62, retirement, to the date of the participant's death at age 63.

DEFINED CONTRIBUTION PLANS

Postretirement Automatic Qualified
Joint and Survivor Annuity

Under the final regulations, defined contribution plans (profit-sharing, money-purchase, or stock bonus plans) were required to provide for the automatic payment of a postretirement qualified joint and survivor annuity only if a life-time annuity is offered under the terms of the plan.[27] The automatic form must be operative even if the annuity offered by a plan is an optional form of payment and not the automatic form. However, as with defined benefit plans, qualified defined contribution plans are no longer required to provide qualified joint and survivor annuities in the normal form of benefit if they offer a life annuity option. Benefits may be paid in the form of a life annuity only if the participant has elected not to take the qualified joint and survivor annuity. Again, these changes do not affect the early survivor annuity requirements.

Thus, a company could avoid the qualified joint and survivor annuity and related administrative requirements by providing that its plan will distribute only lump-sum distributions and/or installment payments for a fixed period of time, with no provision for lifetime annuity payments. Under this arrangement, a retiree could purchase an annuity on his own which will accommodate his particular financial needs.

Defined contribution plans which are subject to the joint and survivor requirements must follow the rules concerning eligibility, applicable benefits, election periods, and disclosure of information described earlier for defined benefit plans.

The regulations specify that the estimated future annuity payments reported to a participant seeking additional information on options may be based on the participant's account balance as of the most recent valuation date.

With respect to both post- and preretirement qualified annuity elections, eligible participants of a defined contribution plan include those persons for whom the company is currently obligated to make a contribution or would be so obligated if it made any contribution to the plan at that time.[28]

Preretirement Survivor Annuity

Defined contribution plans are not obliged to offer preretirement survivor annuities if they distribute survivors' benefits which are at least equal to participants' vested account balances. These survivor benefits must be payable when a participant dies at any time while employed by the employer maintaining the plan. Presumably, this survivor's benefit can be limited to surviving spouses.[29]

[27] Code Reg. Section 1.401 (a)-11 (a) (1).
[28] Code Reg. Section 1.401 (a)-11 (f).
[29] Code Reg. Section 1.401 (a)-11 (c) (2) (i) (C) (2).

If a plan does not provide for this type of death benefit, it must allow participants to elect to have their vested account balances converted to a lifetime annuity for their spouses in the event of their death in the preretirement period. The rules concerning the preretirement survivor annuity that were previously explained for defined benefit plans would also govern these defined contribution plans.

PLAN DESIGN AND EMPLOYEE COMMUNICATIONS

Many defined benefit plans are required to offer both an election out of the postretirement automatic form of annuity and an election in favor of the preretirement survivor annuity. The following factors relating to the administration of these options should be important considerations:

Administrative Systems.   A system that regularly provides the names of participants, their marital status, and early retirement dates for the purpose of distributing the necessary information and election forms will be necessary. Up-to-date election forms and explanatory materials must also be maintained.

Accrued Benefits Data.   A major concern should be the availability of data providing the current amount of accrued benefit for each eligible individual and materials explaining the significance of such amounts.

Flexible Election Periods and Coordinated Disclosure.   Probably the easiest election period to explain and administer is one which extends from the time the appropriate information is received by the participant until a date shortly before benefits commence or service ends, where appropriate. The advantages of waiting periods should be weighed. Where they are imposed, feasible election periods must be devised. Issuing explanations of post- and preretirement annuities in one package may be practical since required dates for disclosure will often coincide.

Even though it may be administratively practical to limit the period during which additional information will be provided, this approach may be too hard on employees who receive initial joint and survivor information on options many years in advance of their actual retirement dates.

APPENDIX E

Disclosures to Plan Participants and Beneficiaries

INTRODUCTION

Under ERISA, plan participants are entitled to receive a variety of informative materials concerning their pension and welfare benefits.

These include:

1 *Summary Plan Description (SPD).* This report explains pension and welfare plan provisions and benefits in detail.

2 *Summary Annual Reports (SAR).* This report summarizes a plan's financial condition based upon the plan's full annual report that is filed with the IRS and DOL.

3 *Individual Benefit Statements.* Information about a participant's accrued and vested retirement benefits must be provided when requested.

4 *Information Regarding Survivor Benefits and Optional Forms of Benefit Payments.* Under ERISA most married pension plan participants are entitled to receive certain detailed information on spouses' benefit coverage. In addition, the plan may provide for other optional benefit forms necessitating various elections and the distribution of related information.

5 *Notice to Interested Parties.* Employees must be notified of the retirement plan sponsor's request for a determination from the IRS as to the plan's qualified status.

6 *Claims Procedure Notices.* These are required notices regarding denial of benefit claims and of a denied claim.

7 *Documents on Request.* Plan members and beneficiaries must be permitted to obtain or to inspect copies of almost all plan-related documents.

8 *Notice of Plan Termination.* Each of these disclosure items is discussed below.

9 *Suspension of Benefits Notice.* Plans must give suspension of benefits notices to working participants eligible to retire unless benefits are paid or are actuarially adjusted when they begin or resume.

10 *Notice to Terminated Vested Recipients.* Notice must be given to participants and the IRS, on Schedule SSA, concerning terminated participants' accrued benefits.

SUMMARY PLAN DESCRIPTION

The summary plan description (SPD) is a detailed description of a plan's terms and conditions. It is sent to both participants and to the U.S. Department of Labor.

Types of Plans Which Must Issue an SPD

All pension benefit plans must issue an SPD except the following exempt programs or plans:

unfunded or uninsured plans maintained for a select group of management or highly compensated employees

government plans

church plans

excess benefit plans

plans maintained outside the United States primarily for the benefit of persons substantially all of whom are *not* U.S. citizens.

Who Must Receive the SPD and When

An SPD for a new plan must generally be distributed within 120 days after the plan becomes subject to Part I of Title I of ERISA, which is generally the first day on which an employee is credited with an hour of service. If the plan's effective date depends on a certain condition being met (such as the receipt of a favorable IRS determination letter on the plan's qualification) or a potential event occurring, the 120-day period starts to run when the condition is satisfied or the event occurs. The initial SPD deadline for a previously existing plan (one which becomes subject to ERISA before July 19, 1977) was November 16, 1977, or in some cases, 90 days after a letter of determination for the plan was issued by the IRS after the plan was restated to justify ERISA.

When the initial SPD is distributed, it must be furnished to active plan participants, pension plan beneficiaries receiving benefits, any retirees, and terminated employees who have vested plan benefits. However, an SPD need not be issued a retiree whose entire benefit rights are fully guaranteed by an insurance company, as evidenced by a contract or certificate issued to that individual. Moreover, no SPD is needed for an employee whose total balance in the plan has been completely distributed in one lump sum or in installment payments.

A new plan entrant must receive an SPD within 90 days after becoming a plan participant. In addition, a beneficiary under a pension plan must receive the SPD within 90 days after receiving the first benefit payment.

Method of Distribution

Distribution of SPDs must be "by a method or methods of delivery likely to result in full distribution."

Acceptable SPD delivery methods are:

first-class mail—second or third class is acceptable only if return and forwarding postage is guaranteed, with the SPD to be sent again by first-class mail or hand delivery, if necessary.

personal delivery at worksite—however, it cannot simply be placed for a pickup in a location frequented by participants.

special insert in company or union periodical—as long as the mailing list is up-to-date and a prominent notice appears on the front page advising readers that the issue contains important information about rights under the plan and ERISA, which should be read and kept for future reference.

In some cases a combination of these delivery methods may be necessary to assure full distribution.

Information To Be Included in the SPD

The SPD must contain the following information:

1 *Plan Name.*   Or the commonly recognized name.
2 *Plan Sponsor.*   Name and address of sponsoring employer, employee organization. The names and addresses of principal representatives must be included in the case of a collectively bargained plan or of a multiple employer plan. It must include at least the name and address of the parent or most significant employer, where the plan is maintained by a group of companies. A statement must be included that a complete list of plan sponsors is available, or as an alternative, a statement as to the availability of information as to whether a particular employer or employee organization is a sponsor and, if so, the sponsor's address.
3 *Identification Numbers.*   Employer identification number of the plan sponsor, and the plan number.
4 *Type of Plan.*   Defined benefit, profit-sharing, and so on.
5 *Type of Plan Administration.*   Contract administration, insurer administration, and so on.
6 *Plan Administrator.*   Name, business address, and business phone number.
7 *Agent for Service of Legal Process.*   Name and address of designated agent, and a statement that legal process may be served on the plan administrator or the plan trustee as well.
8 *Plan Trustee.*   Name, title, and principal place of business of each trustee.
9 *Collective-Bargaining Agreement.*   If the plan is maintained pursuant to a collective-bargaining agreement, a statement that it is so maintained and that a copy of the agreement is available on request.
10 *Plan Funding.*   Name and address of organization through which plan benefits are funded.
11 *Eligibility and Benefits.*   Description of requirements relating to eligibility for participation and benefits, as well as a summary of plan benefits. Conditions for receiving benefits must be explained and must be indicated.

12 *Plan Year.* Date the plan's year ends.

13 *Joint and Survivor Benefits.* For pension benefit plans, pre- and postretirement joint and survivor benefits must be explained, as well as related election procedures.

14 *Loss of Benefits.* Statement describing any circumstances which could result in ineligibility, denial, loss, or suspension of benefits.

15 *Years of Service.* For pension benefit plans, a description of how the plan credits service for purposes of eligibility, vesting, benefit accrual, and how a break in service is determined.

16 *Retroactive Amendments.* For pension benefit plans which will make retroactive amendments regarding vesting or benefit accrual, a statement describing which plan provisions will be involved and the nature of the changes, giving specific reference to plan provisions and SPD text which will be affected. This statement may be printed in the SPD or enclosed separately.

17 *Contributions.* Identification of all sources—employer, employee organization and/or employees, and the method for determining contributions. Defined benefit plans may merely state that contributions are actuarially determined.

18 *Claims Procedures.* Procedure for denied claims for benefits and the review procedure for denied claims.

19 *Foreign Language Assistance.* For plans with a certain number of participants literate only in a non-English language, a conspicuous statement, in the appropriate foreign language, offering assistance in interpreting the SPD. This statement must appear in SPDs for:

Plans with fewer than 100 participants at the beginning of a plan year, if 25% or more can read only the same foreign language, and

Plans with 100 or more participants at the beginning of the plan year, if at least 500 or 10%—whichever is less—can read only the same foreign language.

The statement must clearly describe how participants and beneficiaries can receive help in understanding the SPD.

20 *Pension Insurance.* For plans whose benefits are *not* insured by the Pension Benefit Guaranty Corporation (PBGC), a statement of this fact, and the reason the plan is not covered under the PBGC provisions of ERISA. For plans which are covered by the PBGC, the SPD must include a statement of this fact and a summary of PBGC provisions under ERISA, as well as a statement regarding the availability of information regarding PBGC coverage and the PBGC's address.

The model PBGC statement from the regulations follows. Plan administrators may use a different statement if all necessary information is included.

Benefits under this plan are insured by the Pension Benefit Guaranty Corporation (PBGC) if the plan terminates. Generally, the [PBGC] guarantees most vested normal age retirement benefits, early retirement benefits, and certain disability and survivor's pensions. However, the PBGC does not guarantee all types of benefits under covered plans, and the amount of benefit protection is subject to certain limitations.

The PBGC guarantees vested benefits at the level in effect on the date of plan termination. However, if a plan has been in effect less than five years before it terminates, or its benefits have been increased within the five years before plan termination, the whole amount of the plan's vested benefits or the benefit increase may not be guaranteed. In addition, there is a ceiling on the amount of monthly benefit that PBGC guarantees, which is adjusted periodically. For more information on the PBGC insurance protection and its limitation, ask your Plan Administrator or the PBGC should be addressed to the Office of Communications PBGC, 2020 K Street, N.W., Washington, D.C. 20006. The PBGC Office of Communications may also be reached by calling 202-254-4817.

21   *ERISA Rights.*   A consolidated statement of participants' and beneficiaries' rights under ERISA. Use of the DOL's suggested language will satisfy this requirement, although, given its somewhat negative tone, a number of employers have found it desirable to reword this statement. This is permissible so long as the modified version complies in content and meets the requirements as to SPD style.

Information which does not apply to the plan may be omitted, and additional explanation may be included if written in easily understood terms. The DOL prescribed language is reproduced below:

As a participant in (name of plan) you are entitled to certain rights and protections under the Employee Retirement Income Security Act of 1974 (ERISA). ERISA provides that all plan participants shall be entitled to:

Examine, without charge at the plan administrator's office and at other specified locations, such as worksites and union halls, all plan documents, including insurance contracts, collective bargaining agreements and copies of all documents filed by the plan with the U.S. Department of Labor, such as detailed annual reports and plan descriptions. Obtain copies of all plan documents and other plan information upon written request to the plan administrator. The administrator may make a reasonable charge for the copies. Receive a summary of the plan's annual financial report. The plan administrator is required by law to furnish each participant with a copy of this summary annual report.

Obtain a statement telling you whether you have a right to receive a pension at normal retirement age (age __) and, if so, what your benefits would be at normal retirement age if you stop working under the plan now. If you do not have a right to a pension, the statement will tell you how many more years you have to work to get a right to a pension. This statement must be requested in writing and is not required to be given more than once a year. The plan must provide the statement free of charge. In addition to creating rights for plan participants, ERISA imposes duties upon the people who are responsible for the operation of the employee benefit plan. The people who operate your plan, called "fiduciaries" of the plan, have a duty to do so prudently and in the interest of you and other plan participants and beneficiaries. No one, including your employer, your union, or any other person, may fire you or otherwise discriminate against you in any way to prevent you from obtaining a (pension, welfare) benefit or exercising your rights under ERISA. If your claim for a (pension, welfare) benefit is denied in whole or in part you must receive a written explanation of the reason for the denial. You have the right to have the plan reviewed and reconsider your claim.

Under ERISA, there are steps you can take to enforce the above rights. For instance, if you request materials from the plan and do not receive them within 30 days, you may file suit in a federal court. In such a case, the court may require the plan administrator to provide the materials and pay you up to $100 a day until you receive the materials, unless the materials were not sent because of reasons beyond the control of the administrator. If you have a claim for benefits which is denied or ignored, in whole or in part, you may file suit in a state or federal court. If it should happen that plan fiduciaries misuse the plan's money, or if you are discriminated against for asserting your rights, you may seek assistance from the U.S. Department of Labor, or you may file suit in a federal court. The court will decide who should pay court costs and legal fees. If you are successful, the court may order the person you have sued to pay these costs and fees. If you lose, the court may order you to pay these costs and fees, for example, if it finds your claim is frivolous. If you have any questions about your plan, you should contact the plan administrator. If you have any questions about this statement or about your rights under ERISA, you should contact the nearest Area Office of the U.S. Labor-Management Services Administration, Department of Labor.

SPD Style and Format

ERISA requires SPDs to be "written in a manner calculated to be understood by the average plan participant and (to) be sufficiently comprehensive to apprise the plan's participants and beneficiaries of their rights and obligations under the plan." Department of Labor regulations strongly advise plan administrators to consider education and comprehension levels of participants. "Consideration of these factors," regulations state, "will usually require the elimination of technical jargon and of long, complex sentences, the use of clear cross references, and a table of contents." The SPD's general composition and organization must give equal emphasis to all plan elements, and choice of type must uniformly highlight all provisions. ERISA requires the SPD to present fairly all of the plan's benefits as well as all of its restrictions.

Restrictive plan provisions may be described apart from benefit provisions; however, clear page reference to any related limitation or restriction must appear next to the benefit description. In short, arrangement of the format in an attempt to mislead or misinform participants and beneficiaries will violate ERISA.

Updates and Plan Changes

A complete, fully updated SPD must be issued to participants and beneficiaries every five years if plan changes occur or every 10 years if the plan remains unchanged.

The plan administrator must provide participants and beneficiaries with a descriptive summary of a change in the plan or plan information if the change is considered a *material modification.* The description must be issued no later than 210 days after the close of the plan year in which the modification or change was adopted.

The following changes are examples of material modifications:

a change in the benefit formula,

the use of a new funding medium,

a change in the plan administrator's business address or phone number.

In general, any plan modification or change in the information to be included in the SPD must be communicated to participants.

Different Benefits for Different Classes of Employees

If a plan has a different schedule of benefits for different classes of participants, a single SPD covering all participants and all benefits could lead to confusion. For this reason, the regulations permit a plan to provide a different SPD for each class of participants, which may omit information which does not apply to that class. The class of participants for which the SPD is prepared must be identified on the first page. If the classes are too numerous to list on the first page, then they may be identified elsewhere in the text if reference to those pages of the text is made on the first page.

When these SPDs are filed with the Department of Labor, a list identifying each SPD should also be furnished. The name of the plan sponsor and the employer identification number assigned to the plan sponsor should appear on the cover page of each SPD filed and also on the list of such SPDs.

SPDs for Merged Plans

If a plan merger takes place after the successor plan (i.e., the surviving plan) has already distributed its SPDs, it is not necessary for the administrator of the successor plan to reissue an SPD that reflects both merged and successor plan provisions.

Instead, the administrator should, within 90 days after the merger occurs, distribute the following items to participants and beneficiaries of the former and now merged plan(s):

a copy of the successor plan's most recent SPD together with summaries of material changes not described in the SPD; and

a statement which briefly describes the merger, summarizes provisions of both plans that apply to participants and beneficiaries of the merged plan, and informs them of the availability of plan and merger documents.

Updated SPD's furnished after the merger should clearly identify those classes of participants and beneficiaries affected by the merged plan and describe the availability of plan and merger-related documents.

SUMMARY ANNUAL REPORTS

A summary annual report (SAR) is a description of an employee benefit plan's financial status based upon the information contained in the plan's most recent annual return/report (Form 5500, 5500-C, 5500-K or 5500-R). It must be distributed annually to participants and beneficiaries of most pension benefit plans. This includes distribution to terminated plan participants who have vested rights to benefits as well as to retirees for whom an insurance company has not fully guaranteed payments or who have not received the balance to their credit in the plan in the form of one lump-sum payment or in installment payments.

The following types of plans are exempt from this requirement:

plans which are not *funded* by the employer or which provide benefits from an insurer and cover a select group of management; or

certain dues-financed plans.

Format

SARs must follow the formats provided by the regulations for pension plans (Figure 1). For convenience, the final regulations include cross-reference tables which match each SAR item with the corresponding section of the annual report. Although the prescribed forms may not be altered, any items which are inapplicable to the plan, or which are not shown on the plan's annual report, may be omitted.

A copy of the plan's financial statements and accompanying notes (which are part of the annual report) must be furnished to a participant or beneficiary upon request, free of charge. The entire annual report or any portion must also be furnished upon request, although a reasonable charge may be made for this material.

If the plan administrator considers it necessary to elaborate upon the basic SAR information, he may do so by adding a section entitled "Additional Explanation," which may appear after the form itself.

As with the SPD, if a significant number of participants in the plan are not

FIGURE 1

Form for summary annual report relating to pension plans

Summary Annual Report for (name of plan)

This is a summary of the annual report for (name of plan and IEN) for (period covered by this report). The annual report has been filed with the Internal Revenue Service, as required under the Employee Retirement Income Security Act of 1974 (ERISA).

Basic Financial Statement

Benefits under the plan are provided by (indicate funding arrangements).
    Plan expenses were ($).
    These expenses included ($) in administrative expenses and ($) in benefits paid to participants and beneficiaries, and ($) in other expenses. A total of (   ) persons were participants in our beneficiaries of the plan year, although not all of these persons had yet earned the right to receive benefits.
    [If the plan is funded other than solely by allocated insurance contracts:]
    The value of plan assets, after subtracting liabilities of the plan, was ($) as of (the end of the plan year), compared to ($) as of (the beginning of the plan year). During the plan year the plan experienced an (increase) (decrease) in its net assets of ($). This (increase) (decrease) includes unrealized appreciation or depreciation in the value of plan assets; that is, the difference between the value of the plan's assets at the end of the year and the value of the assets at the beginning of the year or the loss of assets acquired during the year. The plan had total income of ($), including employer contributions of ($), employee contributions of ($), (gains) (losses) of ($) from the sale of assets, and earnings from investments of ($).
    [For plans filing Form 5500-K omit separate entries for employer contributions and employee contributions and insert instead "contributions by the employer and employees of ($)."]
    [If any funds are used to purchase allocated insurance contracts:]
    The plan has (a) contract(s) with (name of insurance carrier(s)) which allocate(s) funds toward (state whether individual policies, group deferred annuities or other). The total premiums paid for the plan year ending (date) were ($).

Minimum Funding Standards

[If the plan is a defined benefit plan:]
    An actuary's statement shows that (enough money was contributed to the plan to keep it funded in accordance with the minimum funding standards of ERISA) (not enough money was contributed to the plan to keep it funded in accordance with the minimum funding standards of ERISA. The amount of the deficit was ($)).
    [If the plan is a defined contribution plan covered by funding requirements:]
    (Enough money was contributed to the plan to keep it funded in accordance with the minimum funding standards of ERISA.) (Not enough money was contributed to the plan to keep it funded in accordance with the minimum funding standards of ERISA. The amount of the deficit was ($).)

Your Right to Additional Information

You have the right to receive a copy of the full annual report, or any part thereof, on request. The items listed below are included in that report: (Note—list only those items which are actually included in the latest annual report.)

FIGURE 1 (continued)

1 an accountant's report;

2 assets held for investment;

3 transactions between the plan and parties in interest (that is, persons who have certain relationships with the plan);

4 loans or other obligations in default;

5 leases in default;

6 transactions in excess of 3% of plan assets;

7 insurance information including sales commissions paid by insurance carriers; and

8 actuarial information regarding the funding of the plan.

To obtain a copy of the full annual report, or any part thereof, write or call the office of (name), who is (state title: e.g., the plan administrator), (business address and telephone number). The charge to cover copying costs will be ($) for the full annual report, or ($) per page for any part thereof.

You also have the right to receive from the plan administrator, on request and at no charge, a statement of the assets and liabilities of the plan and accompanying notes, or a statement of income and expenses of the plan and accompanying notes, or both. If you request a copy of the full annual report from the plan administrator, these two statements and accompanying notes will be included as part of that report. The charge to cover copying costs given above does not include a charge for the copying costs of these portions of the report because these portions are furnished without charge.

You also have the legally protected right to examine the annual report at the main office of the plan (address), (at any other location where the report is available for examination), and at the U.S. Department of Labor in Washington, D.C., or to obtain a copy from the U.S. Department of Labor upon payment of copying costs. Requests to the department should be addressed to: Public Disclosure, Room N4677, Pension and Welfare Benefit Programs, Department of Labor, 200 Constitution Avenue, N.W., Washington, D.C. 20216.

literate in English, a statement (in the non-English language common to those employees) must be attached indicating that assistance in understanding the SAR is available.

SAR Timing

The final regulations regarding SARs became effective June 5, 1979. All SARs prepared after that date must be based upon the prescribed format, rather than in accordance with the former, more complicated rules. Therefore, some SARs prepared for plan years beginning in 1977, most SARs prepared for plan years beginning in 1978, and all SARs thereafter will use the new format. SARs must generally be distributed within nine months after the end of the plan year. This is normally two months after the due date of the plan's annual report. When an extension is granted for the filing of the annual report, the SAR deadline is two months after the new extended date.

INDIVIDUAL BENEFIT STATEMENTS

The individual benefit statement provides each plan member with an estimate of his future retirement income. Thus it is perhaps the most important disclosure item required by ERISA. Most defined benefit and defined contribution plans are required to provide these statements. For a list of retirement plans exempt from this disclosure requirement, see Chapter 4, "Plans Covered and Excluded," referring to types of programs exempt from the SPD rules.

The individual benefit statement must contain the following information:

the amount of retirement benefit the participant has accrued to date (e.g., an account balance for a profit-sharing plan or a monthly benefit for a defined benefit plan);

the percentage of the participant's accrued benefit which is vested;

the date on which the participant's nonvested accrued benefit, if any, will become nonforfeitable.

A benefit estimate is generally based upon the participant's current salary level and, where applicable, social security benefit level under present law. In other words, the participant is normally given an idea of what his or her retirement benefit would be if present circumstances remain unchanged.

Final DOL regulations on benefit reports have not been issued as of this printing, although proposed DOL rules concerning the specific content of the statement, timing, procedures, and so forth have been issued. Many of the comments received by the DOL have strongly objected to the proposed regulation's stringent requirements as to the statement's contents and timing. It therefore seems unlikely that the proposed rules will be adopted without significant change.

When To Furnish the Statements

ERISA does not require employers to automatically issue benefit reports to active employees at regular intervals. However, the statement must be provided to an employee upon his request, although no more than one statement need be furnished an employee within a 12-month period.

The proposed regulations would allow an employer to satisfy the disclosure requirement by automatically issuing benefit statements to participants on an annual basis. However, employers who take advantage of this alternative would be required to provide an employee with one duplicate copy of his benefit statement at any time during the year if he or she requests it. In addition special rules are applicable to terminated participants who have deferred vested benefits.

Proposed Contents

In addition to the *accrued benefit* display, the DOL proposed regulations would require the inclusion of an extensive amount of information relating to the calculation of pension benefits.

For example, the following information would have to be included:

number of completed years of service;
cross-reference to the summary plan description;
earnings taken into account for pension calculation purposes;
any optional form of payment elected by the participant.

INFORMATION REGARDING SURVIVOR BENEFITS

Plans providing retirement benefits in the form of a life annuity (defined benefit and certain defined contribution plans) that intend to qualify under the Internal Revenue Code and which must adhere to ERISA's vesting standards must comply with ERISA's rules concerning the financial protection of plan participants' surviving spouses.

Basically, these rules prevent a plan from paying benefits in a life annuity if the participant dies after retiring (i.e., retiring on or after either normal retirement age or early retirement age) or after reaching normal retirement age, while employed, unless the participant has elected not to take survivor coverage for his spouse. Most plan participants must also be given the right to elect financial protection for their spouses in the event they die while employed, after reaching early retirement age. (However, this rule does not apply to a defined contribution plan which provides a survivor benefit equal to the participants' vested account balance.)

In all cases, proper disclosure of information concerning the availability of survivors' coverage must be made. The participant must be made aware of his right to elect or decline a survivor annuity for his spouse, and must receive a thorough description of how these annuities work and the financial effect of making an election for or against the available coverage. Participants must receive this information even though they may already have received a similar explanation in their summary plan description.

Specifically, the following information concerning the *postretirement* joint and survivor annuity must be provided:

a general description of the annuity and the circumstances under which it is paid;
the availability of the election out;
an explanation of the financial effect of making this election illustrated in terms of:

an arithmetic or percentage reduction from a single life annuity, or

a table showing the difference in dollars between the single life annuity and joint and survivor annuity for a hypothetical plan benefit;

a notice that participants may request more information in terms of his particular benefit, as described below, including directions on how this information can be obtained.

Employers may use the following methods of communicating this information:

by mail or personal delivery;

permanent posting (which will remain available throughout the election periods);

repeated publication in a company periodical read by employees.

The additional information to be made available on request includes a written explanation in nontechnical language of the terms and conditions of the joint and survivor annuity of the automatic form and the financial effect upon the individual's benefit of electing out of the automatic form. The dollar differences between forms must be shown. No more than one request has to be honored and that answer must be furnished by mail or personal delivery.

If the plan allows the spouse of a deceased participant to elect out of the survivor annuity, the spouse must be furnished, within a reasonable time after request, with a written explanation in nontechnical language of the survivor annuity and any other benefits which may be selected in its place. The explanation must contain a comparison of the various benefits that can be elected in dollar terms. Only one such request must be honored.

Table I in Appendix D indicates when the required information must be distributed and when election periods must occur.

With respect to the election of the preretirement survivor annuity, eligible participants, before the start of the election period, must be given a general description of the preretirement survivor annuity, election information, and a description of the circumstances under which it will be paid if elected, in addition to a general explanation of the relative financial effect of the election on the participant's benefit.

The regulations are not clear as to whether it is necessary to offer additional information concerning an individual participant's preretirement coverage. In any case, the general information initially distributed to eligible employees will normally provide enough information since it will include a description of coverage charges and the financial effect of the election.

The methods of communicating this information are the same as those described for the postretirement automatic form.

Table II in Appendix D indicates the due dates for disclosure and required election periods.

NOTICE TO INTERESTED PARTIES

Before the IRS will issue an advance determination as to the qualified status of a new plan or the continued qualification of an existing plan (due to plan amendment or termination), the plan sponsor must provide a notice to interested parties.

The notice serves to inform the interested parties that the employer is submitting an application for advance determination as to the qualification of the plan. Each person is advised that he or she is entitled to submit or request the Department of Labor to submit a comment to the IRS on the question of whether the plan meets the qualification requirements.

In general, all present employees of the employer who are eligible to participate in the plan must be notified, as well as those who would be eligible if they met the plan's age and service requirement or if they agreed to make mandatory contributions.

In some cases, other employees are also considered interested parties to whom a notice must be sent, such as those who work at the same location as those who are eligible for plan participation.

Notice by mail must be given not less than 10 nor more than 24 days prior to the date the application is submitted. Notice by posting must be furnished not less than seven nor more than 21 days prior to such date.

CLAIMS PROCEDURE NOTICES

If a claim for a benefit is denied, the plan administrator must provide the employee, within 90 days of the claim, with a written explanation of why the claim was denied. An additional 90 days may be taken provided that the plan administrator informs the claimant of the delay and the reason for it. The notice must include specific references to the plan provisions on which the denial was based and must identify any materials that may be needed to perfect the claim, together with an explanation of why the materials are needed. In addition, information on how the employee may have the claim again reviewed must be supplied.

Claimants must have at least 60 days in which to appeal a denied claim. The claimant has the right to have a representative present to argue the claim. Pertinent documents must be available for review. Claimants must also have the opportunity to present their requests for appeal and arguments in writing.

The decision on appeal must be given to the claimant in writing within 60 days, or within 120 days if the claimant has been notified of the decision's delay and the reason for it. Sometimes a decision may be delayed until the next meeting of the committee in charge of reviewing denied claims.

The written decision concerning a denied claim must contain the specific reasons for its acceptance or denial.

FURNISHING DOCUMENTS ON REQUEST

ERISA protects the right of plan participants and beneficiaries to receive plan-related documents upon their request or to examine them at designated locations. The ERISA Rights Statement contained in the SPD informs participants of their right to receive and inspect pertinent documents.

The following materials must be provided upon written request:

latest updated summary plan description (in addition to the SPD initially distributed without charge);

latest annual report;

any terminal report (to the DOL);

bargaining agreement, trust agreement, contract, or other instruments under which the plan is established or operated.

Documents may be mailed or delivered personally. Recipients of documents may be charged a reasonable fee, not more than $.25 per page, or if less, the actual cost per page to the plan for the least expensive means of acceptable reproduction. No postage or handling charges may be assessed. Upon request, participants and beneficiaries must be given information regarding charges for documents.

The above-mentioned documents must also be available for inspection at the principal office of the plan administrator. In addition, documents must be available at appropriate employer establishments and union meeting halls or offices within 10 calendar days of the individual's request for inspection at that location. A reasonable procedure for requesting inspection of documents at work and union locations may be established.

Plan administrators are required to keep detailed records on plan participants which are sufficient to determine benefits that may become due an individual. DOL regulations indicate that records pertaining to a participant or beneficiary must be available for copying, for his or her inspection, and for examination by his or her personal representative.

NOTICE OF PLAN TERMINATION

An administrator of a defined benefit plan must inform covered employees of an impending plan termination. The notice to employees must state, in writing, the proposed date of termination and the date the notice was filed with the Pension Benefit Guaranty Corporation. It should be posted at the work place, or if the employees are covered by a collective-bargaining contract, the notice should be delivered to the union representative.

If the PBGC institutes proceedings to terminate a plan and appoints a trustee to administer it, the trustee must notify certain interested parties, including the participants and beneficiaries of the plan, of the institution of such proceedings.

NOTICE TO PARTICIPANTS WITH
DEFERRED VESTED BENEFITS

A separated employee must be furnished a statement of his deferred vested benefits, and all the information filed on Schedule SSA must be provided to the separated participant by the plan administrator. Specifically, this individual statement must include: the plan administrator's name and address; the nature, amount, and form of the deferred vested benefit to which the participant is entitled; and such other information as may be required by Code Section 6057(a) or Schedule SSA and instructions.

This individual statement to a separated participant must be furnished on or before the date by which the Schedule SSA is to be filed with the Secretary of the Treasury. It is to be delivered to the participant or forwarded to his last known address. A fine of $50 may be imposed if the plan administrator (1) willfully fails to furnish the statement to the participant in the manner, at the time, and showing the information required, or (2) willfully furnishes a false or fraudulent statement to the participant.

Immediately after the participant's termination, a plan administrator must furnish the participant with a report that is sufficient to inform the employee of his accrued benefits under the plan and the percentage of such benefits that are nonforfeitable under the plan. This also applies for an employee who has a one-year break in service as defined for vesting purposes.

In order to comply with these rules, it is necessary for an employer to maintain records for each employee sufficient to determine the benefits due or which may become due. The plan administrator is to be furnished with the information needed to make the required reports.

Failure to furnish the required information or maintain the required records will subject the employer or administrator to a penalty of $10 for each employee for whom such failure occurs, unless the failure is for a reasonable cause.

SUSPENSION OF BENEFITS NOTICE

Benefit payments may not be withheld unless notice of the suspension is given to the employee during the first calendar month or payroll period in which the plan withholds payments.

The notification must include the specific reasons for the benefit suspension, a general description of the plan provisions relating to the benefit suspension, a copy of such provisions, and a statement that the applicable DOL regulations can be found in Section 2530.203-3 of the Code of Federal Regulations. Furthermore, the notice must also inform the employee of the plan's procedure for affording a review of suspension. Requests for reviews may be considered in accordance with the plan's claims procedure under Section 503 of ERISA.

The final regulation, as amended, provides that, to the extent the SPD contains information substantially similar to that required to be given to retirees, the suspension notice need only refer to the relevant pages of the SPD. The notice must also inform the retiree of how to obtain a copy of the SPD or the relevant pages thereof. Such requests must be honored within 30 days.

METHODS OF DELIVERING DISCLOSURE MATERIALS

The text of the DOL regulation which describes how materials are to be distributed is reproduced below. Note that this rule applies to all situations in which a participant is entitled to plan information under ERISA.

> Where certain material, including reports, statements, and documents, is required under Part I of the Act and this part to be furnished either by direct operation of law or on individual request, the plan administrator shall use measures reasonably calculated to ensure actual receipt of the material by plan participants and beneficiaries. Material which is required to be furnished to all participants covered under the plan and beneficiaries receiving benefits under the plan (other than beneficiaries under a welfare plan) must be sent by a method of delivery likely to result in full distribution. For example, in-hand delivery to an employee at his or her worksite is acceptable. However, in no case is it acceptable merely to place copies of the material in a location frequented by participants. It is also acceptable to furnish such material as a special insert in a periodical distributed to employees such as a union newspaper or a company publication if the distribution list for the periodical is comprehensive and up-to-date and a prominent notice on the front page of the periodical advises readers that the issue contains an insert with important information about rights under the plan and the Act which should be read and retained for future reference. If some participants and beneficiaries are not on the mailing list, a periodical must be used in conjunction with other methods of distribution such that the methods taken together are reasonably calculated to ensure actual receipt.
>
> Material distributed through the mail may be sent by first-, second-, or third-class mail. However, distribution by second- or third-class mail is acceptable only if return and forwarding postage is guaranteed and address correction is requested. Any material sent by second- or third-class mail which is returned with an address correction shall be sent again by first-class mail or personally delivered to the participant at his or her worksite.

PENALTIES FOR VIOLATION
OF DISCLOSURE REQUIREMENTS

Criminal Penalties

A person who willfully violates ERISA's disclosure and reporting requirements (Part I of Title I) can be fined not more than $5,000 or imprisoned not more than one year, or both. Where the entity in violation is not an individual, the fine cannot exceed $100,000.

Civil Enforcement

If an administrator fails to supply the required disclosure materials or refuses to comply with a request for information by the participant or beneficiary within 30 days after such request (unless such failure is due to matters beyond his or her control), he or she may be personally liable to the claimant for up to $100 a day from the date of refusal or failure to supply the information.

A civil action may be brought for redress of violations of the reporting and disclosure provisions of ERISA by a participant, beneficiary, the Secretary of Labor, or a fiduciary. In a civil action by a participant, beneficiary, or fiduciary, the court may allow a reasonable attorney's fee and costs of action to either party.

APPENDIX F

Illustrative Letter Requesting a Copy of the Actuary's Report and Other Information on the Plan

Gentlemen:

In connection with an examination of the financial statements of the XYZ Pension Plan (date of statements) please furnish our auditors, _____, _____, the infor-
       (name)   (address)
mation described below as of (the more recent benefit information date of either _____ or _____). For
  date of the plan year-end   date of beginning of plan year
your convenience, you may supply in response to these requests pertinent sections, properly signed and dated, of your actuarial report and/or Schedule B, if available and if the requested information is contained therein.

1 The actuarial present value of accumulated plan benefits as defined in FASB Statement No. 35, *Accounting and Reporting by Defined Benefit Pension Plans,* classified as follows:

    (a) Vested benefits of participants and beneficiaries
           currently receiving payments $_____
    (b) Other vested benefits $_____
    (c) Nonvested benefits $_____
    (d) Total $_____

2 Date of the valuation of accumulated plan benefits above.
3 A description of the principal assumptions used in determining the actuarial present value of accumulated plan benefits.

4 The minimum annual contribution including the use of any credit balances in the funding standard account available to offset present or future contributions required under ERISA and the actuarial cost method being used, a description of the actuarial assumptions used in computing the funding standard account, and the aggregate effect of any change in such method or assumption(s). Also, indicate whether the alternative funding standard account was elected and whether the full funding limitation is applicable.

Information Requested Which May Be Contained in the Actuarial Report or Other Sources

5 A brief description of the employee group covered.

6 **(a)** A brief general description of the benefit provisions of the plan used in the actuarial calculation.

(b) A description of any benefits, as prescribed by FASB Statement No. 35, not included in the accumulated plan benefits valuation and the reason therefor.

(c) The effective date of the last plan amendment included in this valuation.

7 The following information applies to the employee census data used in performing the actuarial valuation:

(a) Date as of which the census data was collected is _____.

(b)

Participants—	Number of persons	Compensation (if applicable)
Currently receiving payments	_____	_____
Active with vested benefits	_____	_____
Terminated with deferred vested benefits	_____	_____
Active without vested benefits	_____	_____
Other (describe)	_____	_____
TOTAL	_____	_____

Note: If information is not available for each of these categories, indicate which categories have been grouped. Please describe any group or groups of participants not included in the above information.

(c) Requested information for the following specific individuals contained in the census:

Participant's Name or Number	Age or Birth Date	Sex	Salary	Hire Date or Years of Service

Note: The auditor should select information from company records to compare with the census data used by the actuary. In addition, the auditor may wish to have selected certain census data from the actuary's file to compare to the company's records.

8 Describe, if significant (either individually or in the aggregate), the effects of the following factors on the change in the actuarial present value of accumulated plan benefits from the preceding to the current benefit information date. (Effects that are individually significant should be separately identified.)

(a) Plan amendments.

(b) Changes in the nature of the plan (for example, a plan spin-off or a merger with another plan).

(c) Changes in actuarial assumptions.

9 For the current year, the effects of the following on changes in the present value of accumulated plan benefits:

(a) Increase in benefits accumulated.

(b) Increase (for interest) as a result of the decrease in the discount period.

(c) Benefits paid.

10 If an accumulated funding deficiency exists, the amount necessary to reduce the deficiency to zero under ERISA. $_____

11 Have you been notified of a decision by the sponsor company to fully or partially terminate the plan? If so, please describe the effect on the plan.

12 Please describe the nature of the relationship, if any, you may have with the plan or the sponsor company which might appear to impair the objectivity of your work.

13 What is the amount of the unbilled and/or unpaid actuarial or other fees due your firm applicable to the plan year-end and *payable by the plan?*

14 Please supply any additional information which you believe is necessary.

Your prompt attention to this request will be appreciated.

Very truly yours,

_____

(Plan Administrator)

Operational Guidelines for Managing Pension Fund Investments

INTRODUCTION

The success of a pension fund depends significantly upon effective operational procedures and controls.[1] Such controls are important to the efficiency and effectiveness with which plan assets are managed.

In some instances, identifying control weaknesses and developing procedural or policy changes can result in improving the plan's investment performance. Such improvement is translated directly into decreased employer contributions (in a defined benefit plan) or increased retirement benefits (in a defined contribution plan).

This appendix is designed as a guide to conducting an operational controls review and to instituting or modifying controls, where needed, to ensure that the system is operating effectively. Rather than provide a lengthy description of investment policies, systems, and procedures, this appendix is organized in the form of a checklist questionnaire to facilitate quick identification of areas which may require attention in a particular situation.

Where problems are identified (via "no" answers), remedial action should be considered. Such action may involve immediate implementation of needed controls or, where appropriate corrective action is not readily definable, obtaining professional assistance to study particular problem areas more fully. Certain checklist questions are referenced to related "Dollarization Steps" which may be helpful in quantifying, in dollars, the magnitude of potential improvement opportunities.

The checklist covers four categories:

organization and management policies,
buying and selling,
portfolio management,
assessing portfolio performance.

ORGANIZATION AND MANAGEMENT POLICIES

The organization of the investment function and the policies prescribed by management normally have a direct effect on virtually all phases of a pension fund's operations. This section deals with basic (but frequently overlooked) organizational and policy considerations, including factors relating to the selection of and dealings with external money managers.

---

[1] *Operational controls,* sometimes called *administrative* or *management controls,* relate to operational efficiency and effectiveness. They generally differ from *internal controls,* referred to in previous chapters, which relate to the accuracy of financial statements and safeguarding of assets. The latter term is technically called *internal accounting controls.*

1 Does the investment function have:

(a) an organization chart?

(b) job descriptions?

(c) clear-cut assignments of responsibility?

By providing job descriptions and defined responsibilities, people are directed so that their combined efforts are complementary rather than overlapping or inefficiently applied.

Lack of organization may have adverse results; for example, financial analysts may be researching too many industries or categories of securities, thus failing to become proficient in any one area.

2 Are there written policies covering the following areas:

(a) portfolio composition (e.g., concentrated, diversified, high risk, low risk, growth, income)?

(b) limitations or prohibitions as to investment type or technique (e.g., writing or investing in options, real estate, commodities, short sales of securities, unregistered securities, underwriting of securities of other issuers, or leverage techniques such as margin accounts or bank borrowings)?

(c) limitations as to funds available to each portfolio manager where there is more than one manager?

(d) conflicts of interest (to supplement applicable governmental regulations)?

(e) expected investment return (i.e., based on relative market indicators such as New York Stock Exchange Industrial Average or Standard & Poor's Stock Index or on absolute factors such as the percent of expected investment return over a specified period of time)?

(f) formal portfolio review program (establishing the frequency of reviews, review team composition, techniques for following up deficiencies until they are corrected)?

(g) limitations upon portfolio turnover (providing a portfolio manager with guidelines to the amount of trading which is acceptable)?

(h) limitations upon the percentage of funds which may be invested in a particular security or group of securities?

Absence of objectives and policies can subject the organization to poor portfolio management decisions and could subject officers to charges of failure to exercise fiduciary responsibilities effectively. It is important that the policies set forth cover all legal restrictions which apply, including restrictions prescribed in ERISA (see Chapter 4).

3 Are the investment activities of each portfolio manager treated as a separate profit center?

Establishing the activities of each portfolio manager as a separate profit center fixes accountability, responsibility, and authority for a manager's investments and allows for an objective evaluation of each manager's performance.

4 Has management evaluated the alternatives of managing the portfolio internally, compared to engaging one or more external money managers? Factors that should be considered include availability of the necessary talent to manage the portfolio, relative costs involved, and willingness of management to assume direct responsibility for investment decisions and results.

Where it has been decided not to manage the portfolio internally, consideration should be given to engaging several external managers or management companies, rather than one. The purpose of splitting funds is to obtain a range of investment skills, in that certain money managers may excel in particular investment areas. For example, particular banks may be strong in general securities investing, insurance companies in real estate and private placements, investment counselors in aggressive growth stocks, and brokers in mutual funds and other investment vehicles. Other reasons for splitting funds are potential increased motivation on the part of the managers to perform well in order to obtain a larger share of the total portfolio, and the implicit safety that comes with diversification. These reasons for fund splitting must be weighed against counterarguments against it: the use of multiple managers may result in dilution of the quality of investment performance, overdiversification, increased expenses, and increased communication problems.

It should be noted that if no formal study of pertinent factors has been made and no conclusions have been reached, then officials have in effect made a "decision by default."

5 In selecting an outside investment manager, have the following criteria been considered:

(a) whether he has a stated philosophy of operation and, if so, whether it is consistent with the fund's philosophy?

(b) past performance in terms of a market indicator such as the New York Stock Exchange Industrial Average or Standard & Poor's Stock Index?

(c) past performance in terms of ability to meet stated performance goals?

(d) history and approach toward investments?

(e) recommendations of past and present clients regarding ability to perform basic research, ability to execute trades efficiently, and attentiveness to clients' needs?

(f) dollar value, quality, and types of accounts managed (e.g., growth, income, institutional)?

(g) potential conflicts of interest?

(h) fee schedule?

(i) willingness to charge fees based, at least in part, on portfolio performance?

When officials do not consider the above points, they may select a manager whose investment philosophy, abilities, and experience are inconsistent with the needs of the fund, thereby inviting unacceptable portfolio performance.

6 Where an outside investment manager is engaged, are prescribed investment policies communicated to him?

It is important to communicate the fund's policies to the outside investment manager so that he will be aware of the fund's needs and its limitations upon holdings, investment vehicles, and so on. Policies may be communicated to the advisor in a policy statement, in a trust agreement, or in a letter supplementing an agreement.

7 Are controls in effect by which appropriate officials are apprised of changes in the business associations and financial interests of directors, trustees, advisors, and so on, of the fund which would place such persons in a position where conflicts of interest may exist?

An example of such a control is a requirement that all such persons periodically (e.g., annually) submit a signed statement indicating that no conflicts of interest exist. Absence of such a control could lead to conflicts of interest of which the fund is unaware.

8 Are controls in effect by which appropriate officials are apprised of persons or entities considered under ERISA to be fiduciaries and/or parties in interest?

It is important that fiduciaries and parties in interest be identified to enable prohibited transactions to be avoided (see Chapter 4 for details).

BUYING AND SELLING

In order for the decision-making process to be meaningful, buy-sell decisions must be carried out accurately and promptly. This section deals with the mechanics of executing securities transactions and related matters, including accuracy of brokerage charges, timing of payments, minimizing commissions, and controlling trading activity.

9 Are controls in effect to ensure that purchase and sale orders are executed accurately?

Errors by stockbrokers, such as purchasing or selling the wrong stock or the wrong number of shares, can have a direct adverse effect. The fund should be in a position to detect errors promptly so that corrections can be made quickly. (See dollarization step 1, Error Control.)

10 Are controls in effect to verify that securities transactions are executed promptly?

Significant differences should not normally exist between the market price at the time orders are placed and the price at which transactions are executed. Failure to control and analyze the effectiveness with which transactions are executed may lead to unfavorable changes in price. (See dollarization step 2, Prompt Execution.)

11 Where applicable, are controls in effect to verify that securities are traded within the day's high–low range?

Typically, the fund should determine that securities are not sold below the day's low quote, nor purchased above the day's high quote. Management should also be alert to situations where purchases are *consistently* executed at or near the day's high price and sales are *consistently* executed at or near the day's low price; such a situation may point to the need for an evaluation of trading practices. (See dollarization step 3, Unfavorable Trade Prices.)

12 Are controls in effect to verify the correctness of commission cost, stock transfer tax, accrued interest, and any other items charged on securities transactions?

Commissions may be traced to memoranda regarding negotiated rates, stock transfer taxes may be checked to published tables, and interest accrued may be recalculated. Failure to verify the correctness of such charges could lead to overpayments. (See dollarization step 1, Error Control.)

13 Are payments for purchase transactions deferred until the settlement date in order to gain greater use of funds?

Failure to time payments to maximize the use of available funds could result in lost income. The settlement date is generally the fifth full business day following the transaction; stretching the settlement date to its maximum legal limits by using weekends and holidays is a useful technique to gain additional use of funds. (See dollarization step 4, Early Payments.)

14 Are brokerage commissions negotiated?

The failure to take advantage of negotiating may result in higher commission payments than would otherwise be necessary, as well as a possible breach of fiduciary responsibilities. (See dollarization step 5, Excess Commissions.)

15 Are controls in effect to avoid excessive trading with related excessive commissions?

While the portfolio manager may have discretion as to the frequency of trades, a situation where excessive commissions are generated without adequate related gains should be avoided. Controls should highlight situations where the same securities have been bought and sold within a limited time (e.g., one week, one month) so that the reasonableness of such transactions can be examined; and the portfolio turnover rate should be monitored in terms of prescribed policies and objectives.

16 Where the fund is purchasing or selling a large number of shares of a security in smaller lots, is the commission negotiated on the basis of the total transaction?

It is not unusual for trades involving large blocks of stock to be broken up into smaller lots to minimize the effect on the market price of executing a large transaction. When this is done, a lower commission cost can usually be negotiated with the broker, based on the total transaction. (See dollarization step 5, Excess Commissions.)

17 Where an outside investment manager is responsible for portfolio transactions, does he obtain the benefit for the fund of lower commission charges by combining transactions for the same security for several of his investment clients?

When an outside investment manager is purchasing the same security for several of his clients, he can sometimes negotiate a lower total commission, and the savings can be passed on to his clients. (This practice of combining transactions for more than one client is known as *bunching*.)

18 Does the fund utilize "secondary" markets for very large transactions to effect the transaction at the most favorable price?

Where a very large transaction is contemplated, the fund should consider making the transaction in a secondary market (i.e., not through a securities exchange) so that the market price of the security is not adversely affected by an abrupt change in the available market demand for or supply of the security.

PORTFOLIO MANAGEMENT

This section deals with controls necessary for efficient and effective management of a fund's portfolio. It is divided into four subsections: "Management Information," which covers data normally required for making informed decisions; "Decision Control," which deals with controls over the portfolio decision-making process; "Revenue and Expense," which deals with means of controlling certain revenue and expense activities; and "Tax Considerations."

Management Information

19 Are cash requirements and cash flow projections prepared on a regular basis to enable portfolio managers to maximize the use of funds?

Failure to monitor and project cash requirements and flows may lead to the necessity to dispose hurriedly of securities to satisfy cash requirements, or to an unexpected inflow of funds creating an idle cash situation. (See dollarization step 6, Idle Funds, and step 7, Premature Sales.)

20 Do portfolio managers have the following information immediately accessible and current (i.e., daily):

(a) portfolio listing showing for each holding and each designated investment grouping the current market value in dollars and percentage to the total, and the range of prices for each stock during the preceding period (e.g., day, week, or month)?

(b) strategy grouping? (This involves grouping securities held, and those contemplated for purchase, by their expected reaction to certain events. The purposes of such grouping are to determine the risks involved in holding securities whose market prices are likely to be directly affected by a particular event, and to facilitate prompt action when such an event occurs.)

(c) funds available for investment?

Failure to maintain the above information places portfolio managers in a position where they must make investment decisions on incomplete or noncurrent information.

21 Do portfolio managers have available, on a timely and periodic basis (e.g., weekly), reports containing the following information required for short-term market strategy decisions:

(a) portfolio concentration by industry showing the dollar and percentage investment in particular industries?

(b) portfolio holdings experiencing higher than normal trading activity?

(c) portfolio performance reports (e.g., realized and unrealized gains and losses, investment income, rate of return, and so forth)?

(d) tax basis of securities and holding periods, where necessary to determine whether a potential transaction will have tax implications (e.g., long-term vs. short-term, wash sales)? (Applicable only where the fund does not have tax-exempt status.)

Failure to make available the above information to portfolio managers on a timely basis places them in a position where they must make investment decisions on incomplete or noncurrent data.

22 Are reports that are issued to portfolio managers periodically reconciled with accounting records to ensure that managers are basing their decisions on accurate data?

The portfolio managers' effectiveness is dependent on the accuracy of information received.

23 Has management considered using computer capabilities to produce required information for portfolio managers on a timely basis?

Where large volumes of data are processed and reports must be generated quickly, the computer can be a useful tool. Where an in-house computer cannot be cost-justified, use of a service bureau might be considered. Considering the utilization of a computer may be particularly important where the answers to Questions 20 through 22 are negative.

24 Where there is more than one portfolio manager, is there adequate communication so that the managers do not work at cross-purposes?

There should be sufficient interaction between portfolio managers to avoid situations where: one manager is buying a security that another manager is selling, several managers are buying heavily in a particular security or industry without knowledge of the others' transactions, and the like. Failure to maintain adequate communication could lead to poor portfolio decisions, unnecessary commission expenses, and inadvertent concentration of risk within one security or industry.

Decision Control

25 Does the investment function have a formal long-range investment strategy?

A long-range investment strategy should be developed based upon economic data, forecasts, market research, potential legislation, and so on. Absence of overall strategy may result in the making of one portfolio decision which negates the effect of another, and in failure to recognize pertinent events and to take appropriate action.

26 Does management provide guidelines, based on long-range strategy, with respect to investment vehicles, industries, or even specific securities for buying or selling during a specified period?

Providing direction to portfolio managers is necessary to ensure that long-range strategy is translated into specific investment decisions.

27 Are purchase selections of new portfolio managers either subject to approval by management or restricted to a prescribed list of approved securities?

The requisite approval or prescribed list serves to enforce investment policy, and to limit the potential risk associated with new portfolio managers who have yet to establish a successful "track record" within the fund organization.

28 Does management review and approve on a periodic basis (e.g., weekly, monthly) all trading activity and commitments from the previous period?

Failure to review previous activity may result in the prolongation of undesirable trading practices. By reviewing activity promptly exposure is limited.

29 Is the size of the portfolio, or of that portion of the portfolio assigned to a particular manager, maintained at a manageable level?

Unless very large pools of money are broken into smaller, more manageable funds, a situation may be created where the volume of a particular transaction, in order to have a desired effect, would be so large as to affect the market price of the security being traded; that is, market supply and demand forces tend to push down the price of an unmatched sale order, and push up the price of an unmatched purchase order.

30   Do portfolio managers engage in arbitrage when the opportunity is available?

Arbitrage is the dealing in securities where an "automatic" profit can be earned through price differentials between: two or more markets over which a security is traded; realizable value of a security convertible into another security, and the market price of the latter security; and so on. While profits can be generated through arbitrage, for arbitrage to be beneficial, such profits must exceed the related trading costs and the costs involved in monitoring price fluctuations of many securities.

Revenue and Expense

31   Are cash balances maintained at a level consistent with normal working requirements, whereby contingency and other reserves are invested?

Portfolio managers sometimes tend to maintain cash balances to cover unexpected payments that may be required. Usually such contingency reserves should generate revenue by being invested, preferably in prime grade, highly liquid, short-term debt securities. On the other hand, cash balances should not be so low that securities must be sold prematurely to meet financial obligations. (See dollarization step 6, Idle Funds, and step 7, Premature Sales.)

32   Are controls in effect to ensure that proceeds from sales of securities, dividends, interest, and other cash receipts are:

(a)   received when due?

(b)   recorded in a manner whereby portfolio managers are informed promptly that such funds are available for investment?

Failure to control receivables and related cash receipts properly may result in lost income on funds which should have been, but were not, available for investment. (See dollarization step 8, Late Receipts.)

33   Are brokers and advisors paid only for services which have been requested and received?

Services by brokers and advisors may or may not be "bundled." Where additional services (e.g., research) are included within the basic fee structure, the fund should be sure that it, in fact, requires and receives such additional services and that it is willing to pay the price. Where such services are not required, an effort should be made to arrange for services on an "unbundled" basis. (See dollarization step 9, Investment Expenses.)

34   Where the fund utilizes the services of an outside organization (e.g., a bank) to handle cash receipts and disbursements, and custodian functions, is an analysis periodically performed to determine whether the fees paid are consistent with the services received?

The fund should establish that fees or other forms of remuneration (e.g., compensating balances) for the above-mentioned services are negotiated and are consistent with services received. The failure to be cognizant of the ability to negotiate proper remuneration could be costly. (See dollarization step 9, Investment Expenses.)

Tax Considerations

The questions in this section are pertinent only with respect to funds which do not have tax-exempt status.

35 Is adequate consideration given to such potential tax savings opportunities as:

    (a) using the specific identification method of determining the cost of securities sold? (This enables a fund to gain maximum flexibility with respect to assigning costs to securities sold and thereby affecting taxable gain or loss.)

    (b) timing sales of securities so as to maximize the excess of net long-term capital gains over net short-term capital losses?

    (c) utilizing techniques such as acquiring a put option or selling short against the box to fit the economic gain or loss while postponing the tax impact?

    (d) selling and repurchasing appreciated securities to offset capital losses or to obtain the benefit of a capital loss carryover which is about to expire? (The wash sale rules do not apply to gains.)

    (e) investing in preferred stocks of domestic corporations rather than bonds, where advantage can be taken of the 85% dividends-received deduction?

    (f) expensing transfer taxes on securities transactions?

These are only a few examples of tax-planning opportunities that may be available. The intent of this question is to determine whether management is cognizant of such opportunities; the question is not designed to take the place of more comprehensive tax checklists or of analysis and planning of tax specialists.

36 Are controls in use to ensure that tax-planning decisions are effected?

It is important not only to arrive at appropriate tax-planning decisions (see Question 35) but also to ensure that such decisions are carried out. For example, when utilizing the specific identification method of costing securities sold, it is necessary that the appropriate block of stock be indicated; similarly, controls should be in effect to prevent wash sales which might negate the desired tax effect of an earlier transaction.

37 Has adequate consideration been given to state and local tax planning?

Although usually of relatively minor importance, there are situations in which state and local taxes (e.g., income, receipts, and use taxes) can be significant. In such cases, appropriate tax-planning techniques should be considered. For example, since most states tax obligations of other states but not their own obligations, purchase of the securities of the fund's own state should be considered. Similarly, if a state or municipality levies investment income taxes based on the issuer's operations allocated to its jurisdiction, consideration should be given to purchasing securities of issuers with low allocation percentages.

ASSESSING PORTFOLIO PERFORMANCE

Periodic review of performance in relation to investment philosophy and goals, by appropriate management personnel, enables management to take corrective action where necessary. This section deals with the nature of certain techniques for assessing portfolio performance.

38 Is portfolio performance evaluated in terms of:

    (a) an absolute measurement of performance (e.g., rate of return on investment)?

    (b) a measurement of performance relative to current market standards?

The rate of return on investment is the basis on which most other performance evaluators are founded. Also known as the *dollar weighted, discounted, average compounded,* and *yield to maturity* rate of return, this and related techniques consider total return from investment income and realized and unrealized capital gains.

Selected market indicators have long been a standard for measuring relative investment performance. Such market indicators include Standard & Poor's Stock Index, Dow Jones Common Stock Averages, Dow Jones Bond Averages, and Moody's Common Stock Average. While there is disagreement as to the degree to which indicators are meaningful, these performance guides have long been present. The particular market indicator used as a yardstick against which performance is measured is not as important as the consistent use of the indicator. Frequent changes from one indicator to another might signify that an effort is being made to show the fund's performance in the most favorable light.

39 Are portfolio managers evaluated only with regard to items over which they have control, via the utilization of further appropriate techniques, as:

    (a) time-weighted rate of return?

    (b) unit-value method?

There are many different methods that can be used to evaluate portfolio managers' performance. The most popular and easiest to use, the rate of return and the market comparisons, are discussed in Question 38. These methods are suitable for evaluating total portfolio performance, but, because they do not allow for segregation of matters beyond a portfolio manager's control, they may not be sufficiently accurate to be used in evaluating a portfolio manager's performance.

A technical description of the time-weighted rate of return and the unit-value method is beyond the scope of this appendix. Of primary importance is the fact that they have the ability to desensitize the effect of cash flow. Although precise calculation using either of these two methods is time consuming and requires much data, both approaches are valid and should be considered.

DOLLARIZATION STEPS[2]

1. Error Control

a. Select a sample of purchases and sales executed. (Consider segregating data by broker.)
b. For each selected transaction, verify the accuracy of:
security
number of shares or par value
transaction price
commission cost
stock transfer tax
accrued interest
any other items
computation of net amount of transaction

The name of the security, number of shares or par value, and (frequently) price may be traced to a record of the order placed by the portfolio manager. Commission costs may be traced to memoranda regarding negotiated rates; stock transfer taxes may be traced to published tables; and accrued interest and net amount may be recalculated.

c. For any discrepancies noted in (b), complete the following schedule:

Security	Actual Amount	Correct Amount	Difference
_____	$ _____	$ _____	$ _____
_____	_____	_____	_____
_____	_____	_____	_____
_____	_____	_____	_____
_____	_____	_____	_____
_____	_____	_____	_____
_____	_____	_____	_____
	$ _____		$ _____

[2] The applicability of extrapolation to any particular finding must be carefully weighed.

d. Calculate the total excess charges by extrapolating the above calculation as follows:

$$\begin{array}{c} \text{Total} \\ \text{Sample} \\ \text{Difference} \end{array} \times \dfrac{\begin{array}{c}\text{Total Dollar Value}\\\text{of All Transactions}\end{array}}{\begin{array}{c}\text{Total Dollar Value}\\\text{(i.e., Actual Amount)}\\\text{of Transactions in}\\\text{Sample}\end{array}} = \begin{array}{c}\text{Total}\\\text{Difference}\end{array}$$

2. Prompt Execution

a. Select a sample of transactions of varying dollar amounts. (Consider segregating data by broker.)

b. Compare the time the order was placed with the time it was executed. For those trades with a time lag exceeding a specified period (e.g., one-half business day), compare the price at which the trade was executed with the market price at the time the order was placed (where such data are available). Complete the following schedule, offsetting the favorable effect of such price differentials against the unfavorable:

Security Traded	Trade Price	Market Price When Order Placed	Dif- ference	Number of Shares	Extended Dif- ference
_____	$ _____	$ _____	$ _____	_____	$ _____
_____	_____	_____	_____	_____	_____
_____	_____	_____	_____	_____	_____
_____	_____	_____	_____	_____	_____
_____	_____	_____	_____	_____	_____
_____	_____	_____	_____	_____	_____
_____	_____	_____	_____	_____	$ _____

c. If a significant unfavorable difference exists, extrapolate the total extended difference computed in (b) to reflect the total potential difference between the actual value of transactions executed and the value of the transactions had they been executed at the market price when the order was placed.

$$\begin{array}{c} \text{Total} \\ \text{Extended} \\ \text{Difference} \end{array} \times \dfrac{\begin{array}{c}\text{Total Dollar Value}\\\text{of All Transactions}\end{array}}{\begin{array}{c}\text{Total Dollar Value}\\\text{of Transactions in}\\\text{Sample}\end{array}} = \begin{array}{c}\text{Total}\\\text{Difference}\end{array}$$

Caution: With respect to transactions of securities with limited market activity, a lengthy delay between the time an order is placed and the time it is executed may be justified. Furthermore, in many instances, the broker has little control over the final trade price, and he cannot be held responsible for rapid, sharp fluctuations in market prices. However, transactions should be placed within a reasonable period of time after the order is placed, and, on the average, the trade price should not vary significantly from the market price when the order is placed.

3. Unfavorable Trade Prices

a. Select a sample of purchases and sales. (Consider segregating data by broker.)
b. Compare the price at which the trade was executed to the average high/low trading price for the day, and multiply the difference by the number of shares. (Favorable differences should be shown as offsets.) Complete the following schedule:

Security	Actual Price	Day's Average High/ Low	Dif- ference	Number of Shares	Extended Dif- ference
_____	$ _____	$ _____	$ _____	_____	$ _____
_____	_____	_____	_____	_____	_____
_____	_____	_____	_____	_____	_____
_____	_____	_____	_____	_____	_____
_____	_____	_____	_____	_____	_____
_____	_____	_____	_____	_____	_____
_____	_____	_____	_____	_____	$ _____

c. If the total extended difference is unfavorable, extrapolate the above results as follows:

$$\text{Total Extended Difference} \times \frac{\text{Total Dollar Value of All Purchases and Sales}}{\text{Total Dollar Value of Purchases and Sales in Sample}} = \text{Total Difference}$$

4. Early Payments

a. Select a sample of cash disbursements, and obtain the related supporting documentation.

b. Determine the number of days, if any, by which disbursements preceded the date required for payment. Take into account the method of payment (check, wire transfer, etc.), and appropriately identify weekends and holidays in making the determination. Complete the following schedule:

Payment Description	Amount	Date Paid	Date Payment Required	Days Lost	Lost Revenue
_____	$ _____	_____	_____	_____	$ _____
_____	_____	_____	_____	_____	_____
_____	_____	_____	_____	_____	_____
_____	_____	_____	_____	_____	_____
_____	_____	_____	_____	_____	_____
_____	_____	_____	_____	_____	_____
_____	_____	_____	_____	_____	_____
	$ _____				$ _____

$$\text{Lost Revenue} = \text{Amount} \times \text{Rate} \times \frac{\text{Days Lost}}{360}$$

The rate used in this formula should be based on the rate obtained by the fund on its short-term investments or, if such data are not readily available, on an appropriate standard such as the average Treasury bill rate in effect during the period.

c. Extrapolate the total lost revenue computed in (b) above, as follows:

$$\text{Total Lost Revenue per Sample} \times \frac{\text{Total Cash Disbursements}}{\text{Cash Disbursements (i.e., Amount) in Sample}} = \text{Total Lost Revenue}$$

5. Excess Commissions

a. Select a sample of transactions. All transactions for a particular security on a given day should be grouped together and treated as one transaction for the purpose of negotiating commissions.

b. For each transaction selected in (a), compare actual commissions paid with an industry average for similar transactions. One such average that may be used is included in the "Analysis of Negotiated Rates," compiled and distributed quarterly by the Economist's Office of the New York Stock Exchange. The comparison may be made as follows, summarizing transactions by broker, and offsetting favorable differences against unfavorable ones:

Security Traded	Gross Dollar Value of Trade	Commission Paid	Commission per Industry Average	Difference
	$	$	$	$
	$			$

c. Extrapolate the total difference computed in (b) to reflect the excess commissions paid:

$$\text{Total Difference per Sample} \times \frac{\text{Total Gross Dollar Value of All Trades}}{\text{Total Gross Dollar Value of Trades in Sample}} = \text{Total Excess Commissions Due to Negotiation Practices}$$

Caution: The industry averages do not reflect differences in services (e.g., research) received from brokers, so caution must be exercised before concluding that commissions paid are excessive. These data may, however, indicate that a problem may exist with respect to commission costs.

6. Idle Funds

a. Determine average cash balance during most recent fiscal period. Where cash does not fluctuate significantly, month-end or quarter-end balances may be used in calculation.

b. Compute the excess average cash balance maintained:

Average cash balance per (a) above	$
Less: Normal working capital requirements	
Less: Compensating balances or other restricted cash balances	
Excess average cash balance	$

c. Compute the lost revenue by applying an appropriate estimated rate of return to the excess average cash balance. The rate used should be based on that obtained by the fund on its short-term investments or, if such data are not readily available, on an appropriate standard such as the average Treasury bill rate in effect during the period.

7. Premature Sales

a. Ascertain whether any short-term debt investments (e.g., commercial paper, Treasury bills, etc.) were disposed of before maturity date during most recent fiscal period.

b. For the items identified in (a), determine the revenue lost due to disposal of an investment before maturity. This determination should be made by comparing the revenue actually received with the revenue that would have been received had the fund purchased a shorter term investment that could have been held to maturity:

Investment	Actual Dollar Revenue	Potential Revenue of Shorter-Term Investment	Lost Revenue
	$	$	$
			$

The potential revenue of the shorter term investment should be based on a like investment to that actually purchased.

Caution: This step should normally only be applied to certain short-term debt investments where an effective "penalty" is levied by the market if such an investment is sold rather than held to maturity. Such a penalty is relatively insignificant with respect to long-term debt investments, which may be sold at a substantial profit or loss when wide fluctuations in interest rates occur.

8. Late Receipts

a. Select a sample of cash receipts and obtain the related supporting documentation.

b. Determine the time lag, if any, between (1) when the receipt was due and when it was actually received, and (2) when it was actually received and when the portfolio manager received information indicating that such funds were available for investment. (Proceeds from the sale of securities are generally due on or before the fifth business day following the trade date. Dividend and interest payments are generally mailed by the distributing corporation before the payable date so as to be received by the investor on the payable date.) Complete the following schedule:

Payment Description	Amount	Time Lag per b(1) Above, in Days	Time Lag per b(2) Above, in Days	Lost Revenue per b(1) Above	Lost Revenue per b(2) Above
_____	$ _____	_____	_____	$ _____	$ _____
_____	_____	_____	_____	_____	_____
_____	_____	_____	_____	_____	_____
_____	_____	_____	_____	_____	_____
_____	_____	_____	_____	_____	_____
_____	_____	_____	_____	_____	_____
_____	$ _____	_____	_____	$ _____	$ _____

$$\text{Lost Revenue} = \text{Amount} \times \text{Rate} \times \frac{\text{Time Lag}}{360}$$

The rate used in this formula should be based on the rate obtained by the fund on its short-term investments or, if such data are not readily available, on an appropriate standard such as the average Treasury bill rate in effect during the period.

c. Extrapolate the total lost revenue figures computed in (b) above, as follows:

$$\text{Total Lost Revenue per (b)(1)} \times \frac{\text{Total Cash Receipts}}{\text{Cash Receipts (i.e., Amount) per Sample}} = \text{Total Lost Revenue Due to Late Receipts}$$

$$\text{Total Lost Revenue per (b)(2)} \times \frac{\text{Total Cash Receipts}}{\text{Cash Receipts (i.e., Amount) per Sample}} = \text{Total Lost Revenue Due to Late Reporting of Receipts}$$

9. Investment Expenses

a. Based upon examination of the fund's records, determine the dollar amount of investment expenses applicable to the investment program. Consider such items as management fees, advisory fees, custodian fees, and commissions.

b. Ascertain whether an adverse trend is developing with respect to such expenses:

Expense	19— Dollar Amount	19— % to Total Average Investment	19— Dollar Amount	19— % to Total Average Investment	19— Dollar Amount	19— % to Total Average Investment
Management fees	$	%	$	%	$	%
Advisory fees						
Custodian fees						
Commissions						
	$	%	$	%	$	%

APPENDIX H

Special Analysis: Employee Benefit Provisions of the Tax Equity and Fiscal Responsibility Act of 1982

RESTRICTIONS ON TOP HEAVY PLANS

Parity Between Corporate and HR 10 Plans

To achieve parity between qualified plans maintained by corporate and non-corporate employers, the law eliminates most of the special restrictions that currently apply to plans maintained by sole proprietors, partnerships and Subchapter S corporations and extends other restrictions to all qualified plans. Requirements for top heavy plans are substituted for the restrictive rules previously imposed on HR 10 plans and plans maintained by Subchapter S corporations.

Top Heavy Plan Requirements

Beginning in 1984, new restrictions apply to any top heavy plan, whether the plan is maintained by a corporation, partnership, or sole proprietorship.

Top Heavy Plan and Key Employee Defined

A *defined benefit plan* is top heavy under the new law if the present value of accrued benefits of key employees exceeds 60% of the present value of accrued benefits of all plan participants. A *defined contribution plan* is top heavy if more than 60% of the account balances have been accumulated on behalf of key employees. Under certain circumstances, two or more plans maintained by the same employer must be aggregated to determine whether the plans, as a group, are top heavy. Under other circumstances, aggregation is optional.

Officers, 5% owners, 1% owners earning more than $150,000, and employees owning the 10 largest interests in the employer are considered key employees.

Restrictions

Top heavy plans are subject to special rules affecting vesting, contributions, and benefits. The rules will require:

Special Vesting. Either 100% vesting after 3 years of service with a participation requirement that does not exceed 3 years, or a 6 year graded vesting schedule (20% after 2 years of service and 20% for each subsequent year) with a participation requirement that does not exceed 1 year.

Minimum Benefits for Nonkey Employees.   For *defined benefit plans,* a minimum nonintegrated benefit for each nonkey employee equal to 2% of average annual compensation per year of service, not to exceed 20%; for *defined contribution plans,* a minimum nonintegrated contribution equal to 3% of compensation for each year in which a key employee receives an allocation of at least 3%.

Compensation Limit.   Compensation in excess of $200,000 (as adjusted for future cost of living increases beginning in 1986) may *not* be taken into account in computing contributions or benefits under the plan.

Premature Distribution Penalty.   A distribution to a key employee prior to the attainment of age 59½ will be subject to a 10% penalty tax, unless the distribution is made on account of death or disability.

Age 70½ Rule.   A distribution to a key employee, whether or not he or she has retired, must commence no later than the tax year in which he or she attains age 70½.

Special Limit for Multiple Plans.   The aggregate dollar limit applicable to a key employee covered by a defined benefit and a defined contribution plan maintained by the same employer is 100% instead of 125% of the otherwise applicable separate dollar limits if the following conditions are *not* met:
   an additional nonintegrated benefit is provided for nonkey employees (for defined contribution plans, a minimum annual contribution of 1% of compensation; for defined benefit plans, a minimum benefit of 1% of average annual compensation per year of service, not to exceed 10%) and not more than 90% of accrued benefits are for key employees.

Parity for All Plans.   Under the new law, the qualified plan rules will base distinctions on whether a plan primarily benefits key employees (i.e., whether the plan is top heavy). Whether the employer maintaining a plan is a corporation, partnership, or sole proprietorship generally will have no relevance.

Need for Plan Amendments.   All plans will have to be amended to incorporate the new top heavy plan provisions.

Widespread Impact on Small Corporate Plans.   Although the restrictions on top heavy plans are substituted for rules applicable to HR 10 plans, the new rules will also affect tens of thousands of small plans currently maintained by corporations. Many plans maintained by companies with 100 employees or less will be subject to the newer rules, and these companies will have to develop effective strategies for compliance. As indicated in Figure 1, affected companies should examine a number of alternatives if they are to minimize the cost of compliance with the new rules.

Most Top Heavy Plans Should Remain Beneficial.   Although the new rules generally will increase costs for employers maintaining top heavy plans, the benefits for key employees will still be substantial in most situations. Top heavy plans will continue to provide immediate deductions for contributions, tax-free accumulations of trust earnings, and favorable income tax treatment for certain plan distributions.

FIGURE 1
Plan of action for affected employers

Test Existing Plans

Companies maintaining qualified plans should test to determine if their plans are top heavy under the new law. To make this determination, key employees must be identified and the accrued benefit of each participant calculated. As indicated earlier, a plan will be considered top heavy if more than 60% of accrued benefits are provided for key employees.

Examine Existing Plan Provisions and Alternatives

Vesting and benefit provisions of plans which are considered to be top heavy should be examined to determine whether they satisfy the new rules without modification. Before necessary amendments are made, companies need to consider alternative provisions to minimize the costs of complying with the new rules.

REPEAL OF HR 10 RULES: GREATER OPPORTUNITIES FOR DEFERRAL BY SELF-EMPLOYED PERSONS

Since the focus now is on whether or not the plan is top heavy, the new law eliminates nearly all of the differences in the rules applying to HR 10 and corporate plans. As a result, larger contributions and benefits under HR 10 plans will be permitted for self-employed persons. (Larger contributions and benefits will also be permitted for Subchapter S plans and SEPS.) The restrictive deduction rules and most of the special qualification rules applicable to HR 10 plans have been repealed. The rule which limits accruals for self-employed persons has been repealed, and this will allow defined benefit HR 10 plans to provide past service benefits. This change will provide the same flexibility and latitude in the design of HR 10 plans that has been enjoyed by corporate plans.

It is noteworthy that the new law retains, and extends to all qualified plans, the special HR 10 requirement that distributions commence in the year in which the participant attains age 70½ or in which he or she retires, if later, as well as the requirement that benefits generally must be paid out within five years of death.

Under the law, HR 10 and corporate plans will be subject to the same deduction limits. The effect of this change is summarized in Figure 2.

Professional Corporation Advantages Eliminated

The repeal of the HR 10 rules and the addition of top heavy plan restrictions will effectively eliminate the differences in the rules applying to corporate and noncorporate plans. Only minor differences remain. As a result, in the future

FIGURE 2
Deduction limits—HR 10 plans

Limit Under	Defined Contribution	Defined Benefit
Current law	Lesser of 15% of earnings or $15,000.	Effectively limited by restrictions on accruals for self-employed.
New law	Profit sharing plans—lesser of 15% of aggregate compensation or $30,000;[1] Money purchase plans—lesser of 25% of compensation or $30,000.[1]	Actuarially determined—same as corporate defined benefit plan limits.

1 For self-employed individuals, earnings have been redefined so that these percentage limitations apply to net earnings less *all* deductible contributions to the plan.

there will be no advantage for professionals to incorporate their practices to obtain greater retirement benefits.

Treatment of Certain Existing Professional Service Corporations

In addition to discouraging the formation of professional service corporations, the new law affects existing professional corporations. The IRS will be permitted to disregard the corporate tax status of certain personal service corporations in which substantially all of the services are performed by employee-owners for or on behalf of another corporation, partnership, or entity (including related parties). This provision aims at individuals who have incorporated principally for tax advantages. In these situations, income, deductions, credits, exclusions, etc., of the corporation may be allocated to the employee-owners (i.e., more than 10% owners of the outstanding stock).

This change may encourage existing personal service corporations to liquidate. The law includes a transitional rule for 1983 and 1984 under which these corporations may complete a one-month liquidation under Code section 333 without risking taxation on unrealized receivables. Income represented by unrealized receivables will retain its character as ordinary income and will be recognized by the shareholder upon collection or other disposition. The rules become effective in 1983.

MODIFICATION OF PLAN INTEGRATION RULES

The new law eliminates the special rules which have limited the ability of HR 10 plans to integrate contributions and benefits with social security. In the future, defined benefit plans of noncorporate employers may integrate benefits with social security in accordance with the rules presently applicable to corporate defined benefit plans. However, the new law modifies the rules for the integration of all defined contribution plans so that contributions on behalf of an employee can be reduced by no more than an amount equal to the employee's taxable wage base multiplied by the social security (OASDI) tax rate (5.4% for 1982). Accordingly, beginning in 1984, the permissible integration margin for all defined contribution plans will be 5.4%. For example, a money purchase pension plan could provide for an annual contribution of 10% of total compensation plus 15.4% of compensation in excess of the taxable wage base.

LIMITATIONS ON CONTRIBUTIONS AND BENEFITS

Reduced Dollar Limitations

Under previous law, a participant in a qualified defined benefit plan may receive an annual benefit, expressed as a single life annuity, up to the lesser of 100% of his average compensation or $136,425. (Average compensation is based on the participant's highest three consecutive years.) Similarly, annual allocations under qualified defined contribution plans may not exceed the lesser of 25% of compensation or $45,475. The new law reduces the maximum dollar limits to $90,000 for defined benefit plans and to $30,000 for defined contribution plans. In addition, an interest rate of at least 5% or the rate specified in the plan, if greater, must be used in converting other benefit options to a single life annuity for purposes of applying the $90,000 dollar limit.

This change is intended to scale back the benefits derived by highly paid individuals from qualified plans. Other plan participants will be affected by the percentage of compensation limitations rather than the dollar amounts. For example, a participant earning $30,000 annually is subject to the percentage limitation and would not be affected by the reductions to the dollar amounts. If he or she participated only in a defined contribution plan, he or she would be limited to an annual allocation of $7,500 (25% of $30,000); if he or she participated only in a defined benefit plan, he or she would be limited to a $30,000 single life annuity (100% of compensation). Of course, additional multiple plan limitations would apply if he or she participated in both a defined benefit and a defined contribution plan.

Dollar Limitations Temporarily Frozen

The new dollar limitations are frozen for calendar years 1983 and 1984 and adjusted for cost of living increases for later years according to the Social Security benefit index formula then in effect. Since the first adjustment will be made in 1986, the new dollar limitations remain applicable for three calendar years.

Deductions Limited

The new law codifies the existing IRS position that contributions to defined benefit plans may not be based on anticipated cost of living increases to the dollar limits. Deductions for such contributions are not permitted.

Early and Delayed Retirement Adjustments

Under current law, the maximum dollar limitation for defined benefit plans need not be reduced unless benefits begin before age 55. Under the new law, where benefits begin before age 62, the new $90,000 limit must be actuarially reduced, but not below $75,000 at age 55 or later. Moreover, unlike current law, the new law provides that the dollar limit be actuarially increased where benefits begin after age 65. Certain limitations are provided as to the interest rate that may be used for any adjustment to the dollar limit.

Under the new law, the benefits of highly paid participants are subject to stringent limits when benefits begin before age 62. At age 60, for example, the $90,000 limit would be reduced to $75,000. (Based on actuarial reduction factors set forth in Rev. Rul. 81-57, the limit would be reduced to $73,800 at age 60. However, at age 60, the reduction is subject to a $75,000 floor.) Under current law, an annual benefit of $136,425 could commence at age 60 or even at age 55.

Multiple Plans

The new law reduces the aggregate dollar limit applicable to participants covered by both a defined contribution and a defined benefit plan maintained by the same employer from 140% to 125% of the otherwise applicable separate dollar limits. Because the reduction applies only to participants subject to the dollar limitations, rather than the percentage of compensation limits, it generally will affect only highly paid employees.

Example

An employee with annual compensation of $300,000 participates in a defined benefit plan which provides a single life annuity of 50% of average compensation at age 65. Her employer has just installed a profit sharing plan in which allocations are based on compensation. Under current rules, the defined benefit plan annuity is limited to $136,425. Since this represents 100% of the applicable dollar limit, the defined contribution plan allocation is currently limited by the multiple plan rule to 40% of the otherwise applicable limit. Therefore, the profit sharing plan allocation could not have exceeded $18,190 (40% × $45,475). Under the new law, the defined benefit plan annuity would be limited to $90,000. The profit sharing plan allocation would be limited to $7,500 (25% × $30,000).

Plan Amendments and Effective Date

Plans must be amended to reflect both the new dollar limits applicable to single plans and the new aggregate limit applicable to multiple plans. The required reduction to the $90,000 limit where benefits begin before age 62 should also be stated in the plan. However, since IRS rules allow a plan to incorporate cost of living adjustments to the dollar limits (though contributions may not be based on anticipated future adjustments), plan amendments will not be necessary each time future adjustments are made.

These new limitations are effective in 1983 for existing plans. However, plan amendments implementing the changes are not required before 1984. Plans which exceed the amended limits in 1983 (but satisfy the earlier limits) will not be disqualified, but employers may not deduct contributions based on the excess amounts in 1983 or any subsequent year.

Transitional Rules—Current Benefits Protected

The law provides transitional rules to protect accrued benefits of current plan participants from reduction because of the limits on contributions and benefits. Employers are required to fund these accrued benefits which currently exceed the limits, and future accruals in some cases will be frozen until the limits, increased by future cost of living adjustments, exceed current accrued benefits. For example, a participant in a defined benefit plan currently entitled to a $130,000 life annuity commencing at age 65 will not lose the right to this benefit. However, future accruals will cease until the $90,000 limitation has been increased above $130,000.

Restoration of Reduced Benefits

Employers and executives may wish to consider the use of alternative arrangements to restore benefits no longer provided by qualified plans because of the reduced limits. Because they are not subject to ERISA type nondiscrimination requirements, unfunded nonqualified plans could be a possible approach for selected executives. If the plan is properly structured, the executive would not be taxed until the deferred compensation is received, and the employer would be entitled to a deduction at that time. Excess benefit plans and supplemental pension agreements represent two effective methods of restoring the benefits. In Figure 3 we show a plan of action for affected companies to consider the restoration of benefits.

Excess Benefit Plans

An excess benefit plan is designed solely to restore a benefit which cannot be provided by a qualified plan because of the maximum limitations on contributions and benefits. A typical excess benefit plan would provide a benefit equal to the benefit which would be provided under the employer's qualified plan if the maximum limits were not applicable, less the benefit actually provided by the plan.

Unfunded excess benefit plans are exempt from ERISA's reporting, participation, vesting, funding and fiduciary requirements.

Careful planning is required to properly utilize excess benefit plans. For example, an excess benefit plan can more efficiently restore an annuity payable from a defined benefit plan than a lump sum distribution payable from a defined contribution plan which is eligible for favorable rollover or ten-year averaging tax treatment. Annuity payments from both qualified defined benefit and nonqualified excess benefit plans are taxed as ordinary income. Therefore, reductions which are necessary to comply with the overall limit applicable to multiple plans should generally apply first to the defined benefit plan. This will maximize the defined contribution plan lump sum which could be eligible for favorable tax treatment.

Supplemental Retirement Plans

In contrast to an excess benefit plan, a supplemental retirement plan (SRP) generally defines the executive's total retirement benefit without regard to the limits on contributions and benefits. Frequently included as part of an employment agreement, a typical supplemental agreement would provide for a lifetime retirement income of some specified percentage of "final salary" less the executive's benefit from the employer's qualified plan(s) and his or her social security benefits. Survivor and disability income and early retirement benefits may also be provided.

Supplemental retirement plans have become popular in the last few years for several reasons:

Social security benefits are geared toward lower and middle income workers. They replace only a small portion of final earnings at the executive level.

Private pension benefits, considered as a percentage of earnings, often favor

FIGURE 3
Plan of action for affected employers

Identify Affected Employees and Examine Existing Benefit Levels

Employers should identify employees who are affected by the new qualified plan limits and the size of any benefit reductions. Employment agreements and other documents implementing existing excess benefit plans or SRPs should be examined to determine whether the plans are self-adjusting so that they will automatically compensate for reduced qualified plan benefits. Employers may wish to consider including newly affected employees in nonqualified arrangements and amending nonqualified arrangements which are not self-adjusting to maintain existing benefit levels.

New Benefit Levels and Financing

Employers may also wish to determine whether existing benefit levels are appropriate. This decision will, of course, be based on the employer's philosophy towards retirement income and its view of "adequate" income replacement, the level of retirement income considered competitive, and the level of projected costs to provide supplemental benefits. If present benefit levels are not adequate, supplemental arrangements can be effectively designed, or existing arrangements can be redesigned. If benefit levels are increased, separate consideration should be given as to how to finance new supplemental benefits. This requires an analysis of the risks and potential savings associated with corporate-owned life insurance as well as other financing vehicles.

lower paid employees. Even though employers may "integrate" plan benefits with social security, IRS rules generally do not allow benefit differentials large enough to make a substantial difference for highly paid executives.

Some executives may not complete enough service to accumulate sufficient retirement income from their employer's basic qualified plan.

Often the qualified plan will use only basic salary when computing an employee's pension benefit, excluding bonuses or other incentive pay which may comprise a substantial part of an executive's total earnings.

With the new reductions in the ERISA limits on contributions and benefits, SRPs should become even more attractive.

If unfunded and maintained by an employer to provide deferred compensation for a select group of management or highly compensated employees, SRPs are exempt from most ERISA requirements. Only minimal reporting requirements apply.

LOAN RESTRICTIONS

The new law restricts borrowing by participants from tax-sheltered annuities and qualified plans by treating certain loans as distributions. A loan to a plan participant will not be treated as a distribution if it is required to be repaid within five years, but only to the extent that the amount of the loan, when added to the participant's outstanding borrowing under all plans maintained by the employer or certain related employers, exceeds the lesser of $50,000 or one-half of the present value of the participant's nonforfeitable accrued benefit (but not less than $10,000). Loans used to buy or improve the principal residence of the participant or his or her family member, however, need not meet the five-year repayment provision. Loans in excess of applicable limits made before August 13, 1982 will not be affected unless subsequently renewed or renegotiated. A special one-year transitional rule exempts loans after this date used to make a principal repayment on an existing loan that is due before August 13, 1983, where the loan is repaid by August 13, 1983.

Since the usual income tax rules governing distributions from qualified plans allow participants to recover nondeductible employee contributions first, excess loans will be taxed only to the extent that they exceed the amount of nondeductible contributions the participant may have made.

Repayments of loans treated as distributions will not be subject to the overall limits on contributions and benefits.

The new loan restrictions could discourage participation by low and middle income employees in contributory plans. Decreased participation by these individuals could threaten the qualified status of thrift plans and §401(k) cash or deferred plans.

WITHHOLDING REQUIREMENTS

Amount Withheld

Starting in 1983, withholding will be required on the taxable portion of distributions made under qualified plans, IRAs and nonqualified deferred compensation plans where payments are not considered "wages." Withholding on periodic payments is to be computed as if the payments were "wages." Where no withholding certificate is in effect, the payee will be treated as a married individual claiming three withholding exemptions.

Ten percent withholding will apply to nonperiodic distributions, but special tables will be provided for lump sum distributions to reflect favorable 10-year averaging tax treatment. Special tables reflecting the income tax exclusion for employer provided death benefits will also be provided for total distributions payable upon death.

Where a distribution consists of employer securities, the new law provides that the securities will not have to be sold merely to satisfy the withholding rules.

Although the withholding requirements become effective in 1983, payors may not be subject to civil and criminal penalties for failure to withhold on payments made before July 1, 1983 if a good faith effort to withhold is made.

Recipient Elections

Recipients will be allowed to elect *not* to have taxes withheld. For periodic payments, an election "out" will be binding until revoked; annual elections will not be required.

The essential change is to place upon retirees the burden to elect "out" of the withholding system, rather than allowing them to elect to have amounts withheld.

Notice

Notice of the right to elect "out" of withholding must be provided to recipients of periodic payments not more than six months prior to the first payment and annually thereafter. Notices are to be provided to recipients of nonperiodic distributions at the time of the distribution.

The new election and notice procedures will create significant administrative costs for employers. Employers and other payors will have to develop special forms and procedures for the required notices and elections.

Reports

New reporting requirements are imposed on employers and plan administrators. Regulations will specify precisely what information must be reported to the IRS with respect to taxable distributions. It is expected that at a minimum the reports will include information sufficient to identify the total amount of the distribution, the portion attributable to employee contributions (both deductible and nondeductible), and the portion eligible for capital gains treatment.

Penalties will be imposed where the data base needed for the reports is not maintained. Employees and plan administrators will be subject to an annual penalty of $50 for each affected individual up to a maximum of $50,000. An exception will be made where the failure to maintain the information is due to reasonable cause and not willful neglect. In addition, where reasonable effort for correction has been made, no penalty will be imposed for pre-1983 failures.

MEDICAL COVERAGE OF CERTAIN OLDER EMPLOYEES

The new law amends the federal Age Discrimination in Employment Act to require employers of more than 20 persons to offer employees aged 65 through 69 and their dependents the same health benefit plan offered to younger workers. Medicare will become the secondary payor for employees covered by the plans.

A number of companies currently provide health benefits for older employees only after Medicare benefits are exhausted. By requiring these companies to become the primary payor for older employees, the new law will significantly add to the costs of maintaining medical benefits for older workers.

NONDISCRIMINATION REQUIREMENTS FOR GROUP TERM INSURANCE PROGRAMS

The new law also provides that the income exclusion for employer-provided group term life insurance will not be available to key employees if the life insurance is provided under a program that discriminates in their favor. An employer-provided group-term life insurance program will not be considered discriminatory as to *coverage* if:

it benefits at least 70% of all employees,
at least 85% of all participating employees are *not* key employees, or
the program benefits a nondiscriminatory classification of employees.

In testing for adequate coverage, certain employees, such as those who have not completed three years of service, may be excluded from consideration.

A group life program will not be considered discriminatory as to *benefits* if the insurance coverage provided bears a uniform relationship to compensation. This provision will be effective starting in 1984.

Group-term life insurance plans should be reviewed and tested against these new requirements. Changes in some plans will be needed to take advantage of the income exclusion under section 79. It will also be important to examine alternative methods to provide coverage in excess of $50,000. In this regard, Treasury will be revising the tables for computing the amount includable in an employee's income.

BARGAIN ELEMENT OF ISOs SUBJECT TO NEW MINIMUM TAX

The new law makes the bargain element of an Incentive Stock Option a preference item which may, in certain situations, trigger the new *alternative* minimum tax that will be higher than the regular income tax.

The new alternative minimum tax expands the old alternative minimum tax and also includes most of the preference items that were formerly subject to the add-on minimum tax, which has now been repealed. The new tax applies a flat 20% rate to all "minimum taxable income" in excess of $30,000 (single) or $40,-000 (married filing jointly). Like the old alternative minimum tax, it is incurred only when it exceeds the regular income tax.

In calculating the tax, preference amounts will be added to adjusted gross income, and deductions will be allowed for charitable contributions, medical and casualty deductions to the extent that each exceeds *10%* of adjusted gross income, home mortgage interest, other interest to the extent of investment income, and net operating losses not attributable to preferences.

If the option stock is sold less than a year after exercise, with the result that the gain is taxed as ordinary income rather than long term capital gain, the bargain element of the option will not be a preference item for the alternative minimum tax.

The new tax is likely to affect far more people than the old alternative minimum tax because of the greatly increased list of preference items. Those who potentially have large tax preferences will have to give careful consideration to the new minimum tax and make it an essential element in their tax planning.

An individual who has an Incentive Stock Option with a large bargain element should carefully plan when it should be exercised and when the stock should be sold. Consideration should be given to exercising ISOs this year since the bargain element will not be considered a tax preference until 1983. After 1982, in many cases it will be desirable to spread the exercise over several years. This is clearly illustrated in the example shown in Figure 4, where an individual with $150,000 of salary income exercises an ISO with a bargain element of $300,000 and incurs additional tax of $31,300 (the difference between the alternative minimum tax and the regular income tax that would have been incurred if the ISO had not been exercised). This additional tax could have been avoided or substantially reduced if the exercise had been spread over a number of years.

FIGURE 4

Example

Year Option Is Exercised

Adjusted Gross Income	$150,000
Bargain Element at Date of Exercise	300,000
Less: Allowable Itemized Deduction	(30,000)
Specific Exemption	(40,000)
Alternative Minimum Taxable Income	$380,000
Alternative Minimum Tax	$ 76,000 [1]
Regular Tax Liability	$ 44,700 [2]
Excess Alternative Minimum Tax	31,300
Total Tax Liability	$ 76,000

Year Stock Is Sold

Tax on Capital Gain Assuming No Appreciation in Value	$ 59,590 [3]
Excess Alternative Minimum Tax Upon Exercise of Option (above)	31,300
Total Tax Burden	$ 90,890
Effective Tax Rate	30% [4]

Calculations

1 $380,000 × 20% = $76,000.

2 The 1983 tax rate for a married couple filing jointly applied to adjusted gross income of $150,000 less allowable excess itemized deductions of $26,600 and two exemptions.

3 Same as in [2] except the net long-term capital gain of $120,000 (40% of $300,000) is added to adjusted gross income and tax rates after 1983 are used. The tax attributable to the capital gain is the difference between $102,100 and $42,510. Although the new law makes the deduction for long-term capital gain a preference item, the minimum tax will generally not be applicable in the year the option stock is sold.

4 $\dfrac{\$\ 90,890}{\$300,000} = 30\%.$

OTHER MISCELLANEOUS PROVISIONS

For individuals dying after December 31, 1982 an aggregate $100,000 limit will be imposed on the estate tax exclusion currently applicable to certain amounts payable under qualified plans, tax-sheltered annuities, or IRAs. Currently, no dollar limit applies to this exclusion.

The new law expands the class of employers in affiliated service groups who are to be treated as a single employer when testing for plan discrimination. Beginning in 1984, where one organization performs management functions for another they may be treated as a single employer. Moreoever, certain individuals performing services under a leasing agreement between a company and a third party will be treated as the company's employees when testing for plan discrimination.

The new law conforms the rules governing IRA distributions upon death to the new rule applicable to all qualified plans so that the entire interest must be distributed within five years of death. An exception is made where distribution over a period certain commenced before death. Moreover, a beneficiary, other than a surviving spouse, may not contribute to or roll over an IRA acquired on account of death.

Employers will be able to make and deduct contributions to defined contribution plans on behalf of disabled rank and file employees. These contributions, which must be fully vested, will be based on the employee's rate of pay before becoming disabled. This change allows defined contribution plans to pay disability benefits without reducing benefits otherwise payable to the disabled participant. Defined benefit plans can provide payments to a disabled participant without reducing the accrued benefit. Under a defined contribution plan, however, disability payments are made from the participant's account balance and therefore reduce his or her accrued benefit. This change allows defined contribution plans to restore part or all of the account balance of a participant receiving disability payments.

Tax-free rollovers of less than the total amount of an IRA distribution will be allowed.

The exclusion allowance will be increased under a tax-sheltered annuity for a church employee with adjusted gross income that does not exceed $17,000. In addition, the tax-sheltered annuity tax rules are extended to retirement income accounts maintained by churches.

Favorable tax treatment is granted to certain state judicial plans.

The new law insures that the tax-exempt status of a group trust is not affected solely because of participation by a state or local retirement plan.

Index